RISK TAKERS

THE PRENTICE HALL SERIES IN FINANCE

Alexander/Sharpe/Bailey
Fundamentals of Investments

Andersen
Global Derivatives: A Strategic Risk Management Perspective

Bear/Moldonado-Bear
Free Markets, Finance, Ethics, and Law

Berk/DeMarzo
*Corporate Finance**

Berk/DeMarzo
*Corporate Finance: The Core**

Bierman/Smidt
The Capital Budgeting Decision: Economic Analysis of Investment Projects

Bodie/Merton/Cleeton
Financial Economics

Click/Coval
The Theory and Practice of International Financial Management

Copeland/Weston/Shastri
Financial Theory and Corporate Policy

Cornwall/Vang/Hartman
Entrepreneurial Financial Management

Cox/Rubinstein
Options Markets

Dorfman
Introduction to Risk Management and Insurance

Dietrich
Financial Services and Financial Institutions: Value Creation in Theory and Practice

Dufey/Giddy
Cases in International Finance

Eakins
Finance in .learn

Eiteman/Stonehill/Moffett
Multinational Business Finance

Emery/Finnerty/Stowe
Corporate Financial Management

Fabozzi
Bond Markets, Analysis and Strategies

Fabozzi/Modigliani
Capital Markets: Institutions and Instruments

Fabozzi/Modigliani/Jones/Ferri
Foundations of Financial Markets and Institutions

Finkler
Financial Management for Public, Health, and Not-for-Profit Organizations

Francis/Ibbotson
Investments: A Global Perspective

Fraser/Ormiston
Understanding Financial Statements

Geisst
Investment Banking in the Financial System

Gitman
*Principles of Managerial Finance**

Gitman
*Principles of Managerial Finance——Brief Edition**

Gitman/Joehnk
*Fundamentals of Investing**

Gitman/Madura
Introduction to Finance

Guthrie/Lemon
Mathematics of Interest Rates and Finance

Haugen
The Inefficient Stock Market: What Pays Off and Why

Haugen
Modern Investment Theory

Haugen
The New Finance: Overreaction, Complexity, and Uniqueness

Holden
Excel Modeling in the Fundamentals of Corporate Finance

Holden
Excel Modeling in the Fundamentals of Investments

Holden
Excel Modeling in Investments

Holden
Excel Modeling in Corporate Finance Book and CD-ROM

Hughes/MacDonald
International Banking: Text and Cases

Hull
Fundamentals of Futures and Options Markets

Hull
Options, Futures, and Other Derivatives

Hull
Risk Management and Financial Institutions

Keown/Martin/Petty/Scott
Financial Management: Principles and Applications

Keown/Martin/Petty/Scott
Foundations of Finance: The Logic and Practice of Financial Management

Keown
Personal Finance: Turning Money into Wealth

Kim/Nofsinger
Corporate Governance

Levy/Post
Investments

May/May/Andrew
Effective Writing: A Handbook for Finance People

Madura
Personal Finance

Marthinsen
Risk Takers: Uses and Abuses of Financial Derivatives

McDonald
Derivatives Markets

McDonald
Fundamentals of Derivatives Markets

Megginson
Corporate Finance Theory

Melvin
International Money and Finance

Mishkin/Eakins
Financial Markets and Institutions

Moffett
Cases in International Finance

Moffett/Stonehill/Eiteman
Fundamentals of Multinational Finance

Nofsinger
Psychology of Investing

Ogden/Jen/O'Connor
Advanced Corporate Finance

Pennacchi
Theory of Asset Pricing

Rejda
Principles of Risk Management and Insurance

Schoenebeck
Interpreting and Analyzing Financial Statements

Scott/Martin/Petty/Keown/Thatcher
Cases in Finance

Shapiro
Capital Budgeting and Investment Analysis

Sharpe/Alexander/Bailey
Investments

Seiler
Performing Financial Studies: A Methodological Cookbook

Solnik/McLeavey
Global Investments

Stretcher/Michael
Cases in Financial Management

Titman/Martin
Valuation: The Art and Science of Corporate Investment Decisions

Trivoli
Personal Portfolio Management: Fundamentals and Strategies

Van Horne
Financial Management and Policy

Van Horne
Financial Market Rates and Flows

Van Horne/Wachowicz
Fundamentals of Financial Management

Vaughn
Financial Planning for the Entrepreneur

Weston/Mitchel/Mulherin
Takeovers, Restructuring, and Corporate Governance

Winger/Frasca
Personal Finance

*denotes  titles

Log onto www.myfinancelab.com to learn more

RISK TAKERS
Uses and Abuses of Financial Derivatives

Second Edition

John E. Marthinsen
Babson College

PEARSON

Prentice Hall

Boston San Francisco New York
London Toronto Sydney Tokyo Singapore Madrid
Mexico City Munich Paris Cape Town Hong Kong Montreal

Editor in Chief: Denise Clinton
Executive Editor: Donna Battista
Assistant Editor: Kerri McQueen
Managing Editor: Nancy H. Fenton
Senior Production Supervisor: Kathryn Dinovo
Design Manager: Joyce Cosentino Wells
Supplements Coordinator: Heather McNally
Senior Media Producer: Bethany Tidd
Senior Marketing Manager: Andrew Watts
Senior Author Support/Technology Specialist: Joe Vetere
Senior Prepress Supervisor: Caroline Fell
Rights and Permissions Advisor: Shannon Barbe
Senior Manufacturing Buyer: Carol Melville
Cover Designer: Christina Gleason
Text Design, Production Coordination, Composition, and Art: Nesbitt Graphics, Inc.

Cover image: © Dave Cutler, images.com/Veer
Photo credits: p. 169, The Orange County Archives; p. 196, PANDIS MEDIA; p. 235,
   James McGoon/CORBIS SYGMA

Library of Congress Cataloging-in-Publication Data

Marthinsen, John E.
   Risk takers : uses and abuses of financial derivatives / John E. Marthinsen. —
2nd ed.
       p. cm. — (The Addison-Wesley series in finance)
   Includes bibliographical references and index.
   ISBN-13: 978-0-321-54256-4
   ISBN-10: 0-321-54256-8
   1. Derivative securities. 2. Risk management. 3. Investment analysis. I. Title.
   HG6024.A3M374 2008
   332.64'57—dc22
                                    2008001237

ISBN-13: 978-0-321-54256-4

ISBN-10: 0-321-54256-8

1 2 3 4 5 6 7 8 9 10—DOH—12 11 10 09 08

Contents

Chapter 9   Amaranth Advisors LLC: Using Natural Gas Derivatives to Bet on the Weather   270

Preface

Introduction

Scandals sell, but crime does not pay. From the start, I have tried to make *Risk Takers: Uses and Abuses of Financial Derivatives* a book about the bad *and* good uses of derivatives (i.e., cases when things went wrong and other cases where they went right), but financial catastrophes are just too interesting. There is much to be learned from the mistakes of others, especially when the errors are so colossal and the personalities behind them so engaging. Fortified with thoughtful feedback from students and colleagues and also with a better understanding of my readership, I have rewritten *Risk Takers* to provide more examples, insight, and background on derivative instruments. Where possible, I have also tried to probe deeper into the financial controversies and characters involved in these famous financial fiascos.

Purpose of the Book

I wrote *Risk Takers* as a practical supplement to the "Risk Management" course that I teach at Babson College in Babson Park, Massachusetts. This book is not intended to be a substitute for the rigorous mathematical and empirical information needed to understand the theoretical backbone of finance or the intricacies of derivative valuation. My goal is more modest, aiming to write an accessible book that helps bridge the gap between theory and practice. Based on my experiences, there are many excellent analyses of derivatives and risk-management techniques, but they are often technical and presume considerable knowledge of the subject. As a result, their strength in rigor is a weakness in terms of accessibility. I tried to make the analyses in this book understandable to readers with even a novice understanding of derivatives. The real-life events provide a contextual framework for understanding and evaluating the potential risks and returns of derivative instruments. These are not traditional case studies that provide brief descriptions of situations or problems and then set the stage for group discussions about possible solutions and approaches. Rather, the chapters thoroughly describe the strategies and events that actually affected companies and municipalities faced with derivative-related decisions, and they cover the outcomes, as well.

This still leaves plenty to discuss, and I hope readers will continue the conversation and form their own opinions about how to prevent derivative use from turning into abuse. When failures occur, it is important to understand their causes, identify the important lessons to be learned, and make the changes needed to reduce the chances of similar misfortunes happening in the future. Unfortunate as they are, financial disasters have been occurring for centuries, and they will be a part of our future. If we learn from them, a healthier more vital economic environment can emerge from the destruction.

Organization of the Book

This book is divided into three parts: a brief introductory chapter on financial derivatives, two chapters on the creative, value-added uses of financial derivatives, and, finally, six chapters on the abuse and misuse of financial derivatives. At the end of the book, a glossary has been included with definitions of all the important terms used in *Risk Takers*.

Part I is an introductory chapter that serves as a primer on the basics of forward, futures, and option contracts. Part II covers the good uses of financial derivatives. Because many readers will be offered options at some point in their careers as part of their employment compensation packages, Chapter 2 focuses on employee stock options—why and how they are used and why employers may value them differently from employees. This chapter is especially important for MBA students because it will empower them in salary negotiations with potential employers. Chapter 3 examines Roche Holding, a Swiss multinational company, and how it successfully developed and implemented an iconoclastic financial strategy, using financial derivatives (e.g., Bull Spread warrants) as part of its approach.

Part III examines, in chronological order, companies that have been commonly associated with the "rogues' gallery" of financial derivative disasters. Chapter 4 analyzes Metallgesellschaft, a German company that reported losses of $1.3 billion in 1993 due to mistakes associated with its offering of energy derivative contracts. Chapter 5 looks, in detail, at two interest-rate swaps that were transacted in 1993 and 1994 between Procter and Gamble (P&G) and Bankers Trust, which resulted in losses for P&G of $157 million and led to some landmark court decisions in financial security law. Chapter 6 considers the investment strategy and events that caused Orange County, California to lose $1.6 billion in 1994, thereby earning it the ignoble reputation as the largest municipal failure in U.S. history. Chapter 7 explains the speculative trades of Nick Leeson, a middle-level bank manager at Barings

Bank's Singapore branch, who, in 1995, lost $1.3 billion, resulting in the bankruptcy of the oldest and most prestigious merchant bank in England. Chapter 8 analyzes Long-Term Capital Management—the company and principals, its strategy to build a market-neutral portfolio, and the chain of events in 1998 that caused the company to lose $4.5 billion in about two months. Finally, Chapter 9 investigates the financial failure of Amaranth Advisors LLC, which (as of early 2008) was the largest hedge fund failure in the history of the world – and maybe the quickest.

What is New in the Second Edition?

The second edition of *Risk Takers: Uses and Abuses of Financial Derivatives* has been fully reworked and updated. In an effort to *stick to the story*, some of the original text has been moved into vignette sections called "Risk Notepads." New end-of-chapter questions have been added, some of the on-line appendices have been pruned, and new appendices have been added.

The first edition assumed that readers had a basic knowledge of financial derivatives. To improve the accessibility of *Risk Takers* and, therefore, make it more of a stand-alone text, Chapter 1 (Primer on Derivatives) has been added to provide readers with the information needed to understand and better appreciate the remaining eight chapters.

In an effort to keep the book as close to 300 pages as possible, something had to be cut. For me, trimming material was the hardest of all tasks – sort of like saying good-bye to an old friend. I eliminated some of the Content Highlights (which are now called Risk Notepads) that were in the first edition and consolidated information, where possible. To make room for the introductory chapter, new chapter on Amaranth Advisors LLC, and glossary, I had to cut "The Three Amigos," which is a true story about how three friends earned incredibly large profits, for the short period they lived near to each other, by using put-call parity. Even though the story is true, feedback from readers was that it seemed contrived. While gone from the book, "The Three Amigos" still survives (south of the border, so to speak) in a special online Web site at **http://www.prenhall.com/marthinsen**.

Chapter 4 on Metallgesellschaft and its use of the stack-and-roll hedge was considered by many readers to be one of the most difficult to understand; so I rewrote many parts of this chapter and also added a numerical example that compares the risks of the stack-and-roll hedge to the risks of an unhedged position and a one-year rolling hedge. Chapter 5 on two derivative transactions between Procter & Gamble Company and Bankers Trust provides examples that explain how to calculate the losses on P&G's interest rate swaps and also the losses on its option-like gambles. Chapter 7 on Nick Leeson and the Barings Bank failure has been thoroughly reworked to provide more insight into the breadth and depth of Leeson's deception and the gross negligence on the part of his supervisors. Chapter 8 on Long-Term Capital Management has been expanded to show how LTCM's failure was the result of a chain reaction involving exogenous macroeconomic shocks that affected the entire hedge fund industry, endogenous, hedge-fund-related reactions that sabotaged many of LTCM's basic risk-management assumptions and measures, and, finally, calamitous feedback effects. The final chapter is on Amaranth Advisors LLC. When **Risk Takers** went to press, Amaranth had already failed, and its financial machinations are described in detail in this book, but the fund's legal and legislative legacies were still unfolding. Price manipulation charges against Amaranth and some of its traders were being prosecuted, and Congress had not yet decided whether to cast a wider regulatory net over derivative exchanges.

Resource and Learning Material

To motivate discussion and thoughtful reflection, I have provided end-of-chapter questions to test readers' understanding of the major principles in the text. To keep the length of the book manageable, Prentice Hall has created a Web site at **http://www.prenhall.com/marthinsen**, where you can find embellishments and extensions of the subject matter in many of the chapters. The material currently on this site includes:

Chapter 2: Employee Stock Options: What Every MBA Should Know

- Appendix 2.1: Employee Stock Options: A Brief History of U.S. Accounting Treatment

Chapter 3: Roche Holding: The Company, Its Strategy, and Bull Spread Warrants

- Appendix 3.1: Should Corporate Treasuries Be Profit Centers?

Chapter 4: Metallgesellschaft AG: Illusion of Profits and Losses, Reality of Cash Flows

- Appendix 4.1: Cash Flow Risks of a Stack-and-Roll Hedge, Unhedged Position, and One-Year Rolling Hedge
- Appendix 4.2: MGRM's Embedded Options

Chapter 5: Swaps That Shook an Industry: Procter & Gamble versus Bankers Trust

- Appendix 5.1: P&G-BT's Landmark Court Opinion
- Appendix 5.2: Disclosure Reform After the P&G-BT Swaps

- Appendix 5.3: Putting P&G-BT in Perspective: Other Derivative Disasters in the 1990s That Led to Financial Reform
- Appendix 5.4: Should Corporate Treasuries Be Profit Centers?
- Appendix 5.5: What Are the Problems with Value at Risk?

Chapter 6: Orange County: The Largest Municipal Failure in U.S. History

- Appendix 6.1: Orange County's Recovery Plan
- Appendix 6.2: What Happened to Orange County's Public Services?
- Appendix 6.3: What Happened to Orange County's Debt Level and Credit Ratings?
- Appendix 6.4: What Happened to the Mountain of Orange County Legal Cases?

Chapter 8: Long-Term Capital Management: "JM and the Arb Boys"

- Appendix 8.1: LTCM's Major Trades
- Appendix 8.2: What Are the Problems With Value at Risk?
- Appendix 8.3: UBS and the LTCM Warrant Fiasco

Chapter 9: Amaranth Advisors LLC: Using Natural Gas Derivatives to Bet on the Weather

- Appendix 9.1: What Are the Problems with Value at Risk?
- Appendix 9.2: Position Limits and Accountability Levels
- Appendix 9.3: Reporting Requirements for Exempt Commercial Markets

In addition to the Web site material, the solutions to all end-of-chapter questions are available for download as Word or PDF files from the Instructor's Resource Center (**http://www.prenhall.com/irc**).

Acknowledgments for the Second Edition

I owe my greatest thanks to students in my "Risk Management" classes, who have read these chapters and offered insightful comments. Thanks also go to colleagues who have provided feedback on the book, especially Dan M. Berkovitz (Counsel, Permanent Subcommittee on Investigations, U.S. Senate), Don M. Chance (William H. Wright, Jr. Endowed Chair for Financial Services, Louisiana State University), John C. Edmunds (Associate Professor of Finance, Babson College), Robert C. Merton (John and Natty McArthur University Professor, Harvard University), James A. Overdahl (Chief Economist, Securities and Exchange Commission), Eric Rosenfeld (Crescendo Partners), and Amareshwar Sahay (Markit).

I am also very appreciative of the help given to me by professors who provided feedback to Prentice Hall and me on specific chapters in the book.

- Don M. Chance, Louisiana State University, Baton Rouge, Louisiana
- Blake LeBaron, Brandeis University, Waltham, Massachusetts
- John A. MacDonald, Central Connecticut State University, New Britain, Connecticut
- Glen L. Stevens, Franklin & Marshall College, Lancaster, Pennsylvania

Poonam Bajaj supplied me with research assistance during the summer of 2007, and I was also helped by Kristin Djorup, Babson's Graduate Instruction Librarian. Thanks also go to the research staff at NYMEX, who provided me with a wealth of data on natural gas futures contracts.

The first edition of **Risk Takers** benefited greatly from the colleagues and students. Among the many who made special contributions were Professors John Edmunds, Craig Ehrlich, Robert McAuliffe, Erik Sirri, and Virginia Soybel, who were valued sources of input and suggestions. Each of the chapters in the first edition was read and commented on by numerous professors from colleges and universities and by industry experts around the world. I benefited enormously from feedback provided by the following reviewers: James Bennett, Jeremy Berkowitz, Antonio Camara, Charles Q. Cao, Dr. Mukesh A. Chaudhry, Patrice Clarke, Anna Dodonova, Imad Elhaj, Ekaterina Emm, Michael S. Haigh, Shantaram Hegde, Ufuk Ince, Francis Laatsch, Stewart Mayhew, Lalatendu Misra, Nicholas Valeio III, Niklas Wagner, Jill Wetmore, and Hongmin Zi.

The crew at Prentice Hall has been terrific. Kerri McQueen ushered the second edition from start to finish. Donna Battista provided timely and helpful feedback on the two new chapters of the book. Christina Gleason was in charge of the cover, Heather McNally organized the supplementary material, Kathryn Dinovo supervised the book's production. Maria McColligan and Janette Krauss at Nesbitt Graphics, Inc. directed, with patience and care, the project management and production coordination of the book.

Despite the time and effort that has gone into making this book error free and ensuring that the arguments are transparent and deductive, there are bound to be instances where errors may have gone undetected. I take full responsibility for the content in this book, and wish to invite readers to contact me (marthinsen@babson.edu) with any comments, insights, and/or constructive criticism they have, so that I might improve the book.

As I did in the first edition, I dedicate this book to my wife, Laraine.

1

Primer on Derivatives

Introduction

Derivative contracts have played a useful role in trade and
commerce for thousands of years. Evidence shows that
forward contracts were used as early as 2000 B.C. in trade
between India and the Arab Gulf, as well as in Mesopotamia.[1]
In Ancient Greece, around 300 B.C., olive growers used
derivative agreements to reduce the price risks associated
with future harvests. In the twelfth century, merchants at
European trade fairs negotiated forward contracts for the
future delivery of their goods. Business owners in
seventeenth-century Amsterdam were also frequent users of
forward and option contracts. In fact, during Amsterdam's
infamous tulip mania in the 1630s, these financial
instruments helped protect some merchants from dramatic
price swings, but they also fuelled speculative increases in
the price of tulip bulbs. Later in the seventeenth century,
Japan developed a forward market in rice.

Derivative markets, as we know them today, began in the
mid-nineteenth century and progressed rapidly during the

---

[1] Edward J. Swan, *Building the Global Market: A 4000 Year History of Derivatives* (London: Kluwer Law
International, 2000).

twentieth century. Looking back over four thousand years of history, it is clear that, even though the number and types of derivative contracts have changed dramatically, their basic function has remained the same. Derivatives exist to transfer risk from those who do not want to bear it to those who are willing to bear it. The growth and development of these financial instruments are examples of the positive effects that come from business ingenuity and competition. By improving the allocative efficiency of our national and international financial systems, derivative instruments have created a bigger pie for everyone to share, thereby demonstrating that not all aspects of life have to be zero-sum games.

Despite the numerous examples of early derivative uses, growth in these markets is often benchmarked relative to the early 1970s, when large fluctuations in exchange rates and interest rates gave rise to the first traded contracts in currency futures and interest-rate futures. Since then, global derivative markets have blossomed and become integrated parts of our burgeoning global financial networks. By any yardstick, the derivatives markets are immense. The Bank for International Settlements estimates that, at the end of 2006, the *notional value* of financial derivatives worldwide was nearly $500 trillion, which was about 10 times larger than global GDP or global stock market capitalization in that year.[2]

Derivatives have proved to be powerful tools in an unstable and turbulent marketplace. These financial instruments have given debtors the ability to reduce their borrowing costs, transfer unwanted risks, and increase financial flexibility. Creditors have been able to increase their risk-adjusted returns, stabilize cash flows, transfer undesired exposures, and focus on the types of risks that they know best.

---

[2]Bank for International Settlements, *"OTC Derivative Markets Activity in the Second Half of 2006." Table 1: The Global OTC Derivatives Market.* 21 May 2007. http://www.bis.org/press/P070521.htm. p. 7. Accessed 6 November 2007. Also see Reuters, "Global Stock Values Top $50 Trln: Industry Data." 21 March 2007. http://www.reuters.com/article/idUSL2144839620070321. Accessed on 11 August 2007.

Intermediaries have earned considerable profits and secured valuable lines of business with important customers by identifying and transforming risk-return profiles, discovering arbitrage opportunities, and creating new derivative instruments. Speculators have been provided with active markets for trading contracts with the potential to earn above-average returns.

Despite the net benefits that derivative instruments have brought, when left in the wrong hands or unmonitored, they can create losses that are serious enough to bankrupt even the largest and most established companies and municipalities. Unfortunately, it is these speculative losses that have received the lion's share of media attention, even though they represent only a tiny minority of overall transactions. We will analyze in this book a few of these derivative-related fiascos, and, in virtually every case, we will discover that the regrettable outcomes could have been significantly mitigated or avoided entirely by a better understanding, communication, and monitoring of derivative risks.

What Are Derivatives?

Derivatives are promises that are made now and carried out in the future. Every derivative contract establishes, from the beginning, both the price and future delivery date for whatever is being traded. The item being traded is called the *underlier* because its value is the foundation for (i.e., it underlies) the value of the derivative contract. In fact, "derivatives" are so named because they *derive* their value from the underlier.

Potentially, almost anything could serve as an underlier. There are just two major requirements for an underlier to be successful. First, it has to be something that can be quantified; second, there have to be many individuals who want to buy and sell derivatives based on this quantified measure.

The most common underliers are commodities (e.g., precious metals, energy, grains, and meats), financial securities (e.g., equities, bills, bonds, and interest-earning deposits), and currencies (e.g., euros, pounds, Swiss francs, and yen). There are also active derivative markets for underliers that cannot be delivered or would be difficult to deliver at maturity. Among them are derivatives based on weather conditions and creditworthiness, as well as stock indices, such as the Dow Jones Index.

Who Buys and Sells Derivatives?

Derivatives are bought and sold by end users, arbitrageurs, and intermediaries. *End users* include all the individuals, companies, and financial institutions that buy and sell derivative instruments to hedge positions or to speculate. By hedging, they reduce or eliminate risk, and by speculating, they intentionally take on risk to earn profits.

Arbitrageurs are different from end users because they are not interested in owning derivatives. Rather, they make small and (virtually) risk-free profits by simultaneously buying and selling derivative instruments. In this way, arbitrageurs benefit from tiny discrepancies in the prices of financially identical (or similar) contracts that are sold on different markets.

Intermediaries make up the final group of participants in the derivative markets. These financial institutions not only connect buyers to sellers but also create innovative derivative solutions for their customers' financial needs. Brokers, banks, exchanges, and an army of financial wizards earn revenues from commissions, fees, and the difference between bid and ask rates on the derivative contracts they buy and sell.

Where Are Derivatives Bought and Sold?

Derivative contracts are traded either over-the-counter (OTC) or on exchanges. *Over the counter* means that trades by dealer networks are connected by a global network of telephone, telex, fax, and high-speed Internet connections. By contrast, exchange-traded derivatives are bought and sold at distinct locations, where trades are made by human outcry, such as on the Chicago Mercantile Exchange (CME) and Singapore International Monetary Exchange (SIMEX), or electronically, such as on the European Exchange (EUREX) and Osaka Stock Exchange (OSE). Currently, the notional value of OTC-traded derivative contracts dwarfs the notional value of exchange-traded contracts by almost six-to-one.[3] Nevertheless, the volume of business done on worldwide derivative exchanges is significant and growing.

---

[3]In 2006, the notional value of OTC-traded derivatives and exchange-traded derivatives (excluding commodity derivatives) equaled $415.2 trillion and $70.5 trillion, respectively. See Bank for International Settlements, *OTC derivative markets activity in the second half of 2006, Table 1: The Global OTC Derivatives Market,* May 2007. http://www.bis.org/press/P070521.htm, p. 7. Accessed 6 November 2007.

Two Major Types of Derivatives

There are two basic types of derivatives: forwards and options. Readers who have had some exposure to derivatives might be saying to themselves: "Hey, what happened to futures and swaps?" Actually, futures and swaps are just versions of forward contracts. If you understand forwards, then you understand futures and swaps. Futures contracts are merely standardized forward contracts that are traded on exchanges, and swaps are a series of forward contracts. Exhibit 1.1 provides a brief explanation of forward, option, futures, and swap contracts; Risk Notepad 1.1, which is at the end of this chapter, provides a more detailed explanation of the similarities and differences between OTC-traded derivatives (i.e., forwards and OTC-traded options) and exchange-traded derivatives (i.e., futures and exchange-traded options).

In this chapter, we will concentrate on forward, futures, and option contracts; so let's begin by defining some terms that are common to all derivative contracts.

TERMINOLOGY THAT IS COMMON TO ALL DERIVATIVES

Every derivative contract has a buyer and a seller, who are called *counterparties* to the deal. Therefore, there is a buyer counterparty and seller counterparty for every derivative contract traded. The buyer is said to be *long* or to have a *long position*, and the seller is said to be *short* or to have a *short position*. All derivative contracts establish on the day of the transaction the price and date on which the underlier will be delivered in the future. If the underlier cannot be delivered, settlement at maturity is made in cash. The price of the underlier on the transaction day (e.g., the day the derivative is opened) is called the *current market price*,[4] and its price at maturity is called the *maturity market price*.[5]

FORWARD CONTRACTS

A forward contact allows counterparties to purchase or sell the underlier at a price agreed upon on the day of the transaction but for delivery and settlement on a specified date or during a specified period in the future. Therefore, unless a collateral requirement has been negotiated, there are no immediate cash flows when a forward contract is initiated. Payment and delivery (if any) take place at maturity. Because promises to pay in the future are not the same as cash in hand, these transactions carry default

[4]The *current market price* is also called the *current spot price*.
[5]The *maturity market price* is also called the *maturity spot price*.

Exhibit 1.1 Derivative Contracts

Derivative Contract	Explanation
Forward contract	• A forward contract is an over-the-counter agreement to buy and sell the underlier at a price determined on the day of the transaction but with delivery on a specific day in the future or during a specified period in the future. The contract terms (e.g., size and delivery date) are negotiable and can be tailored to the customer's needs. • Unless it is offset beforehand, the buyer and seller are obliged to transact the deal at maturity.
Futures contract	• A futures contract is almost the same as a forward contact except it is traded on an exchange using brokers, and the contract terms (e.g., size and delivery dates) are standardized. • Unless it is offset beforehand, the buyer and seller are obliged to transact the deal at maturity.
Swap contract	• A swap is a series of forward contracts that mature sequentially between initiation and the end of agreement. Usually, it involves two simultaneous transactions in which each counterparty pays and receives prearranged amounts (or prearranged terms). • Unless it is offset beforehand, the buyer and seller are obliged to transact the deal at each interim date and final maturity date.

Option contract	• An option gives a *buyer* the right, but not the obligation, to buy or sell the underlier at a price determined on the day of the transaction but with delivery on or before a specified expiration date in the future.
	  • A call option gives a *buyer* the right, but not the obligation, to purchase the underlier at a price agreed upon now but for future delivery.
	  • A put option gives a *buyer* the right, but not the obligation, to sell the underlier at a price agreed upon now but for future delivery.
	• Only the buyer has the option. The seller must transact the deal if the buyer exercises the option at maturity.

risks. As a result, participants in derivative deals must know and accept the creditworthiness of their counterparties.

Forward contracts are usually for relatively short time periods (e.g., one year or less). One of the major benefits of OTC-traded contracts is that their terms can be tailored to meet the needs of customers. At the same time, the benefits that come from customization can vanish quickly if a counterparty wishes to reverse a position before maturity because the secondary market for OTC-traded contracts is very illiquid. To get out of a forward deal, a counterparty usually has to transact a second deal that is equal to and opposite from the unwanted one.

Long Forward

An example might help to clarify a forward contract. Suppose you manage a chain of U.S. retail stores and purchase dinnerware worth £100,000 from Josiah Wedgwood & Sons Limited (i.e., Wedgewood), the British manufacturer. To provide time for you to sell your new inventory of dinnerware, Wedgewood gives you one year to pay. You worry that the pound might rise in value before next year and reduce your profits. To protect yourself, you call your bank and lock in a one-year forward price of $2/£. Your bank requires some sort of protection to ensure that you could complete your end of the deal. Often, companies initiating forward deals already have established lines of credit with banks, and their forward transactions just reduce these lines. For many other forward contracts, collateral is negotiated on a case-by-case basis, and contracts are marked to market daily. Therefore, you might pay nothing today for your forward contract, but in one year, you would have to pay $200,000 to get the £100,000 needed to pay Wedgewood. Because you were buying pounds for forward delivery and protecting a future transaction, your position is called a long hedge.

Let's now turn the clock ahead one year and evaluate the results of your forward contract. Remember that you must pay $2/£ regardless of what the actual rate is in one year (i.e., the maturity market price). Exhibit 1.2a shows the *payoff profile* from your decision to lock in the forward pound price. A *payoff profile* shows the relationship between the price of the underlier (in this case, the pound) and the value of your position.

If the maturity market price were $2/£, then your forward contract would have provided neither savings nor added costs relative to the unhedged position, which means your payoff would equal $0.00 per pound. By contrast, if the maturity market price were $2.20, then your forward contract would save you $0.20 per pound. Finally, if the maturity market price were $1.80/£, then the decision to lock in the forward price

Exhibit 1.2 Payoff Profiles for Long and Short Forward Contracts

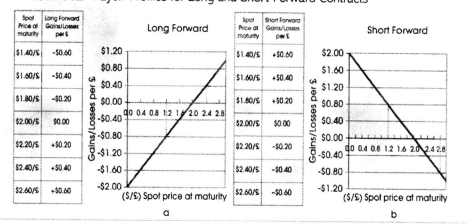

a

b

would require you to pay $0.20 more per pound than if you had done nothing last year and simply bought the pounds when payment was due. Notice that the gains and losses in Exhibit 1.2a are perfectly symmetrical; the payoff profile is an upward-sloping line with a 45-degree angle that emanates from the forward price.

Short Forward

Exhibit 1.2b shows the payoff profile for a short forward position. The slope and shape of this line might be self-evident because they are exactly opposite from the long position, which is shown in Exhibit 1.2a. Again, an example may help to clarify a short forward position. Suppose you manage a U.S.-based health food company that just sold trail mix worth £100,000 to Marks & Spencer, a large English retail chain. The contract calls for Marks & Spencer to pay you in one year, which means that your major worry is that the pound might fall in value before you got paid.

To free yourself from this risk, you could call your bank and lock in a one-year forward price to sell pounds. Because you are selling pounds for forward delivery and protecting a future transaction, your position is called a *short hedge*. As in the last example, suppose that you locked in a forward price of $2/£. In the absence of any collateral requirement, no money would change hands when the forward deal is transacted, but in one year, you would receive $200,000 and be required to pay the bank £100,000, which you would receive from Marks & Spencer.

The payoff profile of this short position (shown in Exhibit 1.2b) is a downward-sloping line that intersects the $2/£ forward price and has a 45-degree angle. If the maturity market price for pounds turns out to be $2/£, then the forward contract provides you with no net benefit or net cost relative to the unhedged position, which means the payoff at $2/£ equals zero.

By contrast, if the maturity market price were $2.20/£, then the forward contract would have cost you $0.20 per pound because the $2 you received for your pounds from the forward contract would be $0.20 less than you would have received without the hedge. Finally, if the maturity market price were $1.80/£, then your forward price would be $0.20 per pound better than if you had not hedged.

OPTIONS

An option gives the *buyer* (i.e., the holder) the right, *but not the obligation*, to buy or sell the underlier at an agreed price on or before a specified date in the future.[6] The price at which the underlier can be purchased or sold in the future is called the *strike price*, and the up-front cost of purchasing the managerial flexibility provided by an option is called the *premium*. The option premium (plus any accumulated interest earned) is kept by the seller regardless of the buyer's decision.

A *call option* gives the option *buyer* the right, but not the obligation, to *purchase* the underlier at the agreed-on (strike) price in the future. If the buyer decides to go through with the deal, then he or she *exercises* the call option. A *put option* gives the option *buyer* the right, but not the obligation, to *sell* the underlier at the agreed-on (strike) price in the future. If the buyer decides to go through with the deal, then he or she *exercises* the put option.

It is important to keep in mind that, unlike forward contracts, which have symmetrical gains and losses, option contracts have asymmetrical gains and losses. The most a call-option buyer can lose is the up-front premium (plus any accumulated interest costs connected to financing the premium), but if the market price rises above the strike price, benefits rise in tandem. By contrast, the most a call-option seller can earn is the option premium (plus any accumulated interest earnings on the premium), but as underlier's price rises above the strike price, the seller's losses rise in tandem.

The same is true for put options. The most a put-option buyer can lose is the up-front premium (plus accumulated interest costs), but if the underlier's price falls below the strike price, the benefits increase until the price of the underlier hits zero. By contrast, the most a put-option seller can earn is the option premium (plus accumulated interest earnings), and as underlier's price falls below the strike price, the seller's losses rise in tandem.

A few examples of call options and put options might help to cement their similarities and differences. To make things easy, let's use the same scenarios as with forward contracts.

---

[6]An American option can be exercised on any date prior to and including the maturity date. By contrast, a European option can be exercised only at maturity.

Exhibit 1.3 Profit/Loss Profiles for Long and Short Calls and Puts

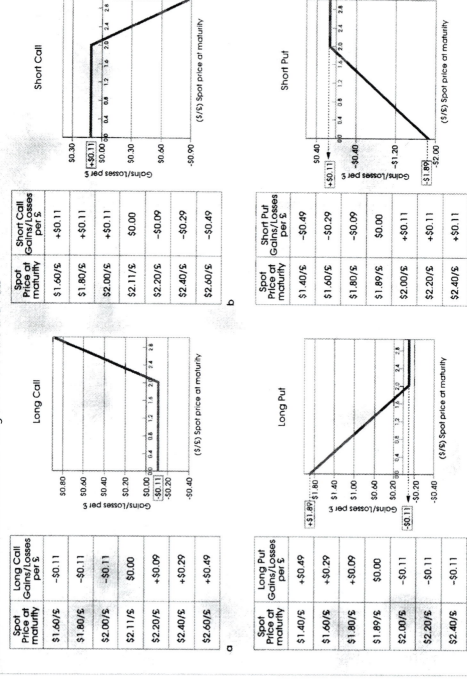

a. Long Call

Spot Price at maturity	Long Call Gains/Losses per £
$1.60/£	-$0.11
$1.80/£	-$0.11
$2.00/£	-$0.11
$2.11/£	$0.00
$2.20/£	+$0.09
$2.40/£	+$0.29
$2.60/£	+$0.49

b. Short Call

Spot Price at maturity	Short Call Gains/Losses per £
$1.60/£	+$0.11
$1.80/£	+$0.11
$2.00/£	+$0.11
$2.11/£	$0.00
$2.20/£	-$0.09
$2.40/£	-$0.29
$2.60/£	-$0.49

c. Long Put

Spot Price at maturity	Long Put Gains/Losses per £
$1.40/£	+$0.49
$1.60/£	+$0.29
$1.80/£	+$0.09
$1.89/£	$0.00
$2.00/£	-$0.11
$2.20/£	-$0.11
$2.40/£	-$0.11

d. Short Put

Spot Price at maturity	Short Put Gains/Losses per £
$1.40/£	-$0.49
$1.60/£	-$0.29
$1.80/£	-$0.09
$1.89/£	$0.00
$2.00/£	+$0.11
$2.20/£	+$0.11
$2.40/£	+$0.11

Long Call

Suppose your import business just purchased dinnerware worth £100,000 from Wedgewood, in England. You have a year to sell your new inventory and to pay the bill. Worried that the value of the pound might rise in value but interested in taking advantage of any reduction in the pound's value, you call your bank and lock in a one-year call option with a strike price of $2.00/£. For this option, you pay an up-front premium equal to $0.10 per pound, which is 5% of the pound's value. Assuming the one-year dollar interest rate is 10%, the total cost at year's end would be $0.11 per pound (i.e., the $0.10/£ premium plus a $0.01 per pound interest cost).

Exhibit 1.3a shows the profit/loss profile of your long call option.[7] If the maturity market price were $2.00, then the option would be *at-the-money*, and there would be no reason to exercise your option because you could do as well (and it would be more convenient) to purchase the currency in the spot market. Similarly, for all exchange rates below $2.00/£, your option would be *out-of-the-money*. You (the buyer) would not exercise the option because you could do better by purchasing the currency in the spot foreign exchange market. Therefore, for options that are at-the-money or out-of-the-money, you would lose the entire $0.11/£ premium.

At any rate above $2/£, your call option would be *in-the-money* and become ever more valuable as the exchange rate rose. For example, at $2.20/£, you could exercise your option and buy the needed pounds for $2.00/£, thereby saving yourself $0.20/£. After subtracting the per pound option premium of $0.11, your net gain would be $0.09/£. As a result, the profit/loss profile of your long call option is a horizontal line equal to −$0.11/£ for all prices from zero to the strike price and then, afterwards, a positively sloped line with a 45-degree angle. Breakeven is at $2.11/£.

Short Call

The profit/loss profile of a short call is just the opposite of the long call. At any price equal to or below the strike price, the option would be either at-the-money or out-of-the-money. As a result, the buyer would not exercise the call option, which means the seller would keep the premium plus any accumulated interest earned. But if the maturity market price rose above the strike price, the option would be in-the-money. When exercised, therefore, the seller would have to purchase the currency at the maturity market price and sell it to the buyer at the lower strike price, thereby incurring losses. These losses would rise as the spot price rose. Exhibit 1.3b shows that the profit/loss profile of your short call option is a horizontal line equal to

---

[7]A profit/loss profile is slightly different from a payoff profile because it includes payoff from the option and its initial cost.

+0.11/£ for all prices ranging from zero to the strike price and, after the strike price, a negatively sloped, 45-degree line. Breakeven is at $2.11/£.

Long Put

Suppose your U.S.-based health food company just sold trail mix worth £100,000 to Marks & Spencer with payment scheduled in one year. Worried that the value of the pound might fall but wanting to benefit if it rose, you call your bank and purchase a put option with a strike price of $2/£ and a premium of $0.10/£. Assuming the U.S. interest rate is 10%, the total premium cost at year's end would be $0.11 per pound (i.e., the $0.10/£ premium plus a $0.01 per pound interest cost).

Exhibit 1.3c shows the profit/loss profile of your long put. If the maturity market price were $2.00/£ or greater, there would be no reason to exercise your option because you could do as well or better by just selling the £100,000 in the spot market. As a result, for all exchange rates equal to and above $2.00/£, the put option would be either at-the-money or out-of-the-money, and you (the put-option buyer) would not exercise it. As a result, you would sacrifice the $0.11/£ option premium.

By contrast, if the spot exchange rate at maturity fell below $2/£, your put option would be in-the-money and become ever more valuable. For example, at a spot price of $1.80/£, you would exercise your option and sell each pound for $2.00/£, thereby earning $0.20/£ more than if you had not purchased the put option. The net profit or loss from the long put would be $0.09/£ (i.e., the $0.20/£ gain on the currency purchased minus the $0.11/£ premium cost of the option). As a result, the profit/loss profile of your long put is a horizontal line at −$0.11/£ for all spot prices that are at and above the strike price, and, below the strike price, it is a positively sloped line with a 45-degree angle. Breakeven is at $1.89/£.

Short Put

The profit/loss profile of the short put is just the opposite of the long put. For all prices that are at and above the strike price, the option would be at-the-money or out-of-the-money. Therefore, the buyer would not exercise the put option, and the seller would earn the premium plus any accumulated interest. But if the spot price were below the strike price, the option would be in-the-money and exercised, forcing the seller to purchase pounds for $2/£ that were worth less than that in the spot market. For example, at a spot price of $1.80/£, the put-option seller would be required to purchase pounds for $2 that could be sold in the market for only $1.80, which would cause losses of $0.20/£. These losses would be partially offset by the $0.11/£ premium,

Risk Notepad 1.1

OTC-Traded Versus Exchange-Traded Derivatives

Let's take a brief look at the similarities and differences between OTC-traded derivatives (i.e., forwards and OTC-traded options) and exchange-traded derivatives (i.e., futures and exchange-traded options).

SIMILARITIES

Forward contracts and futures contracts are similar in function because they allow customers to lock in prices now either for delivery of the underlier or for cash settlement at maturity. With both contracts, delivery is scheduled to take place on a designated day in the future, but it could also occur during a specific time period (e.g., a 10-day window in the future). Similarly, OTC-traded options and exchange-traded options are alike in function because they give buyers the right, but not the obligation, to buy or sell the underlier at an agreed price on or before a specified date in the future.

DIFFERENCES

The major differences between these OTC-traded and exchange-traded derivatives are based on their levels of standardization and the methods used to protect counterparties from credit (i.e., default) risk.

Level of Customization

The markets for OTC-traded derivatives are like financial boutiques that tailor their products to customers' unique specifications (e.g., amounts and maturities). By contrast, exchange-traded derivatives offer off-the-rack contracts that are standardized by exchanges. Customers have to take what is offered, which means their only real flexibility is in the number of contracts they buy or sell, and even that has minimum and maximum limits.

Credit Risk (i.e., Default Risk)

Exchange-Traded Deals

Counterparty risk for the buyers and sellers (i.e., customers) of exchange-trade derivatives is extremely low because their counterparty is the clearinghouse of the exchange. The entire exchange would have to default for their contracts not to be honored. By contrast, counterparty risk faced by an exchange can be significant. To protect itself, the exchange requires brokers (i.e., the clearing members of exchange's clearinghouse) as well as end users and arbitrageurs to post initial margin and to *mark to market* outstanding contracts.

Margin is a fixed dollar amount per contract (or per position) and represents very small percent (e.g., 5%) of the overall value. Normally, it can be posted in cash or acceptable security (e.g., government securities and letters of credit). By law, margin is held by the broker in a customer-segregated account so that margin deposits are sure to be separated from the brokers' operating funds.

(continued)

Exchange-traded contracts are directly between clearing members (e.g., broker) and the clearinghouse. As a result, there are separate margin requirements for the broker relative to the clearinghouse and for the customer relative to the clearinghouse. The exchange sets minimum customer margin requirements, based on factors such as the underlier's price volatility (e.g., worst daily movement) and general market liquidity. The more active and volatile an underlier's price and the less liquid the market, the higher the margin requirement. Brokers are allowed to raise customers' margins above the exchange-required minimum, depending on their perceptions of customers' risks and the volume of business that customers are likely to transact.

Margin is not really a down payment on the underlier as much as it is a performance bond that ensures the broker and exchange that the contract will be settled in due course. For that reason, exchange-traded contracts are marked to market each working day, which means they are revalued, with funds transferred from the losers' margin accounts to the winners' accounts, as if the contracts had been closed out and then reopened. Therefore, even if the underlier's price kept changing by substantial amounts, the daily transfer of funds and periodic replenishment of the margin account ensures that the exchange collects enough cash to pay the winning counterparty when the contract matures.

Marking to market each day is a practical way to protect exchanges from the liability of customers defaulting during the life of the contract. If everything runs smoothly, the clearinghouse should have a perfectly matched book, with winners paying losers on a daily basis from their margin accounts. As a result, exchanges should have very low customer credit risks.

Futures contracts require both buyers *and* sellers to deposit margin, and their contracts are marked to market every working day. By contrast, exchange-traded options require only the option *sellers* (*writers*) to deposit margin with the exchange, and only the sellers' positions are marked to market daily. Option buyers are not required to deposit margin, and their contracts are not marked to market. The reason for this difference is because option buyers pay an up-front premium for the right to walk away from deals when prices move disadvantageously. The most buyers can lose is the premium, which was paid at the beginning of the contract plus any sacrificed interest. By contrast, sellers are exposed to substantial risks throughout the contract.

OTC-Traded Deals

Counterparty risk for OTC-traded derivatives is significant and can be a deal breaker. For this reason, dealers often take precautions to minimize this risk. An important take-away from this section is that these protections are negotiated bilaterally between the two counterparties. Therefore, they vary from customer to customer and from dealer to dealer. The first line of defense for dealers is to establish a line of credit for each counterparty, which puts limits on the amount of business the customer can do with that dealer. Credit lines are based on a customer's creditworthiness; the more creditworthy the customer, the higher the credit line. Usually a customer's *net* exposures are considered, so that offsetting risks, such as long and short positions in the same contract, are considered rather than the gross amount of business transacted. At the same time, both current and potential exposures are (or should be) deducted from an existing credit line.

Crucial to any OTC deal is the master agreement that establishes the terms and conditions for each OTC deal. A master agreement lays out important contractual details, such as representations, warranties, covenants, events that trigger default, as well as conditions for netting, the sale of collateral, and early termination. Increasingly, OTC dealers protect themselves from counterparty risk by collecting up-front collateral from their customers and/or by requiring cash payments whenever a contract suffers substantial losses. Government securities and cash are normally used as collateral, but corporate debt and equities might be accepted. *Haircuts* are applied to most collateral deposits, which means that only a portion of these assets' market value (e.g., 98%) is counted as collateral; the remainder (2%) is the haircut.

Just as dealers protect themselves from relatively weak customers, strong counterparties may employ the same measures to protect themselves from relatively weak dealers. In fact, *one-way* collateral agreements, in which only one counterparty posts collateral, are giving way to *two-way* agreements, in which both counterparties have such obligations.

Profit Risk versus Cash-Flow Risk

When OTC-traded and exchange-traded derivatives are used to modify customers' risk-return profiles, their effects on profitability are very much the same; the gains or losses on the derivative transactions (partly or wholly) offset the losses or gains on existing positions or expected positions. By contrast, the cash-flow effects can be very different, and for anyone using these markets (especially companies in which positive cash flows are vital to survival), this difference should be kept firmly in mind. Many OTC-traded contracts require up-front collateral payments, and, as the contracts mature, they are marked to market daily. All exchanged traded contracts have up-front margin requirements and must be marked to market daily. Collateral and margin payments require a small initial outlay, and the mark-to-market provision holds the possibility of much larger payments as the contracts mature.

Exchanges monitor how much is on deposit for each open contract, and through brokers, they demand and get additional funds from customers who are on the losing side of any price change. By contrast, customers whose margin accounts increase above the minimum level can withdraw and use the excess funds. For those whose accounts fall below the *maintenance margin* (often called *variation margin*) requirement, a *margin call* is issued, and their accounts must be brought immediately up to the full initial margin level. If the margin call is not met with the funds required, contracts are closed out by the broker and excess margin (if any) is returned to the customer. Dealers also monitor vigilantly the collateral and positions of their OTC counterparties, they collect additional collateral, if necessary.

Exhibit RN 1-1 summarizes the most important differences between the OTC-traded derivatives and exchange-traded derivatives

(continued)

Exhibit RN1.1	Differences between OTC-Traded and Exchange-Traded Derivatives

OTC Markets (Forwards and OTC-Traded Options)	Exchanges (Futures and Exchange-Traded Options)
Traded over the counter	Traded on an exchange
Customized terms	Standardized terms
Counterparty risk: risk could be high	Counterparty is the exchange: low risk
Up-front collateral negotiated on a case-by-case basis	Margin is required
Mark-to-market requirement negotiated on a case-by-case basis	Marked to market daily
Delivery or cash settlement often occurs at maturity	Delivery at maturity is rare (positions are usually closed before maturity)

---

causing a net loss of only $0.09/£. At $1.60/£, the net loss would be $0.29/£ (i.e., a $0.40/£ loss on the option, which is offset partially by the $0.11/£ premium). Exhibit 1.3d shows that the profit/loss profile of your short put option is a horizontal line equal to +$0.11/£ for all prices equal to or greater than the strike price and, below the strike price, a negatively sloped line with a 45-degree angle for all maturity spot prices. Breakeven is at $1.89/£.

Conclusion

Now that we have reviewed the basic types of derivatives, their payoff or profit/loss profiles, as well as the similarities and differences between OTC-traded and exchange-traded derivatives, let's use this information to investigate both the good use and bad use of these financial instruments.

Review Questions

1. Must the underlier of a derivative transaction be an asset that can be delivered at maturity? If so, explain why. If not, explain what happens when the contract matures. What are the two major requirements for an underlier to be successful?

2. Suppose forward price for a contract maturing on December 15 is $50/share.

a. Draw the payoff profile of a short forward contract. How much would you earn or lose if the spot price at maturity was $68/share? How much would you earn or lose if the spot price at maturity was $48/share?

b. Draw the payoff profile of a long forward contract. How much would you earn or lose if the spot price at maturity was $68/share? How much would you earn or lose if the spot price at maturity was $48/share?

3. Define the following terms: call option, put option, long call, short call, long put, short put, at-the-money call, at-the-money put, in-the-money call, in-the-money put, out-of-the-money call, out-of-the-money put, premium, strike price, exercise, margin, maintenance margin, and margin call.

4. Suppose it is July 10, and the current spot price of a Microsoft share is $40. Rank the following call options from the most valuable to the least valuable.

a. September 10 Microsoft call option with a strike price of $45/share.

b. September 10 Microsoft call option with a strike price of $40/share.

c. September 10 Microsoft call option with a strike price of $35/share.

5. Suppose it is July 10, and the current spot price of a Microsoft share is $40. Rank the following put options from the most valuable to the least valuable.

a. September 10 Microsoft put option with a strike price of $45/share.

b. September 10 Microsoft put option with a strike price of $40/share.

c. September 10 Microsoft put option with a strike price of $35/share.

6. Draw the profit/loss profiles of the following options and explain their risks.

a. Long September 16 call @ $100/share = $4.

b. Short September 16 call @ $100/share = $4.

c. Long September 16 put @ $100/share = $4.

d. Short September 16 put @ $100/share = $4.

7. Suppose that one year ago you bought a call option with a strike price of $2/euro and a premium of $0.10/euro. The option expires today, and the spot price of the euro is $2.05. Calculate your profit or loss from exercising this option. Should you exercise the option?

8. What payoff profile would you get if you combined a long call option with a short call option that has the same underlier, strike price, and maturity?

9. What payoff profile would you get if you combined a long forward contract with a short forward contact that has the same underlier, forward price, and maturity?

10. How do exchanges protect themselves from counterparty risk?

11. Are the following sentences true or false? If they are false, explain why.

   A major difference between exchange-traded derivatives and OTC-traded derivatives is:

   a. Exchange-traded derivatives have underliers, and OTC-traded derivatives do not have underliers.

   b. OTC-traded derivatives are standardized, and exchange-traded derivatives are customized.

   c. Exchange-traded derivatives require up-front margin payments, but OTC-traded derivatives require no up-front payments.

   d. Exchange-traded derivatives are marked to market, and OTC-traded derivatives are not marked to market.

   e. Exchange-traded derivatives have high credit (i.e., counterparty) risk compared to OTC-traded derivatives.

   f. OTC-traded derivatives require delivery at maturity, but exchange-traded derivatives do not require delivery.

Bibliography

Chance, Don M., and Robert Brooks. *An Introduction to Derivatives & Risk Management*, 7th ed. Mason, Ohio: Thomson South-Western, 2007.

Edward J. Swan, *Building the Global Market: A 4000 Year History of Derivatives*. London: Kluwer Law International, 2000.

Hull, John C. *Options, Futures and Other Derivatives*. 5th ed. Upper Saddle River, New Jersey: Prentice Hall, 2005.

Kolb Robert W., and Overdahl, James A. Futures, Options, and Swaps, 5th ed. Malden, MA: Blackwell Publishing, 2007.

McDonald, Robert L. *Derivatives Markets*. Second Edition, Boston, MA: Pearson Addison Wesley, 2006.

2

Employee Stock Options

What Every MBA Should Know

Introduction

Between its founding in 1975 and 2003, Microsoft Corporation offered all its employees stock options as part of their compensation packages. If you had been offered a job at Microsoft during those years and the going market wage for someone with your qualifications was $80,000, Microsoft's offer would have included a base salary of $40,000 to $48,000 (i.e., 50% to 60% of the market wage) and stock options worth $40,000 to $32,000 (i.e., 50% to 40% of the market wage).

Microsoft's compensation plan turned many of its employees—from the secretaries to the senior executives—into multimillionaires and at very early ages. To understand why, suppose you began working for Microsoft in 1986 (the year it went public), earning a yearly base salary of $48,000 and collecting 2,050 yearly call options worth $32,000. Suppose further that these call options had 10-year maturities and were offered at-the-money.[1] Because Microsoft's share price at the time was $28, the options would have given you the right, but not the obligation, during the next 10 years to

---

[1] Most U.S. employee stock options are granted at-the-money and have 10-year maturities.

buy Microsoft shares for $28, regardless of how high the market price rose.

During the decade between 1986 and 1996, Microsoft's share price rose by 6,500% (i.e., about 52% per year).[2] If you had waited and exercised your options in 1996, you would have received a windfall of almost $3.7 million in additional compensation, bringing your total compensation (just for 1986) to $3.75 million.[3] Conversely, if Microsoft had gone the way of many other companies, and the share price had remained at or below $28, your options would have expired worthless, and you would have ended up earning in 1986 just your base salary of $48,000.

In July 2003, Microsoft surprised the business community when it announced that it would break its 28-year tradition by replacing the company's stock option compensation plan with one that rewarded employees with restricted shares.[4] Some market analysts interpreted this decision as a punctuating event for Microsoft, marking a transition in the company's culture from prioritizing capital gains and the potential for huge future wealth to putting greater weight on cash compensation and more stable future assets.[5] The change in policy was also interpreted as an admission by Microsoft that its stock price was unlikely to rise at its past stratospheric rates.[6]

Microsoft's decision raises many questions. What are the advantages and disadvantages for companies using employee

---

[2]Between 1986 and 1996, Microsoft's share price rose from $28 to slightly over $100, but that was after five stock splits. Adjusted for stock splits, the price of a Microsoft share during the decade from March 1986 to March 1996 increased by slightly less than 6,500% (i.e., from $0.194 on 13 March 1986 to $12.61 on 13 March 1996).

[3]Because you would be receiving $3.75 million 10 years after you received the $48,000 base pay, this multimillion-dollar figure should be discounted to reflect its present value—but it is still a bundle of cash!

[4]Restricted shares give employees (actual) stock as compensation but only after the employees have remained with the company for a required period of time (i.e., the vesting period).

[5]Jonathan Weil, "Microsoft's Move on Restatement Seems Unusual," *Asian Wall Street Journal* (11 July 2003), M1.

[6]Ibid. In fact, that is exactly what happened. From 2003 to 2007, Microsoft's share rose less rapidly than the Dow Jones Industrial Average, NASDAQ Composite Index, and Standard and Poor's 500 Index.

stock options in their compensation plans? What are the benefits, costs, and risks to employees who receive stock options in lieu of outright pay? How do shareholders fare in all of this? Do employee stock options make managers think like stockholders? How would you (or should you) react to an offer with stock options rather than one with salary compensation alone? The answers to these questions depend, in part, on the individuals and the companies involved because people who seek, welcome, and accept option compensation reveal a lot about their tolerance for risk, and the companies that offer stock options reveal a lot about the incentives they feel will best motivate their employees.

The goal of this chapter is to address each of these questions and to provide an overview of the major issues relating to employee stock options so that you are able to form your own opinion about this controversial form of compensation. This chapter explores facets of the risk-return matrix that convince employees to trade off current income for the possibility of earning higher future income and that convince companies to tie employee compensation to their share prices.

Employee Stock Options: A Major Pillar of Executive Compensation

Executive compensation typically is composed of four pillars: a base salary, annual performance bonus, stock options, and long-term incentive plan.[7] The stock option component of these compensation plans is usually in the form of call options, which give an employee the right, but not the obligation, to buy a company's shares at a predetermined price (called the strike price or exercise price) during a given period of time (or on a given date in the future). If the stock price remains at or below the strike price, the options expire worthless, and the employee ends up earning just the base pay. But if the

[7]This chapter is about employee stock options, in general, but its focus is on executive stock options. See Kaye A. Thomas, *Consider Your Options: Get the Most from Your Equity Compensation* (Lisle, IL: Fairmark Press, 2007). An excellent source on this topic is Kevin J. Murphy, *Executive Compensation.* http://papers.ssrn.com/sol3/papers.cfm?abstract_id=163914, April 1998 (posted to database: 19 May 1999). Accessed 9 November 2007.

stock price rises above the strike price (i.e., the options are in-the-money), and the employee exercises the options, the rewards can be significant.

The beauty of owning call options is that they never put you in a position where you end up owing something if the share price falls or remains below the strike price, and you gain for each cent the share price rises above the strike price. Of course, eliminating the downside risk is of little comfort to those who sacrifice higher paying jobs elsewhere for the chance to strike it rich with options in their current jobs. Because the final values are so uncertain, stock options are less attractive to individuals who are risk-averse[8] or foresee declining economic activity (e.g., a recession). By contrast, more adventuresome individuals might prefer having elements of risk that offer upside compensation potential.

Why Do Companies Use Employee Stock Options?

Companies that use stock options in their compensation plans usually do so for one or more of the following reasons: aligning incentives, hiring and retention, adjusting compensation to employee risk tolerance levels, employee tax optimization, and cash flow optimization.

ALIGNING INCENTIVES

The finance and economics literature has long acknowledged that most large corporations are managed by executives who, for the most part, are not major shareholders. As a result, managers' goals are not necessarily the same as the goals of shareholders.[9] The hope is that, by giving employees a piece of the corporation, stock options will build membership and commitment, encourage employees to constantly refresh their skills, and promote decision-making that is consistent with corporate strategy and with the ultimate goal of maximizing shareholder value. The fear is that, without such incentives, employees will pursue more self-serving goals, such as increasing their salaries and power bases, extravagantly beautifying their workspaces, as well as excessively entertaining clients and traveling at company expense.[10]

---

[8]*Risk aversion* is an individual's dislike for unexpected results. A risk-averse person, who is faced with two alternatives, both having the same expected return but different risks, will choose the alternative with the lower risk.

[9]The classic treatment of this topic can be found in Adolph A. Berle and Gardner C. Means, *The Modern Corporation and Private Property* (New York: Macmillan, 1932). For readers interested in the principal-agent theory discourse, a more complete list of references is provided in the bibliography to this chapter.

[10]John Kenneth Galbraith, *The New Industrial State* (Boston: Houghton Mifflin, 1967).

Logic dictates that the more opportunities a company has to invest in value-adding projects, the more important it is to have an incentive system that encourages employees to maximize shareholder value. In fact, empirical evidence supports the claim that companies with greater value-creating opportunities (i.e., projects that contribute to shareholder value) make greater use of employee stock options than those that do not have such growth prospects.[11]

HIRING AND RETENTION

Stock options may be essential for hiring and retaining first-rate employees. Many companies feel that offering employee stock options is necessary in an environment in which competitors offer them.

To more tightly bind employees to a company, many stock option plans have vesting periods, which require employees to wait three to five years (or more) before they can exercise their options and harvest the rewards (assuming there are any). In fact, numerous human resource executives and analysts feel that lengthening both the maturity and the vesting periods of employee stock options are excellent ways to retain key people because they increase an employee's cost of leaving and raise the stakes for covetous competitors trying to hire away quality talent.[12]

Without stock options, young, fast-growing, cash-strapped companies would be hard-pressed to compete aggressively for top-notch employees against established, well-financed competitors. We will have more to say in a later section about the cash flow effects of employee stock options, but, for now, it is important to realize that, if they are not hedged, a company is burdened with no cash outflows when the options are granted. Furthermore, when they expire or are exercised, the magnitude and timing of any negative cash flow effects depend on whether or not the options expire in-the-money, whether or not the company has hedged its exposure, and whether or not the company issues new shares to satisfy the demand by option-exercising employees.

[11]See Sung S. Kwon and Qin Jennifer Yin, "Executive Compensation, Investment Opportunities, and Earnings Management: High-Tech Firms Versus Low-Tech Firms," *Journal of Accounting* 21(2) (Spring 2006), 119–148; and Clifford W. Smith, Jr. and Ross L. Watts, "The Investment Opportunity Set and Corporate Financing, Dividend, and Compensation Policies," *Journal of Financial Economics* 32 (1992), 263–292. It is controversial whether high-opportunity companies actually shift resources toward real investments and the effect it has on firm performance. See Daniel A. Bens, Venky Nagar, and M.H. Franco, "Real Investment Implications of Employee Stock Option Exercises," *Journal of Accounting Research* 40(2c) (May 2002), 359–393.

[12]One problem with long maturities and long vesting periods is that they may inhibit a company's ability to issue new options in the future due to the old issues waiting to mature. Often, those who prefer shorter maturities and shorter vesting periods feel that companies should encourage employees to exercise their options earlier and become shareholders.

ADJUSTING COMPENSATION TO EMPLOYEE RISK TOLERANCE LEVELS

The quantity of stock options paid to an employee as compensation depends on two major factors: the price of each option and the total value of the option compensation. For instance, if you were awarded $32,000 in stock option compensation, and each option was worth $1.00, then you would receive 32,000 options. If the price of each option were $2.00, you would receive only 16,000 options. Call options that are substantially out-of-the-money (i.e., their strike price is much higher than the current market price) have relatively low values because they have little chance of expiring in-the-money.

Companies have the flexibility to choose strike prices that they feel will best motivate their employees, but this choice has a double-edged blade. The higher the strike price, the lower the value of each option because the options have less chance of paying anything. Due to their lower value, employees have to be given more stock options for any predetermined level of compensation. By contrast, a lower strike price increases the option's value, which means that employees receive fewer of them for a given level of compensation, but the chances are greater that the options will be worth something when they expire. By varying the strike price, stock option plans can be adjusted to accommodate different individuals' preferences for either secure income or uncertain future gains. Young, single, energetic college graduates might eagerly choose options that are dramatically out-of-the-money because their lower value means getting more of them. If the share price rose substantially, these young employees could be a millionaires before they are 30. By contrast, married employees with children in college and large mortgages might prefer much lower strike prices and much more secure sources of income.

EMPLOYEE TAX OPTIMIZATION

The tax treatment of employee stock options varies from country to country. Some nations, like the United States, impose no taxes on employee stock options when they are granted, unless the options have intrinsic value (i.e., issued in the money), but then tax any realized appreciation in their value. Other nations, like Switzerland, do just the opposite, taxing employee stock options as ordinary income when they are granted but imposing no tax on their appreciation (i.e., capital gains). In nations where stock option appreciation is recognized as a capital gain (and not as ordinary income), employee stock options can be highly attractive because the tax rate on capital gains is often much lower than the tax rate on ordinary income. The take-away point is always to check about the treatment of *your* employee stock options. It is important and can be messy.

Employee stock options offer recipients considerable control over the timing of their realized earnings. Employees who exercise their stock options can choose either to purchase company shares at the strike price or simply to cash out their profits and earn the difference (per share) between the stock's market price and its strike price. In the United States, when stock options are cashed out, the gains are treated (usually) as ordinary income and taxed at ordinary income tax levels. If employees exercise their options, purchase company shares, and continue to hold them, the profits on any *further* share appreciation are taxed at the capital gains tax rate, which is lower than the rate on ordinary income.

CASH FLOW OPTIMIZATION FOR COMPANIES

Employee stock options become more valuable only if the share price rises above the strike price, and a rising share price usually corresponds with good company performance and favorable expectations about future earnings and cash flows. As a result, one would expect the rising cash outflows associated with exercised employee stock options to coincide with a company's increased ability to pay them.

The cash flow effects of employee stock options should be evaluated at three crucial points: when they are issued, when (and if) they are hedged, and when they are exercised or expire. At issuance, the cash flow effects depend on whether the options are hedged or not. At exercise (or expiration), the cash flow effects depend on the combined conditions of whether or not the options are in-the-money and whether or not the options were hedged.

Cash Flow Effects at Issuance

Employee stock options, regardless of whether a company issues them at-the-money, in-the-money, or out-of-the-money, have no immediate, explicit, negative cash flow effects. In fact, companies using them can be thought to have implicit cash inflows because these options are used as substitutes for higher outright compensation.[13] Nevertheless, if companies cover the exposures created by their employee stock options (i.e., cover their short call positions) by purchasing long call options, then there are cash outflows when the hedge is implemented equal to the price of the option times the number of options purchased.

If a company protects its short call position by purchasing shares in the open market (i.e., increasing its treasury stock), then there are cash outflows at the time the hedge is implemented equal to the price of the share times the number of shares purchased. The increase in demand for shares should

---

[13]Companies must recognize employee stock options as expenses, but a reduction in profits is not the same as cash outflows.

put upward pressure on their price, but simultaneously, by depleting its cash assets, the book value of the company should fall.[14]

Cash Flow Effects at Exercise or Expiration

If the share price remains at or below the strike price, then the options expire worthless, and there are no negative cash flow effects at expiration. Similarly, if a company hedges its employees stock options, then cash outflows from the exercised options are offset by the hedge, and, again, there are no negative cash flow effects.

By contrast, if a company has not hedged its employee stock options, and they expire in-the-money, then the cash flow effects can be positive or negative. Suppose the employee stock options had a strike price of $100 per share, they were exercised when the market price was $150, and employees wanted to own the shares. If it did not issue new shares, the unhedged company would have to pay $150 to acquire each share, and then each of these shares would be transferred to option-exercising employees for only $100. The net effect would be to drain the company's cash reserves by $50 times the number of exercised stock options. Alternatively, if employees had no interest in purchasing shares and wanted only a cash payment, then the company would not need to purchase shares in the open market and would simply make a net payment to the employees of $50 per exercised option.

Finally, if the options expired in-the-money and the company issued new shares to meet the demand, there would be net cash inflows because the company would issue new equity and receive an amount of cash equal to the number of exercised options (i.e., shares purchased) times the strike price. The cash proceeds would be simply added to the company's current assets and paid-in capital, and the number of outstanding shares would increase.

Option Valuation Differences and Human Resource Management

Stock options can create an illusion by presenting two different images of the same reality. An example of this illusion occurs when current or potential employees value options differently from the companies offering them. These discrepancies can be highly important because they can mean the

---

[14]Because companies do not report their balance sheets on a daily, weekly, or monthly basis, the source of the increased demand for shares and the loss of cash assets will probably not be known immediately by investors.

Risk Notepad 2.1

What Effect Do Employee Stock Options Have on Profits? Should They Be Recorded as Expenses?[15]

Since 2005, U.S. companies have been *required* to report as expenses the *fair value*[16] of their equity-based compensation for employee services. This change in accounting treatment was due to the December 2004 release of Rule 123 (R) by the U.S. Financial Accounting Standards Board (FASB).[17] Implementation of the new Rule started in 2005, with the beginning of each company's new fiscal year.

Under FAS 123 (R), equity-based compensation could be paid in two basic forms: equity instruments or liability instruments. Equity instruments, such as stocks, stock options, phantom stocks, and stock appreciation rights (SARs), are valued at their grant date, and liability instruments, such as cash-settled SARs and cash-settled stock compensation, are measured at their settlement date.[18] These costs are then amortized over the estimated life of the employee services, which is normally the vesting period, and a *fair-value-based method* is to be used for appraising the value of these options (rather than the intrinsic-value method).[19]

Before 2005, companies had a choice. They could report *as expenses* either the fair value or the intrinsic value of their employee stock options. Companies choosing the intrinsic value method were still required to report the fair value of their equity-based compensation, but they could do so in the footnotes of their financial statements rather than as explicit expenses. Most companies chose the intrinsic value method because at-the-money options (the usual form of employee compensation) have no intrinsic value. Therefore, choosing this valuation method lowered costs and raised profits above where they would have been. Many observers were concerned that, by lowering U.S. companies' reported earnings, FAS 123 (R) would hurt share prices, but that does not seem to have occurred.[20]

---

[15]For readers interested in a brief historical overview of the accounting treatment for U.S. employee stock options, see Online Appendix 2.1: *Employee Stock Options: A Brief History of U.S. Accounting Treatment* at http://www.prenhall.com/marthinsen.

[16]A *fair value* means that an option's value is measured using a *fair-value-based method* that accounts for the intrinsic value and time value of an option.

[17]Financial Accounting Standards Board, *Statement of Financial Accounting Standards No. 123 (revised 2004): Share-Based Payment* (December 2004). See http://www.fasb.org/news/nr121604_ebc.shtml. Accessed on 9 November 2007. FAS 123 (R) provides accounting guidance for a wide range of equity-based compensation instruments. See Anne L. Leahey and Raymond A. Zimmermann, "A Road Map for Share-Based Compensation," *Journal of Accountancy* 203(4) (April 2007), 50–54; and Tim V. Eaton and Brian R. Prucyk, "No Longer an 'Option'," *Journal of Accountancy*, 199(4) (April 2005), 63–68.

[18]Because liability instruments compensate employees *after* they have performed their services, companies choosing this form of compensation are required to value these liabilities at each reporting date.

[19]Only under certain circumstances (e.g., due to complexity or the lack of comparables for nonpublic firms) can companies use intrinsic value as their method of valuation.

[20]See David Aboody, Mary E. Barth, and Ron Kasznik, "Firms' Voluntary Recognition of Stock-Based Compensation Expense," *Journal of Accounting Research* 42(2) (May 2004), 123–150; and Zvi Bodie, Robert S. Kaplan, and Robert C. Merton, "For the Last Time: Stock Options Are an Expense," *Harvard Business Review* 81(3) (March 2003), 62–71.

(*continued*)

In February 2004, the International Accounting Standards Board (IASB), whose rules are followed by companies in many European countries, issued International Financial Reporting Standards No. 2 (IFRS 2),[21] which required European companies to expense the grant-date value of employee stock options using a fair-value-based method. Therefore, one of the benefits from FAS 123 (R) has been to bring U.S. accounting rules closer to European standards, thereby simplifying international financial comparisons.

One of the burning issues since the passage of FAS 123 (R) and IFRS 2 has been finding the proper way to value employee stock options. The most popular fair-value-based methods have been the Black-Scholes formula, binomial lattice model, and Monte Carlo approach, but regulators have given companies considerable discretion in this area.[22] For instance in 2007, the U.S. Securities and Exchange Commission permitted Utah-based Zions Bancorporation to publicly auction relatively small amounts of Employee Stock Option Appreciation Rights (ESOARS), which had all the payoff characteristics of Zions' employee stock options, to get a market-based value for the company's employee stock options.[23]

For most academic and business audiences, options are costs whether they are explicitly recognized in a company's reported financial statements, disclosed only in footnotes of the financial statements, or not reported at all. To argue that option costs affect share values only when they are disclosed openly is to argue that the stock markets act in systematic but irrational ways for long periods of time. At the same time, better reporting clarity allows the market system to operate more efficiently and effectively. The recognition of options as a compensation cost was (and is) supported by FASB, IASB, many members of the academic community (e.g., Myron Scholes and Robert Merton, who won the 1997 Nobel Prize in Economics for their part in developing the Black-Scholes formula), as well as numerous central bank, government, and business leaders (e.g., former Federal Reserve Chairman Alan Greenspan and investor-billionaire Warren Buffett).

In the end, the pressure of logic and the demand for transparency prevailed so that fully expensed employee stock option compensation must now be recorded and disclosed.[24] Perhaps the sentiment behind FAS 123 (R) was best expressed by Warren Buffett when he said, "If options aren't a form of compensation, what are they? And if compensation isn't an expense, what is it? And if expenses shouldn't go into the calculation of earnings, where in the world should they go?"[25]

FAS 123 (R) is a step toward better accounting transparency, relevancy, and consistency. If it is successful, the main beneficiaries will be not only shareholders, analysts, and regulators but also employees and managers because the new standard neutralizes

[21]IFRS 2 stands for *International Financial Reporting Standards No. 2, Share-Based Payment.*

[22]See Greg Regan, Matt Lombardi, and Michael Gray, "FAS 123R: Accounting for Stock Options," *California CPA* 75(8) (March/April 2007), 12–15.

[23]It is a matter of debate why the market value of Zions' ESOARS was lower than the theoretical value estimated by the Black-Scholes formula. See Floyd Norris, "What Seller Wants a Low Price?" *The New York Times* (1 June 2007), C1.

[24]Junning Cai, "Accounting for Employee Stock Options and Mandatory Expensing: An Economics Perspective," *Journal of Derivatives Accounting* 2(2) (September 2005), 137–154.

[25]Warren Buffett, "Stock Options and Common Sense," *The Washington Post* (9 April 2002), A19.

the accounting treatment of stock option plans. As a result, plain-vanilla stock option plans (i.e., at-the-money call options) will no longer be treated differently from more innovative plans, such as index options (which will be discussed later in this chapter). FAS 123 (R), therefore, has cleared a path for greater creativity and flexibility in designing and administrating employee stock option plans.

difference between landing or retaining quality talent and losing the talent to competitors—often after extended searches and after investing thousands of dollars and hundreds of hours in fruitless recruitment efforts.

To better understand the illusion created by options, imagine yourself trying to decide between two attractive job offers. One position offers you pure salary compensation, and the other is a combination of salary and stock options. How would you go about deciding which one to accept? To make the choice even more interesting, suppose that, on paper, the salary-with-options offer was about 10% higher than the pure-salary offer. The following dialog puts you in the shoes of someone who was in just this position. It explains how she systematically decided which offer was better *for her*. In the process, you will gain a better appreciation for the way in which many companies arrive at the values *they put* on employee stock options and how these values may be quite different from the value *employees put* on them. Hopefully the ideas that emerge from this dialog will be helpful to you if (and when) you negotiate a future contact.

Helvetia Holding, a pharmaceutical company located in Boston, Massachusetts, spent nine months identifying the scientist it wanted to head corporate-wide research and development activities, but the candidate was also being pursued by Zentrum Inc., an equally important U.S. pharmaceutical company located just minutes away in Cambridge. Knowing that Zentrum was offering an outright salary of $550,000, Helvetia countered with a total compensation package worth $600,000: $400,000 in outright salary and $200,000 worth of stock options. Imagine the surprise of Helvetia's human resources chief when the scientist turned down Helvetia's offer because she found Zentrum's deal to be financially more attractive. You might ask: "How can two people put such different values on something so seemingly cut and dried as an option's price?"

To understand the answer to this question, let's roll back the clock to the day before Helvetia made its employment offer. It is highly likely that the director of human resources understood very well the benefits, costs, risks, and returns of call options, but he had no idea how to value them. For that he relied on Helvetia's treasury department. Let's look in on the conversation between Daniel Weiss, Helvetia's human resources chief, and Tom Benson,

Helvetia's assistant treasurer, that took place the day before the offer was made.

Daniel Weiss: Tom, thank you for coming on such short notice, but I need to know, as quickly as possible, the market price of a call option on a Helvetia share. Can you help me, and how long do you think it will take you to figure this out?

Tom Benson: I'd be glad to help, Daniel, and once we agree on a few details, it will take me only a minute or so to enter the information into my computer and figure out the market price of the option, but first I need some information from you. The price of any option depends on six major factors: current share price, the exercise (or strike) price, maturity, expected share price volatility, risk-free interest rate, and expected dividends. I came prepared with most of this information, but I need to know from you the maturity and strike price.

Daniel Weiss: All right. Helvetia's current share price is $50, so could you tell me the price of a five-year call option that has a $50 strike price?

Tom Benson: Fine, then you want to price a five-year, at-the-money call option. That's all I needed to know. Let me just summarize in this table the six variables we will be using in our calculations, just to make sure that what I am entering into my computer is transparent to you.

Helvetia Option Pricing Information	
Current share price	$50
Strike price	$50
Maturity	5 years
Volatility	35%
Risk free interest rate	4.75%
Dividends	$0

Based on this information, the Black-Scholes formula tells us that the market price of this option should be $19.49.

Daniel Weiss: Just for comparison sake, could you tell me the price of a 10-year call option with the same $50 strike price?

Tom Benson: With a 10-year maturity, an at-the-money call option should have a market price of $27.84.

Daniel Weiss: OK. Give me just a second to write down this information. That was much easier than I thought it would be. Thanks for your help, Tom.

> Call Option Prices @ $50 strike price
>
> 5-year call option = $19.49
>
> 10-year call option = $27.84

Armed with this knowledge, Daniel Weiss could now make his offer to Jennifer Smith, a research professor at M.I.T. and head of R&D at Bio-Pharm Associates in Wellesley, Massachusetts. Weiss figured that, if an at-the-money, five-year stock option was worth $19.49, and he wanted to compensate Smith with $200,000 worth of stock option benefits, then the compensation package should include 10,262 stock options.[26] To ease the math and sweeten the deal, Weiss rounded the offer at 10,500 call options. The next morning, he called Jennifer Smith and made his offer. As he explained the offer to her, Weiss stressed that Smith would get raises each year and additional stock options in proportion to her salary.

Jennifer Smith had been anxiously awaiting Weiss' call because Zentrum was actively pressuring her for an answer. Weiss explained to Smith the calculations behind his offer of a base salary of $400,000 and 10,500 call options, and he volunteered the services of Tom Benson if she had any technical questions about how Helvetia valued her options. Smith had no immediate questions about the offer or the option valuation. At first glance, Helvetia's offer looked very attractive. "Imagine," she thought, "being offered over $50,000 more than Zentrum. How can I say no?"

Jennifer Smith didn't really understand any of the nuances of option pricing; so she wasn't sure how to reply to Weiss' offer. All she could think to ask was whether the options had any restrictions, like a vesting period. Embarrassed by the oversight, Weiss answered that all of Helvetia's

---

[26] $200,000 ÷ $19.49 per option = 10,261.67 options ≅ 10,262 options.

employee stock options had three-year vesting periods. Smith knew from experience that this was normal.

From her years in the corporate world, Jennifer Smith had earned a stellar professional reputation using her mind in clever and, at times, ingenious ways, but on numerous occasions, she had been saved from disaster by her instincts, and in this case, her instincts were flashing red. Her mind was telling her that the Helvetia offer was head and shoulders above the Zentrum offer, but if that was the case, why didn't it seem $50,000 better *to her*? Something wasn't right, and she protected herself by asking Weiss for a few days to think over her alternatives. Weiss reluctantly agreed to a three-day decision period.

It took Smith only a day to come to the conclusion that Helvetia's offer was *not* as financially attractive as Zentrum's offer, and by the time she called Daniel Weiss, she had already accepted Zentrum's contract. Weiss was staggered. He was so sure she would accept his offer that he had already notified the CEO to include her name in Helvetia's organization chart. How could Helvetia's offer of over $600,000 not be as attractive "financially" as a competing offer for $550,000?

Weiss asked Smith if he could call her later that day. Realizing that he had lost the battle with Zentrum, he did not want to make the same mistake again. Quickly, he called Tom Benson and asked if Benson could participate in the conversation. Benson was glad to help and curious, as well, about what happened. Later that day, here is how the conversation went.

Daniel Weiss:	Dr. Smith, we are very disappointed to have lost you to our competitor. Are you sure there is nothing we can do to change your mind?
Jennifer Smith:	Thank you, Daniel, but no. I've accepted the Zentrum offer, and I'm happy with my decision.
Daniel Weiss:	I have Tom Benson on the line with me, just so he can help me piece together what went wrong. You will remember that Mr. Benson helped me value your stock options. Did I tell you that we used the Black-Scholes formula to do our valuation?
Tom Benson:	Hello, Dr. Smith. Thank you for allowing me to be a part of this conversation. I'm as interested as Mr. Weiss in understanding how you arrived at your decision.
Jennifer Smith:	I realize you both must think I'm crazy—especially when Nobel prizes were given to the gentlemen who developed the Black-Scholes formula, but all I can say is that what the formula says Helvetia's options *should be* worth is not

what *I feel* they are worth to me. Here's how I arrived at my conclusion. First, let me preface my remarks by admitting that I had some help making up my mind. After our call yesterday, Daniel, I phoned an old friend, John, who is now teaching at a nearby college. John and I met last night for dinner, and he sorted out some of the technical details for me. The first question I asked him was if there was any way I could lock-in immediately the $200,000 of stock option compensation that Helvetia was offering.

Daniel Weiss: That sounds logical enough. What was his answer?

Jennifer Smith: He explained that my call options gave me the right to buy Helvetia shares for $50 any time after the three-year vesting period. One way to lock in the value of the options would be to sell short the Helvetia shares—which I now understand means that I would have to borrow shares, sell them at the current market price, and agree to pay them back in the future.

Daniel Weiss: I've heard of short selling but never really understood what it meant. Usually, when I think of someone making a profit, I think in terms of buying something today and then selling it in the future at a higher price. What you would be doing is just the opposite: selling Helvetia shares today and then buying them in five years at the price guaranteed by your stock options. It's sort of like closing the loop—selling now and then buying later.

Jennifer Smith: Exactly! But once I sold the shares short and collected the proceeds, I'd have to invest the funds in a safe asset, like a U.S. government bond. My Helvetia options had five-year maturities, so I based all of my calculations on investing the funds until maturity.

Daniel Weiss: But, Dr. Smith, would it be legal or ethical to sell short Helvetia's shares in this way?

Jennifer Smith: Imagine my surprise when I found out that, even if I wanted to, I could *not* sell short the Helvetia shares. Apparently, there are rules in the United States that put tight restrictions on short sales of stocks by employees.

Tom Benson: If my memory is correct, Section 16-C of the 1934 U.S. Securities and Exchange Act prohibits officers and directors from selling shares in their companies if they do not already own the securities. There could also be insider-trading issues.

Jennifer Smith: Yes, that's true, but my main point is that even if I could sell short the Helvetia shares, I figured that the most I could lock in—assuming Helvetia shares rose in value, which I'm sure they will—would be only about $137,100, and to do that, I'd have to wait five years! Here's how I did my calculations.

If I sold short 10,500 Helvetia shares at $50 per share, I'd receive $525,000, which then I could invest for five years. Currently, a five-year U.S. government bond yields 4.75%; so $525,000 invested at a compound annual rate of 4.75% would grow to $662,109 in five years. At the end of the five years, if Helvetia's share price rose above $50, I would exercise my options, spend $525,000 to buy back and return the 10,500 shares that I borrowed, and have $137,109 remaining.

Daniel Weiss was frantically trying to write all of this on his pad. He now understood how Jennifer Smith derived her figures, and he was relieved by the thought that he could review his notes later with Tom Benson. Her math made sense. Nevertheless, he called on Tom Benson for confirmation.

<u>To lock in minimum option value</u>

- Short 10,500 shares
  Receive: $10,500 \times \$50 =$
  $525,000

- Invest for 5 years @ 4.75%
  Receive: $525,000 \times (1.0475)^5 =$
  $662,108.95

- In 5 years, buy shares to cover short position
  Pay: $10,500 \times \$50 = \$525,000$

- <u>Net</u>: $662,108.95 - 525,000 =$
  137,108.95
  $\approx \$137,109!$

Daniel Weiss: Mr. Benson, do you agree with Dr. Smith?

Tom Benson: Yes, I do. Here's the problem. An option's initial market value can vary within minimum and maximum limits. The $137,109 figure that Ms. Smith calculated as the amount she could lock in if she sold short Helvetia's shares, works out to $13.06 per option. Discounted, this equals $10.35 per option, which is close to the minimum initial option price. The maximum initial price is Helvetia's current $50 share price. The Black-Scholes formula, for reasons we will not get into here, calculated a market price for the Helvetia option equal to $19.49, which is within this minimum-maximum range. Actually, if Ms. Smith wanted to cover her position, all she could hope to do is to lock in a range of possible future payoffs with $137,109 being the minimum.

Daniel Weiss: If $137,109 is the minimum she could lock in, then how could she earn the maximum value?

Tom Benson: Well, here Dr. Smith has been very diplomatic. To earn more than $137,109, the price of a Helvetia share would have to fall below $50 when she exercised her options in five years, and to earn the maximum, the Helvetia share would have to fall to $0.

Daniel Weiss: I see. The call options give her the right, but not the obligation, to buy Helvetia shares in five years at $50. If the share price fell to $0, she would let the options expire and pay nothing to return the borrowed shares. At the end of five years, the entire investment (principal and interest) of $662,109 would be hers to keep.

Tom Benson: Exactly.

Daniel Weiss: Dr. Smith, I'm no expert on hedging, but I've always thought that to hedge, you had to take a position the exact opposite of the one you had. In other words, take what you have and do the opposite. Since Helvetia would be compensating you with long call options, to hedge this position, I thought you would want to sell options with the same strike price and maturity.

Jennifer Smith: Daniel, you're absolutely right, and, yes, John and I discussed last night the possibility of shorting call options on Helvetia shares. Here's the problem. Helvetia has exchange-traded options in the United States, but they do not have the same maturities or strike prices as the ones you would be giving me. Even if they existed, John told me that I would be exposed to a sizeable cash risk due to margin calls.

<u>To lock in minimum option value</u>

- <u>Short 10,500 shares</u>
  Receive: $10,500 \times \$50 =$
  $\$525,000$

- <u>Invest for 5 years @ 4.75%</u>
  Receive: $525,000 \times (1.0475)^5 =$
  $\$662,108.95$

- In 5 years, <u>buy shares to cover</u>
                 <u>short position</u>
  Pay: $10,500 \times \$0.00 = \$00.00$

- Net: $662,109 - \$00.00 =$
  $\$662,109!$

Daniel Weiss: Margin calls? How is that a risk? The gains from your Helvetia call options should exactly offset the losses on your hedge—or vice versa? No?

Jennifer Smith: In the long run, you're right. It's true that, eventually, the gains or losses from my Helvetia options would offset the losses or gains from my hedges, but in the short run, I could be in for quite a financial roller-coaster ride. The problem is that, if Helvetia's share price rose rapidly, I'd be rich on paper because my long call options on Helvetia shares would be in-the-money. In other words, they'd have a lot of intrinsic value, but I wouldn't collect these profits until I exercised the options—and that wouldn't be for three to five years from now. In the meantime, the exchange-traded options—my hedges—would be repriced daily and their rising price would require me to constantly feed margin to my broker. It could end up draining all of my savings!

Daniel Weiss looked down at the notes he had made on his memo pad. There were only three major points, but a voice deep inside told him that there was more to come.

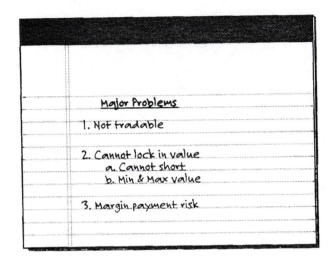

Daniel Weiss: Dr. Smith, you have been very thorough, patient, and generous with your time, but, some time today, I'm going to have to explain to my boss how we lost you; so please answer for me just one question. How was it possible for Helvetia to offer you over $50,000 more than Zentrum but for you to feel that the Zentrum offer was financially more attractive? Is it just because Zentrum was offering you a sure thing, and we were offering you a degree of uncertainty? Did you consider that the uncertainty of our offer also contained the opportunity to strike it rich and become a millionaire?

Jennifer Smith: I can assure you that becoming a millionaire didn't escape my attention, but the fundamental problem I had with Helvetia's offer, was that the price *you put* on the options was not equal to the value *I put* on them. Even after figuring in the advantage I would have over anyone outside the company with regard to timing the exercise of my options, your offer came up short.

Daniel Weiss: We—and by "we" I mean Mr. Benson and I—did not put an arbitrary price on the options. We used the Black-Scholes formula, which is used by virtually everyone. I have always thought that it was considered widely to be an unbiased and highly accurate way of valuing options.

Jennifer Smith: My second major question last night to John was: "What is this Black-Scholes formula, and how is it coming up with an option price that seems so out of whack with my instincts?" Its precision alone was unnerving. Any formula that says an option should be worth exactly $19.49 made me skeptical—or should I say, nervous. As a scientist, I knew that the Black-Scholes formula had to be based on a set of assumptions. I also knew that, in the course of one evening, I had no chance of understanding all the intricacies of option pricing models; so I took a simpler and more direct route. All I wanted to know was whether the assumptions behind the Black-Scholes formula made Helvetia's options look more desirable or less desirable *to me*. It was a simple plus and minus evaluation, and at the end, I asked myself whether the difference was large enough to nullify the $50,000 advantage of Helvetia's offer. For me, the Helvetia offer came up short, so I accepted the Zentrum offer.

Daniel Weiss: I find it amazing that you did all this work in one evening. Now, I am doubly disappointed that you will not be working with us.

Jennifer Smith: Here's what I discovered from John. The Black-Scholes formula was designed for tradable, short-term options rather than nontradable, nontransferable, long-term options, like Helvetia was offering me. John said that you probably based your option prices on past market statistics, plugged the six important parameters into the Black-Scholes formula, and assumed that these factors would remain constant over the maturity of my options.

Daniel Weiss: Yes. That is exactly what we did.

Jennifer Smith: Well, I figured that, with just slight modifications in your assumptions and their constancy over time, my options could be worth either far more or far less than the Black-Scholes formula estimated.

Daniel Weiss: I understand. You questioned not only the factors we entered into the formula but also their stability over time, and because of this risk, you turned down our offer.

Jennifer Smith: Exactly. I was surprised to find over the course of last evening how risk-averse I am. Do you know what else bothered me about Black-Scholes?

Daniel Weiss: Please tell me.

Jennifer Smith: The common sense, or lack of it, behind some of the assumptions used in the formula.

Daniel Weiss: The common sense? Do they have to make common sense?

Jennifer Smith: They do to me. Remember that I'm a research scientist with an analytical education but with little or no training in finance.

Daniel Weiss: Do you have an example?

Jennifer Smith: Take volatility, for instance. I now understand why volatility is important to option pricing, but we have just come out of a tumultuous economic and political period. This increased volatility raised the Black-Scholes price of the options you offered me, but curiously, it lowered their value *to me*.

Daniel Weiss: What is your prediction about the future?

Jennifer Smith: Looking forward, I anticipate calmer conditions—which mean lower volatility—and my expectation has a bizarre, reverse effect on the price of Helvetia's options. It lowers their Black-Scholes price but raises their value *to me*. Sorry, Daniel and Tom, but I don't see how increased volatility and uncertainty help me. For me to place a higher value on Helvetia options, I would need to believe that they would grow at a steady positive rate, so I could exercise them in three to five years at a profit. Increased volatility is a threat to me because the period of time when I would be allowed and want to exercise them might coincide with a gigantic dip in the share price. This led me into the issue of tradability.

Daniel Weiss: So, tradability, again. Are you saying that because these options are not tradable, their value is reduced to you?

Jennifer Smith: Precisely, and, for me, that's a big negative. They're not tradable, and they're not transferable. In other words, only I can exercise them, and when I do, I have to exercise them against Helvetia. John told me that high volatility increases the price of *tradable* options, but it may not increase the value of *non*tradable options like the kind you were offering me. Black-Scholes assumes that it's unwise, or, more formally, "sub-optimal" for investors to exercise call options early because they could always sell them in the market for their intrinsic value *and* time value.

For example, suppose that today I bought a five-year call option on a Helvetia share with a $50 strike price, and then sold it three years later when the market price was $60. I'd get $10 for the amount by which the option was in-the-money—this is called the option's intrinsic value—and I'd get additional compensation for the two years of remaining maturity—this is called the option's time value. The Helvetia options you're offering me can't be sold in the market. I'd have to sell them directly to Helvetia, and then I'd receive only their intrinsic value. In other words, because they aren't tradable or transferable, I'd earn nothing for the time remaining to maturity. Because of their lack of tradability, your offer earned another black mark in my book.

Daniel Weiss: You seem to have gone right to the critical assumptions of the Black-Scholes formula and questioned them in ways that we didn't consider. OK, Dr. Smith, I'm beginning to see your point, so I guess that Mr. Benson and I should go back to the drawing board and—

Jennifer Smith: Hold on! I'm not done. There are more points to take into consideration. Since I have your attention, may I continue?

Daniel Weiss: Please do.

Jennifer Smith: Your vesting period also irked me. I knew that a three-year vesting period was normal—I didn't need John to tell me that—but the vesting period's length was not one of the six factors that John said was used in the Black-Scholes formula. I figured that, if restrictions like this could be entered into the formula, they surely would reduce the price of my options and their value to me. They would not raise it. Look at it this way, Daniel, I could quit or be fired before the three-year vesting period ended, and, if I did quit or was fired, I'd receive nothing! Again, I put this factor in the negative column, but admittedly, I was unsure how much difference it made to my final decision.

Daniel Weiss: I'm humbled by all the work you put into this and by what you have taught me already. Is that all, or is there more?

Jennifer Smith: I'm almost done. By accepting your offer, I would have made my portfolio even more lopsided than it already is because I'd be swimming in Helvetia exposure, with little chance of diversifying until I exercised the options. This increased vulnerability was another reason my valuation of the Helvetia call options may have differed from your valuation. I was also concerned that the Black-Scholes formula assumes a world in which investors pay no transaction costs and have an ability to sell short their shares—which I already mentioned should not be done. Daniel, the more I thought about your offer, the more I realized that the $50,000 premium you thought you were paying was not a premium to me.

Daniel Weiss: What would you have said if I had offered you options with the same strike price but with 10-year, rather than five-year, maturities? Mr. Benson calculated that a 10-year option should have a price of $27.84.

Jennifer Smith: Funny you should mention that. Near the end of our meal last night, John and I began to troubleshoot ways to make your deal look more attractive. We discussed lengthening the maturity of your options because the Black-Scholes formula says that the longer the maturity, the higher the option's price.

Daniel Weiss: I guess that's something we can all agree on!

Jennifer Smith: Not really.

Daniel Weiss: Unbelievable, that cannot be true!

Jennifer Smith: Here's why. First, if you gave me 10-year call options worth $27.84, but still gave me only $200,000 in stock option compensation, then all you'd be doing is reducing the number of options I got from 10,262 to about 7,200. I know that you graciously rounded up my compensation to 10,500 options, but you get the point.

Daniel Weiss: Yes, I see what you mean. In that case, we might have had to make an adjustment.

Jennifer Smith: But, Daniel, that's not my main point. My major problem with increasing the maturity of these options is it would not significantly raise their value to me because the options wouldn't be tradable and because I couldn't short the Helvetia shares. The change in value to you and the Black-Scholes formula from doubling the maturity would be more than $8, but to me the difference, if there were any, would be miniscule.

Daniel Weiss: How is that possible?

Jennifer Smith: I asked myself: "What use would it be to double the length of my options if there was no chance I was going to wait 10 years to cash them in, and no way to sell them so I could take advantage of the remaining time to maturity?"

John mentioned that, in general, the more risk-averse an individual is and the more significant stock options are as a portion of her portfolio, the earlier she is likely to exercise these options. He went on to explain that most people cash in their employee stock options soon after the vesting period ends, which in my case would be three years. He assumed that I'd probably do the same, so whether you gave me a five-year option or a 10-year option, the relevant time period *for me* would remain about three years.

Doubling an option's maturity might have its greatest appeal to someone like Methuselah, who lived to be 969 years old. If I had a well-diversified portfolio and your stock options were only a small part of my total wealth, then the uncertainty surrounding their value would be less important to me. I could afford to wait before exercising, even if the share price fell. Sorry Daniel, but even if you increased the maturity of the options, it probably wouldn't have made much of a difference—but thank you for asking.

Daniel Weiss: Mr. Benson, you have been uncharacteristically quiet through all of this. What do you have to say about Dr. Smith's arguments?

Tom Benson: Actually, I am a little embarrassed because I agree with all of them. Dr. Smith did an excellent job, but in my defense, I tried to answer the question you asked me, which was "What is the *market price* of a five-year option with a $50 exercise price." Sorry, I should have been more alert to why you needed the option's price. Together, we might have been able to head off many of these valuation and communication problems.

Daniel Weiss: Dr. Smith, on behalf of Mr. Benson and me, I want to thank you for your time, openness, and honesty. This conversation has been a real eye-opener for me, but it may take some time for me to digest it all.

Jennifer Smith: It was my pleasure. I'm sure I would have enjoyed working at Helvetia.

Daniel Weiss knew that he had a lot of explaining to do this afternoon when he met with Helvetia's CEO. It was now clear to him that the valuation of stock options was not as black and white as he had thought. In the future, before he assigned a value to Helvetia's employee stock options, he would need to think harder about all the issues Dr. Smith outlined to him.

Major Problems

1. Not tradable

2. Cannot lock in value
   a. Cannot short
   b. Min & Max value

3. Margin payment risk

4. Assumptions questioned
   a. Volatility
   b. Tradability-again!
   c. Vesting period
   d. Not diversified
   e. Transactions costs
   f. Maturity

Problems with Employee Stock Options

As you can see from the discussion among Jennifer Smith, Daniel Weiss, and Tom Benson, the decision to use stock options to compensate executives could lead to difficulties. Shortcomings of the Black-Scholes formula (and other option pricing models) for pricing employee stock options have long been recognized by the academic and business communities, and solutions are being sought. To this end, new option valuation models are being developed that account for the idiosyncrasies of employee stock options.[27] In addition, companies are experimenting with solutions that address some of these specific problems. For example in 2007, Google offered its employees transferable stock options,[28] thereby allowing them to capture the

[27]See for example Charles Baril, Luis Betancourt, and John Briggs, "Valuing Employee Stock Options under SFAS 123R Using the Black-Scholes-Merton and Lattice Model Approaches," *Journal of Accounting Education* 25(1/2) (January 2007), 88–101; Lookman Buky Folami, Tarun Arora, and Kasim I. Alli, "Using Lattice Models to Value Employee Stock Options Under SFAS 123(R)," *CPA Journal* 76(9) (September 2006), 38–43; J. Carr Bettis, John M. Bizjak, and Michael L. Lemmon, "Exercise Behavior, Valuation, and the Incentive Effects of Employee Stock Options," *Journal of Financial Economics* 76(2) (May 2005), 445–470; and John D. Finnerty, "Extending the Black-Scholes-Merton Model to Value Employee Stock Options," *Journal of Applied Finance* 15(2) (Fall/Winter 2005), 25–54.
[28]The original maturity of these options was 10 years, and they could be sold only after a vesting period. Once sold, their maturity dropped to two years, unless there were fewer than two years left until maturity. See Ben Charny, "UPDATE: Google to Let Employees Trade Their Stock Options to Institutions," *Dow Jones Business News* (12 December 2006).

options' intrinsic value *and* time value. Other companies, like Swiss-based Roche Holding and Givaudan SA, offered their employees, for years, exchange-traded options rather than options that could be exercised only against the company.

In addition to valuation dilemmas, there are other important issues such as whether options are the best way to motivate employees, if good companies' share prices always increase rapidly, whether options motivate undesired behavior, if options improve company performance, and whether options that reward absolute performance are the best form of option-based incentive compensation. Let's look more closely at each of these issues.

EMPLOYEE MOTIVATION

To be successful, any pay-for-performance compensation plan should link a company's success drivers to clearly defined, transparent measures that employees understand and are able to influence—but not manipulate. In other words, there must be firmly established goals that employees understand and have authority to influence but that are not open to exploitation.

Many people feel that employee stock options are an ideal way to motivate employees because rewards are given only when the stock price increases, and, therefore, the company is in a position to pay extra compensation. But should options be given to *all* employees?[29] As a generalization, it is true that every employee's actions influence the stock price, but on a more practical, day-to-day level, how many people in a company truly believe that what they do has any direct, identifiable effect on the daily, weekly, monthly, and yearly fluctuations of a share's value?[30] A better incentive for energizing employees and rewarding performance may be setting goals that are more directly under their control, such as targets for increased production, better customer service levels, less returned merchandise, or fewer customer complaints.

Critics ask: "How often do employees working in back-office jobs, maintenance crews, or cost centers reflect on how their productivity affects the share price?" Even in cases where employees may have relatively large degrees of influence on the share price (e.g., high-level executives), the multitude of co-workers with similar titles and responsibilities may make the weight of any individual's decisions and the narrow scope of his responsibilities seem small. Surely, there is a paradox here because it is clear that the

---

[29]Some companies, like Cisco, PepsiCo, Southwest Airlines, and Starbucks, give most or all employees (albeit, often subject to acceptable performance reviews) stock options or the right to purchase shares at reduced prices.

[30]A large portion of the fluctuation in a company's share price is due to external factors outside any employee's control, such as general movements in the industry, stock market, weather, and macroeconomic conditions.

collective actions of a majority of a company's workers do have a direct and significant effect on the share price, but nonetheless, the actions of just one of these individuals is relatively small in most cases.

THE SHARE PRICE OF "GOOD" COMPANIES

Another reason why stock options may not be good motivators of employees is because good companies do not always earn above-average returns for their shareholders. As illogical as this statement may seem, a moment's reflection will show that it is correct. If a company is well run, has good future prospects, and investors recognize all of this, then the market should already factor the quality management and bright prospects into the *current* share price. So long as the company meets (and does not exceed or fall short of) the market's already high expectations, the share should earn just an average return. Only if performance is better than expected will the shares earn above-average returns.[31] For employees working in companies that are the darlings of Wall Street, the prospects of bettering market expectations could be difficult, and therefore, the employees' likelihood of profiting richly from stock option compensation could be low.

MOTIVATING UNDESIRED BEHAVIOR

Employee stock options could encourage shortsightedness in business decisions because they focus on the ultimate goal of increasing share prices rather than on the important enabling factors that cause the share price to appreciate, such as profit margins, sales growth, cost of capital, and discounted cash flows.[32] Establishing stock option plans could encourage managers to artificially inflate share prices by reducing dividend payouts, using cash funds to repurchase outstanding shares, and/or borrowing to finance the repurchase of shares—thereby increasing the company's leverage and level of risk.[33] Furthermore, because the market value of options increases with volatility, there is some reason to speculate whether granting them provides incentives for managers to injudiciously amplify the operating risks and nonoperating risks of their companies. Some industry analysts

---

[31]See Tim Koller, Marc Goedhart, and David Wessels, *Valuation: Measuring and Managing the Value of Companies.* 4th ed. New York: Wiley, 2005.

[32]Ibid.

[33]See George W. Fenn and Nellie Liang, "Corporate Payout Policy and Managerial Stock Incentives." *Journal of Financial Economics* 60, Iss. 1 (April 2001), 45–72. Also see Richard A. Lambert, William N. Lanen, and David F. Larcker, "Executive Stock Options Plans and Corporate Dividend Policy," *Journal of Financial and Quantitative Analysis* 24, No. 4 (December 1989), 409–425; and Hideaki Kiyoshi Kato, Michael Lemmon, Mi Luo, and James Schallheim, "An Empirical Examination of the Costs and Benefits of Executive Stock Options: Evidence from Japan," *Journal of Financial Economics* 78(2) (November 2005), 435–461.

believe that financial misconduct at companies like Enron and WorldCom, where executives seemed narrowly focused on raising the short-term value of their option compensation, was at least part of the motivation for Microsoft and other companies to change their incentive programs away from employee stock options.[34]

A good example of undesirable behaviour is illegally backdating employee stock options. Backdating occurs when a company grants employee stock options on one date (e.g., June 1) and then changes the issue date afterwards (e.g., to March 1) so the options have greater value. Actually, backdating options is a legal practice so long as it is reported promptly and accurately. What is illegal is forging, falsifying, hiding, and/or not reporting material option expenses. Backdating carries special cachet in the current debate because it connects financial transparency with issues related to fair executive compensation and equitable tax burdens.[35]

IMPROVING PERFORMANCE

Fundamental to the question "Why employee stock options?" is a current debate about whether stock option compensation actually improves companies' performance. Critics ask if there is any evidence showing that companies using stock option plans perform better than companies that do not. The United States has had over a decade and a half of intensive experience using this form of compensation. As a result, there is a wealth of information available for evaluating the effects of stock options on corporate performance. Unfortunately, the results are ambiguous, which means the ultimate verdict is still to be determined.[36]

[34]Jonathan Weil, "Microsoft's Move on Restatement Seems Unusual," *Asian Wall Street Journal,* (11 July 2003), M1.

[35]Dow Jones News Service, "Companies Responding to Stock Option Investigations (8/30)," *Dowjones Newswires* 30 August 2007. Also seem Erik Lie, "On the Timing of CEO Stock Option Awards," *Management Science* 51(5) May 2005, 802–812.

[36]Evidence in favor can be found in Marion Hutchinson and Ferdinand A. Gull, "The Effects of Executive Share Options and Investment Opportunities on Firms' Accounting Performance: Some Australian Evidence," *The British Accounting Review* 38(3) (September 2006), 277–297; Eric Schulz, Stewart L. Tubbs, "Stock Options Influence on Manager's Salaries and Firm Performance," *The Business Review* 5(1) (September 2006), 14–19; Swee-Sum Lam and Bey-Fen Chng, "Do Executive Stock Option Grants Have Value Implications for Firm Performance?" *Review of Quantitative Finance and Accounting* 26(3) (May 2006), 249–274; James C Sesil, Maya K Kroumova, Joseph R Blasi, and Douglas L. Kruse, "Broad-Based Employee Stock Options in U.S. 'New Economy' Firms," *British Journal of Industrial Relations* 40(2) (June 2002), 273–294; and D. Yermack, "Good Timing: CEO Stock Option Awards and Company News Announcements," *Journal of Finance* 52(2) (1997) 449–476. Agnostic conclusions can be found in J. Brickly, S. Bhagat, and R. Lease, "The Impact of Long-Range Managerial Compensation Plans on Shareholder Wealth," *Journal of Accounting and Economics* 7(1–3) (1985), 115–129. Also see Kevin J. Murphy, *Executive Compensation.* http://papers.ssrn.com/sol3/papers.cfm? abstract_id=163914, April 1998 (Date posted to database: 19 May 1999) Accessed 8 November 2007, and Hideaki Kiyoshi Kato, Michael Lemmon, Mi Luo, and James Schallheim, "An Empirical Examination of the Costs and Benefits of Executive Stock Options: Evidence from Japan," *Journal of Financial Economics* 78(2) (November 2005), 435–461.

ABSOLUTE VERSUS RELATIVE PERFORMANCE

Another potential problem with stock options is the absolute, rather than relative, nature of their payoffs. A rising tide tends to raise all ships, even those carrying a lot of excess baggage and lacking direction. In rising markets, stock options reward employees even if their performance is worse than competitors. In falling markets, these options provide no compensation even if the company's performance is stellar relative to competitors. This asymmetry and lack of relative comparison introduces an element of uncertainty and unfairness into employees' compensation because it decouples compensation from personal performance and makes compensation dependent on the broader macroeconomic environment. As a result of this asymmetry, in falling markets, stock options give employees with specialized training an incentive to switch employers in order to get new stock options with better upside potential.

Some Innovative Solutions to Employee Stock Option Problems

Some innovative compensation plans that address the shortcomings of "plain vanilla" employee stock options have been proposed and implemented. Let's review the major ones.

PREMIUM-PRICED STOCK OPTIONS

Business acumen is often confused with being in the right place at the right time. Plain, at-the-money stock options reward employees whenever the share price increases, even if the appreciation is less than the average competitor's increase and even if it is due entirely to general market trends (i.e., not because of effective management or superior strategy). One way to level the playing field is by offering *premium-priced stock options,* which have strike prices that are anywhere from 25% to 100% out-of-the-money. To gain any intrinsic value, the share price has to rise above the premium, so this type of option offers a way for companies to raise the performance hurdle for their employees. Suppose a company had a share price of $40, and it offered five-year employee stock options with a premium of 50%. To be in-the-money, the company's share price would have to increase to more than $60 ($40 plus a 50% premium).

The benefit of premium-priced stock option plans is that they are relatively transparent (employees understand them, but not as well as plain, at-the-money options), and they tie payment to a targeted performance level. In other words, they decouple compensation from undistinguished performance and from lucky upticks in a company's share price.

One problem with premium-priced option plans is their potential to dilute shareholder earnings and shareholder control more severely than plain, at-the-money call option plans. Raising the payoff bar makes each call option less valuable; so companies using them should expect to compensate each employee with a larger number of options for any defined level of compensation. If the options are exercised in the future and the company issues new shares to meet the demand for shares, dilution of ownership and dilution of earnings could result.

Premium-priced option plans help to solve the "free rider" problem that occurs when there is *any positive* change in share price, but they do nothing to reward employees who have superior performance in down markets. For a solution to this problem, let's turn to index options.

INDEX OPTIONS

Index options are a way to even-handedly reward employees for *above average* company performance in both up-markets and down-markets because this type of compensation ties the exercise price to a peer index.[37] To see how such a plan might work, suppose that, in 2007, Aztec Microchip, Inc. (AMI) devised an index option plan offering five-year, at-the-money stock options that had a positive payout only when AMI's share price outperformed its four leading competitors. To ensure this result, the strike price on the AMI options was adjusted at maturity by the percentage growth or decline in the index.

At the end of 2006, AMI's share price was $50, and its four competitors had share prices of $15, $20, $25, and $40, respectively, so, at inception, the "Index" against which AMI compared its performance equaled $100.[38] Exhibit 2.1 summarizes the payoffs after five years on AMI's employee call options, assuming AMI's share price rose by an average annual rate of 5% (column 6), and the index changed by annual rates of 10%, 5%, 0%, –5%, or –10% (columns 2, 3, and 4). In Case A, the index rose during the five years by a compound annual rate of 10% (column 4), so AMI's strike price in 2011 would be $80.53, which is the original strike price ($50) inflated by a 10% compound annual rate over five years (column 7). Because AMI's share price rose only by 5% to $63.81 (column 6), the options would expire out-of-the-money, and employees would earn nothing (column 8). In Case B, the payoff would be also zero because the options' strike price rose by the same compound annual rate as the index; so the options would be at-the-money. In Case C, AMI's options would be

[37]See Alfred Rapport, Alfie Kohn, Egon Zehnder, and Jeffrey Pfeffer, *Harvard Business Review on Compensation* (Cambridge: Harvard Press Book, 25 January 2002).
[38]$100 is the sum of AMI's four competitors' share prices (i.e., $15, $20, $25, and $40).

Exhibit 2.1   Example of Index Call Option Plan for Aztec Microchip Inc.

1	2	3	4	5	6	7	8
Case	Index Price End 2006	Index Price 2011	Percentage annual change in the Index 2007–2011	End 2006 AMI share price	2011 AMI share price assuming a +5% annual appreciation	2011 strike price on AMI options*	Payoff per Aztec call option**
A	$100	$161.05	+10%	$50	$63.81	$80.53	$0
B	$100	$127.63	+5%	$50	$63.81	$63.81	$0
C	$100	$100.00	0%	$50	$63.81	$50.00	$13.81
D	$100	$77.38	–5%	$50	$63.81	$38.69	$25.12
E	$100	$59.05	–10%	$50	$63.81	$29.52	$34.29

* AMI's strike price in 2011 = $50 × (1 + Annual percentage change of index price)^5.

** Payoff per AMI call option = Greater of $0 or (Market price in 2011 – Strike price)

in-the-money because its average annual performance (5%) was greater than the Index (0%). As a result, the strike price on AMI's options would remain at $50, and the option payoff would be $13.81 (column 8), which is the difference between the market price of an AMI share and the strike price of the option ($63.81 − $50 = $13.81). In Cases D and E the payoffs are also positive. A falling market causes the strike price to fall at the same compound annual rate as the index and thereby increases the payoff on AMI's options.

All the cases in Exhibit 2.1 dealt with payoffs assuming that the AMI share price rose by 5%. Even if AMI's share price fell over the option's five-year maturity, so long as the percentage decline was lower than the drop in the index, there would be a positive option payoff because the strike price of AMI options would be lower than the market price of its shares.

The use of relative, performance-based incentives makes compensation symmetric regardless of the general share price movement of the market. In this way, index option plans reduce the variance of employee compensation, better tie rewards to performance, and, therefore, increase fairness. For these reasons, many human resource analysts feel that indexed compensation should be incorporated into the third pillar of all executive compensation programs.

Though index options offer companies many advantages, they have their share of drawbacks. One major disadvantage of index plans is their complexity. Employees cannot simply open the newspaper to the financial pages and calculate the intrinsic value of their options from the stock quotes. To do that, they need to compute how their companies fared relative to the companies in the index. The complexity could lead to a waning of enthusiasm for this incentive-based compensation plan, thereby diminishing performance, but companies might combat this potential glitch by creating links on their Web sites with information on option values updated daily.

Another problem with index options is their potential to more severely dilute company earnings and control than plain vanilla stock options. Like premium options, index options are not worth as much as regular (plain vanilla) options because they reward relative performance and not absolute performance. Therefore, companies should expect to pay their employees more of them for any defined level of compensation.[39] As a consequence, if all the extra options were exercised and the company met this increased demand by issuing new shares, rather than hedging with derivatives or buying back its shares in the open market, dilution of shareholder earnings and control could result.[40]

Before adopting an index option plan, companies should be fully aware of the incentives they create. We already mentioned that index options have lower risks than traditional options because they (can) reward employees in up and down markets. But there is much more to consider. For instance, research has shown that, as long as they are not too far out-of-the-money, index options are more sensitive to changes in the underlier's price and to changes in volatility than are traditional options.[41] Therefore, they provide managers with greater incentives to increase risks.

With regard to the effects of volatility, it should be kept in mind that the value of an index option is influenced by idiosyncratic firm-specific risks rather than overall market or industry risks. Filtering out the portion of overall volatility that is common to all firms in an industry increases an index option's sensitivity to risk.[42] As a result, managers have greater incentives to increase their firms' idiosyncratic risks and to pursue activities that reduce the correlation between their firms' performance and the performance of the index. These decisions could change the nature of a company's business and affect important managerial decisions, such as whether and how to diversify

---

[39]See Shane A. Johnson and Yisong S. Tian, "Indexed Executive Stock Options," *Journal of Financial Economics* (July 2000), 35–64. Johnson and Tian show that, under normal conditions, an index option should be worth approximately 34% of a traditional option. Also see A. Louis Calvet and Abdul H. Rahman, "The Subjective Valuation of Indexed Stock Options and Their Incentive Effects," *The Financial Review*, 41(2) (May 2006), 205–227.

[40]During the 1990s, "No" votes by shareholders increased dramatically when they were asked by corporations for stock option authorization. A major source of shareholder concern was the potential dilution of earnings and control.

[41]See Shane A. Johnson and Yisong S. Tian, "Indexed Executive Stock Options," *Journal of Financial Economics* (July 2000), 35–64.

[42]Ibid.

or hedge. Because of these caveats, firms that institute index option plans should closely monitor them and consider installing risk brakes to ensure that operations remain within reasonable bounds.

Index option plans are not panaceas for all the shortcomings of plain-vanilla, option-based compensation plans. Their adoption most certainly would introduce new problems, such as determining the appropriate index to use (e.g., a market index or an industry index) and the date on which to lock in the compensation terms. Nevertheless, index options are worth considering because they remedy one of the major shortcomings of traditional employee stock options, which is they reward managers for factors that are under their control and do not penalize them for factors that are out of their control.

RESTRICTED SHARES

Restricted shares offer employees compensation in the form of rights to receive shares. Unlike stock options, which gain value only if a company's share price rises above the strike price, restricted shares are actual payments in shares, which maintain value (albeit less) even if the share price falls. They could have the added benefit of placing greater emphasis on financial performance for a longer period of time.

Restricted share compensation is not a new idea; rather, it is a well-known compensation alternative that has been eclipsed by stock options. Typically, restricted shares have vesting periods ranging from one to 10 years, but employees receiving them are entitled to full dividend and voting rights. The major restrictions facing employees who receive them relate to the transfer and selling rights of these shares. Accounting treatment can vary, but, in the United States, companies recognize the costs of restricted shares as compensation expenses that are prorated over the vesting period. In addition, employees have to report unrestricted share compensation as taxable income.

OMNIBUS PLANS

Omnibus plans set out a common list of *possible* compensation alternatives and leave it to the compensation committees or the management teams in individual countries to craft agreements that tailor compensation to the preferences, rules, laws, practices, and expectations of the local workforces.[43] Omnibus plans allow for the granting of many different types of awards, ranging from conventional options to stock appreciation rights to restricted stock plans and various types of performance-based awards. These plans make sense for com-

---

[43]Mark W. Sickles, "Managing the Workforce to Assure Shareholder Value," *HR Focus* 76, Issue 8 (August 1999), 1, 14, 15.

panies that are designing equity-based compensation systems for operations in multiple geographic areas. By offering a common palette from which to choose, companies can promote and preserve shared corporate goals.

Conclusion

The popularity of employee stock options as a form of remuneration flourished in the bull market of the 1990s, but it will surely wither on the vine if stock markets suffer prolonged downturns, as they did in the early years of the 21st century. Many companies have embraced employee stock options because they are flexible, encourage workers to increase shareholder value, provide a noncash way to hire and retain quality employees, align cash payments with a company's ability to pay, and provide cash-flow incentives. Employees have also welcomed employee stock options because of their benevolent tax treatment, but mainly because options limit downside risks and offer the potential to make employees fabulously rich.

Because of the distinctive characteristics of employee stock options, the formulas and models that are normally used to value exchange-traded options (e.g., Black-Scholes formula, binominal lattice model, and Monte Carlo model) may be inadequate. But help is on the way. New and innovative methodologies are being developed to account for factors, such vesting periods, relevant maturities, and the lack of transferability and tradability.

Stock option compensation plans tend to be most effective when employees are fully involved in their creation and when the workforce is cognizant of their benefits, costs, and risks. For stock options to align incentives properly, employees must understand the cause-and-effect relationship between what they do and how it affects their companies' share prices. If employee stock option plans are implemented to align employee incentives with those of the public shareholders, companies should be open about this goal and conscious of how hard it is to achieve.

Review Questions

1. Explain the reasoning behind employee stock options as a source of compensation. What do options accomplish that salary and bonus adjustments don't accomplish? Who in a company should receive employee stock options?

2. Develop a brief presentation for the head of your company's human resource department on the advantages and disadvantages of compensating a CEO with at-the-money stock options.

3. Explain why the stock options received by employees may have market prices that are much different from the value placed on them by employees themselves.

4. Explain premium-priced stock options. What are their advantages and disadvantages in terms of aligning employee interests with shareholder value?

5. Explain index options. What are their advantages and disadvantages in terms of aligning employee interests with shareholder value? To what should these options be indexed?

6. What would you expect to happen to corporate dividends (i.e., rise, fall, or stay the same) for companies that introduce stock option plans? Explain.

7. What would you expect to happen to the size and number of stock buy-backs at companies that introduce employee stock option plans? Explain.

8. Suppose Cadbury-Schweppes spins off Snapple as a separate legal entity and lists its shares on the NYSE. The CEO of Snapple decides to compensate top management with $4 million in stock options.

   a. How will the payment of $4 million in stock option compensation affect Snapple's income statement?

   b. When the options are exercised, from where will Snapple get the shares to satisfy the demand by employees? What are the implications?

9. Use the information in the following table, where appropriate, to answer these questions regarding Snapple.

   a. Use the Black-Scholes formula to determine the market price for a Snapple option.

Snapple Option Pricing Information			
Snapple share price	$50	Vesting period	3 years
Risk-free interest rate	4.75%	Volatility	35%
Inflation rate	2%	Dividends	$0
GDP growth rate	4%	Strike price	$50
Maturity	5 years		

b. Using the table and your answer from question 9(a), suppose you were offered $100,000 of stock option compensation. If the options were valued at their market price:

   (i) How many options would you get?

   (ii) Is there a way to lock in immediately the value of these options? If so, how? If not, why not?

   (iii) If, after three years (i.e., at maturity) Snapple's stock price rose by 10%, by how much (if any) will your stock options change in value? If you exercised the options, how much would you receive?

c. Suppose that in five years (i.e., at maturity) Snapple's share price rose to $130. If you exercised your options:

   (i) How much, if anything, will you have to pay if you wanted to own the shares?

   (ii) How much, if anything, will you receive if you cashed out?

   (iii) How, if at all, would your answers to the questions above change if the share price rose to $130 in three years, and you exercised your options (i.e., exercised them in three years rather than five years)?

Further Reading

Please visit http://www.prenhall.com/marthinsen, where you can find the following embellishment on and extension of this chapter:

- Appendix 2.1: Employee Stock Options: A Brief History of the U. S. Accounting Treatment

Bibliography

Aggarwal, R. and Samwick, A. "The Other Side of the Trade-off: The Impact of Risk on Executive Compensation." *Journal of Political Economy* 107 (1999), 65–105.

Anonymous. "The Trouble with Stock Options." *The Economist Magazine* (August 7th 1999), 13–14.

Baril, C., Betancourt, L., and Briggs, J. "Valuing Employee Stock Options under SFAS 123R Using the Black-Scholes-Merton and Lattice Model Approaches." *Journal of Accounting Education* 25(1/2) (January 2007), 88–101.

Bebchuk, Lucian and Fried, Jesse. *Pay without Performance: The Unfulfilled Promise of Executive Compensation.* Cambridge: Harvard University Press, 2006.

Bens, D.A., Nagar, V., and Franco, M.H. "Real Investment Implications of Employee Stock Option Exercises." *Journal of Accounting Research* 40(2c) (May 2002), 359–393.

Berle, Adolph A. and Means, Gardner C. *The Modern Corporation and Private Property*. New York: Macmillan, 1932.

Bettis, J.C., Bizjak, J.M., and Lemmon, M.L. "Exercise Behavior, Valuation, and the Incentive Effects of Employee Stock Options." *Journal of Financial Economics* 76(2) (May 2005), 445–470.

Black, Fischer and Scholes, Myron. "The Pricing of Options and Corporate Liabilities." *Journal of Political Economy* 27 (1973), 637–654.

Bodie, Z., Kaplan, R.S., and Merton, R.C. "For the Last Time: Stock Options Are an Expense." *Harvard Business Review* 81(3) (Mar 2003), 62–71.

Boody, D., Barth, M.E., and Kasznik, R. "Firms' Voluntary Recognition of Stock-Based Compensation Expense." *Journal of Accounting Research*, 42(2) (May 2004), 123–150.

Booth, Richard A. "Other Voices: Views From Beyond the Barons Staff—Payment Optional: Attacking Some Myths About Executive Compensation." *Barron's* (7 December 1998), 52–53.

Brenner, M., Sundaram, R., and Yermack, D. "Altering the Terms of Executive Stock Options." *Journal of Financial Economics* 57 (2000), 103–128.

Brickly, S. Bhagat and Lease, R. "The Impact of Long-Range Managerial Compensation Plans on Shareholder Wealth." *Journal of Accounting and Economics* 7(1–3) (1985), 115–129.

Buffett, Warren. "Stock Options and Common Sense." *The Washington Post*, (9 April 2002), A19.

Cai, Junning. "Accounting for Employee Stock Options and Mandatory Expensing: An Economics Perspective." *Journal of Derivatives Accounting* 2(2) (September 2005), 137–154.

Calvet, A. Louis and Rahman, Abdul H. "The Subjective Valuation of Indexed Stock Options and Their Incentive Effects." *The Financial Review* 41(2) (May 2006), 205–227.

Carpenter, J., "The Exercise and Valuation of Executive Stock Options." *Journal of Financial Economics* 96 (1998), 453–473.

Charny, Ben. "UPDATE: Google To Let Employees Trade Their Stock Options to Institutions." *Dow Jones Business News*, (12 December 2006).

Conyon, M., and Sadler G. "CEO Compensation, Option Incentives and Information Disclosure." *Review of Financial Economics* 10 (2002), 251–277.

Demsetz, Harold. "The Structure of Ownership and the Theory of the Firm." *Journal of Law and Economics* 26 (1983), 375–390.

Eaton, Tim V. and Prucyk, Brian R. "No Longer an 'Option'." *Journal of Accountancy*. 199(4) (April 2005), 63–68.

Fama, Eugene F. "Agency Problems and the Theory of the Firm." *Journal of Political Economy* 88 (1980), 288–307.

Fama, Eugene F. and Jensen, Michael C. "Separation of Ownership and Control." *Journal of Law and Economics* 26 (1983), 301–325.

Fenn, George W. and Liang, Nellie. "Corporate Payout Policy and Managerial Stock Incentives." *Journal of Financial Economics* 60 (1) (Apr 2001), 45–72.

Financial Accounting Standards Board. *Statement of Financial Accounting Standards No. 123 (revised 2004): Share-Based Payment*. (December 2004). http://www.fasb.org/news/nr121604_ebc.shtml. Accessed on 9 November 2007.

Folami, L.B., Arora, T., and Alli, K.L. "Using Lattice Models to Value Employee Stock Options under SFAS 123(R)." *CPA Journal* 76(9) (September 2006), 38–43.

Galbraith, John Kenneth. *The New Industrial State*. Boston: Houghton Mifflin Company, 1967.

Garen, J. "Executive Compensation and Principal-Agent Theory." *Journal of Political Economy* 102 (1994), 1175–1199.

Gibbons, R. "Incentives in Organizations." *Journal of Economics Perspective* 12 (1998), 115–132.

Gilson, Stuart, and Vetsuypens, Michael R. "CEO Compensation in Financially Distressed Firms: An Empirical Analysis." *Journal of Finance* 48(2) (1993), 425–458.

Greene, Thomas M. and Bianchi, Alden J. "Mixing Oil and Water: Backdated Stock Options under IRC Section 409A." *Benefits Law Journal* 20(2) (Summer 2007), 45–50.

Grossman, Sanford J. and Hart, Oliver D. "An Analysis of the Principal-Agent Problem." *Econometrica* 51 (1983), 7–46.

Hall, B.J. and Murphy, K.J. "Stock Options for Undiversified Executives." *Journal of Accounting and Economics* 33 (2002), 3–42.

Hall, B.J., and Murphy, K.J. "Optimal Exercise Prices for Executive Stock Options." *AEA Papers and Proceedings* 90 (2000), 209–214.

Hart, Oliver D. "The Market Mechanism as an Incentive Scheme." *Bell Journal of Economics* 14 (1983), 366–382.

Himmelberg, C., Hubbard, G., and Palia, D. "Understanding the Determinants of Managerial Ownership and the Link Between Ownership and Performance." *Journal of Financial Economics* 53 (1999), 353–384.

Holmström, Bengt. "Managerial Incentive Problems: A Dynamic Perspective." *Review of Economics Studies* 66 (1999), 169–182.

Holmström, Bengt. "Moral Hazard and Observability." *The Bell Journal of Economics* 10 (1979), 74–91.

Hutchinson, Marion and Gull, Ferdinand A. "The Effects of Executive Share Options and Investment Opportunities on Firms' Accounting Performance: Some Australian Evidence." *The British Accounting Review* 38(3) (September 2006), 277–297.

Jenkins, Holman W. Jr. "The Backdating Molehill." *The Wall Street Journal* (7 March 2007), A16.

Jensen, Michel C. and Meckling, William H. "Theory of the Firm: Managerial Behavior, Agency Costs and Ownership Structure." *Journal of Financial Economics* 3 (1976), 305–360.

Jensen, Michael and Murphy, Kevin. "CEO Incentives—It's Not How Much You Pay, but How." *Harvard Business Review* 68, Iss. 3 (May/June 1990), 138–149.

Jensen, Michael C. and Ruback, Richard S. "The Market for Corporate Control: The Scientific Evidence." *Journal of Financial Economics* 11 (1983), 5–50.

Jin, Li. "CEO Compensation, Diversification, and Incentives." *Journal of Financial Economics* 66(1) (October 2002), 1–46.

Johnson, Shane A. and Tian, Yisong S. "Indexed Executive Stock Options." *Journal of Financial Economics* (July 2000), 35–64.

Kahl, M., Liu, J. and Longstaff, F. "Paper Millionaires: How Valuable Is Stock to a Shareholder Who Is Restricted from Selling It?" *Journal of Financial Economics* 67 (2003), 385–410.

Kato, H.K., Lemmon, M., Luo, M., and Schallheim, J. "An Empirical Examination of the Costs and Benefits of Executive Stock Options: Evidence from Japan," *Journal of Financial Economics* 78(2) (November 2005), 435–461.

Koller, T., Goedhart, M., and Wessels, D. *Valuation: Measuring and Managing the Value of Companies,* 4th ed. New York: Wiley, June 2005.

Kulatilaka, Nalin and Marcus, Alan J. "Valuing Employee Stock Options." *Financial Analysts Journal* (November-December 1994), 46–56.

Kwon, See Sung S. and Yin, Qin Jennifer. "Executive Compensation, Investment Opportunities, and Earnings Management: High-Tech Firms Versus Low-Tech Firms." *Journal of Accounting* 21(2) (Spring 2006), 119–148.

Lam, Swee-Sum Lam and Chng, Bey-Fen. "Do Executive Stock Option Grants Have Value Implications for Firm Performance?" *Review of Quantitative Finance and Accounting* 26(3) (May 2006), 249–274.

Lambert, Richard A., Lanen, William N., and Larcker, David F. "Executive Stock Options Plans and Corporate Dividend Policy." *Journal of Financial and Quantitative Analysis* 24(4) (December 1989), 409–425.

Leahey, Anne L. and Zimmermann, Raymond A. "A Road Map for Share-Based Compensation. *Journal of Accountancy*." 203(4) (April 2007), 50–54.

Lewellen, W.G., Park, T., and Ro B.T., "Self-Serving Behavior in Managers' Discretionary Information Disclosure." *Journal of Accounting and Economics* 21 (1996), 227–251.

Merton, Robert C. "Theory of Rational Option Pricing." *Bell Journal of Economics and Management Science* 4 (1973), 141–183.

Milbourn, T. T., "CEO Reputation and Stock-Based Compensation," *Journal of Financial Economics* 68(2) (May 2003), 233–262.

Mirrlees, James A. "The Optimal Structure of Incentives and Authority within an Organization." *Bell Journal of Economics* 7 (1976), 105–131.

Morck, Randall, Shliefer, Andrei, and Vishny, Robert W. "Management Ownership and Market Valuation: An Empirical Analysis." *Journal of Financial Economics* 20 (1988), 293–315.

Morgenson, Gretchen. "Stock Options Are Not a Free Lunch." *Forbes Magazine* 161(10) (18 May 1998), 212–217.

Muelbrock, L. "The Efficiency of Equity-Linked Compensation: Understanding the Full Cost of Awarding Executive Stock Options." *Financial Management* 30 (2001), 5–30.

Murphy, Kevin J. "Executive Compensation," http://papers.ssrn.com/sol3/papers.cfm?abstract_id=163914 (April 1998, posted to database: 19 May 1999), 29.

National Center for Employee Ownership. *The Stock Options Book*. 8th ed. Oakland, CA: National Center for Employee Ownership, February 2007.

National Center for Employee Ownership. *National Employee Ownership and Corporate Performance (ESOPs, etc.) and Corporate Performance*. NCEO Library, http://www.nceo.org/library/corpperf.html. Accessed on 9 November 2007.

Norris, Floyd. "What Seller Wants a Low Price?" *The New York Times* (1 June 2007), C1.

Ofek, E. and Yermack, D. "Taking Stock: Equity-Based Compensation and the Evolution of Managerial Ownership." *Journal of Finance* 55 (2000), 1367–1384.

Perry, Tod and Zenner, Marc. "Pay for Performance? Government Regulation and the Structure of Compensation." *Journal of Financial Economics* 62(3), December 2001, 453–488.

Pfeffer, Jeffrey. "Six Dangerous Myths About Pay." *Harvard Business Review*. Reprint number 98309 (May-June 1998).

Rappaport, A., Kohn, A.K, Zehnder, E., and Pfeffer, J. *Harvard Business Review on Compensation*. Cambridge: Harvard Press Book, 1 November 2001.

Regan, G., Lombardi, M., and Gray, M. "FAS 123R: Accounting for Stock Options." *California CPA* 75(8) (March/April 2007), 12–15.

Rogerson, William. "The First-Order Approach to Principal Agent-Problems." *Econometrica* 53 (1985), 1357–1367.

Rosen, C., Case, J., and Staubus, M. "Every Employee an Owner. [Really]." *Harvard Business Review* 83(6) (June 2005), 122–130.

Ross, Stephen A. "The Economic Theory of Agency: The Principal's Problem." *American Economic Review* 63 (1973), 134–139.

Schulz, Eric and Tubbs, Stewart L. "Stock Options Influence on Manager's Salaries and Firm Performance." *The Business Review* 5(1) (September 2006), 14–19.

Sesil, J.C., Kroumova, M.K., Blasi, J.R., and Kruse, D.L. "Broad-Based Employee Stock Options in U.S. 'New Economy' Firms," *British Journal of Industrial Relations* 40(2) (June 2002), 273–294.

Sickles, Mark W. "Managing the Workforce to Assure Shareholder Value." *HR Focus* 76 (8) (August 1999), 1, 14, 15.

Smith, Clifford W., Jr. and Watts, Ross L. "The Investment Opportunity Set and Corporate Financing, Dividend, and Compensation Policies." *Journal of Financial Economics* 32 (1992), 263–292.

Thomas, Kaye A. *Consider Your Options: Get the Most from Your Equity Compensation.* Lisle, IL: Fairmark Press, 2007.

Yermack, D. "Good Timing: CEO Stock Option Awards and Company News Announcements." *Journal of Finance* 52(2) (1997), 449–476.

3

Roche Holding

The Company, Its Financial Strategy, and Bull Spread Warrants

Introduction

Soren Kierkegaard once said that: "life . . . [is] . . . understood backwards . . . but it must be lived forwards."[1] We all can appreciate this maxim because events are usually more clearly understood with hindsight, but it is particularly appropriate for chief financial officers (CFOs), who choose to borrow using one instrument or another based on their perceptions of the future, but who are held accountable at year's end if they guess wrong. When they get it right, though, CFOs and their companies can achieve history-making financial reputations.

It is just this type of reputation that Roche Holding and its CFO achieved during the decade from 1991 to 2000. On the operational side, Roche developed a global reputation as a

---

[1] The actual quote is: "It is perfectly true, as philosophers say, that life must be understood backwards. But they forget the other proposition, that it must be lived forwards." This quote comes from a page of Kierkegaard's Journals, 1843, p. 89. See Alexander Dru, ed., *The Journals of Kierkegaard* (Harper Torchbooks, 1959).

leader in the research-oriented healthcare industry by means of its strong internal growth, well-stocked pipeline of new products, significant acquisitions, and massive divestitures of nonhealthcare-related businesses that lacked either success or critical mass. On the nonoperational side, the company enjoyed an equally strong reputation as a powerhouse in the global financial community. Roche became one of world's most skillful users of state-of-the-art borrowing techniques,[2] having borrowed on 10 occasions between 1991 and 2000 by issuing structured notes[3] in the euro-markets and Swiss capital markets. The total face value of these debt issues amounted to more than US$13 billion, and many of them (e.g., *Bull Spread, Knock Out, Samurai, LYON, Rodeo,* and *Chameleon*) were heralded for their novelty.

This chapter discusses Roche Holding, a company that was forced to take the unconventional step of transforming its treasury department into a profit center. It also explains the growth strategy crafted by Roche's Chairman and CEO, Fritz Gerber, and his CFO, Henri B. Meier, to navigate the business and financial landmines planted by the convergence of powerful company-specific and industry-specific conditions. The chapter explores the process through which CFOs, in general, and Roche, in particular, decide whether to borrow using straight debt (bonds) or a hybrid issue. Finally, the chapter dissects one of Roche's early deals, its 1991 Bull Spread issue for US$1 billion, first by analyzing expected investor returns, and then turning the tables and analyzing the deal from Roche's perspective.

---

[2]Kari Nars, ed., *Excellence in Debt Management* (London, England: Euromoney Publications, PLC, 1997) showcases some of the world's most sophisticated borrowers. Among this distinguished group of sovereigns, supra-nationals, quasi-sovereigns, and financing institutions, Roche was the only private corporation to which an entire chapter was devoted.

[3]The term "hybrid bond" or "hybrid note" is used synonymously with "structured bond" or "structured note."

Roche Holding AG: Transition from a Lender to a Borrower

Roche Holding AG[4] was founded in 1896 as an entrepreneurial venture dedicated to manufacturing, for worldwide distribution, drugs with uniform strength and quality. In the mid-1990s, after a century of successful operations, the company had become a world leader in diagnostic instruments and reagents, vitamins and fine chemicals, as well as flavors and fragrances.[5] Its pharmaceutical division ranked among the leaders in the industry, with a dominant position in the primary care sector and global leadership in the hospital market.

The road to a global leadership position for Roche was not smooth. During the 1960s and 1970s, the company fell victim to its own success. Awash with funds from Valium,[6] its blockbuster pharmaceutical product, Roche entered into a string of acquisitions, which were tangential to the pharmaceutical industry and drained needed resources (financial and human) from the company's primary focus.[7]

LOSS OF THE VALIUM PATENT IN THE UNITED STATES

In 1985, Valium lost its U.S. patent protection, thereby reducing substantially Roche's major source of funding for working capital, capital expenditures, and acquisitions. Despite the product's brand image and quality assurances, generic products were introduced rapidly, which caused revenues to plummet and operating margins to fall below 5%. The decline of Valium sales made Roche's earlier diversification mistakes even more apparent.

RAPID INCREASE IN R&D COSTS, MARKET GROWTH, AND INDUSTRY CONSOLIDATION

Had the loss of Roche's Valium patent been the only problem, perhaps the company could have taken it in stride, but that was not the case. In addition, Roche needed to react quickly and shrewdly to the combined threats of

---

[4]In German, AG stands for *Aktiengesellschaft*, the English equivalent of an *incorporated (Inc.)* or a *limited (Ltd.)* public stock company.

[5]In April 2000, Roche spun off its flavors and fragrances division, Givaudan Roure, to be run as a separate company, and in September 2002, Roche's Vitamins and Fine Chemicals Division was sold to DSM, a Dutch life science products and performance materials company.

[6]Valium (aka, diazepam) was one of the world's best-known sedatives/tranquilizers. From 1969 to 1982, Valium was the most prescribed drug in the United States.

[7]Roche acquired companies with market positions in industries, like physical instruments, agrochemicals, flavors and fragrances, and liquid crystals.

exploding research and development costs in the pharmaceutical industry, rapid industry consolidation, the biotechnology revolution, and increasing synergies between medical diagnostics and treatment. The pharmaceutical industry was expanding rapidly in the 1970s and 1980s due to the increasing demands of the baby boom generation, and it was also becoming more global in its reach. To survive in this changing competitive environment, Roche needed funding to support international expansion of its existing product lines, development of new products, and synergistic acquisitions.

As rapidly as the cost of funding R&D was reaching stratospheric levels, the chances of success for pharmaceutical products were falling. Pharmaceutical companies faced significant delays (typically, 10 years) before bringing new products to market. The cost of world-class scientists and the increasing scrutiny of regulatory agencies combined to drive up costs and lengthen the gap between invention and market introduction. Pharmaceutical companies faced the prospect of significant negative cash flows for a decade or more, and, in the end, there was a growing probability that their products would not be approved. Even if the products were approved, these companies faced the possibility that follow-on studies, focusing on factors such as a drug's interaction with other medications, would remove them from the market.

ROCHE'S UNIQUE CAPITAL STRUCTURE

Burgeoning costs, declining revenues, and rapid industry consolidation forced Roche to seek external funding, but the company faced a huge financial obstacle due to its highly unusual capital structure—a structure that had been a feature of Roche's corporate governance for decades.[8] Despite Roche's size, its voting shares were majority owned by a relatively small group of investors composed of the Hoffmann and Oeri-Hoffmann families, as well as Dr. Paul Sacher. This group created a formal shareholder pool for the purpose of ensuring its majority voting power over key corporate decisions.[9]

Even though the investor pool had a vested interest in maximizing shareholder value, there would have had to be extraordinary and compelling reasons to sacrifice its majority voting rights. Obviously, to the minds of this group, such extraordinary and compelling reasons never presented themselves. As a result of the investor pool, there could be no increase in Roche's share capital that meaningfully diluted or threatened to dilute the voting block's position. This constraint restricted the company's ability to raise equity capital; so, rather than issue shares, Roche relied on financial creativity, using innovative hybrid debt instruments for its funding.

Limitations on Using Hybrid Debt Instruments

The hybrid debt securities issued by Roche during the 1990s were bonds with warrants linked to the company's voting shares or to its nonvoting equity shares (NES). (see Exhibit 3.1)[10] To ensure that majority ownership remained in the hands of the shareholder pool and to protect against the dilution of earnings, these hybrid instruments were issued without increasing (or the intention to increase) either Roche's shares or NES.

This made Roche the delight of shareholders because to meet the demands of investors who exercised call options on the hybrid debt, the company had to purchase its own shares or NES in the open market, which raised their prices. Of course, such purchases had the potential to seriously erode Roche's profitability and cash flows. The normal corporate practice for companies issuing debt with call options or convertible debt was (and is) to meet the exercise and conversion demands by issuing new shares. Roche was restricted from doing so by the nature of its share structure. As a result, the company faced significant future cash flow exposures and threats to its profitability.

Exhibit 3.1 What are Nonvoting Equity Shares and Dividend Certificate Rights? *(Genußschein)*

Nonvoting equity security and dividend right certificate *(Genußschein)*	A nonvoting equity security and a dividend right certificate are two different forms of equity, but they are so similar that they are often grouped together and called a *Genußschein* (plural: *Genußscheine*). Neither security has voting power. The one small difference between a nonvoting equity security and dividend right certificate lies in their financial rights. Owners of dividend right certificates have the right to participate in dividends only. Nonvoting equity shareholders have the *full* financial rights of shareholders, except the liquidation of nominal capital and voting rights. Under Swiss corporate law, Genußschein securities cannot be used to raise funds.

---

[10]See Risk Notepad 3.1: What Are the Differences Between Warrants and Options?

ROCHE BRINGS IN A NEW LEADER AND REPLACES ITS MANAGEMENT COMMITTEE

To survive, Roche had to change rapidly and dramatically; for that, it needed a new leader. Therefore, in 1978, Roche hired Fritz Gerber to be its chairman and CEO. Gerber was well known throughout Europe and Switzerland as a savvy, no-nonsense businessman.[11] He had a reputation for decisive and clear decision-making and for surrounding himself with extraordinary talent. One of Gerber's earliest decisions at Roche was to clean house at the very top levels of the company. In the mid-1980s, he brought in a fresh group of division and department heads. He also adopted a strategy of boosting profitability by turning Roche's treasury into a profit center, but such an iconoclastic step required hiring a chief financial officer with a proven record of success and who fully understood capital markets from both the borrowing and investment sides.

Gerber chose Dr. Henri B. Meier, former head of the Investment Banking Division of HandelsBank N.W., Zurich. Henri Meier was given considerable latitude to take controlled risks, but these risks could not threaten the solvency of the company. Gerber also made clear that treasury's success or failure rested directly on Meier's shoulders and that he would be held personally accountable to Gerber for all treasury-related decisions.

A NEW FINANCIAL STRATEGY

Gerber's directive to Meier—to turn the treasury into a profit center—meant the risk-return profile of the company's nonoperating assets and capital structure would no longer have to accommodate passively or mirror the exposures of the operating divisions. The treasury department's new job was to borrow funds at the cheapest possible rates (even if they were not needed immediately), actively manage debt throughout its maturity for the purpose of minimizing cash flow payments, and aggressively invest excess funds that were not being used so that they could support later operations or acquisitions.

Meier (as part of the executive committee) devised a five-pronged financial strategy to fund Roche's growth. The facets of this strategy were to (1) build an acquisition war chest by borrowing at opportune times; (2) minimize cash outflows by borrowing with hybrid debt issues; (3) prune divisions and sell off dead wood to increase cash flows; (4) reduce dividends

---

[11]Fritz Gerber became Chairman of Zurich Insurance's management board in 1974; from 1977 to 1995, he served as Chairman of Zurich Insurance's board of directors. In what amounted to a remarkable demonstration of business ingenuity and courage, Gerber remained head of Zurich Insurance after taking over the helm at Roche and presided over an extended period of prosperity for both companies.

to increase cash flows; and (5) improve Roche's financial transparency and stock market profile.

Build an Acquisition War Chest by Borrowing at Opportune Times

Roche began to borrow when funds were cheap and not necessarily when they were needed. The idea of borrowing prior to a clearly defined need might seem preemptive or costly, but acquisition opportunities could not be predicted with accuracy, and having funds on hand increased Roche's speed to market and, therefore, gave the company a negotiating edge. In the end, acquisition decisions would rest heavily on Roche's cost of capital, but the company bet that future acquisition opportunities would clear this hurdle by substantial margins—and they did.[12]

Borrowing in this fashion meant that Roche was walking a capital market tightrope, with any false step resulting in a worsened debt-equity ratio and higher borrowing costs. As financing became increasingly more opportunistic and less related to operations, Roche found itself with a large pool of liquid assets to invest. Meier's tactic created new asset-management responsibilities that had to be administered by Roche's treasury. To earn above average returns on these funds, Roche actively managed them, which meant liberating the treasury to take on tolerable risks for the sake of increased return.

Minimize Cash Outflows by Borrowing with Hybrid Debt Issues

To minimize cash outflows (i.e., coupon and principal payments) and to obtain low-cost, long-term funding, Henri Meier relied on financial hybrid instruments and offered investors nonvoting equity shares (i.e., *Genußscheine*), as equity kickers. At times, Meier was able to spot capital market imperfections, which he was able to arbitrage and thereby reduce borrowing costs. For instance, hybrid securities could be unbundled and sold separately to targeted investor groups. Roche would often identify distinct investor segments with excess demands for securities having particular risk and/or return characteristics and then customize the terms of its hybrid securities to fit the precise needs of these creditors. Moreover, by selectively choosing investment bankers with strong placement powers, Meier was able to steer a healthy portion of each issue away from hedge funds, which, in an effort to hedge their warrant exposures, might have shorted the Roche stock in the spot market and thereby driven down the share price. The company's strategy sought to simultaneously

---

[12]During the late 1980s and 1990s, Roche's major acquisitions included Genentech (pharmaceutical biotechnology) in 1990, Syntex (pharmaceuticals) in 1994, Tastemaker (flavors) in 1997, and Böhringer-Mannheim (diagnostics) in 1998.

maximize the initial sale price of its debt instruments, minimize cash outflows from borrowing, and increase the placement power of its investment banks.

Besides their ability to minimize cash outflows and reduce the cost of funds, hybrid debt securities had an additional and crucial advantage over straight debt or loans. They offered opportunities to take controlled speculative risks by hedging and unhedging positions, thereby driving borrowing costs even lower. Of course, one might say that any company could do the same by setting up a hedge fund and speculating in the market, but there is one major difference. Hybrids offered Roche the chance to compete against the market in its own shares—shares in which it had enormous informational advantages.

Prune Divisions and Sell Off Dead Wood to Increase Cash Flows

The third prong of Roche's financial strategy was to divest itself of divisions and subdivisions that had become financially burdensome and/or did not contribute to the companies' goals and core competencies. To help the process of making hard decisions, such as divestitures, Roche introduced management information systems that put significant pressure on the managers of all divisions to perform. Hurdle rates were woven into all discussions about divisional performance and capital budgeting projects.

Divisions that could not clear the performance bar were sold to the highest bidder.[13] The proceeds from these divestitures were used to finance new acquisitions and reinvigorate ongoing operations. When there were no imminent acquisition targets or obvious ways to support ongoing operations, surplus cash flowed by the billions into Roche's treasury and created an even greater need for an investment arm with professional management capabilities.

Reduce Dividends to Increase Cash Flows

Roche sought to fund internally as much of its expansion as possible. To accomplish this goal, the dividend payout ratio was kept intentionally low (on average around 16% of earnings) and shareholders were rewarded with noncash benefits (typically derivatives that were structured to give capital gains).[14]

Improve Roche's Financial Transparency and Stock Market Profile

Finally, to execute its financial strategy, Roche needed as large a potential shareholder base as possible and a reputation for transparency. To this end,

---

[13]During these years, Roche sold Fluka (specialty chemicals and analytical reagents) and Kontron (instruments) in 1989, and it sold Dr. R. Maag AG & Maag Agrochemicals (plant protection/agrochemicals) and Medi-Physics in 1990.

[14]Returns to investors in the form of capital gains were tax free in most Swiss cantons, and capital gains were usually taxed at levels lower than the income tax rate in other countries, as well.

the company overhauled its corporate and financial structures (1989), listed its shares on the major Swiss stock exchanges (1989), adopted the "single auditor concept" for both local statutory audits and group reporting, and was one of the first Swiss companies to adopt International Accounting Standards with respect to valuation methods, accounting rules, and reporting principles (1990). These changes improved the transparency, quality, and range of Roche's financial reporting and enhanced the control of financial risks, returns, and costs.

Roche's 1991 Bull Spread Issue

Roche's 1991 Bull Spread issue was representative of the financial strategy Henri Meier developed at Roche. These hybrid securities offered Roche long-term funding at a very low coupon rate; they targeted a specific segment of the capital market to profit from any capital market imperfections that might have existed, did not increase the number of shares outstanding, and most importantly, gave Roche's treasury department 10 years of opportunities to profit from controlled speculative risks. The Bull Spread issue had a face value of $1 billion, and its bonds carried 10-year maturities with 3.5% coupons. The warrants (discussed shortly) added to investors' potential returns.

WHY DID ROCHE CHOOSE LONG-TERM, DOLLAR-DENOMINATED DEBT?

There are many possible explanations for why Meier borrowed long-term U.S. dollars, but there is strong reason to believe that the issue was connected to Roche's acquisition of a 60% stake in Genentech, the California biotechnology company.[15] The ongoing operations of U.S.-based Genentech gave Roche a huge, long-term U.S. dollar exposure. Roche financed the Genentech purchase with a short-term U.S. dollar bridge loan, which left the

---

[15]When Roche acquired a majority stake (60%) of Genentech in 1990, the agreement gave Roche the option to redeem all outstanding Genentech shares by 30 June 1995. It also allowed Roche to acquire on the open market an additional 15% of Genentech stock beyond the initial 60% holding. In May 1995, Roche and Genentech agreed to extend Roche's call option on all outstanding Genentech stock at a predetermined price that would rise quarterly and terminate on 30 June 1999. Roche exercised its option in 1999 with the intention to publicly re-sell up to 19% of Genentech shares, and thereby continue the company as a publicly traded, independent legal entity. Roche sold approximately 17% of Genentech shares in July 1999. Then, in October 1999, Roche sold 20 million shares of Genentech's common stock, reducing its interest in the company to approximately 65%. Roche further reduced, to 58%, its Genentech interest in March 2000, when it sold more of its Genentech common stock and granted underwriters an option to purchase additional shares of common stock to cover overallotments.

company vulnerable to increasing interest rates. To protect the Swiss franc value of Genentech's anticipated long-term cash inflows, Henri Meier set up a natural hedge by creating offsetting, long-term liabilities in U.S. dollars.

DETAILS OF THE BULL SPREAD ISSUE

Each of Roche's Bull Spread securities was issued for $10,000 and gave investors 73 Bull Spread warrants. The warrants had a three-year maturity and, at maturity, 100 bull spread warrants could be redeemed for SFr 7,000, if the closing price of a share was less than or equal to SFr 7,000, or, at the option of the company, one share or SFr 10,000, if the closing price was greater than SFr 10,000 (see Exhibit 3.2).

TARGET INVESTOR GROUP

In structuring the Bull Spread issue, Meier made a concerted effort to tailor its provisions to institutional investors, in general, and to Swiss-based institutional investors, in particular. Most of the cards were stacked in Roche's

---

Exhibit 3.2   Summary of Roche's 1991 Bull Spread Issue

16 May 1991
Bull Spread Issue
US$1,000,000,000
$3\frac{1}{2}\%$
Due 16 May 2001
With Bull Spread Warrants

Issuer of the Bonds	Roche Holdings, Inc. USA
The Bonds	US$1,000,000,000 $3\frac{1}{2}\%$. Due in 2001.
Interest Rate	$3\frac{1}{2}\%$ (paid annually on 16 May)
Maturity	16 May 2001
Issuer of Bull Spread Warrants	Roche Investments Limited, Bermuda (RIL)
Warrants	Per US$10,000 = 73 Bull Spread Warrants
Number of Warrants	7,300,000
Exercise Rights	100 Bull Spread warrants entitled the holder on 16 May 1994 to receive (from RIL) SFr 7,000 if the closing price of a bearer share was less than or equal to SFr 7,000, or, at the option of the company (RIL), one share or SFr 10,000, if the closing price was greater than SFr 10,000
Listing	Luxembourg, Zurich, and Basel Stock Exchanges

Risk Notepad 3.1

What Are the Differences Between Options and Warrants?

Warrants are financial instruments that grant financial privileges to their holders. These privileges might be in the form of simple call options that give owners the right, but not the obligation, to buy a specified number of shares (or other underlying asset, such as participation certificates or natural resources) at a predefined price on a predetermined date (or for an established period of time) in the future. They could also be in the form of put option rights that give owners the right, but not the obligation, to sell a specified number of shares or other asset at a predetermined price on a predetermined date (or for a given period of time) in the future. Warrants could also grant a combination of call options, put options, and forward contract rights. The most commonly used warrants grant call option rights.

Warrants are different from options in two important ways. First, they have long-term maturities (i.e., usually for one year and often lasting many years) compared to options that have short-term maturities (usually lasting one year or less). Second, warrants are issued by the firms themselves, rather than by financial intermediaries (e.g., banks, exchanges, and brokers).

Warrants reduce the coupon rate attached to a debt issue because they offer investors financial incentives and opportunities with acceptable risks. It is common for warrants (e.g., call options) to be issued at prices that are considerably out-of-the-money (e.g., by 20% or more) so that substantial capital appreciation must take place before they have any intrinsic value. If a warrant's strike price is reached before maturity, warrant holders face the same incentives as option holders. In-the-money warrants are seldom exercised before maturity because investors can earn more by selling them and receiving the warrants' intrinsic value plus time value, rather than exercising them and extracting only the intrinsic value.

Why would a company be concerned about the uncertain costs of a warrant issue? If its share price rose, couldn't the company simply issue new shares to meet the demand from any exercised warrants, and under these circumstances, wouldn't the funds be essentially free to the company? The answer is an emphatic "no!" The issuance of new shares leads to dilution of earnings and voting power. Existing shareholders are generally better off if the warrants are paid off in cash, and this is one of the major reasons why they often resist company efforts to issue new shares to meet warrant demand.[16]

At maturity, companies that have not hedged their warrant exposures have three basic ways to honor in-the-money warrant obligations. They can issue new shares, and thereby dilute the existing shareholders base, or they can settle in cash, or they can purchase the needed shares in the relatively high-priced spot market and then re-sell them to warrant holders at the lower strike price. Acquiring shares in the open market helps existing

---

[16]For further analysis, see Stephen A. Ross, Randolph W. Westerfield, and Jeffrey Jaffe, *Corporate Finance*, 8th ed. (New York: Irwin-McGraw Hill, 2008), Chapter 24.

shareholders because it drives up the share price and ensures that dividends will be distributed among the current (fixed) shareholders base (i.e., no dilution). The major disadvantages from acquiring the shares at market prices (or settling in cash) are the huge negative cash flows that result from their purchase and the losses the company suffers on the transactions (i.e., buying at the market price and selling at the lower strike price).

Exhibit RN 3.1.1 summarizes the major differences between options and warrants.

Exhibit RN 3.1.1 Differences Between Options and Warrants

Options	Warrants
Short term	Long term
Issued by financial intermediaries	Issued by firms
Issued independently from any other debt instrument	Usually issued in combination with debt issues
Issued at a variety of strike prices	Often issued considerably out of the money and at one strike price per embedded warrant
Financial intermediaries meet the demands of investors exercising their options.	Company meets the demands of investors exercising their options.

favor. The company had a high credit rating, it enjoyed a positive home-country bias, and Roche carried relatively little debt, therefore adding a rarity value to institutional investors who wanted portfolio diversification. Investors also welcomed the guaranteed minimum return and considerable upside potential offered by the Bull Spread securities. The issue was structured to earn at least a 7.7% (before tax) return, which was above the *legally required* return Swiss pension funds had to earn, and it provided an additional incentive to taxpayers because part of its return was taxed at the capital gains rate, which was lower than the rate on normal income.

ANALYSIS OF THE BULL SPREAD'S RETURN TO INVESTORS

The Bull Spread issue can be separated into two main components (see Exhibit 3.3): a 10-year bond and a collection of 73 Bull Spread warrants having three-year maturities and a combination of put, call, and forward provisions. The warrant portion of the Bull Spread issue can be treated as a "side bet" made between the investor and Roche about how high the share price would be on 16 May 1994 (i.e., three years after the securities were

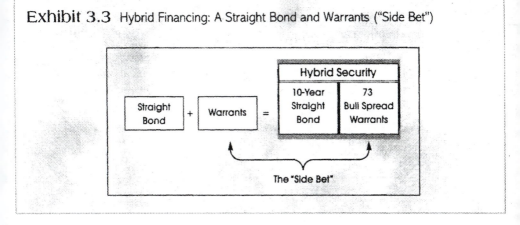

Exhibit 3.3 Hybrid Financing: A Straight Bond and Warrants ("Side Bet")

issued). Once Roche's Bull Spread securities were issued, the bonds and warrants were separated and sold separately on the secondary market.[17] Due to the separability of the Bull Spread issue, Roche was actually offering the public three investment alternatives: (1) a bond without warrants (bond ex warrants), (2) warrants without a bond (warrants ex bond), and (3) a bond with warrants (i.e., bond cum warrants). We will analyze each of the three instruments in the following sections, but before we do, we need to value separately the bond portion and warrant portion of the issue.

Valuing the Bond and Warrant Portions of the Bull Spread Issue

Because an investor's return on the Bull Spread securities was the weighted average of the return on the bond and the return on 73 warrants, a first step in analyzing these instruments is to separate their values. Luckily, there is a relatively easy way to do this. Then, we can calculate the return on each component of the Bull Spread security, as well as the return on the hybrid (i.e., bond and warrants) investment.

In 1991, Roche could have borrowed, outright, 10-year, dollar-denominated funds for about 8.65%. But Roche chose to make a $1 billion Bull Spread issue with an annual 3.5% coupon. Therefore, for each of the 10 years of the issue, Roche had to pay a coupon of $35 million, and then, at maturity, it had to repay the $1 billion principal. Exhibit 3.4 shows these cash outflows, and calculates their present value discounted at 8.65%, the rate at which Roche could have borrowed fixed rate funds. The $664.3 million

---

[17]To increase their attractiveness (i.e., mainly in terms of liquidity and flexibility), hybrid instruments are usually structured so that the bond and the warrant can be separated and sold as independent financial instruments. This "separability" characteristic is important for the analysis in this chapter. See Frank K. Reilly and Keith C. Brown, *Investment Analysis and Portfolio Management*. 8th ed. (Mason, OH, Thomson-Southwestern, 2006), Chapter 23: Swap Contracts, Convertible Securities, and Other Embedded Derivatives.

Exhibit 3.4 Discounted Present Value of the "Fixed" Cash Flows of the Bull Spread Issue

Year	Cash Flow from the 3.5% Coupon Bond (Millions of U.S. Dollars)	Discount Factor @ 8.65%	Discounted Present Value at 8.65% (Millions of U.S. Dollars)
1992	−35.0	0.920	−32.2
1993	−35.0	0.847	−29.6
1994	−35.0	0.780	−27.3
1995	−35.0	0.718	−25.1
1996	−35.0	0.660	−23.1
1997	−35.0	0.608	−21.3
1998	−35.0	0.559	−19.6
1999	−35.0	0.515	−18.0
2000	−35.0	0.474	−16.6
2001	−1,035.0	0.436	−451.5
Value of straight bond portion			**−664.3**

	Issue Amount	Percent of Issue
Value of the hybrid security issue	US$1,000 million	100%
Value of straight bond portion	US$664.3 million	66.4%
Value of warrant portion	US$335.7 million	33.6%

Warrant value = Hybrid value − Straight bond value

discounted present value is the value of the bond portion of Roche's Bull Spread issue. Because the total value of the issue was $1,000 million, the warrants must have been worth $335.7 million, which is the difference between $1 billion and $664.3 million.

Analyzing the Return to Bond Holders

Investors holding only the bond portion of the Bull Spread security earned an 8.65% return, which was composed of a 3.5% annual coupon and a near 50% capital gain for the 10-year period. This capital gain reflected the difference between the purchase price of $664.3 million and the hybrid's full par value ($1 billion) at maturity (see Exhibit 3.5).

An example might help us understand the return earned by the bond-holder. Suppose an investor purchased a Roche $10,000 Bull Spread security, separated the pure bond from the warrants, and sold the pure bond.

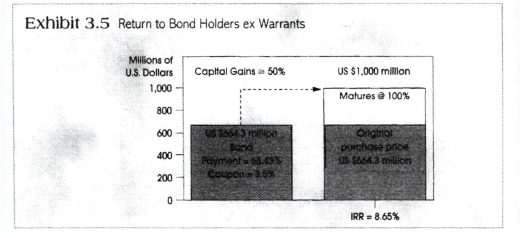

Exhibit 3.5 Return to Bond Holders ex Warrants

What would someone pay for such a bond? Given current macroeconomic conditions and the market's perceptions of Roche's risk level, investors would expect to earn an 8.65% return from Roche debt, just as they would have earned from this company on a straight, fixed-rate bond with a 10-year maturity. If our investor sold the 10-year bond for $6,643, the buyer would earn $350 each year, and then get the full face value, $10,000, in the terminal, tenth year, thereby earning an internal rate of return equal to 8.65% (see Exhibit 3.6).

Analyzing the Return to Warrant Holders

Calculating the return to warrant holders is more complicated than calculating the return to pure bondholders because Roche's warrant payoff was denominated in Swiss francs (not U.S. dollars) and the return on the warrants depended on the price of Roche's share on 16 May 1994. The bond return that was calculated in the last section was a dollar-denominated return, and all the cash flows (i.e., the purchase price of the bond, 3.5% coupon, and repaid principal) were denominated in dollars. By contrast, the warrants were paid for in dollars, but the exercise price was denominated in Swiss francs. As a result, investors who purchased the warrants faced the threat that, at expiration (three years later), the value of the Swiss franc would depreciate.

On the date of issue (16 May 1991), the warrant portion of each $10,000 note was worth $3,356.63, and the spot exchange rate was approximately SFr 1.44 per U.S. dollar. Therefore, the Swiss franc value of the warrants was SFr 4,833.55 (i.e., $3,356.63 × SFr 1.44/$ = SFr 4,833.55), and because each $10,000 Bull Spread bond had 73 warrants attached, each warrant was worth SFr 66.21 (i.e., SFr 4,833.55 ÷ 73 = SFr 66.21).

Exhibit 3.6 US$ Cash Flows Connected to the Bond Portion
of Roche's Bull Spread Security

Year	Bond Cash Flows (US$)
1991	−6,643
1992	350
1993	350
1994	350
1995	350
1996	350
1997	350
1998	350
1999	350
2000	350
2001	10,000 + 350 = 10,350
Internal Rate of Return	**8.65%**

Given this information, let's look at possible rates of return on Roche's Bull Spread warrants assuming the exchange rate did not change, and, in the following section, see what happens if the exchange rate does change.

- **Return if the share price were at or below SFr 7,000** The put option gave investors the right, but not the obligation, to sell 100 warrants and receive SFr 7,000. Because each warrant was worth SFr 66.21, the value of 100 warrants at inception was SFr 6,621. Therefore, Roche was guaranteeing investors a return equal to, at least, SFr 379,[18] which is equal to a 1.9% annual return for three years (see Exhibits 3.7 and 3.8).[19]

- **Implications if the share price were at or above SFr 10,000** Roche's Bull Spread warrant gave Roche the right, but not the obligation, on 16 May 1994 to purchase 100 warrants from investors for a maximum price of SFr 10,000. As a result, regardless of how high Roche's share increased, the most investors could earn was SFr 3,379 or 14.7%,[20] which reflects the difference between the SFr 10,000 strike

[18] SFr 7,000 − SFr 6,621 = SFr 379.
[19] $(1 + 379/6,621)^{(1/3)} - 1 = 1.9\%$. The same answer can be derived by calculating the internal rate of return.
[20] $(1 + 3,379/6,621)^{(1/3)} - 1 = 14.7\%$. The same answer can be derived by calculating the internal rate of return.

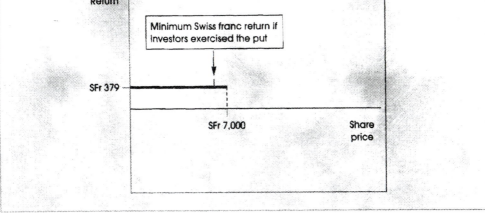

Exhibit 3.7 Warrants: Swiss Franc Profit-Loss Profile if Roche's Share Price Were Below SFr 7,000 on 16 May 1994

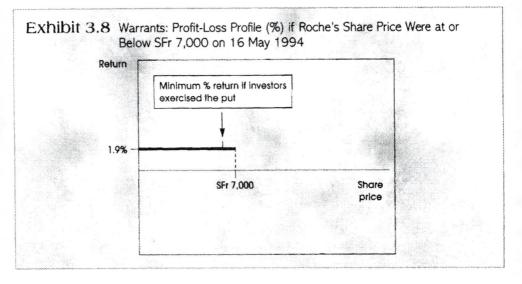

Exhibit 3.8 Warrants: Profit-Loss Profile (%) if Roche's Share Price Were at or Below SFr 7,000 on 16 May 1994

price and SFr 6,621 (i.e., the value of 100 warrants on 16 May 1996, when the issue was sold). Exhibits 3.9 and 3.10 show the profit-loss profiles of the short call if the share price were greater than or equal to SFr 10,000.

• **Implications if the share price were above SFr 7,000 but below SFr 10,000** At maturity, if the share price were above SFr 7,000 but below SFr 10,000, investors would receive one-for-one earnings for each Swiss franc the share price rose above SFr 7,000. Exhibit 3.11 shows the profit-loss profile of this one-for-one profit between SFr 7,000 and SFr 10,000.

Exhibit 3.9 Warrants: Swiss Franc Profit-Loss Profile if Roche's Share Price Were Above SFr 10,000 on 16 May 1994

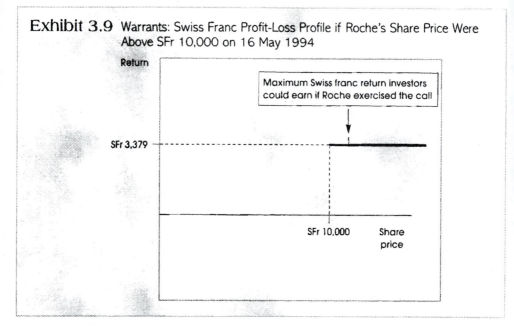

Exhibit 3.10 Warrants: Profit-Loss Profile (%) if Roche's Share Price Were at or Above SFr 10,000 on 16 May 1994

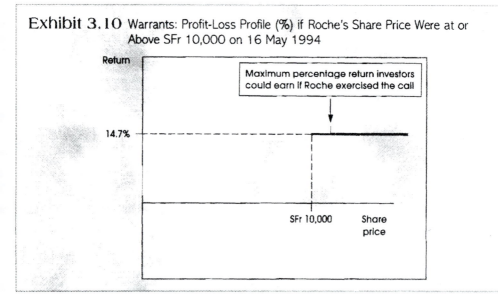

Exhibits 3.12 and 3.13 combine the profits and losses of the three share price ranges and show that the morphed hybrid form is that of a Bull Spread instrument.

The Foreign Exchange Risk of Roche's Warrants

Because the warrants were purchased with U.S. dollars but the return was in Swiss francs, investors faced a foreign exchange exposure. Exhibit 3.14

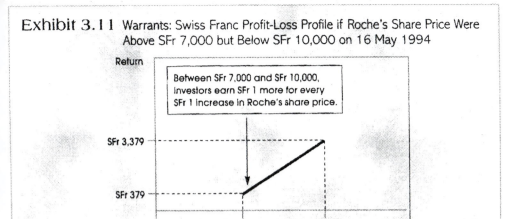

Exhibit 3.11 Warrants: Swiss Franc Profit-Loss Profile if Roche's Share Price Were Above SFr 7,000 but Below SFr 10,000 on 16 May 1994

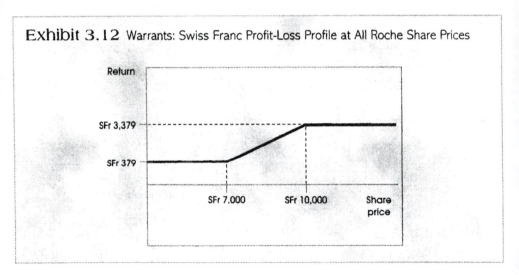

Exhibit 3.12 Warrants: Swiss Franc Profit-Loss Profile at All Roche Share Prices

shows the effect that changes in the dollar value of the Swiss franc would have on the dollar return to warrant holders. Notice that, as the Swiss franc becomes stronger, the dollar return increases. Notice, as well, that it is possible for the warrant return to be negative if the Swiss franc weakens too much.

Analyzing the Return to Bondholders and Warrant Holders (i.e., Bond Cum Warrants)

Investors holding the hybrid (i.e., the bond and warrant) earned an average rate of return that reflected two major factors. First, the bond portion of the

Exhibit 3.13 Warrants: Profit-Loss Profile (%) at All Roche Share Prices

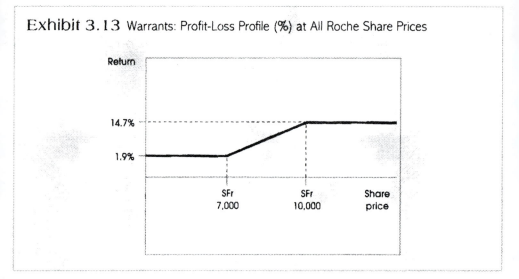

Exhibit 3.14 Return on the Warrants at Various Share Prices and Exchange Rates

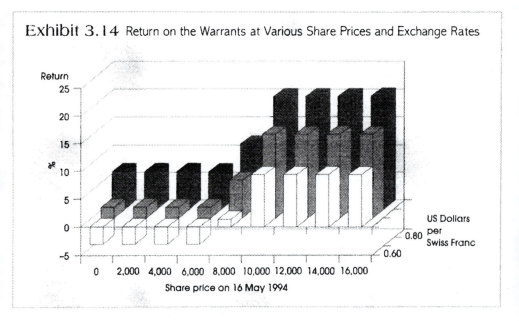

issue was 66.4% and the warrant portion of the issue was 33.6%; therefore, the bond dominated the hybrid's return (see Exhibit 3.4). Second, the bond return lasted for 10 years, but the warrant return was paid at the end of three years. Exhibit 3.15 shows the internal rates of return for the bond ex warrant, warrants ex bond, and bond cum warrants. Notice that bond's return was constant at 8.65% (see Exhibit 3.6) and the warrants' return varied between 1.90% and 14.70% (see Exhibit 3.13). As a result, the

Exhibit 3.15 Swiss Franc Return on the Warrants, Bond, and Bond cum Warrants

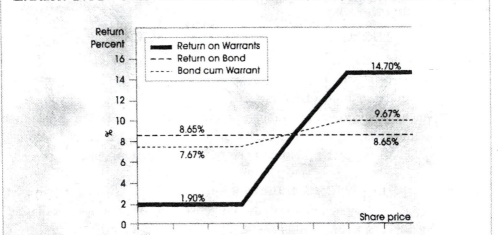

return on the bond cum warrants (i.e., the weighted average return) varied between 7.7% and 9.7%.[21]

- **The foreign exchange risk of the bond cum warrants** Exhibit 3.16 shows the effect that changes in the value of the Swiss franc have on the bond cum warrant's return. Because the warrant payoffs

Exhibit 3.16 Return on the Bond cum Warrants at Various Share Prices and Exchange Rates

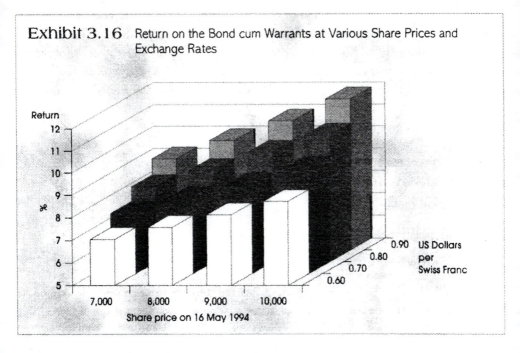

[21]Calculations of the weighted average return on the bond cum warrant are explained in Risk Notepad 3.2: Calculation of the Weighted Average Return on Roche's Bond cum Warrants.

were denominated in Swiss francs, the stronger the Swiss franc (i.e., the weaker the dollar), the greater the U.S. dollar return.

ANALYZING THE BULL SPREAD ISSUE FROM ROCHE'S SIDE

Why did Henri B. Meier decide to borrow by means of a complicated Bull Spread issue rather than a straight bond issue? Was it simply a matter of cost, and if so, how was he able to compare the all-in costs of a hybrid issue, which are uncertain, to a straight issue, where all the cash flows are known up front? Did the Bull Spread issue offer Meier any greater flexibility, and if so, did Roche pay a penalty in terms of increased risk and uncertainty?

Comparing the Costs of the Bull Spread Issue to a Straight Issue

To make valid evaluations of cost differences between two sources of funding, it is important to compare likes to likes, but how is that possible if the cash flows connected to the straight bond issue are known from the start and the cash flows from the hybrid, which depend on the share price, are only known at the end? The answer is we have to figure out the cost of hedging the uncertain cash flows of the hybrid and add the hedging costs to the hybrid's overall cost of funds. In that way, we would be comparing the cost of two sources of financing whose cash flows would be known from the beginning.

An example might help to clarify this point. Had Roche borrowed using a straight, 10-year issue, it would have paid 8.65%. By contrast, Roche made a Bull Spread issue that carried only a 3.5% coupon, but investors were willing to accept the lower coupon because they were given the prospect of earning more than they could have earned on a straight bond. As well, the

Risk Notepad 3.2

Calculation of the Weighted Average Return on Roche's Bond Cum Warrants

INTRODUCTION

The weighted average return to the bond cum warrant holder (see Exhibit 3.15) was calculated the following way. In 1991, an investor paid $10,000 for the Bull Spread security. The bond was worth $6,643.37, and the 73 warrants were worth $3,356.63. In 1994, when the warrants expired, it took 100 warrants to receive a minimum of SFr 7,000 or a maximum of SFr 10,000. As a result, calculations for the weighted average return were based on an investor, who in 1991 paid $10,000 for the Bull Spread issue and received 73/100 of the warrant payoff in 1994. In 1991, the Swiss franc–U.S. dollar exchange was SFr 1.44/US$.

IRR IF ROCHE'S SHARE PRICE ON 16 MAY 1994 WERE LESS THAN OR EQUAL TO SFR 7,000

If Roche's share price on 16 May 1994 (i.e., the expiration date of the warrant) were less than or equal to SFr 7,000, the internal rate of return (IRR) for the bond cum warrant would be equal to 7.7% (see Exhibit RN 3.2.1). Notice that investors receive each year a 3.5% coupon on the $10,000 face value of the security, and, in 1994, they receive the payoff from the warrants. If Roche's share price were below SFr 7,000 on 16 May, investors could exercise their put options and receive SFr 5,110 (i.e., 73/100 x SFr 7,000). Assuming the exchange rate did not change (i.e., it remained at SFr 1.44/US$), investors would receive $3,548.61 (i.e., SFr 5,110 ÷ SFr 1.44/US$) in 1994 from the warrants. Therefore, their total cash inflows in 1994 would be $3,898.61 (i.e., $350 + $3,548.61 = $3,898.61). Putting together all the cash flows from 1991 to 2001, Exhibit RN 3.2.1 shows that the internal rate of return if Roche's share price were less than or equal to SFr 7,000 would be 7.7%.

Exhibit RN 3.2.1 Internal Rate of Return on Bond cum Warrants (Assumes Roche's Share Price on 16 May 1994 was Less Than or Equal to SFr 7,000 and the Exchange Rate Did Not Change)

Year	Bond Cash Flows	Warrant Cash Flows (For 73 warrants @SFr 1.44/US$)	Total Cash Flows
1991	−$6,643.37	−$3,356.63 = −SFr 4,833.55	−$10,000
1992	$350		$350
1993	$350		$350
1994	$350	(73/100 × SFr 7,000) ÷ (SFr 1.44/$) = SFr $3,548.61	$3,898.61
1995	$350		$350
1996	$350		$350
1997	$350		$350
1998	$350		$350
1999	$350		$350
2000	$350		$350
2001	$10,350		$10,350
IRR			7.7%

IRR IF ROCHE'S SHARE PRICE ON 16 MAY 1994 WERE GREATER THAN OR EQUAL TO SFR 10,000

The same procedure can be used to calculate the IRR on the bond cum warrants assuming Roche's share price on 16 May was greater than or equal to SFr 10,000. The only cash flow to change is in 1994, when the investor would receive warrant-related cash inflows equal to SFr 10,000 for every 100 warrants. Assuming the exchange rate did not change, the dollar value of these warrant-related cash flows would be $5,069.44 (i.e., (73/100) × SFr 10,000 ÷ SFr 1.44/US$ = $5,069.44), and total cash flows in 1994 would be $5,419.44 (i.e., $350 + $5,069.44 = $5,419.44). Under these conditions the IRR would increase to 9.7% (see Exhibit RN 3.2.2).

IRR IF ROCHE'S SHARE PRICE ON 16 MAY 1994 WERE GREATER THAN SFR 7,000 BUT LESS THAN SFR 10,000

For all other Roche share prices above SFr 7,000 and below SFr 10,000 on 16 May 1994, the method of calculation would be the same as in Exhibits RN 3.1.1 and RN 3.2.2. One of these share prices is left as a review question.

Exhibit RN 3.2.2 Internal Rate of Return on Bond cum Warrants (Assumes Roche's Share Price on 16 May 1994 Was Greater Than or Equal to SFr 10,000 and the Exchange Rate Did Not Change)

Year	Bond Cash Flows	Warrant Cash Flows (For 73 warrants @SFr 1.44/US$)	Total Cash Flows
1991	–$6,643.37	–$3,356.63 = –SFr 4,833.55	– $10,000
1992	$350		$350
1993	$350		$350
1994	$350	(73/100 × SFr 10,000) ÷ (SFr 1.44/$)	
		= SFr $5,069.44	$5,419.44
1995	$350		$350
1996	$350		$350
1997	$350		$350
1998	$350		$350
1999	$350		$350
2000	$350		$350
2001	$10,350		$10,350
IRR			**9.7%**

Bull Spread issue was attractive to Roche because the attached warrants reduced its *coupon rate*, which lowered the company's cash outflows and supported its overall financial strategy.

We determined earlier in the chapter that the pure bond portion of the Bull Spread issue was worth $664.3 million and the Bull Spread warrants were worth $335.7 million. If the capital markets were perfectly arbitraged, the cost to hedge the Bull Spread exposure (e.g., by transacting a set of off-setting puts and calls) would be $335.7 million, which is exactly the value of the warrants. In percentage terms, the cost to hedge in a perfectly arbi-traged market would be 5.15%, which is the difference between the 8.65% cost of a straight issue and the 3.5% coupon. Under these circumstances, the company might be indifferent to the straight issue costing 8.65% and a hedged hybrid costing 8.65%. In short, if capital markets were perfectly arbitraged, then two identical assets (or liabilities) could not be bought and sold simultaneously to make riskless profits.[22] There should be no differ-ence between the two.

By contrast, if the capital markets were not perfectly arbitraged, the cost to hedge the warrant issue would be greater or less than $335.7 (i.e., 5.15%). For example, if the hedging cost were only $200 million, Roche could have reduced its all-in borrowing costs by issuing Bull Spread securi-ties with a 3.5% coupon and covering the warrant exposure for $200 mil-lion. If the expense to hedge were $200 million, the cost of these funds would have been 6.25%, a full 2.4% below the straight issue. In effect, Roche would have been paying a 3.5% coupon and then hedging at a cost of only 2.75%, instead of the 5.15% it would have paid if the markets were perfectly arbitraged. On an annual basis, a 2.4% savings on $1 billion of debt is worth $24 million!

Henri Meier may have chosen a Bull Spread issue because he spotted a market imperfection that allowed him to arbitrage the capital markets and borrow at a lower cost than if he had gone the easier route and borrowed with a straight bond issue. It is equally likely that he chose a hybrid debt issue over a straight bond issue because of the opportunities it gave him to play the market by hedging and unhedging his warrant exposures during the three-year maturity of the warrants.

There is a big difference between reducing costs by arbitraging the market at the time of issue and playing the market (i.e., speculating) to reduce costs during the maturity of the issue. Arbitraging capital market imperfections reduces costs up front and without any uncertainty because it locks in the lower costs at the time of the issue. By contrast, choosing a hybrid issue because the *expected* all-in cash outflows at the end of the period (i.e., *ex post*)

| [22]The prices of the two homogeneous assets should differ by no more than their transaction costs.

will be less than a straight issue is a speculation that a company makes against the market and executes for the duration of the issue. Not until the maturity of the issue, or until the warrant exposure has been hedged, or until the terminating covenants have been exercised would a company know fully the actual all-in costs. Only then would it be able to determine if its cash outflows were less than it would have paid using a simple straight bond issue (or fully hedged hybrid security issue).

What are the Sources of Capital Market Imperfections?   In a purely competitive world, where market imperfections do not exist, warrants should be priced fairly and offer no immediate source of subsidy to the borrower, but in the real world, distortions can and do occur. Due to the gigantic size of the hybrid issues, spotting any pricing imperfections could save a company millions of dollars in borrowing costs during the lifetime of the issue. The more severe and long lasting the market imperfections, the greater the potential for companies to profit from temporary market aberrations.

How can a CFO or an investment banker identify these opportunities before an issue is made? To get an idea for whether warrants are fairly priced, and therefore if the hybrid is cheaper or more expensive than the straight issue, a way is needed to calculate the cost of hedging a potential warrant exposure. This task would be easy if warrants or options with identical features were already sold on an over-the-counter (OTC) market or on an exchange. Under such conditions, the cost to hedge could be read directly from spot quotes in the financial press or obtained by calling an investment bank.

Unfortunately, flourishing markets in warrants or options with risk-return profiles identical to newly issued warrants do not always exist. As a result, some other valuation method has to be used. One way of generating feedback about a warrant's value is to use option valuation formulas, such as a contingent claims pricing model, a variation of the Black-Scholes formula, or Binominal Lattice Pricing Model. These formulas calculate option prices using information such as the relationship between the current share price and the strike price, expected dividend payments, risk-free interest rate, maturity of the warrant, and expected volatility of the underlier.

Another technique is to employ a practice commonly used for initial public offerings, called "book building," whereby investment bankers derive information about market demand by sampling large investors to determine the amounts of hybrid securities they would purchase at various prices and maturities. First, the investment bankers establish a range of possible prices based on the risk, maturity, and size of similar recent issues. Then, market participants are contacted to get a sense of their demand for the issue at various prices.

What imperfections might create arbitrage distortions in the market for bonds and warrants? Some of them are government-induced distortions, such as differential taxes on various debt instruments, uneven regulations, and preferential subsidies. Others are created by informational imperfections, such as investors' relative familiarity with different companies, investment biases (e.g., preference for local companies over foreign companies), and diverse perceptions of company risks and/or market risks.

Usually, imperfections in the capital markets that would allow arbitrage to take place are remedied or neutralized swiftly. An enormous amount of arbitrage-based capital can flow quickly to realign prices. The arbitrage forces that create this convergence are enhanced when investors have the ability to separate the components of the hybrid issue and sell them separately in the capital markets.

A Few Last Words about Arbitraging Capital Markets   If capital market imperfections are the source of cost differences between hedged hybrid issues and straight bond issues, then these cost differences are known up front. Nevertheless, just because a hedged hybrid security is less expensive than a straight bond does not mean that a CFO will hedge the warrant exposure. Hedging is a decision and not a requirement. When a CFO decides explicitly not to hedge a new position, this decision might have been because the new position offset (i.e., hedged) an existing exposure.

At the same time, it is equally likely that the decision not to hedge was prompted by the willingness to take calculated risks because not paying the hedging costs means a CFO can free funds for other purposes. A conscious choice not to hedge may mean that the CFO is willing to increase the level of company risk in hopes of raising profitability by speculating with the excess funds. By doing so, the CFO is pitting his talents (and those of his staff) against the market.

Because CFOs have the opportunity to hedge or not hedge their hybrid exposures, these debt instruments provide greater financial flexibility than straight issues. Unfortunately, they also make the evaluation of debt costs (and, therefore, the performance of CFOs) less transparent. CFOs are provided with greater latitude to exercise their core competences and thereby influence the level of company risk and return; as a result, this greater latitude places added responsibility on the company's president, CEO, and board of directors.

Every time CFOs decide against hedging the derivative risk in their hybrid debt issues, they introduce risks that would not have been present if they had borrowed by means of a straight issue or hedged hybrid. There are two important facets of this risk to consider. The first facet relates to how hybrid issues affect a company's debt-to-equity ratio because hybrid securities affect the debt-equity ratio differently from straight bonds. If a hybrid debt were left unhedged, then a company's debt-equity ratio would vary during the issue's maturity as the warrants were marked to market. The second facet of this risk is how the hybrid securities affect companies' investment decisions. If a company, like Roche, needed significant funding to hedge its hybrid issue (e.g., funds to purchase shares in the open market and to put in the treasury), then these funds might have been siphoned from other projects with higher value-added. This opportunity cost could be significant and should be considered.

ROCHE'S BULL SPREAD ISSUE: THE RESULT

On 16 May 1994, Roche's share price closed at SFr 12,500, which was SFr 2,500 above the strike price of the embedded call option. As a result, Roche exercised the Bull Spread warrants and paid SFr 730 million to the owners. The outcome was the best for all participants. Investors earned the highest possible returns because, for 100 warrants, they received the maximum SFr 10,000. Even the exchange rate cooperated to raise investors' all-in return. Between 16 May 1991 and 16 May 1994, the Swiss franc appreciated by about 1.04% (i.e., from $0.6940 per Swiss franc rate on 16 May 1991 to $0.7012 on 16 May 1994).

Roche also benefited from the deal because its treasury was able to deliver on two important prongs (i.e., build an acquisition war chest by borrowing at opportune times and minimize cash outflows by borrowing with hybrid debt issues) of the company's financial strategy (see Exhibit 3.17).

It is hard to determine whether Roche would have been better off if it had made a straight 10-year, U.S. dollar issue yielding 8.65% because Henri B. Meier's team is likely to have hedged and unhedged its Bull Spread warrant positions on numerous occasions during their three-year life in order to benefit from temporary opportunities. It is also possible that Henri Meier hedged the entire issue from the beginning, and due to a temporary capital market imperfection, was able to lock in a lower cost of funds than was otherwise available. We are only left with conjectures, but one fact stands out

Exhibit 3.17   Roche's Financial Strategy

1. Build an acquisition war chest by borrowing at opportune times

2. Minimize cash outflows by borrowing with hybrid debt issues

3. Prune divisions and sell off dead wood to increase cash flows

4. Reduce dividends to increase cash flows

5. Improve Roche's financial transparency and stock market profile

Exhibit 3.18 Comparison of Roche's Outstanding Shares, NES, and Stock Market Capitalization 1991 and 1994

	1991	1994	Change
Number of Shares	1,600,000	1,600,000	0
Number of Nonvoting Equity Shares (Genußscheine)	7,025,627	7,025,627	0
Total	8,625,627	8,625,627	0
Equity as Percent of Assets	59.7%	47.7%	−12.0%
Market Capitalization (Millions of Swiss Francs)	24,254	62,467	38,213
Percent			157.6%

Source: Roche Group: Annual Report and Group Accounts 1994 (Basel, 1994), 90 & 117.

among all others. In terms of performance and value creation, Roche's execution was excellent.

As Exhibit 3.18 shows, between 1991, when the Bull Spread warrants were issued, and 1994, when they were exercised, Roche's stock market capitalization rose by an astounding SFr 38.2 billion (158%)! During the same period, the company's equity as a percent of total assets declined by 12% but still remained a healthy 48%. This change in the equity ratio was understandable because Roche accomplished this feat with no change in the number of outstanding shares or nonvoting shares (i.e., Genußscheine).

Conclusion

Roche's decision to transform its treasury into a profit center and to use its financial resources as tactical weapons in the company's overall strategy was highly iconoclastic. Chairman Fritz Gerber and CFO Henri Meier knew that the company would face new risks, which were much different from those of its operating activities (i.e., manufacturing, marketing, and distribution). Implementation of this strategy rested on two vital assumptions:

- The risk-return profile from treasury activities was more attractive than other strategic options, and

- Roche could develop the financial skills needed to profit from both the asset side and the liability side of the balance sheet.

For many nonfinancial companies, the tactical step that Roche took is anathema to the general canons of conservative finance because the major sources of competitive advantage (especially for pharmaceutical companies) are thought to be derived from other factors, such as new products, research and development, novel applications, extensions of old product lines, quickness to the market with new products (e.g., finding ways to streamline the drug application and approval process), pruning unprofitable products, strengthening marketing and distribution, and undertaking joint marketing and/or research ventures.

Given this image of the key success factors, it is easy to understand how conventional wisdom would argue the treasury's role should be to stabilize cash flows to support long-term research and development. The conventional view was (and is, even to this day) the treasury should make sure funds were available when they were needed and ensure that a risk-management system was in place that would alert the company to any cash flow threats.[23] Taking on additional financial (i.e., nonoperating) risks to increase profitability was discouraged—even if the company's CFO and treasury team had clear competitive advantages over rivals. Rather, hedging the company's average operating margins (which in the pharmaceutical industry can be very high) was recommended as the best possible way for the treasury to complement the relatively high-risk operating activities.

Casey Stengel, legendary manager of the New York Yankees, once said: "I'd always heard it couldn't be done, but sometimes it don't always work."[24] Stengel's aphorism is appropriate for Roche because it reinforces the conclusion that there is not one best solution for every corporation. Rules of thumb are good advice for reasonably average companies that are operating in normal circumstances, but to thrive and survive, some companies must look for more creative solutions. In such cases, survival may depend on modifying, bending, and breaking rules of thumb. As CFO Henri Meier often said, why should a company's profit ambitions be limited to only one portion of its assets (i.e., operational assets) and thereby exclude any profits from the rest (e.g., liquid assets)?

Roche made sophisticated use of financial hybrids as part of its financial strategy. To be successful, the company needed a highly skilled staff that understood the ever-changing menu of derivative instruments and had a sense for when to hedge and unhedge positions. It also needed decision-makers who understood the risks taken and who did not view

---

[23]Kenneth A. Froot, David S. Scharfstein, and Jeremy C. Stein, "A Framework for Risk Management," *Harvard Business Review* (November-December 1994), 91–102.

[24]R. Thomas Berner, *St. James Encyclopedia of Pop Culture*, "Casey Stengel." Available at http://findarticles.com/p/articles/mi_g1epc/is_bio/ai_2419201158. Accessed 14 December 2007.

financial risks in isolation from the company's overall strategic position. Success was part skill, part instinct, and part luck—somewhat akin to winning a slalom race at the Olympics or introducing a new product. CFO Henri Meier stressed repeatedly in his presentations to investors that he would run Roche's financial business as the least risky of the company's activities.

From 1991 to 2000, Roche Holding used derivative instruments in ways that enhanced shareholder value. Driven by a highly idiosyncratic capital structure and market forces, CFO Henri Meier took calculated risks by using hybrid security issues, like the Bull Spread issue, and he exploited market imperfections to earn millions of Swiss francs for Roche. One of the keys to his success was an ability to monitor on a constant basis his exposures and to take risks only when the odds were highly in Roche's favor. The Bull Spread issue is just one example of many such deals Roche transacted during the 1990s that shows how analytical risk management tools can be combined in creative and constructive ways.

Review Questions

1. Summarize the reasons Roche transformed its treasury into a profit center. What are the major benefits of a treasury that operates as a profit center? What are the major disadvantages?

2. Fully explain what the following sentence in the chapter means: "Meier was able to steer a healthy portion of each issue away from hedge funds, which, in an effort to hedge their warrant exposures, might have shorted the Roche stock in the spot market and thereby driven down share prices." Assuming the warrants were long call options on Roche shares, explain how shorting Roche's shares would have hedged the hedge funds' positions.

3. Fully explain what the following sentence in the chapter means: "The ongoing operations of U.S.-based Genentech gave Roche a huge, long-term U.S. dollar exposure. Roche financed the Genentech purchase with a short-term U.S. dollar bridge loan, which left the company vulnerable to increasing interest rates. To protect the Swiss franc value of Genentech's anticipated long-term cash inflows, Henri Meier set up a natural hedge by creating offsetting, long-term liabilities in U.S. dollars." Why was Roche vulnerable to increasing interest rates? Explain what a natural hedge is and how Roche used it.

4. Explain how Roche's in-the-money Bull Spread put options with a strike price of SFr 7,000 were equivalent to fixed interest-earning securities. Why might investors be more interested in owning securities with put options than owning interest-earning securities having identical rates of return? Why might the Swiss government object to the issuance of securities with in-the-money put options?

5. Why were investors, like Swiss pension funds that could not invest in stocks, interested in Roche's Bull Spread issue?

6. Why do many shareholders feel threatened when their companies make hybrid debt issues? Explain why Roche shareholders did not feel threatened by the 1991 Bull Spread issue.

7. Analyze the following Bull Spread issue from the investors' perspective. Suppose in 1991, Roche could have borrowed, outright, 10-year, dollar-denominated funds for 9%. Suppose further that Roche offered a $1 billion Bull Spread issue with an annual 4% coupon and the same warrant terms as the 1991 issue (i.e., each US$ 10,000 bond came with 73 Bull Spread warrants, and 100 Bull Spread warrants entitled the holder to receive SFr 7,000 if the closing price of a bearer share in three years was less than or equal to SFr 7,000, or one share or SFr 10,000, if the closing price was greater than or equal to SFr 10,000).

   a. Calculate the value of the bond portion of the issue and value of the warrant portion of the issue.

   b. Calculate the return to the bondholders.

   c. Calculate the range of returns to the warrant holders.

   d. Calculate the range of returns to the bond cum warrant holders.

   e. Explain how a change in the Swiss franc/U.S. dollar exchange rate would affect the returns to bondholders, warrant holders, and bond cum warrant holders.

   f. Explain how Roche could hedge its warrant exposure.

   g. If the market were perfectly arbitraged, what would it cost Roche to hedge its warrant exposure?

   h. Suppose the actual cost to hedge this warrant exposure were $200 million. Calculate Roche's effective interest cost from using the Bull Spread issue.

   i. What market imperfections might cause disequilibrium hedging costs of $200 million.

8. When comparing the all-in cost of a straight bond issue to the all-in cost of a hybrid, what is wrong with waiting until the end of the

issue and then comparing how much is actually paid on each of the two issues?

9. Using the figures in this chapter, calculate the return to the bond cum warrant holders if Roche's share price on 16 May 1994 were equal to SFr 9,000.

Further Reading

Please visit http://www.prenhall.com/marthinsen, where you can find the following embellishment on and extension of this chapter:

- Appendix 3.1: Should Corporate Treasuries Be Profit Centers?

Bibliography

Froot, Kenneth A., Scharfstein, David S., and Stein, Jeremy C. "A Framework for Risk Management." *Harvard Business Review* (November-December 1994), 91–102.

Marthinsen, John. "Buried Treasure: Risks and Value-Added from Using Corporate Treasuries as Profit Centers," Streben Nach Wertschöpfung, Basel, Switzerland: Schwabe AG, Verlag, Basel, Weber-Thedy Corporate & Financial Communications, 178–197, 2006.

Nars, Kari (ed.). *Excellence in Debt Management.* London, England: Euromoney Publications, PLC, 1997.

Reilly, Frank K., and Brown, Keith C. *Investment Analysis and Portfolio Management.* 8th ed. Mason, OH: Thomson-Southwestern, 2006.

Roche Group: Annual Report and Group Accounts 1994. Basel, 1994.

Roche Group: Annual Report and Group Accounts 1995. Basel, 1995.

Ross, Stephen A., Westerfield, Randolph W., and Jaffe, Jeffrey. *Corporate Finance.* 8th ed. New York: Irwin-McGraw Hill, 2008.

4

Metallgesellschaft AG

Illusion of Profits and Losses, Reality of Cash Flows

Introduction

The story of Metallgesellschaft AG [1] (MGAG) is not one
of unabashed success or unmitigated failure. It is, instead, the
tale of a first-rate company that became an industry leader in
energy derivatives[2] by introducing innovative and much-
needed derivative-hedging products, only to have the venture
collapse because of a failure to understand, and an inability
to manage, the risks of the products it was selling. During the
course of three years, from 1991 to December 1993, MGAG's
U.S. affiliate, Metallgesellschaft Refining and Marketing
Company (MGRM), managed to lose $1.3 billion on energy-
derivative activities despite an enthusiastic customer base,
rapidly increasing sales, a dominant industry position, and
highly valued products. MGAG's story is important on many
levels, but it is especially valuable for showing persuasively

---

[1] In German, AG stands for *Aktiengesellschaft*, which is the English equivalent of an *incorporated (Inc.)* or
limited (Ltd.) public stock company.
[2] The energy-derivatives market is for contracts, such as forwards, futures, options, futures options, and
swaps, on crude oil, heating oil, gasoline, natural gas, and electricity. This chapter focuses on crude oil
and natural gas. Forwards, options, and swaps are traded on the over-the-counter market, whereas
futures, options, and futures options are traded on various exchanges (e.g., New York Merchantile
Exchange [NYMEX] and IntercontinentalExchange [ICE]). Settlement varies, depending on the contract, and can be in the form of cash or actual physical delivery of the commodity. Exchange-traded
contracts are standardized. For example, the NYMEX crude oil contract is worth 1,000 barrels of oil.

that the ability to identify and manage risks is as important to success as imagination, creativity, and entrepreneurship.

Metallgesellschaft: Evolution of the Company and Its Product Lines

In the early 1990s, with approximately $15 billion in annual sales generated by its 250 domestic and foreign affiliates, MGAG was one of Germany's largest multinational conglomerates. It had an established reputation in the dirty, slow-moving businesses of mining and smelting nonferrous metals, but growth was difficult in these slumbering industries, and high price volatility made planning decisions precarious.[3]

In 1989, MGAG selected Austrian-born Heinz Schimmelbusch as its new chief executive officer, and almost immediately, he and his management team developed a strategy to increase sales growth and profitability. Their approach was to diversify into high value-added lines of new businesses and to prune deadwood from existing activities by means of divestitures. Schimmelbusch started by splitting MGAG into three parts: *raw materials*, *services*, and *industry*, focusing particular attention on trading, foreign sales, and the rapidly growing pollution-abatement industry. By the early 1990s, MGAG had already spent more than a billion German marks to acquire fresher lines of business, which expanded the company's enterprise portfolio to include a wide variety of products, ranging from energy derivatives, to pollution-abatement equipment,[4] to explosives, to oil.

Schimmelbusch's diversification strategy came under almost immediate pressure after it was put in place because sales growth and profitability in MGAG's core lines of business continued to deteriorate. One of the main reasons for declining sales was a sharp drop in metals prices (e.g., aluminum, nickel, and lead), which was caused, in large part, by former Soviet countries selling metals on world markets at bargain-basement prices. Rising costs also eroded profits; Germany's expensive labor force, the strong German mark, and MGAG's inability to use a few of its new smelters[5] added fuel to the fires of distress. It also fell victim to its own timing mistake, as the company chose

---

[3]MGAG produced and sold mainly chemicals and metals, along with engineering and trading services. In addition, the company produced a wide variety of products including (*inter alia*) heating supplies, castings, stainless steel, aircraft accessories, plastics, and automotive components.

[4]MGAG aggressively expanded its position in the pollution-abatement industry, spending DM 1.5 billion in 1992 alone to acquire companies in the environmental field. The results were impressive. For example, MGAG developed Europe's first complete system for recycling automobile batteries, built leading-edge desulphurization plants, and designed systems for recycling steel dust and salt slag. See Anonymous, "Dreaming of Butterflies," *The Economist* 327 (7817) (26 June 1993), 65–71.

[5]MGAG had problems with the smelting of zinc and lead at its Rheinische Zinkgesellschaft plant.

the early 1990s to upgrade many of its production facilities with costly, state-of-the-art, low-emission equipment. Together, these influences battered MGAG's sales and profitability; as a result, pressure mounted for its new lines of business to pick up the slack.

Energy Derivatives at MGRM

Of the new lines of business, one of the most promising was creating a market for long-term, fixed-rate forward contracts in oil and gas. MGAG's commitment to provide the market with these novel, energy-related derivatives began in earnest in 1991, when it hired W. Arthur Benson, a former Louis Dreyfus Energy executive, to run its U.S. affiliate, MGRM. The German parent hoped to introduce a range of innovative energy-related financial derivatives by leveraging Benson's industry understanding and management skills with MGAG's huge financial resources. Benson accepted the challenge and brought with him about 50 of his former colleagues at Louis Dreyfus Energy.

Arthur Benson had made his name at Louis Dreyfus Energy in the jet fuel market during an era of rising energy prices, but any doubts as to whether he could identify opportunities in this new, declining price environment were soon laid to rest. He and his team offered a palette of highly popular energy derivatives, and by September 1993, MGRM had already sold 185 million barrels[6] of its fixed-rate, long-term forward contracts to about 100 independent heating oil and gasoline retailers.[7]

ENERGY MARKETS ON A ROLLER-COASTER RIDE

Between 1988 and 1994, energy prices changed dramatically (see Exhibit 4.1) and so did the relationship between spot and forward energy prices. As a result, hedges that were supposed to protect MGRM's forward oil and gas deals hemorrhaged cash, causing the company's trading strategy to appear wildly speculative. To understand why, let's begin by investigating the supply and demand conditions that changed absolute and relative energy prices. Afterwards, we will link these price changes to MGRM's hedging strategy and the company's massive cash outflows.

Rising Energy Prices and Backwardation

From 1988 to 1990, just prior to Benson's move to MGRM, energy prices rose. The increase in prices was stimulated from both demand- and supply-related factors. On the demand side, a long global economic expansion encouraged oil

---

[6] A barrel of oil has 42 gallons.

[7] A spokesman for MGAG explained that MGRM's position was equivalent to 85 days of Kuwait's output.

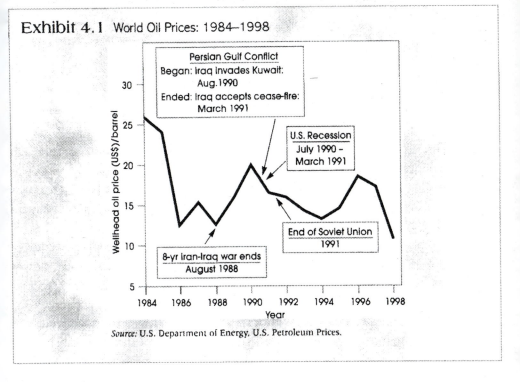

Exhibit 4.1 World Oil Prices: 1984–1998

Source: U.S. Department of Energy, U.S. Petroleum Prices.

consumption and raised oil prices. On the supply side, the double-barreled effects of turmoil in Eastern Europe (e.g., the Berlin Wall fell, there were mass uprisings in Czechoslovakia, and the Soviet Union began to collapse) and fear of a Persian Gulf War created oil line disruptions that helped to escalate oil prices to over $20 per barrel.

Due to uncertainty over a possible Gulf War, energy users put a premium on holding physical inventories of oil and gas rather than having claims on future deliveries. As a result, spot energy prices rose above forward energy prices. When this happens, the markets are in *backwardation*, and a convenient way to discuss backwardation is in terms of an underlier's (in this case, oil's and gas') *basis*. Basis is the difference between an underlier's spot price and forward price. Therefore, when a market is in backwardation, the underlier's basis is positive (see Exhibit 4.2)[8]

Falling Energy Prices and Contango

From 1990 to 1994, energy prices fell continuously and dramatically due to a combination of macroeconomic and industry-related factors. One of the major reasons for the reduction in energy demand was an eight-month recession in the United States that began in July 1990. The recession reduced real

[8]Risk Notepad 4.1. *What is the Difference between Contango and Backwardation?* explains in greater detail why backwardation is an anomalous state.

Exhibit 4.2 Backwardation and Contango Defined

Backwardation	Spot Price > Forward Price	Basis = Spot − Forward > 0
Contango	Spot Price < Forward Price	Basis = Spot − Forward < 0

U.S. GDP by 0.5%, but, fortunately, it was not matched by a global recession (the world economy grew by nearly 3%); so the decline in energy prices was gradual rather than abrupt. At the industry level, the decline in oil prices was exacerbated by overproduction due to post–Gulf War quota disputes among OPEC members.

Normalcy returned to the oil and gas markets after United Nations' forces defeated Saddam Hussein's army in Kuwait during February 1991. Lower levels of global risk reduced or eliminated the premium that energy users put on the physical possession of oil and gas relative to owning energy contracts for future delivery. With fears of a global energy shortage gone, the spot demand for oil and gas fell relative to forward demand, causing the energy markets to move from backwardation to contango and the basis to move from a positive to a negative value (see Exhibit 4.2).

Risk Notepad 4.1

What Is the Difference Between Contango and Backwardation?

Should there be a difference between the spot price and forward price of a commodity? If there is, should the spot price be greater than or less than the forward price? When the forward price of an underlier is greater than the spot price, the market is said to be in contango. When the reverse is true (i.e., the spot price is greater than the forward price), the market for the underlier is said to be in backwardation.

NET INTEREST EXPENSE

Common sense would lead most of us to believe that the forward price of a commodity like oil, should always be greater than the spot price, but we will find that this is not always the case. To understand the common sense of the relationship, let's look at a company trying to increase its oil reserves and considering whether to purchase them on the spot market or forward market.

Suppose the oil market was in backwardation, with the spot price of oil at $20 per barrel, the one-year forward price at $18 per barrel, the one-year Treasury bill rate at 10%, and a company wished to purchase an additional $160,000 of oil for its reserves. In considering whether to purchase the oil on the spot or forward market, the company might reason as follows: *Why should I buy 8,000 barrels of oil today for $20 a barrel, when I could negotiate a long forward contract today that locks in the one-year delivery price of oil at $18 per barrel? In the meantime, I could use my $160,000 to invest in a risk-free government security earning 10%, and, at the end of the year, I would have $176,000 (i.e., my $160,000 investment plus 10% interest). After a year, I could use $144,000 of the $176,000 to settle my forward obligation to buy 8,000 barrels of oil, and I would still have $32,000 left over. This seems like a much better alternative than purchasing 8,000 barrels of oil now for $160,000 and next year having only the 8,000 barrels of oil (i.e., no extra cash).*

The rule-of-thumb conclusion we might draw from this example is that, when markets are in backwardation, rational individuals and institutions wishing to stockpile would always purchase commodities in the forward markets and never purchase them in the spot market.[9]

OTHER FACTORS THAT INFLUENCE FORWARD PRICES: STORAGE COSTS AND CONVENIENCE VALUE

So far, we have considered only net interest expense (i.e., interest cost minus earnings) in the relationship between spot and forward prices, but two other important factors—storage costs and convenience value—should also be taken into account.

Storage Costs

Storage costs are important when deciding whether to buy an underlier on either the spot or forward market because, if a company bought a commodity, like oil, on the spot market, it would have to pay for storage, and these costs would reduce profits. Companies that purchase commodities in the forward markets do not incur this cost. Of course, there are assets, such as stocks and bonds, that have trivial or no storage costs, but then there are others, such as oil or precious metals, for which storage costs can be significant.

Because of storage costs, one would expect, even without considering net interest expenses, the forward price to be higher than the spot price by the compound value of the storage costs. For example, suppose the spot price of oil were $20 per barrel, risk-free interest rate were 0%, forward price were $20 per barrel, and yearly storage costs $1 per barrel (paid up front). Given these conditions, a company looking to purchase oil for inventory would prefer to buy in the forward market. Buying a barrel of oil now would mean spending $21 per barrel for the purchase and storage of this asset. By contrast, purchasing a barrel of oil in the forward market would cost only $20.

Convenience Value

Convenience value reflects the worth an individual attributes to having, on hand, an asset that has some practical use in trade, production, and/or consumption. It is the advantage of possessing an asset and not just having the right to buy it in the future. In this regard,

---

[9] They could also earn riskless profits by selling the commodity short in the spot market, investing the proceeds, and covering themselves by buying in the forward market. Such opportunities should be the exception rather than the rule.

there is a big difference between investment assets that have no practical use, such as government securities or corporate bonds, and assets that can be used in production and/or consumption activities, such as oil, copper, silver, or gold. Ready supplies provide individuals with flexibility to take advantage of opportunities as they appear from time to time. Perhaps more importantly, ready supplies ensure companies (e.g., oil refiners) that they will have available inventories of materials needed for their business operations. When there is a benefit from having supplies on hand, this positive value is called an asset's convenience value.

Net interest expense and storage costs are typically combined and called the cost of carry. Taking into account cost of carry and convenience value, the relationship between the spot and forward price of an asset should be as shown in Equation 4.1.

Forward Price = Spot Price + Cost of Carry − Convenience Value   Eq. 4.1

Where:

"Cost of Carry" is the compound value of all interest expenses minus the compound value of all investment returns plus the compound value of all storage costs, and "Convenience Value" is the compound value that individuals attach to having an asset on hand and their expectations about its future availability.

MGRM'S INNOVATIVE ENERGY DERIVATIVE PRODUCTS

MGRM was an innovator in offering much-needed energy-related financial derivatives to its customers—a fact that is often forgotten. The main source of demand for these contracts came from independent oil and gas retailers trying to lock in long-term supply contracts at the relatively low prices. During the 1980s and early 1990s, intense competition in U.S. petroleum retailing pitted independent fuel oil companies and filling stations against large brand companies and their distributors; but, the independents were losing the war. As a result, the number of independent filling stations and oil retailers (along with their market shares) was declining. The relative success of the brand distributors was largely because their supplies were guaranteed, and, during lean times, they could count on financial support from their large multinational parents. In the end, it came down to a battle of margins (i.e., the difference between the retail price of oil products and the wholesale price paid by filling stations and oil retailers), and the independents could not compete.[10]

MGRM's forward contracts offered these independents an opportunity during the early 1990s to stabilize their future margins by locking in

[10]See Ed Krapels, "Re-examining the Metallgesellschaft Affair and Its Implications for Oil Traders." Oil & Gas Journal (26 March 2001), 70–77.

(relatively low) oil prices for extended periods of time (up to 10 years).[11] The problem with the industry before MGRM entered the picture was the demand for long-term, forward, fixed-rate oil contracts was not matched by counterparties who were willing and able to supply them. The forward and futures markets that existed were mainly used to hedge (or to speculate) in relatively short-term maturities. At the time, approximately 90% of the contracts in the oil futures market expired within four months, which meant that any sizeable movement in the demand for (or supply of) long-dated contracts would result in significant price changes.[12] Insufficient liquidity in long-dated energy derivatives also caused prohibitively large bid-ask spreads. In this environment, MGRM felt confident that it could use its energy market expertise, hedging know-how, and huge financial resources to make a profitable business by selling long-term, fixed-rate, forward energy derivatives.[13]

Due to the energy industry's need for long-term hedging products and the relative absence of viable alternatives, MGRM was able to generate substantial increases in sales of its forward products. These sales were stimulated, as well, by the bargain rates at which MGRM offered its forward products. Because MGRM did not account for all the risks of its derivative products (especially liquidity risk), it failed to properly value the contracts, and customers responded to these underpriced contracts with enthusiasm.

The resulting large exposures put MGRM in a position where even the smallest error could (and did) result in considerable losses. The problem was the risks that MGRM overlooked or failed to consider seriously were not trivial, and, as a result, when market conditions changed disadvantageously, cash outflows were significant. To understand these risks, let's investigate MGRM's hedging strategy.

---

[11]In September 1993, about 64% of MGRM's contracts were *firm-fixed*, which means customers were required to take delivery of oil or gas on fixed contract dates. The other 36% of MGRM's contracts were *firm-flexible*, which means customers could alter the timing of deliveries but had to purchase any deferred quantities by the end of the contract period. Approximately 90% of MGRM's forward contracts in September 1993 had 10-year maturities; the rest had five-year maturities. These contracts also had termination options in them. MGRM's options and their effects are explained in the online appendix to this book (see Appendix 4.2: MGRM's Embedded Options at http://www.prenhall.com/marthinsen.)

[12]On New York Mercantile Exchange (NYMEX), 76% of the volume was in the nearest two contract months, and 90% were transacted in the first four months. See Ed Krapels, "Re-examining the Metallgesellschaft Affair and Its Implications for Oil Traders," *Oil & Gas Journal* (26 March 2001), 70–77.

[13]Customers could ask for physical delivery if they gave MGRM 45 days' notice. See Ed Krapels, "Re-examining the Metallgesellschaft Affair and Its Implications for Oil Traders," *Oil & Gas Journal* (26 March 2001), 70–77.

Understanding How MGRM Hedged Its Forward Exposures

Arthur Benson was hired to energize MGAG's sales growth and to help revitalize the company's bottom line. His strategy involved taking large bets on the *relationship* between spot and forward (or futures) energy prices, and he executed this strategy using stack-and-roll hedges (which will be explained shortly). Customers welcomed the derivative products offered by MGRM, but many market analysts were concerned about the speed with which MGRM had increased sales and net exposures. Did MGRM have the expertise to hedge such large net positions? Were there markets of sufficient size to allow MGRM to lay off its unwanted risks?

PAYOFF PROFILE OF SHORT FORWARD POSITIONS

MGRM sold fixed-rate, forward oil and gas contracts with maturities that stretched out monthly for as long as 10 years. Exhibit 4.3 shows the downward-sloping payoff profile of a short forward position. Unhedged, this exposure results in losses if the spot price at maturity exceeds the forward price, which was determined when the forward contract was initiated

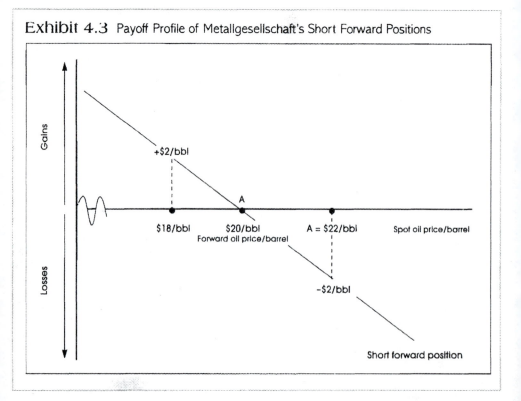

Exhibit 4.3 Payoff Profile of Metallgesellschaft's Short Forward Positions

Exhibit 4.4 MGRM's Monthly Short Positions Extending Out 10 Years

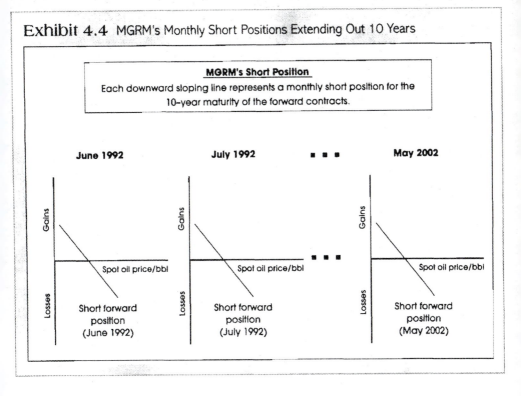

months or years earlier (see point A in Exhibit 4.3). Positive returns occur if the spot price at maturity is less than the forward price. For example, if MGRM agreed to sell oil next year at $20/bbl, it would earn $2/bbl if the maturity spot price in one year were $18/bbl, and it would lose $2/bbl if the maturity spot price in one year were $22/bbl.

Exhibit 4.4 is a depiction of MGRM's position in 1992, with its numerous short forward exposures represented by the series of (monthly) downward-sloping lines (payoff profiles) that extend from June 1992 to May 2002.

THE IDEAL HEDGE WAS NOT AVAILABLE

The ideal hedge for these short exposures (i.e., the series of monthly contracts to sell oil and gas that extended out 10 years) would have been for MGRM to offset them by entering into a series of long forward or futures contracts with identical quantities and maturities (see Exhibit 4.5). But that was impossible because the forward markets and futures markets were illiquid beyond one year. Therefore, these markets could not accommodate MGRM's massive needs.

The paucity of hedging counterparties in the long-dated oil and gas markets was not hard to understand. After all, offering long-dated forward contracts was supposed to be MGRM's novel contribution to the industry.

Exhibit 4.5 The Ideal Hedge: One Long Forward or Futures Contract for Each Short Forward Contract

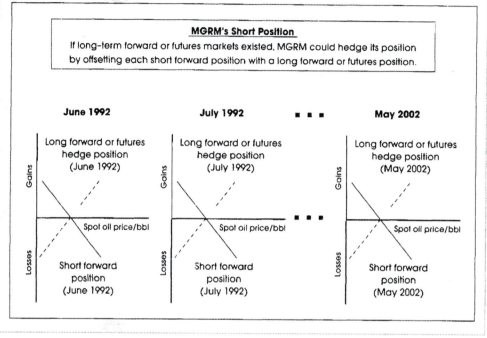

MGRM was "the" innovator, market maker, and leader in this field. Nevertheless, even though MGRM had substantial financial resources and energy expertise at its fingertips, it would have been pure lunacy for the company to take on such large exposures without hedging at least part of them. For this reason, MGRM relied on the *stack-and-roll* hedge.

STACK-AND-ROLL HEDGE

The *stack-and-roll* hedge is often used to neutralize long-term exposures when derivative markets do not have long-term maturities or when liquidity levels (i.e., transaction volumes) are too low for any substantial business to be conducted. At such levels of liquidity, large buy or sell orders can move derivative prices significantly and in unwanted directions. Moreover, in markets where liquidity is low, futures dealers usually protect themselves from losses by quoting wide bid-ask spreads, thereby increasing the cost to hedge.

A stack-and-roll hedge involves stacking enough futures contracts in the near-dated maturities to offset the total exposure of the series of long-term forward contracts.[14] For example, suppose that an independent oil refinery

---

[14]Most of MGRM's hedging contracts were for the next-to-expire futures contracts in unleaded gasoline, No. 2 heating oil, and West Texas Intermediate sweet crude.

Exhibit 4.6 Stack-and-Roll Hedge

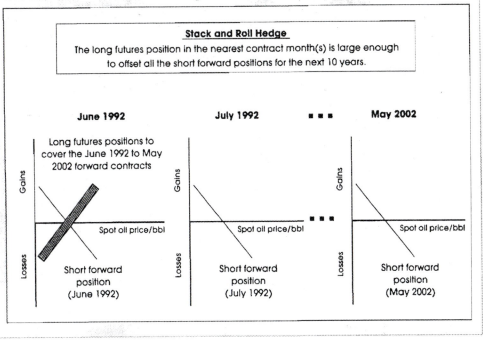

signed a contract with MGRM in June 1992. The 10-year contract called for 100,000 barrels of oil a month, which is 1.2 million barrels a year or 12 million barrels for the 10-year period. Suppose further that MGRM hedged this commitment to deliver by purchasing 12,000 futures contracts in the nearest maturity. Because each oil futures contract is for 1,000 barrels, MGRM's commitment to purchase 12 thousand oil contracts would equal the commitment to deliver 12 million barrels of oil.

In Exhibit 4.6, the stack of near-dated futures contracts to purchase oil (i.e., long contracts) is represented by the rectangle of upward-sloping lines that are front-loaded in June 1992. For each short forward contract (i.e., downward-sloping line) stretching out over the 10-year period, there is a long futures contract (i.e., upward-sloping line) in the stack.

At the end of each month, three important transactions take place, and once they are understood, the stack-and-roll hedge is easier to comprehend.

1. One of MGRM's short forward contracts matures, thereby requiring MGRM to deliver 100,000 barrels of oil at the agreed forward price and requiring MGRM to purchase the oil in the spot market.

2. The entire stack of MGRM's futures contracts, amounting to 12 million barrels, matures, so MGRM has to close out these contracts by

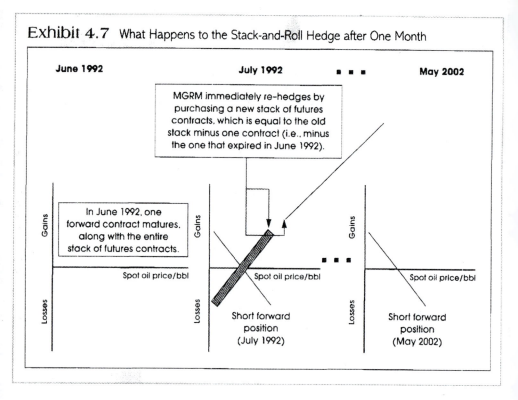

Exhibit 4.7 What Happens to the Stack-and-Roll Hedge after One Month

reversing its position (i.e., by calling its broker and selling 12,000 futures contracts, which is 12 million barrels of oil).

3. MGRM re-hedges its position, but because one of its forward contracts matured, when it re-hedges, the stack of long futures positions is lower by 100,000 barrels of oil, which is one month's worth of contracts. Notice in Exhibit 4.7, that the stack moved forward one month, and it is smaller by one long forward contract (i.e., its size is 11.9 million barrels of oil). In other words, one short forward contract from the 10-year series vanishes, and so does one long futures contract from the stack.[15]

HOW EFFECTIVE IS A STACK-AND-ROLL HEDGE?

An example might help to explain the risk-reducing potential of a stack-and-roll hedge. Let's compare the stack-and-roll hedge to two alternatives: a completely unhedged position and a one-year rolling hedge that covers

---

[15]This example is a simplification, because it gives the impression that MGRM would enter into 10 years of forward contracts, hedge them, and then not enter into any new contracts after that. In reality, new contracts would be opened continuously and old ones would be closed; so the amount of futures contracts needed to re-hedge the total forward position would depend on the net ebb and flow of contracts. Nevertheless, for pedagogical reasons, the explanation here is the best way to understand the risks of the stack-and-roll hedge.

Exhibit 4.8 Example Assumptions: Comparing a Stack-and-Roll Hedge to an Unhedged Position and a One-Year Rolling Hedge *(Figures in dollars)*

	Year 0	Year 1	Year 2
Year 0	$S_0 = 30$ $_0F_1 = {_0}F^*_1 = 29$ $_0F_2 = 28$ $_0B_1 = (30 - 29) = +1$ $_0B_2 = (30 - 28) = +2$ *Backwardation*		

	Basis falls	**Basis rises**
Oil price falls	$S_1 = 25$ $_1F^*_2 = 26$ $_1B_2 = -1$	$S_1 = 25$ $_1F^*_2 = 23$ $_1B_2 = +2$
Oil price rises	$S_1 = 35$ $_1F^*_2 = 36$ $_1b_2 = -1$ *Contango*	$S_1 = 35$ $_1F^*_2 = 33$ $_1B_2 = +2$ *Backwardation*

Year 2		
Oil price falls		$S_2 = 21$
Oil price rises		$S_2 = 39$

just the next period.[16] The one-year rolling hedge may take some clarification. Given the relatively short-term maturities in the futures markets during the MGRM debacle, a natural question to ask is, "If futures markets having sufficient liquidity only existed for contracts with maturities less than one year, then why didn't MGRM just hedge the forward contracts maturing during the coming year and leave the rest unhedged? Then, as time passed, previously unhedged forward contracts would fall within the one-year time horizon and could be hedged in the futures market." This iterative process of rolling hedges forward as the maturities become available is a one-year rolling hedge.

To simplify our task of comparing the three hedging alternatives, let's assume that MGRM sold five million barrels of forward oil contracts to an independent oil refinery, and the forward contracts had maturities of only one and two years. The first forward contract had a one-year maturity (i.e., delivery in Year 1) and was for one million barrels of oil. The second contract had a two-year maturity (i.e., delivery in Year 2) and was for four million barrels of oil. Exhibit 4.8 shows the spot and forward prices of oil for Year 0, Year 1, and Year 2, as well as the relevant basis figures for Year 0 and Year 1. The abbreviations used in Exhibit 4.8 are as follows.

---

[16]The relationships in this section are derived algebraically in Appendix 4–1, *A Comparison of the Cash Flow Risks of a Stack-and-Roll Hedge, Unhedged Position, and One-Year Rolling Hedge*. Available at http://www.prenhall.com/marthinsen.

Exhibit 4.9 Comparison of Cash Flow Effects for Three Hedging Strategies: Unhedged, Stack-and-Roll Hedge, and One-Year Rolling Hedge (Figures in dollars)

Column 1	Column 2	Column 3	Column 4	Column 5	Column 6
Type of hedge	Action	Price Falls & Basis Falls	Price Falls & Basis Rises	Price Rises & Basis Falls	Price Rises & Basis Rises
Unhedged					
Year 0	• Sell one million barrels of oil forward for one-year delivery at $29/bbl and sell four million barrels of oil forward for two-year delivery at $28/bbl				
Year 1	Close out forward	$1M \times (29 - 25) = +4M$	$1M \times (29 - 25) = +4M$	$1M \times (29 - 35) = -6M$	$1M \times (29 - 35) = -6M$
Year 2	Close out forward	$4M \times (28 - 21) = +28M$	$4M \times (28 - 21) = +28M$	$4M \times (28 - 39) = -44M$	$4M \times (28 - 39) = -44M$
	Result	$= +32M$	$+32M$	$= -50M$	$= -50M$
Stack-and-Roll Hedge					
Year 0	• Sell one million barrels of oil for one-year forward delivery at $29/bbl and sell four million barrels of oil for two-year forward delivery at $28/bbl • Buy five million barrels of oil in the futures market for one-year delivery at $29/bbl				
Year 1	Close out forward	$1M \times (29 - 25) = +4M$	$1M \times (29 - 25) = +4M$	$1M \times (29 - 35) = -6M$	$1M \times (29 - 35) = -6M$
	Close out futures	$5M \times (25 - 29) = -20M$	$5M \times (25 - 29) = -20M$	$5M \times (35 - 29) = +30M$	$5M \times (35 - 29) = +30M$
	Net cash flow after Year 1	$-16M$	$-16M$	$+24M$	$+24M$
	Re-hedge	Buy four million barrels of oil in the futures market for one-year delivery			

(Continued)

Exhibit 4.9 (Continued)

Year 2				
Close out forward	4M × (28 − 21) = +28M	4M × (28 − 21) = +28M	4M × (28 − 39) = −44M	4M × (28 − 39) = −44M
Close out futures	4M × (21 − 26) = −20M	4M × (21 − 23) = −8M	4M × (39 − 36) = +12M	4M × (39 − 33) = +24M
Net cash flow: Year 2	+8M	+20M	−32M	−20M
Net cash flow: Year 1 + Year 2	−8M	+4M	−8M	+4M

One-Year Rolling Hedge

Year 0
- Sell one million barrels of oil for one-year forward delivery at $29/bbl and sell four million barrels of oil forward for two-year delivery at $28/bbl
- Buy one million barrels of oil in the futures market for one-year delivery at $29/bbl.

Year 1				
Forward	1M × (29 − 25) = +4M	1M × (29 − 25) = +4M	1M × (29 − 35) = −6M	1M × (29 − 35) = −6M
Futures	1M × (25 − 29) = −4M	1M × (25 − 29) = −4M	1M × (35 − 29) = +6M	1M × (35 − 29) = +6M
Re-hedge	Buy four million barrels of oil in the futures market for one-year delivery			
Net cash flow after Year 1	0	0	0	0

Year 2				
Close out forward	4M × (28 − 21) = +28M	4M × (28 − 21) = +28M	4M × (28 − 39) = −44M	4M × (28 − 39) = −44M
Close out futures	4M × (21 − 26) = −20M	4M × (21 − 23) = −8M	4M × (39 − 36) = +12M	4M × (39 − 33) = +24M
Net cash flow: Year 2	+8M	+20M	−32M	−20M
Net cash flow: Year 1 + Year 2	+8M	+20M	−32M	−20M

107

- S_X is the spot price of oil in Year X;
- $_XF^*_Y$ is the futures price of a contract initiated in Year X and maturing in Year Y;
- $_XF_Y$ is the forward price of a contract initiated in Year X and maturing in Year Y;
- $_XB_Y$ is the basis of a contract initiated in Year X and maturing in Year Y.

Exhibit 4.9 considers the cash flow effects for the three hedging alternatives when the price of oil falls or rises and when the basis falls or rises.[17] From 1991 to 1993, MGRM faced decreasing oil prices and a falling oil basis. In fact, the basis on oil contracts changed from backwardation (positive) to contango (negative). Therefore, the detailed analysis that follows focuses on the actual scenario facing MGRM, and, afterwards, the conclusions are generalized to include all the scenarios.

Cash Flow Effects of the Unhedged Position

If MGRM were completely unhedged, then it would be required to purchase oil at the maturity spot price to fulfill its forward contracts that expire in Year 1 and Year 2. MGRM is committed to sell one million barrels of oil for $29/bbl at the end of Year 1 and to sell four million barrels for $28/bbl at the end of Year 2. What happens to MGRM's cash flows if the price of oil falls or rises?

Price of Oil Falls Let's consider Columns 3 and 4 of Exhibit 4.9 where the effects of falling prices are analyzed.[18] Suppose the price of oil fell from $30/bbl in Year 0 to $25/bbl in Year 1 and then to $21/bbl in Year 2. In Year 1, MGRM would have to pay $25 for each barrel of oil, but it would receive $29/bbl due to the forward contract it signed in Year 0. As a result, net cash inflows would be $4 million for the one-million-barrel delivery. Similarly in Year 2, MGRM would have to pay only $21/bbl each barrel of oil delivered, but it would receive $28/bbl due to the forward contract signed two years prior in Year 0. Net cash inflows on each barrel would be $7, which means that total cash inflows on four million barrels of oil would be $28 million. As a result, the cumulative (noncompounded) cash inflows for Year 1 and Year 2 would be $32 million (i.e., $4 million in Year 1 plus $28 million in Year 2).

Price of Oil Rises Columns 5 and 6 of Exhibit 4.9 show what would happen if the price of oil rose from $30/bbl in Year 0 to $35/bbl in Year 1 and then to $39/bbl in Year 2. Cumulative cash outflows would equal $50 million. MGRM would pay $6 million in Year 1 because its forward contract for one million barrels of oil would cost $35/bbl in the spot market, but

[17]The case in which the basis on oil contracts remains the same is left for two end-of-chapter review questions.
[18]Because we are analyzing unhedged contracts, it does not matter whether the basis rises or falls.

MGRM would earn only \$29/bbl from its forward contract. Similarly in Year 2, net cash outflows would equal \$44 million because MGRM would receive the \$28/bbl forward price for each of the four million barrels of oil it delivered, but it would pay \$39/bbl to purchase the oil in the Year-2 spot market. Therefore, the cumulative (noncompounded) cash outflows from Year 1 and 2 would equal \$50 million (i.e., −\$6 million in Year 1 and −\$44 million in Year 2).

Cash Flow Effects of a Stack-and-Roll Hedge

If MGRM used a stack-and-roll hedge, its range of possible cash-flow outcomes would be much narrower relative to the unhedged position. Let's consider the case in which oil prices fall and the basis falls.

Price of Oil Falls and Basis Falls Column 3 of Exhibit 4.9 shows what would happen if the price of oil fell from \$30/bbl in Year 0 to \$25/bbl in Year 1 and then to \$21/bbl in Year 2, and the basis on a one-year forward and futures contract fell from +\$1/bbl in Year 0 to −\$1/bbl in Year 1. To execute a stack-and-roll hedge, MGRM would purchase five thousand futures contracts[19] in Year 0 for one-year delivery. These contracts would exactly offset MGRM's Year 1 and Year 2 oil delivery obligations.

Year 1: Cash Flows from the Forward Contracts If the price of oil fell to \$25/bbl in Year 1, MGRM would need to pay \$25 million on the spot market to obtain one million barrels of oil that it has to deliver, but the company would receive \$29 million from its forward contract. As a result, MGRM would have cash inflows equal to \$4 million.

Year 1: Cash Flows from the Futures Contracts At the end of Year 1, MGRM would pay the one-year futures price of \$29/bbl, which was negotiated in Year 0. The total expenditure for five million barrels of oil would be \$145 million. If the price of oil fell in Year 1 to \$25/bbl, MGRM would be able to close out its expiring futures position by selling the five million barrels of oil at the spot price.[20] The proceeds from this sale would equal \$125 million; therefore, the net cash outflows from MGRM's purchase and sale of futures contracts would equal \$20 million.

Year 1: Net Cash Flows In Year 1, the cash inflows from MGRM's forward contracts were \$4 million, and the cash outflows from its stack of futures contracts were \$20 million. Therefore, MGRM's net cash outflows for Year 1 were \$16 million.

---

[19]Each futures contract is for 1,000 barrels of oil; so 5,000 contracts is equivalent to five million barrels of oil.

[20]Normally, physical delivery of oil is not made in futures market. The counterparty (e.g., MGRM) would just close out its futures position and take the cash gain. In this case, *closing out its futures position* means taking an offsetting (sell) position. On the day the futures contract matures, the futures price (for delivery that day) must equal the spot price. Otherwise, there would be an opportunity to engage in risk-free arbitrage.

Before analyzing the Year 2 cash flows, it is important to remember that, at this point, MGRM's Year-2 oil deliveries (i.e., four million barrels of oil) would be completely unhedged. Therefore, MGRM would need to re-hedge its position by purchasing four million barrels of oil in the one-year futures market that extends from Year 1 to Year 2. The one-year futures price in Year 1 (i.e., the price of a contract taken out in Year 1 that expires in Year 2) is equal to $26/bbl. Except for the initial margin requirement, which earns interest, there would be no other cash outflows connected to its re-hedging transaction.

Year 2: Cash Flows from the Forward Contracts If the price of oil fell from $25/bbl in Year 1 to $21/bbl in Year 2, then MGRM would need to pay $21/bbl on the spot market in Year 2 to obtain the four million barrels of oil needed to fulfill its forward contract from Year 0. MGRM would receive the forward price from Year 0, which was $28/bbl. Therefore, net cash inflows on the two-year forward contracts maturing in Year 2 would be $7/bbl on four million barrels of oil for net cash inflows equal to $28 million.

Year 2: Cash Flows from the Futures Contracts Finally, let's consider the futures transactions in Year 2. At the end of Year 1, MGRM re-hedged its position by purchasing four million barrels of oil in the one-year futures market (i.e., from Year 1 to Year 2) at the futures price of $26/bbl. Therefore, at the end of Year 2, MGRM would close its stack of futures contracts by purchasing four million barrels of oil for $26/bbl and selling them at the spot rate of $21/bbl. The net cash outflows would be $5/bbl; so, on 4 million barrels of oil, the net cash outflows would equal $20 million.

Year 2: Net Cash Flows MGRM's net cash inflows from its forward contracts in Year 2 were $28 million, and its outflows from the Year-2 futures contracts were $20 million. Therefore, net cash inflows for Year 2 would equal $8 million.

Summary of Cumulative Cash Flows in Year 1 and Year 2 Net cash outflows from MGRM's forward and futures contracts in Year 1 were $16 million, and net cash inflows from these contracts in Year 2 were equal to $8 million. Therefore, the cumulative (noncompounded) cash outflows for the two-year period equaled $8 million.

Generalizing the Net Cash-Flow Effect after Two Years Looking across all the scenarios for the stack-and-roll hedge in Exhibit 4.9 (i.e., Columns 3 to 6), we see that, as the price of oil rises or falls and as the basis rises or falls, the cumulative two-year cash flows vary from −$8 million to +$4 million. This range of possible outcomes varies only by $12 million, which is considerably less variation (by almost 85%) than the range of possible outcomes for the unhedged position (i.e., $82 million).

Cash Flow Effects of the One-Year Rolling Hedge

If MGRM used a one-year rolling hedge, its range of possible outcomes would be narrower than an unhedged position but wider than a stack-and-roll hedge. Let's consider the example in Column 3 of Exhibit 4.9, where the price of oil falls and the basis falls. Afterwards, we generalize our results.

Year 1: Cash Flows from the Forward Contracts As was the case with the stack-and-roll hedge, MGRM sold a one-year forward contract in Year 0 for one million barrels of oil at $29/bbl and a two-year forward contract for four million barrels of oil at $28/bbl. If the price of oil fell to $25/bbl in Year 1, MGRM would pay $25/bbl on the spot market to obtain one million barrels of oil, but it would receive $29/bbl from its forward contract. As a result, its net cash inflows would equal $4 million.

Year 1: Cash Flows from the Futures Contracts Because the futures market had a maximum maturity of one year, MGRM hedged only its first year's exposure, leaving the remaining four million barrels of oil unhedged. Therefore, at the end of Year 1, MGRM would close its futures contracts for one million barrels of oil. Because the price of oil decreased to $25/bbl, MGRM would have to purchase oil at the previously established futures price of $29/bbl and sell it for only $25/bbl. Net cash outflows would be $4/bbl and, therefore, $4 million for the million barrels of oil in total that it purchased and sold.

With the first year's hedge now closed out, MGRM would re-hedge its position. Because the futures market now extends from Year 1 to Year 2, MGRM would buy four million barrels of oil in the one-year futures market at $26/bbl. Notice that, except for the initial margin requirement, there would be no other cash outflows connected to its re-hedging transaction.

Year 1: Net Cash Flows In Year 1, the gains from MGRM's one-year forward contract would exactly match the losses on its futures contract. Therefore, net cash flows in Year 1 would equal zero.

Year 2: Cash Flows from the Forward Contracts If the price of oil fell from $25/bbl in Year 1 to $21/bbl in Year 2, MGRM would pay $21 million in the Year-2 spot market for the four million barrels of oil needed to fulfill its forward contracts from Year 0. Because the two-year forward price (in Year 0) was $28/bbl and the market price in Year 2 was $21/bbl, MGRM's cash inflows from the forward contracts maturing in Year 2 would equal $7/bbl and $28 million for all four million barrels of oil.

Year 2: Cash Flows from the Futures Contracts Finally, MGRM would close the stack of futures contracts (i.e., four million barrels of oil) that it purchased at the end of Year 1. If the market price of oil were $21/bbl in Year 2 and the one-year futures price at the end of Year 1 was $26/bbl, MGRM would have net cash outflows equal to $5/bbl and $20 million for all four million barrels of oil.

Year 2: Net Cash Flows MGRM's net cash inflows from its forward contracts in Year 2 were $28 million, and outflows from its Year 2 futures contracts were $20 million. Therefore, net cash inflows in Year 2 were $8 million.

Summary of Cumulative Cash Flows in Year 1 and Year 2 In Year 1, MGRM's net cash flows equaled zero, and in Year 2, net cash inflows equaled $8 million. Therefore, the cumulative (noncompounded) cash inflows for the two-year period equaled $8 million.

Comparing Results: Unhedged, Stack-and-Roll Hedge, and One-Year Rolling Hedge

Some important conclusions can be drawn from an analysis of Exhibit 4.9. Looking across all four combinations of price and basis combinations (Columns 3 to 6), let's consider the cash flow effects at the end of Year 1 and then consider them at the end of Year 2. These results are summarized in Exhibit 4.10.

Cash Flows at the End of Year 1: Insights into Why MGAG Panicked

Given the four scenarios of price and basis changes in Exhibit 4.9, net cash flows for the unhedged position ranged from a low of −$6 million to a high of +$4 million, which is an absolute difference of $10 million. By contrast, the cash-flow outcomes for the stack-and-roll hedge ranged from a low of −$16 million to a high of +$24 million, which is an absolute difference of $40 million. Finally, cash flow effects for the one-year rolling hedge were $0, with no range. It may be shocking to discover that the range of

Exhibit 4.10 Range of Outcomes for the Three Hedging Alternatives

Type of Hedge	Range of Net Cash Flows after Year 1	Range of Net Cash Flows after Year 2
Unhedged	−$6 million to +$4 million (Range = $10 million)	−$50 million to +32 million (Range = $82 million)
Stack-and-Roll Hedge	−$16 million to + $24 million (Range = $40 million)	−$8 to + $4 million (Range = $12 million)
One-Year Rolling Hedge	$0 million (Range = $0 million)	−$32 million to +$20 million (Range = $52 million)

stack-and-roll outcomes was four times higher than the unhedged position, and it appeared to be infinitely higher than the one-year rolling hedge. For this reason, we must keep in mind that it is dangerous to make judgments before maturity about the risk-abating potential of the stack-and-roll hedge.

By considering only the net cash flows in Year 1, we can gain a better perspective into why MGAG, the German parent, may have considered MGRM's stack-and-roll hedges to be highly speculative. Had MGRM not hedged, it would have received cash inflows equal $4 million, and if it had entered into a one-year rolling hedge, it would have broken even. The stack-and-roll hedge created cash outflows equal to $16 million! But remember, we get this conclusion only if we consider Year 1 in isolation. Let's see what happens when we consider Year 2.

Cash Flows at the End of Year 2 The benefits of a stack-and-roll hedge are evident if we consider cumulative cash flows after Year 2. Exhibit 4.10 shows that the range of possible outcomes changes significantly. The stack-and-roll hedge's range ($12 million) is about 85% lower than the unhedged range ($82 million) and almost 77% lower than the one-year rolling hedge ($52 million).

Was a Stack-and-Roll Hedge the Best Strategy for MGRM?

Exhibit 4.10 shows that, of our three alternatives, the stack-and-roll hedge created net cash flows with the lowest volatility after the two-year period, but this does not mean that the stack-and-roll hedge always produces the best results for every company. For example in the early 1990s, oil and gas prices fell and the energy markets moved from backwardation to contango. Clearly, if MGRM had perfect foresight, its best move would have been to leave all forward positions unhedged. Exhibit 4.9 shows that, of the three alternatives, net cash flows after two years from the unhedged position equaled +$32 million, the one-year rolling hedge earned cash inflows of $8 million, and the stack-and-roll hedge caused cash *outflows* of $8 million. The problem is that companies do not have perfect foresight, which is precisely why they hedge in the first place.

If we strip away the numbers, a key take-away point emerges from Exhibit 4.9. Companies that choose not to hedge expose themselves to *spot price risk*. In the case of MGRM, its short unhedged forward positions made it the beneficiary of any spot price reductions and the victim of any spot price increases. Because there were more oil contracts in Year 2 than in Year 1, the risks associated with Year-2 price increases were greater than Year-1 increases. By contrast, a one-year rolling hedge faces *futures price risk*. In MGRM's case, any increases in the futures price hurt the one-year rolling hedge and any decreases helped it.

The risks associated with a stack-and-roll hedge are different from an unhedged position and from the one-year rolling hedge because it substitutes *basis risk* for spot price risk or futures price risk. If the basis remains the same, it makes no difference with a stack-and-roll hedge whether energy prices rise or fall. The stack-and-roll hedge improves if the basis rises, and it worsens if the basis falls. Usually (but not always), basis risk is lower than spot or futures price risk. Unfortunately for MGRM, during the early 1990s, the basis for energy contracts was highly volatile. Therefore, if MGRM was trying to minimize the variance of its oil payoffs, the stack-and-roll hedge was the best choice only if the basis fluctuated less than the spot-price or futures price.

Stack-and-Roll Hedge Ratios MGRM used a one-to-one hedge ratio for its stack-and-roll hedges, which means it matched each short forward contract (extending out 10 years) with a near-dated long futures contract. Using a one-to-one hedge ratio is a decision and not a law; companies can and should modify this ratio based on their financial goals. Clearly, if risk minimization were MGRM's goal, then its optimal hedge ratio would be different from the ratio that maximized potential profits.[21]

There are two major ways to fine-tune a company's hedge ratio. The first is to analyze past data, uncover predictable movements in the oil and gas basis, and then forecast how the basis is expected to change in the future. Another way to fine tune the hedge ratio is by *tailing the hedge*, which means adjusting the hedge ratio for the expected interest paid (or earned) on the losses (or gains) from marking futures contracts to market on a daily basis. Tailing would have been especially important for MGRM given its huge positions and the asymmetric cash-flow effects of forward contacts, which were not marked to market, and futures contracts, which were marked to market.

MGRM'S LARGE POSITIONS CREATE PROBLEMS

There is little doubt that the shift from backwardation to contango was mainly the result of market forces, but there are strong reasons to believe that the absolute and relative size of MGRM's positions on the New York Mercantile Exchange (NYMEX) in relationship to the total number of energy

---

[21]MGRM's one-to-one stack-and-roll hedge ratio may have been more speculative than a totally unhedged position. Based on oil and gas price data from 20 March 1989 to 20 June 1994, the hedge ratio that would have minimized MGRM's payoff variances may have been well below one-to-one (closer to 0.5-to-1). One study showed that MGRM's payoffs could have been 70% to 80% lower and its cash outflows in 1993 could have been only a fraction of their eventual size if MGRM had used proper variance-minimizing hedge ratios. See Stephen Craig Pirrong, "Metallgesellschaft: A Prudent Hedger Ruined, or a Wildcatter on NYMEX?" *The Journal of Futures Markets* 17(5) (1997), 543–578.

futures contracts traded on the exchange worked against its best interests. At the time, the average trading volume in the heating oil and unleaded gasoline futures markets was between 15,000 and 30,000 contracts per day. MGRM held positions amounting to 55,000 contracts. Because the stack-and-roll hedge required MGRM to roll over its positions each month and because these contracts were such a large portion of the total exchange volume, the company's buy orders were substantial enough to raise futures prices relative to spot prices. It did not help MGRM's cause that the markets knew full well that the company had to enter the futures market each month as a massive buyer. Clever traders began to use this knowledge to their own benefit by intentionally distributing their buy and sell orders throughout the month to take advantage of the spike in futures prices at the end of the month due to MGRM's incessant needs.[22]

The reduction in energy prices and shift to contango caused MGRM's stack of futures positions to hemorrhage cash, as they were marked to market daily at substantial losses and then rolled over. MGRM's cash outflows reached DM 347 million. Because the company was hedging 185 million barrels worth of forward contracts, margin calls in some months approached $90 million.[23] The combined effect of margin calls and MGRM's reported losses sent an alarm through MGAG that served as a wake-up call for the company's management board, board of directors, and major shareholders.[24] To stem the tide of red ink, Heinz Schimmelbusch, MGAG's CEO, and Ronaldo Schmitz, Chairman of MGAG's board, decided MGRM's futures' positions had to be liquidated immediately.[25]

MGRM BUTTS HEADS WITH NYMEX AND THE CFTC

The cash woes of MGRM became a concern not only to the board of directors (supervisory board) of MGAG but also to the New York Mercantile Exchange (NYMEX) and the Commodity Futures Trading Commission (CFTC). To transact the volume of business it was doing, MGRM needed special permission

[22]Ed Krapels, "Re-examining the Metallgesellschaft Affair and Its Implications for Oil Traders," *Oil & Gas Journal* (26 March 2001), 70–77. Krapels argues there is evidence that coordinated trading efforts by the street were responsible for MGRM being squeezed.
[23]The stack-and-hedge rollovers required MGRM to pay $88 million in October and November 1993. See Anonymous, "Metallgesellschaft: Germany's Corporate Whodunit," *The Economist* 334 (7900) (4 February 1995), 71.
[24]Major shareholders included Deutsche Bank AG, Dresdner Bank AG, Daimler-Benz, Allianz, Allgemeine Verwaltungsgesellschaft für Industriebeteiligung GmbH, Kuwait Investment Authority (20%), Australian Mutual Provident Society (5%), and M.I.M. Holdings, Ltd (1%).
[25]See Jay Lorsch and Samantha Date Graft, *Governance at Metallgesellschaft (A)*. Product number: 9-495-055 (Harvard Business School, 10 July 1996) and Jay Lorsch and Samantha Date Graft, *Governance at Metallgesellschaft (B)*. Product number: 9-495-056 (Harvard Business School, 8 July 1996).

from NYMEX to exceed the exchange's trading limits. When MGRM's positive cash flows turned massively negative, the exchange tightened the reins on MGRM by imposing super margin requirements, which only added to MGRM's negative cash flow problems.

The CFTC charged MGRM with illegally selling off-exchange, energy-related futures products (i.e., contracts that had the attributes of futures contracts, but that were not listed on an exchange and so were not regulated by the CFTC) and labeled MGRM's contracts as "speculative" because delivery of the physical assets rarely took place.[26] These charges served only to increase the perceived risk of MGRM's future business prospects and to challenge the entire line of business in which MGRM was involved.[27]

To many observers, the CFTC's charges were absurd. Of course MGRM was selling off-exchange energy-related futures products. That was its strategy, and that was the value added MGRM brought to the market.

MGRM'S PROFITABILITY: IT'S ALL IN HOW YOU ACCOUNT FOR IT

Declining prices and the shift from backwardation to contango had asymmetric effects on the reported earnings of U.S.-based MGRM and German-based MGAG. German companies followed *lower-of-cost-or-market* (LCM) accounting rules, which required companies to report material gains and losses on derivative transactions *when they occurred*. Therefore, when absolute and relative oil and gas prices moved unfavorably, MGAG was required to report immediately the losses from its stack of near-dated futures contracts (i.e., the hedges) but could not offset them with the expected gains (at current prices) on MGRM's 10-year string of forward contracts. In the United States, "qualified companies,"[28] could use *hedge accounting standards*, which allowed them to net the losses/gains on their hedges (e.g., MGRM's stack of futures contracts) with the gains/losses on identified transactions (e.g., the 10-year string of forward energy contracts). The symmetry created by combining the effects of these offsetting transactions stabilized company earnings.

As a result, evaluating the performance of MGRM differed greatly depending on the accounting lens you used. To the German parent, MGRM had become a huge anchor dragging down quarterly profits, but to MGRM,

---

[26] Ed Krapels, "Re-examining the Metallgesellschaft Affair and Its Implications for Oil Traders," *Oil & Gas Journal* (26 March 2001), 70–77.
[27] *Order Instituting Proceedings Pursuant to Sections 6 and 8a of the Commodity Exchange Act and Findings and Order Imposing Remedial Sanctions*, CFTC Docket No. 95-14 (21 July 1995).
[28] The term *qualified companies* has been put in italics, because U.S. hedge accounting rules require companies to satisfy a number of criteria before a hedge can receive hedge accounting treatment.

profitability was hardly affected by the changing market conditions. These accounting differences help to explain MGAG's reaction (or overreaction) to MGRM's trading strategy.

MGRM'S CREDIT RATING

The market did not react well to the losses reported by the German parent and to the U.S. affiliate's excessive cash outflows. Consequently, MGAG's credit rating was lowered, which increased the company's borrowing costs and resulted in many of its counterparties (i.e., swap and forward) requiring increased collateral and margin to back MGAG's transactions that were now perceived to be more risky. Because MGRM was suffering mainly from a liquidity problem and not a long-term profitability problem, the downgrade of MGAG's credit rating could not have come at a worse time. It just added to the company's cash flow troubles.

THE EFFECTS OF AN ITCHY TRIGGER FINGER

It is unclear whether MGAG's management board and board of directors understood that Arthur Benson's strategy added less risk to MGAG's *long-term profitability* compared to its effect on *short-term* liquidity. MGRM became a market maker in long-dated energy derivatives, and in so doing, it staked out a position that required the company to accept commodity price risk in crude oil, gasoline, and heating oil.

Unfortunately, when the smoke cleared and the situation could be assessed under calmer conditions and in the light of better perspective, MGAG's reaction to MGRM's losses and negative cash flows appears to have been too blunt and too draconian. In short, Schimmelbusch and his team (supported by the MGAG board of directors) appear to have overreacted, resulting in considerable self-inflicted injuries.

What MGAG's management failed to grasp was that stack-and-roll hedges with properly weighted hedge ratios can be an effective defense against volatile price fluctuations. It also failed to appreciate that MGRM's cash outflows and losses were short term, and not a reflection of the affiliate's long-term profitability. In other words, liquidity was the main problem, and not long-term viability or asset quality. This conclusion should have the ring of common sense. After all, MGRM was hedging a long-term series of short forward contracts with a stack of long futures contracts, which meant that any losses on its futures positions were expected to offset, as closely as possible, the profits incurred on the company's forward positions (and vice versa).

Was MGRM Hedging or Speculating?

Was MGRM hedging or speculating? What was in the minds of Arthur Benson and his MGRM colleagues? Were they consciously betting on rising prices? Were they wagering that the oil market would remain in backwardation, or were they ignorant of the risks inherent in their strategy and simply hedging forward transactions at what they thought would be profitable margins?

It appears in retrospect that MGRM tried to hedge its 10-year chain of monthly, fixed-rate forward contracts. The problem was that these hedges were effective mainly at stabilizing *U.S.* profits and not the company's cash flows, which meant that MGRM was still exposed to the risks associated with rollovers and liquidity, as well as changing price structures and funding rates. By not hedging, or at least mitigating, the most important risks connected to its long-term derivative contracts, MGRM was speculating with shareholder funds. To the extent that MGRM over-hedged its position (i.e., using a one-to-one hedge ratio instead of something smaller), it was also speculating.

The opinion that these losses were the result of unintended speculation is a possible explanation, but not an excuse, for Benson's oversight because he and his team at MGRM were supposed to be experts at using state-of-the-art knowledge to offer customers forefront risk management products. As experts, they should have been aware of these cash-flow risks and communicated them to MGAG's managers and board of directors; so, upper management could have made informed decisions about the levels of risk to bear. The company's German management should not have felt blindsided by the cash flow effects of changing economic conditions (i.e., declining oil prices and contango).

Corporate Governance Issues

Who in MGAG should have had ultimate responsibility for controlling MGRM's activities? The answer to this question is crucial because it addresses the issue of corporate governance and the role played by MGAG's board of directors and management committee. If MGRM's transactions were speculative in nature, then the board of directors (i.e., the MGAG supervisory board) was culpable for not having established risk management systems that would have brought exposures of such significant magnitude to light, and its management committee was to blame for not monitoring more closely the trading activities of MGRM. The most embarrassing aspect of the episode was that losses of $1.3 billion seem to have come as an enormous surprise to MGAG's board of directors and management committee. If the board was deceived, as it claims, then there is an explanation for the surprise, but not an excuse for it.

Boards of directors are not supposed to be involved in the operations of companies. They are there to protect shareholders by ensuring that early-warning (risk management) systems are in place to identify important risks and catch exposures before they become too large. Such systems do not appear to have been in place, and, on these grounds, MGAG's Board can be criticized.

The Board can also be criticized for its knee-jerk response to the MGRM problem once it became known. In retrospect, a slower, more considered reaction would have been better.[29] Fearing that MGRM's losses could amount to as much as $50 billion (yes, that's *billions*), MGAG's board of directors fired MGRM's CEO and CFO and put new management into place. The marching orders for the new management were to liquidate, as soon as possible, the company's huge *speculative* exposures and rescue the company from bankruptcy.

The quick action of MGAG's board and MGRM's new management was controversial. Some leading financial experts[30] and many industry analysts criticized MGAG for compounding the problem by acting impulsively and hurting long-term profitability for the sake of temporary liquidity relief. By liquidating MGRM's futures positions, it left the company with unhedged forward positions that extended 10 years into the future. These critics had a good point because after all was said and done, MGRM's competitive advantage was supposed to emanate from its experienced, talented staff, hedging know-how, *and the substantial financial resources* of MGAG. If the critics were correct, then MGAG realized greater losses than it would have if it had done nothing.

The new management of MGRM liquidated positions when oil and gas prices were at their lowest levels, which meant the point at which MGRM's futures market losses were at their highest levels. As illustration, in December 1993, when much of the liquidation took place, WTI[31] oil prices were approximately $14 per barrel. By August 1994, they had increased to nearly $19.50 per barrel. Gas prices followed the same pattern. Had MGAG found a way to finance MGRM's liquidity problems and to unwind its positions

---

[29]Christopher L. Culp and Steve H. Hanke. "Derivative Dingbats," *The International Economy* 8 (4) (July-August 1994), 12–19.

[30]Among the critics was Robert Merton. co-recipient of the 1997 Nobel Prize in Economics along with Myron Scholes. Merton and Scholes received this award for their research (which was done in collaboration with the late Fischer Black) on derivatives and stock option valuation.

[31]WTI is an abbreviation for West Texas Intermediate sweet crude oil.

gradually over an extended period, many of its sizeable losses would have turned into sizeable gains. Of course, in the board's defense, everything is obvious in hindsight, but if the board had a stronger understanding that MGRM's troubles were related to short-term liquidity rather than long-term profitability, it might have acted differently.

In December 1993, MGRM declared losses of approximately $1.3 billion. These losses almost exhausted MGAG's equity capital. The company survived only after negotiating an equity-refinancing package with existing shareholders.[32]

Conclusion

MGRM's financial debacle taught some important lessons, such as *hedging is important*, and *the type of hedge employed matters*. It also taught that applying an effective hedge is not enough. Management must also fully understand and transparently communicate the effect these hedges have on cash flows *and* profitability. MGRM failed on all accounts to do this.

There is an old adage that *profit is an opinion but cash is a fact;* MGRM learned the hard way the truth of this aphorism. Metallgesellschaft AG has been placed on many analysts' Wheel of Misfortune, but its predicament was related more to liquidity problems than it was to long-term profitability problems. The major factors that contributed to these liquidity (i.e., negative cash flow) problems were as follows:

1. MGRM's massive exposures in the oil and gas futures markets, combined with falling oil and gas prices in the early 1990s and the shift in the structure of oil and gas prices from backwardation to contango, forced MGRM to make enormous margin payments to NYMEX, which resulted in burdensome cash outflows, funding difficulties, and solid reasons for questioning and eventually down-grading MGAG's credit rating.
2. The damaged credit rating increased MGAG's financing costs.
3. German-based MGAG was forced to report immediately the losses from MGRM's U.S. operations because German accounting standards required companies to account for transactions using the lower-of-cost-or-market method rather than the hedge accounting method that was used in the United States. Therefore, MGAG could not offset the losses on the futures contracts with the profits from forward deals it was hedging.

[32]Ed Krapels, "Re-examining the Metallgesellschaft Affair and Its Implications for Oil Traders," *Oil & Gas Journal* (26 March 2001), 70–77.

4. MGRM's relatively large share of the NYMEX market caused the company to bid up futures prices against itself and offered traders the opportunity to informally conspire against MGRM because they knew the company had to roll over its hedge contracts and therefore was a "must buyer" at the end of each month.

5. The super-margin requirements imposed by the CFTC added to MGAG's cash flow woes.

In the end, MGRM failed because it violated three of the most fundamental rules of risk management: identify all the risks inherent in the products you offer; limit the variety of risks to those you can efficiently manage; and keep the risks you are willing to bear to reasonable levels. Consequently, a company with more than 100 years of experience and the creator of a truly innovative line of derivative products suffered losses that resulted in the dismissal of MGRM's top level management and nearly pushed the German parent into bankruptcy.

Epilogue

What Happened to the Key Players in the MGRM/MGAG Disaster?

Unlike Proctor and Gamble after its calamitous interest rate swaps in 1994, heads rolled at MGAG. Exhibit 4.E.1 provides a brief summary of the key players in the MGAG debacle and what happened to them after the dust settled.

Exhibit 4.E.1 What Happened to the Key Players in the MGRM/MGAG Drama?

Name	Position	What Happened?
Heinz Schimmelbusch	Chairman of the Executive Board and chief executive officer of MGAG	Schimmelbusch was fired on 17 December 1993, along with most of his management team, for faulty internal controls and an inability to keep MGAG board members fully informed of material events. No criminal charges were filed against him. He later founded Allied Resource Corporation, a U.S.-based company. In 1997, Schimmelbusch and MGAG reached an out-of-court settlement

(Continued)

Exhibit 4.E.1 *(Continued)*

		over his dismissal. He is purported to have received DM1.5 million ($920,000) as compensation. As a condition for the settlement, Schimmelbusch (and Meinhard Forster) accepted managerial responsibility for MGRM's losses in 1993.
Meinhard Forster	Chief Financial Officer	Forster was fired on 17 December 1993 along with Heinz Schimmelbusch. In 1997, he received DM 160,000 for past bonuses due to him. As a condition for the settlement, Forster (and Heinz Schimmelbusch) accepted managerial responsibility for MGRM's losses in 1993.
W. Arthur Benson	President of MGRM Inc.	At first, W. Arthur Benson was reassigned to head MGAG's physical marketing operations, but afterwards, on 4 February 1994 (49 days after Heinz Schimmelbusch), he was fired. Benson sued MGAG for $500 million in 1994 on grounds of defamation and civil conspiracy, but in 1996 a panel of arbitrators ruled in favor of MGAG.
Ronaldo Schmitz	Chairman of MGAG's Board of Directors and member of Deutsche Bank's managing board.	No major consequences.
Metallgesellschaft AG (MGAG)		MGAG changed its name in 2000 (after 119 years) to MG Technologies AG due to the shift in its focus from metals, trading, and construction to specialty chemicals, plant, and process engineering.
Metallgesellschaft Refining and Marketing Company (MGRM)		MGRM was sold in 1999, with half of the company spun off on the London Stock Exchange as MG PLC and the remaining half sold to Enron.

Review Questions

1. What major risks did MGRM identify? What major risks did MGRM fail to identify?

2. Was MGRM's decision to use stack-and-roll hedges the reason for its colossal losses? What risks cannot be hedged with stack-and-roll hedges?

3. Would MGRM have had the same cash-flow problems if it had been able to buy and sell energy derivatives in the forward market (i.e., rather than using the futures market to cover its net forward positions)?

4. What are contango and backwardation, and why were they important to MGRM's situation? Why is there often backwardation in the oil markets?

5. Explain how MGRM's cash flows would have changed if the basis had increased (rather than fallen) and if oil prices had increased (rather than fallen).

6. Explain how MGRM's cash flows would have changed if the basis had increased (rather than fallen) and if oil prices had fallen (as they did).

7. Assume MGRM was required to use lower-of-cost-or-market accounting. Answer either question 5 or 6, but this time, explain the profit-and-loss effects under the given conditions.

8. Assume MGRM was able to use hedge accounting standards. Answer either question 5 or 6, but this time, explain the profit-and-loss effects under the given conditions.

9. Assume MGRM used a stack-and-roll hedge. Use Exhibit 4.9 in this chapter to explain what would have happened to MGRM's cash flows in Year 1 and Year 2 if the oil basis did not change and prices rose from $30/bbl in Year 0 to $35/bbl in Year 1 to $39/bbl in Year 2.

10. Assume MGRM used a stack-and-roll hedge. Use Exhibit 4.9 in this chapter to explain what would have happened to MGRM's cash flows in Year 1 and Year 2 if the oil basis did not change and prices fell from $30/bbl in Year 0 to $25/bbl in Year 1 to $21/bbl in Year 2.

11. Why is the size of the stack so important to the cash-flow effects of the stack-and-roll hedge but less important to the profit-and-loss effects when hedge accounting is used?

12. In common-sense terms, explain why the profit-and-loss effects of a stack-and-roll hedge do not depend on the direction of change in oil prices when hedge accounting is used.

13. What corporate governance changes could MGAG's management have made to reduce the chances of being surprised in the future by mishaps, like MGRM?

14. What should the MGAG's board of directors have done differently? Did corporate governance fail?

15. On what grounds, if any, can the CFTC be criticized for aiding and abetting the MGRM disaster?

16. Was MGRM hedging or speculating?

Further Reading

Please visit http://www.prenhall.com/marthinsen, where you can find the following embellishments on and extensions of this chapter:

- Appendix 4-1: Cash Flow Risks of a Stack-and-Roll Hedge, Unhedged Position, and One-Year Rolling Hedge
- Appendix 4.2: MGRM's Embedded Options

Bibliography

Anonymous. "Dreaming of Butterflies." *The Economist* 327(7817) (26 June 1993), 65–71.

Anonymous. "Irony of Metallgesellschaft AG." *The Manage Mentor*. http://www.theman-agementor.com/kuniverse/kmailers_universe/finance_kmailers/if/hedging2.htm.

Anonymous. "Metallgesellschaft: Germany's Corporate Whodunit." The Economist 334 (7900) (4 February 1995), 71.

Mello, Antonio S., Parsons, John E., Culp, Christopher L., and Miller, Merton H. "Maturity Structure of a Hedge Matters: Lessons from the Metallgesellschaft Debacle." Journal of Applied Corporate Finance 8(1) (Spring 1995), 106.

Culp, C.L. and Hanke, Steve H. "Derivative Dingbats." *International Economy* 8(4) (July-August 1994), 12–19.

Culp, Christopher and Miller, Merton. *Corporate Hedging in Theory and Practice: Lessons from Metallgesellschaft* (London: Risk Publications, 1999).

Culp, C. and Miller, Merton. *"Hedging a Flow of Commodity Deliveries with Futures: Lessons from Metallgesellschaft." Journal of Applied Corporate Finance* 7 (1994), 62–76.

Edwards, Franklin S. and Canter, Michael S. "The Collapse of Metallgesellschaft: Unhedgable Risks, Poor Hedging, or Just Bad Luck?" *The Journal of the Futures Market* 15 (1995) 211–264.

Group of Thirty Global Derivatives Study Group. *Derivatives: Practices and Principles* (Washington, D.C.: The Group of Thirty, July 1993).

Krapels, Ed. "Re-examining the Metallgesellschaft Affair and Its Implications for Oil Traders." Oil & Gas Journal (26 March 2001), 70–77.

Lorsch, Jay and Graff, Samantha Kate. *Governance at Metallgesellschaft (A)*. Product number: 9-495-055. (Harvard Business School, 10 July 1996), 13.

Order Instituting Proceedings Pursuant to Sections 6 and 8a of the Commodity Exchange Act and Findings and Order Imposing Remedial Sanctions. CFTC Docket No. 95-14 (21 July 1995).

Pirrong, Stephen Craig. "Metallgesellschaft: A Prudent Hedger Ruined, or a Wildcatter on NYMEX?" *The Journal of Futures Markets* 17(5) (1997), 543–578.

Shirreff, David. "In the Line of Fire." *Euromoney* 299 (March 1994), 40–49.

Taylor, Jeffrey and Sullivan, Allanna. "German Firm Finds Hedges Can Be Thorny." *The Wall Street Journal*, Eastern Edition (10 January 1994), C1.

W. Arthur Benson vs. Metallgesellschaft Corp. et. al. Civ. Act. No. JFM-94-484. U.S. District Court for the District of Maryland (1994).

Wolfert-Elmendorff Deutsche Industrie-Treuhand GmbH und C&L Treuarbeit Deutsche Revision. *Special Audit of Metallgesellschaft Aktiengesellschaft* (1995).

5

Swaps That Shook an Industry

Procter & Gamble versus Bankers Trust

Introduction

Between 1993 and 1994, Procter and Gamble (P&G) entered into two seemingly innocuous over-the-counter derivative agreements with Bankers Trust (BT). On the surface these interest rate swaps appeared to have low risks; nevertheless, within five months of signing the first deal, P&G was forced to charge $157 million to its pre-tax earnings ($102 million to after-tax earnings), making this the largest swap-related loss ever recorded by a U.S. industrial company.

The P&G-BT swaps (P&G-BT, for short) are now infamous, but not for the reasons you might, at first, suspect. Both counterparties were in sound financial health, and their credit ratings were high. BT was well known in the investment banking industry as an expert in managing financial risk, having earned $144 million from its client financial risk management business during the first quarter of 1994 alone. P&G was a globally recognized name in the consumer products industry. In contrast to companies, like Metallgesellschaft and Long-Term Capital Management, which faced near bankruptcy due to their losses of $1.3 billion and $4.5 billion, respectively, or Barings, which was forced to declare bankruptcy because of derivative-related losses totaling $1.3 billion, P&G suffered relatively minor losses, which had little or no negative, long-term impact on the company's share price.[1] Clearly, the $157 million hit to P&G's earnings in 1994[2] was an unwelcome shock, but for a company with more than $25.5 billion in assets and annual sales in excess of $30 billion, this non-cash charge to earnings was far from life threatening. In fact, for fiscal year 1994, P&G's net income (even after the swap write-offs) was more than $2.2 billion, and its share price rose as the market shrugged off these derivative losses as one-time aberrations.

If the losses were relatively small, then why did P&G-BT become such a punctuating event for the 1990s? Why is it among the first cases investment bankers cite when discussing issues about whether corporate treasuries (finance departments) should be profit centers or whether corporations should actively use structured derivatives in their asset and liability management?

One reason the case became so visible was because it resulted in a landmark court ruling.[3] In an unusual twist for a case settled out of court,[4] United States District Judge John Feikens in May 1996 wrote a court opinion that provided a rich set of clarifications on the broad class of derivative transactions in which P&G and BT engaged. A second reason P&G-BT gained widespread attention was because it helped to spur accounting reforms that increased corporate disclosure of off-balance-sheet transactions.

A final reason for the case's visibility and notoriety was because it provided rare and unflattering glimpses at the

[1] Dawn DiMartino, Linda Ward, Janet Stevens, and Win Sargisson. "Procter & Gamble's Derivatives Loss: Isolated Incident or Wake Up Call?" *Derivatives Quarterly* 2 (3) (Spring 1996), 10–21.
[2] This loss was prior to the out-of-court settlement in 1995, when P&G's losses were reduced to $35 million.
[3] *The Procter & Gamble Company, Plaintiff, v. Bankers Trust Company and BT Securities Corporation,* Defendants, No. 925 FS –pp 1270 (S.D. Ohio 1996). Judge Feikens, District of Detroit, took over the case from Judge Carl Rubin, District of Cincinnati, after Judge Rubin died.
[4] The case was settled out of court in 1995, and usually, under such circumstances, the court issues no formal legal opinion.

behind-the-scenes world of investment banking and corporate finance. From 6,500 taped conversations and 300,000 pages of written evidence, BT's investment bankers portrayed themselves as duplicitous weasels, who would walk over their grandmothers for any sale that earned them a small profit.[5] P&G's finance staff came across as having committed the cardinal transgression of taking uncalculated, uncontrolled risks and then suing its investment banker (BT) for losses that resulted from P&G's own lack of risk-management skills. It was easy for the public to vilify both sides without having to delve into the details of the transactions. Deciding whether these stereotypes and characterizations were fair is left for the reader.

With this brief introduction to set the stage, let's take a deeper look at P&G-BT. We will investigate P&G's motivation for engaging in these deals, the provisions in the swap transactions that led to P&G's shocking losses, and some of the most important associated issues, which were addressed by the landmark court ruling. There is much to be learned from mistakes of such magnitude.

P&G's Motivation for the Swaps

Why was P&G, a company that was supposed to specialize in the production of soaps, deodorants, diapers, cosmetics, food, beverages, and oral care, involved in derivative-related deals in the first place? Were they in the best interests of P&G shareholders? Was the use of swaps consistent with P&G's internal policies and procedures? Were shareholders adequately informed of how much risk P&G was taking with its derivative trades? More to the point, could they have obtained an accurate picture of P&G's financial risks by reading the company's accounting statements? Were the derivative deals intended to hedge cash flows, lower borrowing costs, or reduce balance sheet gaps, or were they a means of providing P&G with an independent source of profitability from the finance department?

---

[5]From the tapes, we learned acronyms and pejoratives, such as ROF, which meant "rip-off factor"—as in *"Great! BT will make $1.6 million on the deal, including a 7 [basis point] ROF."* See Kelley Holland, Linda Himmelstein, and Zachary Schiller, "The Bankers Trust Tapes," *Business Week* (16 October 1995), 106–111.

2

P&G's two controversial interest rate swaps were not the first derivative deals the company had ever executed. In P&G's 1994 annual report, the financial statement footnotes showed approximately $2.4 billion worth of derivative contracts on the books. Some of these off-balance-sheet positions were transacted in order to reduce P&G's nonoperating exposures; but others were motivated by a desire to lower overall borrowing costs and increase net returns, for example, by swapping (i.e., exchanging) fixed-rate interest payments for floating-rate payments (or vice versa) based on P&G's perceptions of future interest rate movements.

MOTIVES FOR THE U.S. DOLLAR–DENOMINATED INTEREST RATE SWAP

In early November 1993, P&G transacted the first of its infamous interest rate swaps. The goal of P&G's treasury in transacting this swap was to reduce borrowing costs to 40 basis points below the commercial paper rate on an expiring five-year interest rate swap that had a $100 million notional principal.[6] If it achieved this goal, P&G's annual savings would have amounted to $400,000,[7] which is not a lot compared to the company's total annual interest expenses in 1994 of about $500 million. In light of P&G's eventual losses, these potential savings seem insignificant.

Had economic conditions stayed where they were in November 1993, when the deal was signed, P&G would have ended up borrowing at 75 basis points *below* the commercial paper rate, which was 35 basis points better than its goal. The problem was an embedded option that expired in six months and had the potential to substantially increase P&G's interest costs. We will find shortly that this embedded option was highly leveraged and had unusual characteristics. Basically it was P&G's high-stakes bet that U.S. interest rates would fall or not rise substantially. From P&G's perspective, the potential risks of the embedded option were under control because the company intended to unwind the swap position, if needed, prior to maturity, thereby settling for the 40 basis point advantage it desired. Unfortunately, P&G guessed wrong, and as a result, incurred substantial losses.

MOTIVES FOR THE GERMAN MARK–DENOMINATED INTEREST RATE SWAP

The second of P&G's interest rate swaps was a German mark-denominated deal signed in mid-February 1994. It had a notional value of DM 162,800,000 (about $93 million)[8] and was structured to "overlay" a pre-existing German

---

[6]District Court, S.D. Ohio, Western Division, The Procter & Gamble Company, Plaintiff v. Bankers Trust Company and BT Securities Corporation, *Defendants, First Amended Complaint for Declaratory Relief and Damages Jury Demand Endorsed*, Civil Action No. C-1-94-735, 6 February 1995.
[7]40 basis points is 0.40%. Therefore, $400,000 = 0.40% × $100 million notional principal.
[8]DM is an abbreviation for Deutschemark (i.e., German mark), the German currency unit until 2001.

mark swap that P&G had done with another counterparty. Therefore, BT's payments to P&G were tailored to match exactly what P&G had to pay in the other deal. As was the case with its 1993 dollar-based swap, P&G embedded a highly leveraged option in its German mark swap, which made the deal a high-stakes bet that German interest rates would fall or not rise significantly. Again, P&G was wrong, and the consequences were severe.

MOTIVES FOR USING THE OVER-THE-COUNTER MARKET

Why did P&G decide to transact over-the-counter (OTC) deals with BT rather than use an exchange-traded derivative, for example, on the Chicago Board of Trade (CBOT)? A few reasons are possible. For instance, using the futures market may not have occurred to P&G, or, perhaps, the liquidity in the futures markets may have been too shallow for P&G to transact the volume of business desired without moving prices to its disadvantage. It is more likely the decision was driven by the accounting treatment of exchange-traded derivatives prevailing at that time.

Prior to 1995, U.S. accounting rules gave companies (not just P&G) a strong incentive to prefer structured OTC transactions to exchange-traded transactions. We will see shortly that the options P&G embedded into its dollar-denominated and mark-denominated swaps can be viewed as short calls, but U.S. accounting rules do not recognize written options as hedges, which means they do not qualify for hedge accounting. Therefore, P&G would have had to recognize immediately the profit, loss, and cash-flow effects of its exchange-traded options. At initiation, there would have been premium income to report and accounting recognition of the margin posted to the exchange. Then, during the life of the options, P&G would have had to mark its positions to market, thereby paying or collecting variation margin. Finally, P&G would have had to report any gains or losses when it closed out the positions or when the options were exercised at maturity.

For many structured OTC deals, companies were not required to post initial margin, and their positions were not marked to market. Rather than paying an up-front premium, payments were made periodically and netted against other cash flows in the deal. As a result, there was no reportable accounting event when the contract was initiated, and premiums were amortized over the life of the contract. If an embedded option in an OTC deal was amended, unwound, or expired, the financial consequences could be simply incorporated into the net interest payments and receipts, which were then spread over the life of the contract. Similarly, the effect of value changes could be netted and booked as interest income or interest expense. Finally, the notional value of these OTC transactions was reported off balance sheet as an aggregate figure in the footnotes, which made the value of any individual deal opaque. Therefore, if a position soured, it could be reversed with little or no shareholder concern and analyst notice.[9]

Regardless of P&G's motives to use the OTC market for its side bets with BT, the decisions appear to be misguided because P&G ended up selling far too much risk insurance for far too low a price. There is evidence that, if P&G had written call options on CBOT-traded U.S. Treasury bonds for the equivalent premium income as it got from BT, potential losses on its dollar-denominated swap would have been cut by a third or more.[10]

The U.S. Dollar–Denominated Swap

The first of P&G's two interest rate swaps with BT occurred on 2 November, 1993. The deal was denominated in U.S. dollars, and had a $200 million notional principal and a five-year maturity. Embedded in this interest rate swap was a huge bet that U.S. interest rates would fall or not rise significantly.

P&G's 1993 swap was a complicated transaction, but as Exhibit 5.1 shows, the deal can be simplified by dividing it into two major parts: (1) a plain vanilla swap, and (2) a speculative gamble on interest rates.

PLAIN VANILLA SWAP

The risks associated with the plain vanilla swap were small and transparent. During the five-year period, BT agreed to pay P&G a fixed annual rate of

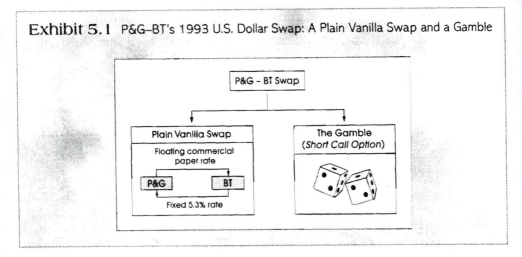

Exhibit 5.1 P&G–BT's 1993 U.S. Dollar Swap: A Plain Vanilla Swap and a Gamble

[9]An insightful review of all these accounting considerations can be found in Donald Smith, "Aggressive Corporate Finance: A Close Look at the Procter & Gamble–Bankers Trust Leveraged Swap." *Journal of Derivatives* 4 (4) (Summer 1997), 67–79.
[10]See D. Smith, Ibid. pp. 74–75.

5.3% on a $200 million notional principal, and, in return, P&G agreed to pay BT a floating annual rate of interest tied to the average daily yield on 30-day commercial paper. Payments were semiannual, commenced in May 1994, and ended in November 1998.

On the plain vanilla side of the P&G-BT deal, there was nothing particularly unusual or risky. One small anomaly was that P&G tied its floating interest payments to the commercial paper rate rather than the normally used London Interbank Offered Rate (LIBOR). Another small variance with standard swap agreements was the commercial paper rate used in the swap was calculated as a daily average rather than the rate on a particular day and at a specific time. Finally, P&G replaced a maturing $100 million swap with one double its size. None of these irregularities added materially to the risks of the deal. Had P&G stopped there and been content with the plain vanilla portion of the deal, the company's eventual losses resulting from rising U.S. interest rates would have been trivial; unfortunately, as we know, there was also a speculative side-bet, and it is to this side-bet that we now turn our attention.

P&G'S GAMBLE: THE SPECULATIVE SIDE-BET

P&G's speculative side-bet was responsible for virtually all of its losses, and the devil was definitely in the details of this transaction. No premium was paid to P&G in November 1993 when the deal was signed. Rather, premium-like payments began in May 1994 (six months later), when the option matured. Under the terms of the agreement, P&G would receive from BT 75 basis points per year (i.e., 0.75%/year) paid semiannually (i.e., 0.375%/half year) for the next 4.5 years, with payments based on the notional principal of $200 million.

In return for BT's semiannual payments, P&G would make payments based on a custom-made formula, and the rate would be set in May 1994, six months after the deal was signed. The spread formula used in the deal is shown below. Because it was based on the yield of a *five-year U.S. Treasury note* and the price of a *30-year U.S. Treasury bond*, the P&G-BT deal was called the *5s/30s Swap*.[11]

---

[11] The *five-year U.S. T-Note yield (CMT)* is the yield on a five-year constant maturity U.S. Treasury note, and the *Price of a 30-Year U.S. T-Bond* is the average bid/ask clean price of a 30-year, 6.25% coupon, U.S. Treasury bond maturing on 15 August 2023. If you were asking yourself "*Where did the constant terms (i.e., 98.5 and 5.78%) in the formula come from?*" you are not alone. It might be easiest to consider 98.5 as the price of a five-year Treasury note, with a similar order of magnitude as the 30-year Treasury bond. Therefore, movements of the 30-year bond price change the formula one-to-one, but movements of a five-year Treasury note's price occur only when there are changes in a relative scaling factor equal to the five-year Treasury note yield divided by 5.78%.

$$\text{Spread} = \text{Max} \left\{ 0, \ \dfrac{98.5 \times \dfrac{\text{5-year U.S. T-Note yield (CMT)}}{5.78\%} - \text{Price of a 30-year U.S. T-Bond}}{100} \right\}$$

This side-bet called for cash settlement, so when the fixed interest payments were determined six months after the deal was signed, no ownership rights to U.S. Treasury securities had to be delivered or received. The spread formula just set the cash payments for the remainder of the deal.[12]

In a nutshell, here is what the formula meant. In May 1994 (six months after the deal was signed), if the spread formula's value (i.e., the spread) were zero or negative, P&G would pay nothing for the next 4.5 years, but it would receive $1.5 million each year from BT (i.e., 0.75% of the $200 million notional principal). By contrast, if the value were positive, P&G would be required to pay BT the spread, which would be offset (partially or wholly) by the 0.75% payment from BT.

Viewing P&G's Speculative Side-Bet as a Short Call Option

It is illuminating to view P&G's side-bet as a short call option with a strike price equal to zero, an annual premium equal to 0.75%, and the price of the underlier equal to the spread.[13] Because the value of an option declines as its maturity falls, P&G had time on its side. If economic conditions did not change, P&G could wait and unwind its position by purchasing a relatively low-priced call and locking in the gain. Of course, problems can (and did) occur if economic conditions change.

Exhibit 5.2 shows the profit and loss profile of P&G's short call option. Under the terms of the deal, if the spread on 4 May 1994 (when the option matured) were equal to or less than zero, the option would expire at-the-money or out-of-the-money; P&G would keep the premium, and it would pay nothing for the remainder of the five-year deal. Therefore, all the points to the left of and including zero are fixed at 0.75%. To the right of zero, P&G would break even when the spread equaled 0.75% (i.e., +0.0075), and for higher values, it would incur losses. For instance,

---

[12]This point will be very important when we discuss the court opinion regarding this case.

[13]This deal can also be viewed as a cash-settled short call option on the *yield* of a five-year Treasury note that is indexed to the price of a 30-year Treasury bond. A third way to view it is as a short put option on the *price* of a 30-year Treasury bond that is indexed to the yield of a five-year Treasury note. In fact, BT used this third way to explain the option in its legal deposition. See Donald Smith, "Aggressive Corporate Finance: A Close Look at the Procter & Gamble-Bankers Trust Leveraged Swap," *Journal of Derivatives* 4 (4) (Summer 1997), 67–79. Also see, District Court, S.D. Ohio, Western Division, The Procter & Gamble Company, Plaintiff v. Bankers Trust Company and BT Securities Corporation, Defendants, *Defendants' Answer to the First Amended Complaint and Defendant Bankers Trust Company's Counterclaims.* Civil Action No. C-1-94-735, 27 February 1995.

Exhibit 5.2 P&G's Side-Bet Viewed as a Short Call Option

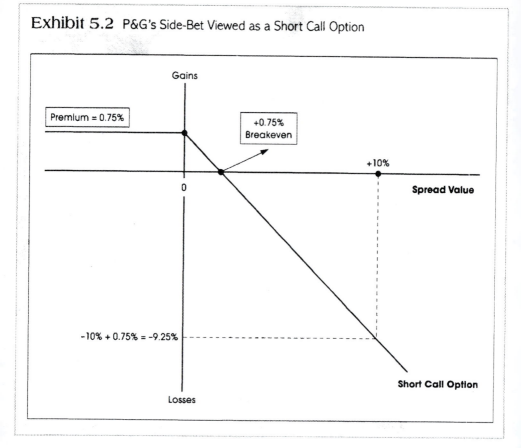

if the spread were +0.10, then P&G would be required to pay BT an annual rate of 10% and receive only 0.75% from BT, thereby incurring a net cost of 9.25%.

If yields moved against P&G, the company's potential payments were unlimited, and because of the highly leveraged nature of the formula, they increased rapidly. P&G had no way of knowing, when the contract was signed, what it would eventually pay, and because P&G doubled the notional principal of the replacement swap, this deal appears to be largely a speculative bet on the directional shift of the U.S. yield curve.

Let's take a closer look at the spread formula. The biggest threat is an upward shift of the U.S. yield curve because the five-year Treasury note yield increases, the price of the 30-year Treasury bond decreases, *and* these changes have an amplified (i.e., leveraged) effect on the spread.[14] By contrast, a flatter or steeper yield curve has an ambiguous effect on the spread because changes in the Treasury note yield and Treasury bond yield have

---

[14]See Risk Notepad 5.1, *Security Yield versus Price.*

Risk Notepad 5.1

Security Yield versus Price

Exhibit RN5.1.1 shows the relationship between the yield and price of a 30-year zero coupon bond. Notice how yields and prices are inversely related.

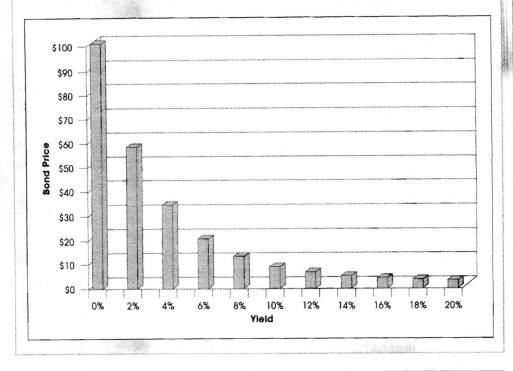

Exhibit RN5.1.1 Relationship Between Yield and Price of a 30-Year Zero-Coupon Bond

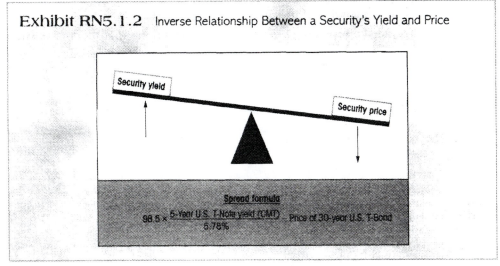

Exhibit RN5.1.2 Inverse Relationship Between a Security's Yield and Price

One must keep this inverse relationship in mind when considering P&G's spread formula because an upward shift of the yield curve causes the spread to increase for two reasons. First, a higher yield on the five-year note increases the first term in the formula (i.e., 98.5 × 5-year note yield/5.78%); second, a higher yield on the 30-year bond causes its price to fall (see Exhibit RN5.1.2). Because the price of a 30-year Treasury bond enters the spread formula with a negative sign, any reduction in its value increases the spread.

different relative impacts.[15] Consider a steeper yield curve. If the Treasury note yield fell and the Treasury bond yield remained the same, then the spread value would fall, and P&G would be helped. If the Treasury bond yield rose (i.e., the Treasury bond price fell) and the Treasury note yield remained the same, then the spread value would rise, and P&G would be hurt. Finally, if the steeper yield curve were caused by a combination of changes in the Treasury note yield and Treasury bond yield, then the net effect would depend on the magnitude of these changes and the relative sensitivity of the spread value to changes in these yields.

The Effect of Rising U.S. Interest Rates

Between November 1993 and May 1994, the U.S. Federal Reserve preemptively tightened monetary conditions. U.S. interest rates rose and the difference between the short-term and long-term interest rates fell, indicating a flattening of the yield curve (Exhibit 5.3). During these six months, the yield on 30-year U.S. Treasury bonds rose by 1.29%, from 6.06% to 7.35%, causing the long-term bond price to fall from 102.58 to 86.84. At the same time, the yield on five-year Treasury notes rose by 1.69%, from 5.02% on 2 November 1993 to 6.71% on 4 May 1994. As a result, P&G's floating interest rate soared, and its embedded option began to spill red ink.

BT contacted P&G on 22 February 1994 with news that the 5s/30s swap spread had already increased to the point where P&G would have to pay 4.6% above the commercial paper rate. This meant that P&G's goal of borrowing at 40 basis points below the commercial paper rate was up in flames. P&G decided to stay with its position rather than lock in an early rate. In part, the decision was based on forward yields for five-year and

---

[15]For all combinations of Treasury bond and Treasury note yields, a 1% increase (decrease) in the Treasury note yield causes a 17.04% increase (decrease) in the spread. Conversely, the effect that changes in the Treasury bond yield have on the spread varies inversely with the level of Treasury bond yield (i.e., as the Treasury bond yield rises, its impact on the spread value falls). At Treasury bond yields below approximately 5.2%, a 1% change in the Treasury bond yield has a greater impact on the spread than a 1% change in the Treasury note yield. Above 5.2%, the Treasury bond yield's effect is smaller.

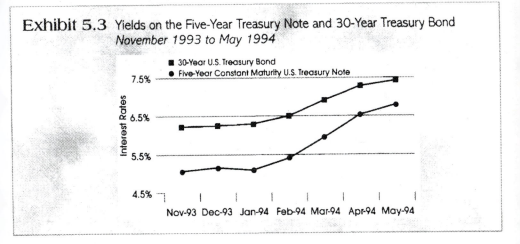

Exhibit 5.3 Yields on the Five-Year Treasury Note and 30-Year Treasury Bond
November 1993 to May 1994

30-year Treasury securities, which indicated moderating interest rates in the future. The decision was also based on, what P&G felt was, a small likelihood that the Federal Reserve's Open Market Committee (FOMC) would substantially increase U.S. interest rates or disadvantageously tilt the yield curve during the next few months. Normally, the FOMC meets about once every six weeks, and, when changes are needed, it adjusts the federal funds rate by increments of 0.25%. Based on past Fed actions, P&G bet that yields would not rise enough to wipe out its 75 basis point advantage.

Exhibit 5.4 compares the payments P&G would have made in November 1993, when the deal was signed, to the payments in May 1994, just six months later, when the terms of the deal were *supposed to be* set. On 2 November 1993, the yield on five-year Treasury notes was 5.02%, and the price of a 30-year Treasury bond was 102.58. Therefore, the spread

Exhibit 5.4 Five-Year Treasury Note Yield, 30-Year Treasury Bond Price, and Spread

	Yield Five-year Note	Price 30-Year Bond	Spread
2 November 1993	5.02%	102.578125	−17.03%
4 May 1994	6.71%	86.843750	+27.50%

$$\text{Spread formula} = \frac{98.5 \times \dfrac{\text{5-year T-Note yield}}{5.78\%} - \text{Price of 30-Year T-Bond}}{100}$$

November 1993 = [[(98.5) × (0.0502)/0.0578] − 102.578125]/100 = −0.1703 = −17.03%

May 1994 = [[(98.5) × (0.0671)/0.0578] − 86.84375]/100 = +0.2750 = 27.50%

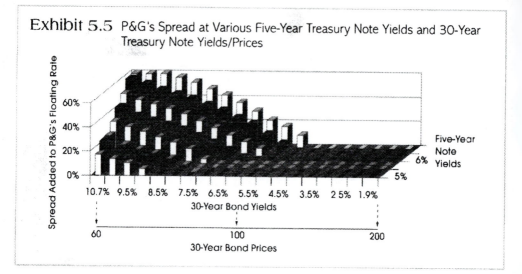

Exhibit 5.5   P&G's Spread at Various Five-Year Treasury Note Yields and 30-Year Treasury Note Yields/Prices

equaled −17.03%, which was out-of-the-money. All these rates, P&G would have paid nothing to BT for the 4.5 years remaining until maturity but would have received a yearly 75 basis point payment from BT. In stark contrast, if P&G had waited until 4 May 1994 (it didn't), the company would have paid an annual rate of 27.50% and received only 0.75% in return, for a net payment of 26.75%, which is $53.5 million a year!

Exhibit 5.5 generalizes the results and shows that, so long as the yields on the 30-year Treasury bond and five-year Treasury note remained below (about) 6% and 6.5%, respectively. P&G's spread would have equaled zero. In other words, there was a lot of flat terrain (i.e., yield-price combinations) over which P&G could have earned 75 basis points each year and paid no net interest expense. Under these circumstances, combining the two parts of the P&G-BT transaction (i.e., the plain vanilla swap and the gamble), P&G would have ended up paying 75 basis points below the floating commercial paper rate on a $200 million notional principal, which at that time would have been a borrowing rate better than the U.S. government paid. By contrast, if interest rates rose, the premium paid by P&G increased rapidly. Exhibit 5.5 shows how steeply P&G's costs increased with every marginal rise in yields.

Fortunately, P&G did not experience such severe losses because it was able to mitigate them in two ways. First, on 20 January 1994, the company renegotiated the terms of the swap so that BT paid a premium of 88 basis points per year instead of the 75 basis points in the original agreement.[16]

---

[16]The rate-setting deadline was postponed to 19 May 1994 from 4 May 1994. This postponement was important because a FOMC meeting was scheduled for 17 May 1994, just two days before the new date. Therefore, the additional 13 basis points P&G received can be viewed as additional compensation for the option's increased maturity and the greater interest rate uncertainty.

Exhibit 5.6 P&G's Short Call Option: Results on 29 March 1994

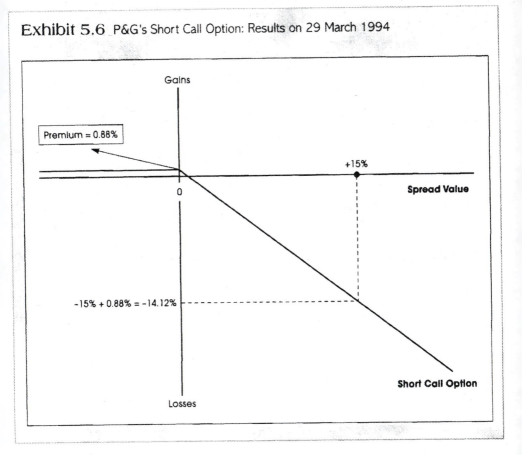

Second, P&G hedged its open position on 29 March 1994, about a month before the spread-setting date of 4 May 1994. As a result, it locked in a spread equal to 15%.[17] Subtracting the (new) annual premium of 0.88%, this amounted to yearly net payments of 14.12% (see Exhibit 5.6).

So, how much did P&G finally lose on its bet? Exhibit 5.7 calculates the discounted present value of P&G's losses based on the 29 March 1994 spread value of 15%. P&G's semiannual payments to BT began in November 1994 and continued until November 1998. BT's semiannual payments to P&G began in May 1994 and also continued until November 1998. P&G was required to pay BT an annual rate of 15% (i.e., 7.5% semiannually) on a notional principal of $200 million, and BT was required to pay P&G an annual premium of 0.88% (i.e., 0.44% semiannually). Discounted at a 7% annual interest rate (i.e., 3.5% semiannually), the present value of P&G's net payments to BT amounted to an astonishing $105.8 million! And

---

[17]P&G locked $50 million of the notional principal at 11.43% on 10 March 1994, another $50 million at 12.86% on 14 March 1994, and the final $100 million at 17.85% on 29 March 1994.

Exhibit 5.7   Loss on P&G's $200 Million Side-Bet

Date	Outflow (Million $)	Inflows (Million $)	Net Cash Flows (Million $)	Annual Discount Factor 7.00%	DPV (Million $)
29 March 1994	0.00	0.00	0.00	1.00	0.00
4 May 1994	0.00	0.88	0.88	0.993	0.9
4 November 1994	15.00	0.88	−14.12	0.959	−13.5
4 May 1995	15.00	0.88	−14.12	0.927	−13.1
6 November 1995	15.00	0.88	−14.12	0.895	−12.6
6 May 1996	15.00	0.88	−14.12	0.865	−12.2
4 November 1996	15.00	0.88	−14.12	0.836	−11.8
5 May 1997	15.00	0.88	−14.12	0.808	−11.4
4 November 1997	15.00	0.88	−14.12	0.780	−11.0
4 May 1998	15.00	0.88	−14.12	0.754	−10.6
4 November 1998	15.00	0.88	−14.12	0.728	−10.3
				Sum	−105.6

More accurate results could be derived by discounting using the yield curve, but the difference is immaterial.

remember that this deal was undertaken in the first place to save P&G 40 basis points in annual interest costs ($400,000 per year) on a maturing $100 million swap.

LOSSES ON P&G'S U.S. DOLLAR INTEREST RATE SWAP

Most of our attention has focused on P&G's side-bet with BT, but what happened to the plain vanilla interest rate swap in which P&G received an annual rate of 5.3% and paid the floating commercial paper rate? To calculate P&G's loss on the swap, we need to compare the swap's value before and after interest rates changed. At initiation, an interest rate swap normally has a zero value. We know this because the cash flows in a fixed-for-floating rate swap are identical to the cash flows from simultaneously selling a floating-rate security and purchasing a similarly sized fixed-rate security. In P&G's case, its swap cash flows were equivalent to selling a $200 million, five-year note yielding the commercial paper rate and using the funds to purchase a $200 million, five-year note yielding 5.3%. At inception, this deal would be an exchange of equals with no net value.

Exhibit 5.8 Loss on P&G's Plain Vanilla Interest Rate Swap

Date	Inflow (Million $)	Discount Factor @ 7.00% (Million $)	Discounted Present Value @ 7% (Million $)
29 March 1994	0.00	1.00	0.0
4 May 1994	5.30	0.993	5.3
4 November 1994	5.30	0.959	5.1
4 May 1995	5.30	0.927	4.9
6 November 1995	5.30	0.895	4.7
6 May 1996	5.30	0.865	4.6
4 November 1996	5.30	0.836	4.4
5 May 1997	5.30	0.808	4.3
4 November 1997	5.30	0.780	4.1
4 May 1998	5.30	0.754	4.0
4 November 1998	205.30	0.728	149.5
		New value of the swap at 7%	190.9
		Original value of the swap	200.0
		Change in swap value	**−9.1**

More accurate results could be derived by discounting using the yield curve, but the difference is immaterial.

Exhibit 5.8 shows what happened to P&G when interest rates rose to 7%. The discounted present value of P&G's stream of fixed cash inflows fell from $200 million to $190.9 million, which was a drop of $9.1 million.[18] If we compare P&G's swap-related losses with the losses on the side-bet, it is clear that the interest rate swap was much safer. For the same increase in interest rates, the side-bet lost about 12 times more than the interest rate swap.

We saw earlier that, almost immediately after P&G transacted its $200 million interest rate swap in November 1993, U.S. interest rates began to move against its position (see Exhibit 5.3). Nevertheless, P&G remained convinced that interest rates would fall; so in February 1994, the company placed another costly wager, making essentially the same bet on German interest rates as it did on U.S. interest rates. Let's turn our attention to P&G's German mark swap.

[18]The floating commercial paper rate kept the value of the variable rate note equal to $200 million at each interest resetting date.

German Mark-Denominated Interest Rate Swap

On 14 February 1994, P&G increased the ante by transacting a 4.75-year interest rate swap, which turned out to be a huge bet that German interest rates would fall or not rise significantly. The terms of the P&G-BT German mark swap in 1994 were as idiosyncratic as the 1993 U.S. dollar swap. The deal ran from 16 January 1994 (backdated) to 16 October 1998 and had a notional principal of DM 162,800,000 (i.e., about $93 million). From January 1994 to January 1995, BT agreed to pay P&G the German mark *two-year* constant maturity swap rate.[19] (i.e., DM two-year swap rate) plus a 233 basis point premium. These payments exactly matched what P&G owed on the overlaid swap. For the same period, P&G agreed to pay BT the DM two-year swap rate plus a 133 basis point premium. If you are scratching your head wondering whether you misread the last sentence, rest assured that your math is correct. For the year running from 16 January 1994 to 16 January 1995, BT promised to pay P&G a net premium of 1% on the notional swap principal. It was a good deal for P&G.

During the second year, the terms changed, and here is where P&G made its interest rate bet. From January 1995 to October 1995, BT continued to pay P&G the DM two-year swap rate pus 233 basis points, but now P&G added a spread to its usual payment. The payments changed once again, but only slightly, from October 1995 to maturity in 1998. Instead of basing their periodic payments on the DM *two-year* swap rate, BT paid DM *three-month* LIBOR plus 233 basis points, and P&G paid DM three-month LIBOR plus the spread. This change was made to ensure that the new swap mirrored exactly the payments that P&G had to make on its old swap.

Here is how the spread formula worked. An interest rate band was established with its lower and upper limits pegged at 4.05% and 6.01%, respectively, for the *four-year* German mark swap rate. This interest rate band became known as the "wedding band." On 25 February 1994, the upper limit of the wedding band was raised from 6.01% to 6.10%; so let's use the revised rate for our discussion (Exhibit 5.9).[20] If the DM four-year swap rate remained within the band for the entire year, P&G's spread would equal zero. As a result, it would have no additional interest costs for the remainder of the agreement, which means it would have received a net 1% payment each year from BT—a savings of DM 1,628,000 per year.[21]

---

[19] The *swap rate* for an interest rate swap is the market interest rate paid by the party responsible for the fixed payment

[20] P&G and BT also negotiated a postponement of the spread-setting date from 16 January 1995 to 16 April 1995.

[21] DM 162,800,000 (notional principal) × 1%/year = DM 1,628,000/year.

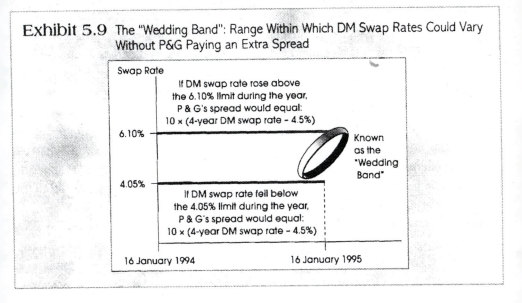

Exhibit 5.9 The "Wedding Band": Range Within Which DM Swap Rates Could Vary Without P&G Paying an Extra Spread

Swap Rate

If DM swap rate rose above the 6.10% limit during the year, P & G's spread would equal: 10 × (4-year DM swap rate − 4.5%)

6.10% ———————————

Known as the "Wedding Band"

4.05% ———————————

If DM swap rate fell below the 4.05% limit during the year, P & G's spread would equal: 10 × (4-year DM swap rate − 4.5%)

16 January 1994   16 January 1995

However, if the band was breached, P&G's spread would equal 10 times the difference between the DM four-year swap rate (on the rate-setting date) and 4.5%[22] (i.e., spread formula = [10 × (4-year DM swap rate − 4.5%)]. Tying its spread payments to a leverage factor of 10 greatly increased the risks for P&G. Notice, however, that P&G's spread could have been positive (costing it more) *or* negative (costing it less). For example, if interest rates went outside the limits during the year, P&G would pay more if the DM four-year swap rate on the rate-setting date was above 4.5% and less if it was below 4.5% (see Exhibit 5.10).

It is important to remember that, because the notional principal was denominated solely in German marks, P&G's 1994 swap was an interest rate swap and not a cross-currency swap. If the transaction were a cross-currency swap, then equivalent notional principals in German marks and

Exhibit 5.10 Summary: Additional Spread Owed by P&G to BT after First Year of the Swap

Spread = 0%,

- *If the German mark swap rate remained within the range of 4.05% to 6.10% during the year*

- *If the limits were breached during the year and the DM four-year swap rate on the rate-setting date were 4.5%*

Spread = 10 × (4-Year DM Swap Rate on 16 January 1995 − 4.50%),

- *If the German mark swap rate moved outside the 4.05% to 6.10% band during the year*

[22]This rate, 4.50%, is not a typo, and should not be confused with the bottom border of the wedding ring, which is 4.05%.

U.S. dollars would have been established up front, and there would have been an exchange of principals at the termination of the contract. By contrast, P&G was taking mainly an interest rate bet with only a small wager on the dollar value of the net German mark interest payments it would receive or pay. Therefore, the risks were much smaller than they would have been with a cross-currency swap.

In the beginning of February 1994, the DM swap rate was about 5.35%, but on February 4th (just 10 days before P&G transacted its swap), the U.S. Federal Reserve tightened significantly U.S. monetary policy. As a result, U.S. interest rates soared, causing international interest rates, including the German mark swap rate, to rise.

On 1 March 1994, BT informed P&G that its DM swap was approaching the upper limit of the band; if P&G wished to unwind the deal, it would cost a whopping 11.9%. P&G was confident of its interest rate forecast and decided not unwind the deal or to renegotiate any of its conditions, such as the upper limit or settlement date. By the next morning (only 15 days after the swap was signed), the DM four-year swap rate already exceeded the wedding band's upper limit. P&G was in trouble and knew it, but it waited until April 11th to unwind the position; by that time, the spread had increased to 16.40%, and the swap had lost more than $60 million in value!

The Suit Against Banker's Trust

P&G was fighting mad, and brought charges against Bankers Trust Co. and BT Securities Corporation[23] on grounds of racketeering, fraud, misrepresentation, breach of fiduciary duty, negligent misrepresentation, and negligence.[24] The original suit, which included only the 1993 U.S. dollar interest rate swap, was filed on 27 October 1994. On 6 February 1995, P&G amended its lawsuit to include the German mark swap, which was transacted on 14 February 1994. On 1 September 1995, the court permitted P&G, once again, to amend its complaint. BT rose to the challenge by demanding that P&G pay the amount it owed on the two swaps, which (BT claimed) was more than $200 million.

---

[23]Bankers Trust Co. and BT Securities Corporation were two wholly owned subsidiaries of Bankers Trust New York Corporation, the seventh largest bank holding company in the United States.
[24]*The Procter & Gamble Company*, Plaintiff, v. *Bankers Trust Company and BT Securities Corporation*, Defendants, No. C-1-94-735, United States District Court of the Southern District of Ohio, Western Division, 925 F. Supp. 1270; 1996 U.S. Dist. LEXIS 6435; Comm. Fut. L. Rep. (CCH) P26,700; Fed. Sec. L. Rep. (CCH) P99,229, 8 May 1996, Decided. See http://www.afn.org/~afn05451/proctor.html. Accessed 26 December 2007.

Managing a large portfolio of off-balance-sheet positions and, at the same time, taking on a considerable number of newly structured deals can be challenging; so, it is easy to understand how P&G might have relied heavily on the price estimates, market information, advice, and position tracking of its investment bankers, in general, and BT, in particular. P&G was convinced that it could lock in advantageous rates on its swaps long before maturity simply by contacting BT and unwinding the deals. In fact, the company looked to BT for support with the timing, pricing, and execution of such deals. But if this were so, why did P&G wait so long to unwind its positions and, in the end, lose so much?

P&G claimed that it was a victim of not understanding how seriously its position had deteriorated. The cost to unwind P&G's structured deals with BT came from a proprietary, multivariate pricing model developed by BT. P&G argued that it never agreed to the formula in the first place and, because it was a proprietary black box, could not check the objectiveness or accuracy of BT's assumptions and conclusions. Had it known the high cost to unwind the 5s/30s swap, P&G claimed it never would have entered into the German mark deal. To P&G, BT's refusal to reveal its pricing model and assumptions amounted to non-disclosure of material information and, therefore, was grounds for P&G's charges of fraud.[25]

BT agreed that its pricing model was proprietary but asserted that it was P&G's responsibility to actively manage its own derivative positions. In fact, BT advised P&G on the day the 5s/30s swap was signed to mark the deal to market and proactively manage it so as not to "get burned."[26] Furthermore, BT offered, on numerous occasions, to quote P&G a price for any amendments it wanted make to the option-like component of the 5s/30s swap. The bank also offered to provide P&G with hard copies of any swap valuation analyses and subsequently sent P&G a diskette with BT's pricing algorithm and embedded assumptions so that P&G could calculate any spread scenarios it wanted. In early March 1994, BT claimed that it offered to send a representative to P&G's Cincinnati headquarters with the computer model, but P&G canceled the visit stating that it was not needed.

From P&G's perspective, BT was the professional and had a fiduciary responsibility to its *relatively* unsophisticated users. BT rebuffed this assertion by citing numerous other swaps in which P&G was a party—some of

---

[25]See John M. Quitmeyer, "Fiduciary Obligations in the Derivatives Marketplace," *S&P's The Review of Securities & Commodities Regulation* 28 (18) (25 October 1995), 179.

[26]District Court, S.D. Ohio, Western Division, The Procter & Gamble Company, Plaintiff v. Bankers Trust Company and BT Securities Corporation, Defendants, *Defendants' Answer to the First Amended Complaint and Defendant Bankers Trust Company's Counterclaims.* Civil Action No. C-1-94-735, 27 February 1995, p. 8.

Risk Notepad 5.2

Value at Risk

One technique that might have helped P&G quantify the risks of its swaps with BT is value at risk (VaR) analysis. VaR is a statistical technique that estimates the minimum amount a company can expect to lose on a portfolio over a given time and with a defined level of certainty. Using this technique, treasurers can make statements like: *Based on historic returns and volatilities, we at P&G are 95% sure that our portfolio will lose no more than $10 million over the next week, which means that there is a 5% chance we could lose $10 million or more.* A study based on P&G-BT was conducted a few years after the case was settled.[27] It found that a VaR analysis would have provided P&G with timely warning signals about the risks of its U.S. dollar-denominated swap. Using a six-month time horizon (i.e., the interest payment period) and a 95% confidence interval, the study determined that the VaR on P&G's swap was approximately seven to 10 times greater than the initial $6.65 million value of the swap contract. As it turned out, P&G lost much more than the VaR analysis estimated, which only goes to show that companies should beware of the unknown risks lurking in the upper 5% tail of the VaR distribution. Nevertheless, had P&G known the VaR exposure on its U.S. dollar swap, perhaps that knowledge would have deterred the company from entering into the transaction, or P&G would have closed out its position far earlier.

which had even higher degrees of leverage than the P&G-BT deals and earned above-market rates. BT indicated that P&G received advice regularly from other financial advisors and investment bankers, such as Merrill Lynch, Goldman Sachs, and J.P. Morgan, who were competitors of BT and with whom P&G did many deals. To BT, P&G was a very sophisticated player in the world of high finance and was fully capable to mark its positions to market using the formulas agreed to in the swap agreements.

It is clear that *pricing* derivative contracts can be very difficult, may require advanced mathematical expertise, and involve sophisticated proprietary models, but tracking their gains and losses (i.e., marking positions to market) once they are up and running is not very complicated. All that is needed is an ability to do basic discounted present value analysis—a skill possessed by anyone with an introductory course in finance and access to a calculator or a computer spreadsheet (e.g., EXCEL). Even if P&G were unable to determine the exact price to unwind its positions, just the daily act of marking positions

---

[27]See Sanjay Srivastava, "Value-at-Risk Analysis of a Leveraged Swap," *The Journal of Risk* 1 (2) (Winter 1998/1999), 87–101. Srivastava based his analysis on the Heath-Jarrow-Morton model of the term structure. The $6.65 million swap value is the discounted present value of the premium payments. Also see *Appendix 5.5: What Are the Problems with Value at Risk?*, which can be found on the Prentice Hall Web site at http://www.prenhall.com/marthinsen.

to market should have served as fair warning to P&G that its swaps had sailed into treacherous waters.

The P&G-BT Settlement

The P&G-BT lawsuit was eventually settled out of court, with both sides claiming victory. BT claimed victory because P&G agreed to pay BT $35 million of the nearly $200 million it owed, and P&G assigned to BT the benefits of another disputed derivative investment that was valued between $5 million and $14 million. P&G claimed victory because it recovered approximately 83% of its total losses,[28] but it is clear that the victory was costly to both sides because of the collateral damage done to their reputations.

How Did BT Fare After the Swaps?

Most of this chapter has focused on the risk-management practices and losses of P&G. Little or nothing has been said about BT, but there are some important points to consider. Typically, when a swap dealer takes a position (as BT did with P&G), it tries to hedge the transaction as soon as possible. In this way, the dealer earns a spread whether interest yields rise or fall, and the risk is neutralized. As BT mentioned in its legal response to P&G's accusations, it "did not need P&G to lose money in order for Bankers Trust to profit, or vice versa.[29]

If BT had hedged the P&G deal, then there would have been a major problem when P&G refused to pay its losses because most of these payments would have been earmarked for the counterparties BT lined up to hedge the P&G deal. For example, if P&G owed BT $200 million on the two swaps, then BT would owe most of those funds to its counterparties and would have to pay them regardless of whether or not P&G paid its side of the swap (Exhibit 5.11). Remember that the contingent nature of this contract only released BT from paying P&G if P&G defaulted on its side of the deal. P&G's default would have had no impact on the independent hedging transactions that BT did with other counterparties.

There was speculation that BT had a vested interest in doing this deal with P&G because BT needed to hedge an inventory of existing positions.

---

[28]The $5 million to $14 million recovered by BT was not counted by P&G when it claimed victory because P&G argued the funds were tied to a different lawsuit.

[29]District Court, S.D. Ohio, Western Division, The Procter & Gamble Company, Plaintiff v. Bankers Trust Company and BT Securities Corporation, Defendants, *Defendants' Answer to the First Amended Complaint and Defendant Bankers Trust Company's Counterclaims*. Civil Action No. C-1-94-735, 27 February 1995, p. 5.

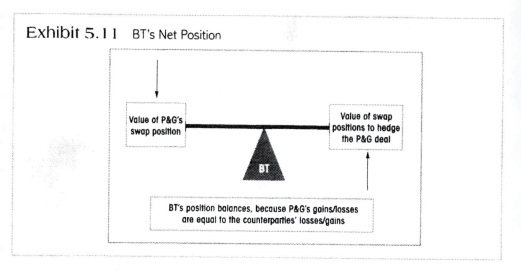

Exhibit 5.11   BT's Net Position

Value of P&G's swap position

Value of swap positions to hedge the P&G deal

BT

BT's position balances, because P&G's gains/losses are equal to the counterparties' losses/gains

According to this view, BT purposely deceived P&G into believing the swaps were benign.[30] P&G openly speculated that BT entered into more than $3 billion in counterparty transactions after the P&G deal was completed to fully hedge its exposure, which may explain why P&G was shocked at the cost of locking in a fixed rate after conditions turned sour.[31] We will probably never know if BT had an existing exposure or if BT hedged the P&G swaps after signing the documents. The case was settled out of court, so it never went through the discovery phase, which is when all the internal files, memos, and e-mails would have been entered into the public record. Regardless, if BT was hedged, the out-of-court settlement with P&G must have been a severe blow to its earnings.

P&G-BT from an Investor's Perspective

It is highly unlikely that an investor who was sensitive to risk and considering whether to invest in P&G would have gleaned any information about the risk-return profile of the company's off-balance-sheet (derivative) transactions from studying P&G's 1993 annual report. For instance, in 1993, P&G reported a $17 million gain on the derivative positions it took to hedge foreign exchange risks, but it made no mention of a $122 million loss on

---

[30]See Saul Hansell, "A Bad Bet for P. & G.," *The New York Times*, late edition, sec. D., col. 1 (14 April 1994), 6.
[31]The PR Newswire Association, Inc., "P&G Amends Suit Against Bankers Trust to Add Deutschmark Swaps to U.S. Treasury Swap; P&G Suit on Derivatives Adds Federal Securities Claims" (6 February 1995). http://web.lexis-nexis.com/universe/. Accessed 26 December 2007.

interest-related derivatives.[32] P&G was not the exception. Many companies revealed in the footnotes of their financial reports only the notional values of their derivative positions; some mentioned their maturities, but few revealed important details, such as swap payments, swap receipts, and credit risks. On the asset side, companies that purchased structured notes for investment purposes provided little or no information about their liquidity or riskiness. Structured securities were just lumped together with other interest-earning assets and put into categories with names like *cash and marketable securities.*

Perhaps one of the positive results of the P&G-BT swap was that it provided clear evidence of how poorly corporations reported their off-balance-sheet positions (i.e., forwards, futures, options, and swaps). This lack of transparency was a primary stimulus behind the recommendations and subsequent accounting reforms (e.g., FASB-133)[33] made by the U.S. Financial Accounting Standards Board in 1995.[34]

The Landmark P&G-BT Court Opinion[35]

Some of the most important legacies of the P&G-BT swaps were the published court opinions that resulted from this case because they were among the first clarifications of legal controversies dealing with swaps. This section reviews the most important court opinions connected to swap transactions.

MAJOR LEGAL ISSUES

One of the key issues addressed by the court was whether swaps are securities. If they are, then swaps can, and should, be subject to regulatory supervision by agencies such as the Securities and Exchange Commission (SEC) and Commodity Futures Trading Commission (CFTC). By contrast, if they

---

[32]See Michael Quint, "P&G Meets the Derivatives Monster," *The New York Times*, sec. 3, col. 3 (9 October 1994), 11.

[33]FASB-133 is a complex document almost 250 pages in length and with a mountain of interpretations. It is a challenge to read, even for the most conscientious accountants and auditors, but it is significant in the history of finance because of its direct and unequivocal statement that disclosure of off-balance-sheet transactions is crucial to understanding the financial health of any company.

[34]See *Appendix 5.2: Disclosure Reform After P&G-BT*, which can be found on the Prentice Hall Web site at http://www.prenhall.com/marthinsen.

[35]*Appendix 5.1: P&G-BT's Landmark Court Opinion*, which can be found on the Prentice Hall Web site at http://www.prenhall.com/marthinsen, covers in greater detail the court opinion in the P&G-BT case. This section draws on the published court opinion. See *The Procter & Gamble Company*, Plaintiff, v. *Bankers Trust Company and BT Securities Corporation*, Defendants, No. 925 FS—pp 1270 (S.D. Ohio 1996).

are over-the-counter transactions, then swaps are (and should be) outside the jurisdiction of these regulators.[36]

Another major issue addressed by the court was whether investment bankers have a fiduciary responsibility to their customers. Fiduciaries are expected to act on behalf of their customers in a transparent, loyal manner and in ways that intentionally avoid self-dealing. A higher standard is expected from fiduciaries than merely acting in good faith because their transactions with customers are not at arm's length. Examples of relationships where agents have fiduciary responsibilities are attorneys to clients, trustees to beneficiaries, executors to inheritors of estates, guardians to children, and directors to shareholders. For a company as large and seemingly well run as P&G to claim that it did not fully understand its multi-hundred-million-dollar transactions and, therefore, deserved fiduciary treatment raises some very uncomfortable questions.

If swap dealers do not have a fiduciary responsibility, then what legal and ethical disclosure obligations, if any, do they owe to their customers? For instance, if an investment banker fails to disclose important information in a swap transaction, can this transgression be prosecuted by customers on the common-law grounds of fraud?

AN UNUSUAL COURT OPINION

On 8 May 1996, Judge John Feikens of the Southern District Court of Ohio in Cincinnati rendered an opinion on P&G's amended charges against BT.[37] The court opinion was unusual for two reasons. First, it was issued *after* P&G and BT had settled out of court, which is rare. Second, the opinion was unusual for what it did not say. In cases decided by summary judgment, the facts of the case are not in dispute, so these "facts" should be the focus of the decision. Judge Feikens' opinion was very forthright in its conclusions, but it was not specific about the facts in the case that led him to his conclusions. For instance, he found that BT did not have a fiduciary relationship with P&G, but he did not explain what facts in the P&G-BT relationship established this finding.

---

[36]P&G's argument that swaps were securities may have been self-defeating because U.S. securities law requires companies to account for securities in their financial statements. One could ask, if P&G had been successful in convincing the court that swaps were securities, then was it inconsistent not to report them as such? Could P&G have been accused of ordinary negligence, gross negligence, or accounting fraud? Even though this outcome was possible, it would have been highly unlikely because charges of negligence or fraud on such grounds were not common in the 1990s.

[37]See *The Procter & Gamble Company, Plaintiff, vs. Bankers Trust Company and BT Securities Corporation, Defendants,* No. 925 FS—pp 1270 (S.D. Ohio 1996).

SUMMARY OF THE COURT OPINION

Judge Feikens had already ruled that P&G's charges against BT under the Organized Crime Control Act of 1970 (i.e., the Racketeer Influence and Corrupt Organizations [RICO] Act) were groundless because P&G failed to prove that BT was part of a corrupt organization distinct from the parent holding company;[38] so, his opinion on 8 May focused on securities law and fiduciary duties of investment bankers. As far-fetched as the racketeering charge might seem, its early resolution was important to BT because, if P&G had been successful in proving these charges, P&G could have then sued BT for treble damages (as much as $600 million), and a jury might have been willing to award P&G that much money.

In his written opinion, Judge Feikens concluded that P&G-BT's "5s/30s and DM swap agreements [were] *not securities* as defined by the Securities Acts of 1933 and 1934 and the Ohio Blue Sky Laws; that these swap agreements [were] *exempt from the Commodity Exchange Act*; that there [was] no private right of action available to P&G under the antifraud provisions of that Act; and that the...choice of law provision in the parties' agreement preclude[d] claims under the Ohio Deceptive Trade Practices Act"[39] (emphasis added). With regard to P&G's charges regarding BT's negligent misrepresentation, breach of fiduciary duty, and negligence, Judge Feikens concluded, "that as a counterparty to swap...agreements, *BT owed no fiduciary duty to P&G*. P&G's claims of negligent misrepresentation and negligence [were] redundant"[40] (emphasis added). In short, the court found that P&G should not be relieved or protected from the harsh ramifications of its own poorly negotiated deals. At the same time, Judge Feikens ruled that dealers, who had superior knowledge and information relative to their customers, had a legal responsibility to disclose material information.

Disclosure Reform After P&G-BT

The financial accounting standards practiced in the United States today are the result of a concerted effort by the Financial Accounting Standards Board

---

[38]The two affiliates sued by P&G (i.e., Bankers Trust Co. and BT Securities Corporation) were wholly owned subsidiaries of Bankers Trust New York Corporation. Therefore, they were considered to be part of the single Bankers Trust organization.

[39]The charges were dismissed under Federal Rule of Civil Procedure ("Fed.R.Civ.P.") 12(b)(6). *The Procter & Gamble Company*, Plaintiff, v. *Bankers Trust Company and BT Securities Corporation*, Defendants, No. 925 FS—pp 1270 (S.D. Ohio 1996).

[40]Ibid.

(FASB) throughout most of the 1990s and early 2000s to improve the clarity of corporate financial reporting. Even prior to the P&G-BT swap debacle, FASB had been trying to determine the proper accounting treatment for derivatives. It was apparent to most observers that U.S. accounting standards for off-balance-sheet transactions were inadequate. P&G-BT helped to accelerate the pace of reform because it focused the public eye on the downside risks of misunderstood and/or unattended derivative transactions. P&G-BT, plus many other blatant examples of derivative abuse in the 1990s, highlighted the incomplete and potentially misleading job U.S. companies were doing reporting their financial conditions.

After P&G-BT was settled, FASB and the SEC passed and implemented a bevy of reforms (e.g., FAS 119, FAS 133, and FAS 138) with respect to the measurement, recognition, and disclosure of accounting information on derivative financial transactions.[41] FASB and the SEC were by no means at the end of their accounting reforms, but they had come a long way toward making financial transactions more transparent to investors and regulators.

Should Corporate Treasuries Be Profit Centers?[42]

Ever since the legal battle between P&G and BT in 1994 and 1995, many investment bankers and investment analysts have been very critical of corporations that are perceived to be speculating in derivative instruments to enhance corporate profits. Nevertheless, these same investment bankers agree that prudently managed derivative transactions are an effective way to control market, credit, and liquidity risks. On one side, P&G felt betrayed by BT, but on the other side, BT maintained that P&G fell victim to its own decision to run the company's treasury (finance) department as an independent profit center or hedge fund.

Should the finance departments of manufacturing companies be profit centers? Was P&G foolish to have expected profits from a group that should have been more concerned about borrowing, hedging, and managing cash flows? When finance departments become profit centers, do they increase or decrease the volatility of a company's cash flows and/or net income?

Companies like P&G that transform their treasuries into profit centers and use their financial resources as tactical strategic weapons must accept

---

[41] *Appendix 5.2: Disclosure Reform After P&G-BT*, which can be found on the Prentice Hall Web site at http://www.prenhall.com/marthinsen, covers in greater detail the accounting reforms that took place from 1996 to 2000 due to P&G-BT and other derivative fiascos.

[42] *Appendix 5.4: Should Corporate Treasuries Be Profit Centers?*, which can be found on the Prentice Hall Web site at http://www.prenhall.com/marthinsen, provides a fuller discussion of these issues.

the consequences of new risks, which are much different from those typi-cally connected to the core of their operating activities (i.e., manufacturing, marketing, and distribution). To many observers, any nonfinancial com-pany that takes this tactical step is acting in direct opposition to the general canons of conservative finance.

Conclusion

P&G-BT was a punctuating event in the 1990s, a period of rapid develop-ment in derivatives industry. Rarely do you hear the chief financial officer of a multibillion dollar company admit that he and his staff lacked a clear understanding of transactions that were in excess of $200 million. When the messy details of the P&G-BT swap were investigated, two major conclu-sions emerged. First, P&G made large bets on the directional movement of U.S. and German interest rates. If it had been correct, the company would have borrowed at rates better than governments can achieve. But P&G's forecasts were incorrect, the company cut its losses too late, and, in the end, it was clear that the compensation P&G negotiated with BT was inadequate for the risks assumed. Second, once the swaps were priced and accepted by both parties, P&G seemed incapable of tracking their market risks (or unwilling to do so); as a result, losses on the combined notional principals of a bit less than $300 million mounted until P&G closed out its positions with pre-tax losses of $157 million. This was a whopping loss for a deal of that size.

P&G-BT was also significant because it helped fuel the drive for account-ing disclosure reform with regard to off-balance-sheet transactions and because it resulted in a significant District Court opinion that ruled on vital issues related to swap transactions. Judge John Feikens ruled that:

- Swaps are not securities; and
- Swaps dealers do not owe a fiduciary responsibility to their customers; at the same time, they do have a legal responsibility to disclose material information, especially when swap dealers have superior knowledge and information.

This chapter also discussed an important, but unresolved, issue dealing with whether company treasuries (finance department) should be profit cen-ters. Since P&G-BT, many Wall Street practitioners and academic analysts have opposed corporate treasuries being profit centers. Nevertheless, this issue will keep weaving in and out of discussions for years to come because so many companies continue to put their treasuries (intentionally or uninten-tionally) in this position.

Epilogue

What Happened to the Players in P&G-BT?

What happened to the P&G and BT employees who transacted these infamous swaps? Was it the case that "the employer absorbed the upside and

Exhibit E 5.1 Where Are They Now?

Procter and Gamble Employees

Name	Position	What Happened?
Edwin L. Artzt	Chairman	Artzt's salary rose by 8% to $2.29 million in 1994. Only his bonus of $420,000 was reduced by $100,000.
Raymond Mains	Vice President and Treasurer	Put on "special assignment" but retired before he took on the new responsibilities.
Erik G. Nelson	Chief Financial Officer	Determined not to be as responsible as Raymond Mains because he did not know about the swaps until after they were completed.[1]
Dane Parker	Treasury Analyst	Reassigned, but he ended up taking a job with another employer.
Victoria Tylman	Supervisor of Dane Parker	Reassigned

Bankers Trust Employees

Name	Position	What Happened?
Kevin Hudson	Salesman	Unknown
Jack A. Lavin	Managing Director, BT Securities, Corporate Derivative Sales	Continued working at BT
Gary S. Missner	Managing Director, BT Securities, Corporate Derivative Sales (Reported to Jack Lavin)	Left BT
Three executives not named		Reassigned and/or left BT

[1] Jeff Harrington. "Papers Disclose Censures at P&G." Cincinnati Enquirer 11 (10), sec. C., number 95-95768, (10 October 1995), 13.

the employees absorbed the downside."[43] Exhibit E5.1 lists some of the important participants and what happened to them. In most cases, the P&G employees were reassigned because management decided their actions were not dishonest or fraudulent.

Review Questions

1. In its 1993 and 1994 interest rate swaps, was P&G speculating or hedging? Explain.
2. In its 1993 dollar-denominated interest rate swap, how much did P&G expect to gain? How much did it eventually lose? Is there any way to justify this tradeoff on financial grounds?
3. Why did P&G use the OTC market and not an exchange to transact its derivative-related deals?
4. For a bank, what has a higher credit risk: a $100 million loan or a $100 million interest rate swap?
5. Explain the gamble P&G took on its 1993 dollar-denominated interest rate swap.
6. Explain the "wedding band" in P&G's 1994 German mark interest rate swap.
7. Was P&G's 1994 German mark swap an interest rate swap or a cross-currency swap? Explain.
8. Summarize what went wrong and caused P&G to lose such large amounts on its interest rate swaps.
9. Present arguments why BT should have been required to give P&G its pricing model. Then present arguments to the contrary.
10. Present arguments why BT should have been required to track the gains and/or losses on P&G's swaps. Then present arguments to the contrary.
11. In the lawsuit between P&G and BT, who won? Explain how both counterparties might have lost.
12. If BT had hedged its U.S. dollar interest rate swap with P&G, explain how BT would have lost twice when the deal collapsed.
13. Why was accounting transparency an important issue in the P&G-BT swap controversy?
14. Are swaps securities? Why is this important?
15. What is a fiduciary? Do swap dealers have fiduciary responsibilities to their customers? Why is this important?
16. Present arguments why corporate treasuries (finance departments) should not be profit centers. Then present arguments to the contrary.

---

[43]Matt Murray and Thomas Paulette, "Management After the Fall: Fingers Point and Heads Roll," *Wall Street Journal* (23 December 1994), B1.

Further Reading

Please visit http://www.prenhall.com/marthinsen, where you can find the following embellishments on and extensions of this chapter.

- Appendix 5.1: P&G-BT's Landmark Court Opinion
- Appendix 5.2: Disclosure Reform After the P&G-BT Swaps
- Appendix 5.3: Putting P&G-BT in Perspective:Other Derivative Disasters in the 1990s that Led to Financial Reform
- Appendix 5.4: Should Corporate Treasuries Be Profit Centers?
- Appendix 5.5: What Are the Problems with Value at Risk?

Bibliography

Ashley, Lisa and Bliss, Robert. "Chicago Fed Letter: Financial Accounting Standard 133—The reprieve." No. 143 (July 1998), 1–3.

BT Securities Corp., Release Nos. 33-7124, 34-35136 (22 December 1994).

BT Securities Corporation, CFTC Docket No. 95-2 (22 December 1994).

Code Civ. Proc., section 437c; Mann v. Cracchiolo 38 Cal. 3d 18, 35 (1985). Available at: http://www.lectlaw.com/def2/s102.htm. *The Lectric Law Library's Lexicon on Summary Judgment.* Accessed 26 December 2007.

DiMartino, Dawn, Ward, Linda, Stevens, Janet, and Sargisson, Win. "Procter & Gamble's Derivatives Loss: Isolated Incident or Wake Up Call?" *Derivatives Quarterly* 2 (3) (Spring 1996), 10–21.

District Court, S.D. Ohio, Western Division, The Procter & Gamble Company, Plaintiff v. Bankers Trust Company and BT Securities Corporation, Defendants, *First Amended Complaint for Declaratory Relief and Damages Jury Demand Endorsed,* Civil Action No. C-1-94-735, 6 February 1995.

District Court, S.D. Ohio, Western Division, The Procter & Gamble Company, Plaintiff v. Bankers Trust Company and BT Securities Corporation, Defendants, *Defendants' Answer to the First Amended Complaint and Defendant Bankers Trust Company's Counterclaims.* Civil Action No. C-1-94-735, 27 February 1995.

Financial Accounting Standards Board. *FASB Statement 39—Financial Reporting and Changing Prices: Specialized Assets-Mining and Oil and Gas—a supplement to FASB Statement No. 33* (Issued: October 1980).

Financial Accounting Standards Board. *FASB Statement 80—Accounting for Futures Contracts* (Issued: August 1984).

Financial Accounting Standards Board. *Summary of Statement No. 133—Accounting for Derivative Instruments and Hedging Activities* (Issued: June 1998). Available at: http://www.fasb.org/st/summary/stsum133.shtml. Accessed 26 December 2007.

Froot, Kenneth A., Scharfstein, David S., and Stein, Jeremy C. "A Framework for Risk Management." *Harvard Business Review.* Product Number: 94604 (November-December 1994), 91–102.

Hansell, Saul. "A Bad Bet for P. & G." *The New York Times,* Late Edition, sec. D., col. 1 (14 April 1994), 6.

Harrington, Jeff. "P&G case about keeping secrets." *Cincinnati Enquirer* 41 (10), sec. A (9 October 1995), 1.

Harrington, Jeff. "P&G charges 'pattern of fraud.'" *Cincinnati Enquirer* 15 (39), sec. B (4 October 1995), 8.

Harrington, Jeff. "Papers Disclose Censures at P&G," *Cincinnati Enquirer* 11 (10) sec. C., number 95-95768 (10 October 1995), 13.

Loomis, Carol J. "Untangling the Derivative Mess." *Fortune* 131 (5) (20 March 1995), 50–68.

Murray, Matt and Paulette, Thomas. "Management: After the Fall: Fingers Point and Heads Roll." *Wall Street Journal* (23 December 1994), B1.

Ohio Rev. Code § 1707.01 (B) (1992).

PriceWaterhouseCoopers *The New Standard on Accounting for Derivative Instruments and Hedging Activities (FAS 133): An Executive Summary* (30 September 1998), 19 pages.

Quint, Michael. "P&G Meets the Derivatives Monster." *The New York Times*, sec. 3, col. 3 (9 October 1994), 11.

Quitmeyer, John M. "Fiduciary Obligations in the Derivatives Marketplace." *S&P's The Review of Securities and Commodities Regulation* 28 (18) (25 October 1995), 179.

Regulation S-X and Regulation S-K of the Securities and Exchange Commission. 17 CFR Parts 210, 228, 229, 239, 240, and 249 [Release Nos. 33-7386; 34-38223; IC-22487; FR-48; International Series No. 1047; File No. S7-35-95]. RIN 3235-AG42, RIN 3235-AG77. *Disclosure of Accounting Policies for Derivative Financial Instruments and Derivative Commodity Instruments and Disclosure of Quantitative and Qualitative Information about Market Risk Inherent in Derivative Financial Instruments, Other Financial Instruments, and Derivative Commodity Instruments.*

Reves v. Ernst & Young, 494 U.S. 56, 61 n.1, 108 L. Ed. 2d 47, 110 S. Ct. 945 (1989).

SEC v. Howey, 328 U.S. 293, 90 L. Ed. 1244, 66 S. Ct. 1100 (1946).

Securities and Exchange Commission, 17 CFR Parts 210, 228, 229, 239, 240, and 249 [Release Nos. 33-7386; 34-38223; IC-22487; FR-48; International Series No. 1047; File No. S7-35-95]. RIN 3235-AG42, RIN 3235-AG77. *Disclosure of Accounting Policies for Derivative Financial Instruments and Derivative Commodity Instruments and Disclosure of Quantitative and Qualitative Information about Market Risk Inherent in Derivative Financial Instruments, Other Financial Instruments, and Derivative Commodity Instruments.*

Smith, Donald. "Aggressive Corporate Finance: A Close Look at the Procter & Gamble-Bankers Trust Leveraged Swap." *Journal of Derivatives* 4 (4) (Summer 1997), 67–79.

Srivastava, Sanjay, "Value-at-Risk Analysis of a Leveraged Swap." *Journal of Risk* 1 (2) (Winter 1998/1999), 87–101.

The PR Newswire Association, Inc., "P&G Amends Suit Against Bankers Trust to Add Deutshmark Swaps to U.S. Treasury Swap; P&G Suit on Derivatives Adds Federal Securities Claims" (6 February 1995). Available at: http://web.lexis-nexis.com/universe/. Accessed 11 June 2003.

The Procter & Gamble Company, Plaintiff, vs. Bankers Trust Company and BT Securities Corporation, Defendants, No. C-1-94-735, United States District Court of the Southern District of Ohio, Western Division, 925 F. Supp. 1270; 1996 U.S. Dist. LEXIS 6435; Comm. Fut. L. Rep. (CCH) P26,700; Fed. Sec. L. Rep. (CCH) P99,229, 8 May 1996, Decided. Available at: http://www.afn.org/~afn05451/proctor.html. Accessed 26 December 2007.

United Housing Foundation, Inc. v. Forman, 421 U.S. 837, 848, 44 L. Ed. 2d 621, 95 S. Ct. 2051 (1975).

6

Orange County

The Largest Municipal Failure in U.S. History

Introduction

In December 1994, the County of Orange in California filed for bankruptcy. Reporting a $1.5 billion loss on a net investment portfolio of $7.6 billion, the county earned the ignominious distinction as the largest municipal bankruptcy in U.S. history. During the six weeks after bankruptcy was declared, administrators sold off Orange County's portfolio of investments at fire-sale speed, turning its unrealized losses of $1.5 billion into realized losses of more than $1.6 billion.

News of the insolvency shocked national and international financial markets, which were already reeling from previous derivative-related failures, such as Metallgesellschaft[1] and Procter and Gamble.[2] Many feared that if Orange County, a rich, thriving, conservative, community of about 2.6 million people, could default, then who was safe?

[1] From 1991 to 1994, Metallgesellschaft AG lost approximately $1.3 billion on energy derivatives.
[2] From 1993 to 1994, P&G lost $157 million on two interest rate swap transactions.

Even though the Orange County debacle was similar, in many ways, to the other derivative-related failures of the 1990s, it maintained its own special character because a county government, not a company, had failed, and the rules governing such bankruptcies were nebulous. In addition, the Orange County failure was disconcerting because it materialized quickly, almost from nowhere—like a massive submarine surfacing next to an unsuspecting rowboat—and challenged common perceptions of what "safe" meant.

Robert Citron and the Orange County Board of Supervisors

Most observers believed that Orange County's investments were being managed wisely and well by treasurer–tax collector Robert Citron, a 35-year resident of Orange County and an elected, seven-term incumbent with 24 years of experience as treasurer. Robert Citron was generally considered to be a level-headed, hard-working public official, who lived a comfortable but modest life and derived great pleasure from providing his constituency, the people of Orange County, with financial rewards beyond their expectations. Citron lacked a formal university degree, but he was far from uneducated. He learned on the job, and his professional ascent in Orange County was rapid.

Hired as Orange County's deputy tax collector in 1960, Citron was elected in 1970 as tax collector; in 1973, the tax collector and treasurer positions were combined. Citron was not an articulate speaker, and his written explanations of Orange County's investment strategies were opaque, but most people in Orange County were willing to forgive these failings and let his

Robert Citron

performance do the talking for him. After all, his performance was impressive: For the first 22 years of his tenure as Orange County's treasurer–tax collector, Citron earned an average return of 9.4% compared to the 8.2% return on the state of California's pool. For the 12-year period prior to the collapse in 1994, Citron's return was nearly double the return on the state of California's portfolio (7.8% versus 4.2%, respectively).[3]

---

[3]Philippe Jorion, "Lessons from the Orange County Bankruptcy," *Journal of Derivatives*, 4(4) (Summer 1997), pp. 61–66. Merton H. Miller and David J. Ross, "The Orange County Bankruptcy and its Aftermath: Some New Evidence," *Journal of Derivatives*, 4(4) (Summer 1997), p. 54.

Orange County had no mayor, chief executive officer, or chief financial officer; so Citron reported, but was not directly accountable, to the Orange County Board of Supervisors, a group of five popularly elected officials (see Exhibit 6.1). He also reported to the Orange County Administrative Officer. Although supervision appeared to be adequate, in fact, it was relatively weak. Of the five board members, only one had any formal training in finance, and some of them were convinced (incorrectly) that the board had no legal supervisory powers over the treasurer–tax collector's position.[4]

Most of the Orange County Board felt that Citron's financial reports lacked timeliness (Citron reported only yearly) and quality, but no one was willing to rock the boat and challenge his proven record of success. The Chairman of Orange County's Board of Supervisors summed up the feelings

Exhibit 6.1 Orange County Board of Supervisors: 1994

Name	Background
1 Thomas Riley	A 20-year-incumbent on the Orange County Board of Supervisors, who was due to retire in January 1995
2 Roger Stanton	The longest-serving member of the Orange County Board of Supervisors. A full professor of management at California State University, Long Beach, he was elected in 1980 after serving seven years on Fountain Valley's City Council. Stanton was Chairman of the Board of Supervisors at the time of the bankruptcy.
3 William Steiner	Appointed to the Orange County Board of Supervisors in March 1993 and elected in 1994. Formerly, an Orange County councilman, president of the Orange Unified School District, and head of the Orangewood Children's Home for abused and neglected children. Steiner also taught a class on child abuse at Chapman University.
4 Gaddi Vasquez	Hired in the 1960s as an Orange County policeman. Later appointed as executive assistant to Bruce Nestande, Orange County Supervisor (1980–1984). Vasquez also worked as an executive at Southern California Edison (1984–1985). In April 1987, he was appointed to the Orange County Board of Supervisors; in 1988 and 1992, he won election to the Board. Vasquez was widely recognized as one of the most prominent Hispanic politicians in the U.S. with bright political prospects.
5 Harriet Weider	A long-standing incumbent due to retire in January 1995

[4]Actually, California Government Code Section 25303 *required* boards of supervisors to control any independently elected officials, like Citron. See Jean O. Pasco, "Article 16: Exercise of Power: Board Had the Right to Interfere," *Orange County Register* (31 December 1994), A16.

of the group in 1994 when he said: "[Citron] is a person who has gotten us millions of dollars. I don't know how in the hell he does it, but he makes us all look good."[5]

Whether by dint of success or by virtue of familiarity, Citron gradually assumed the role of Orange County's authoritarian, albeit benevolent, financial godfather. Unopposed in six elections, he was well regarded as a man who would go out of his way to support good projects and worthy causes. Having been in the treasurer–tax collector's job as long as he was, Citron must have been very familiar with the county's assets and liabilities, as well as the back alleyways between the various accounts. At times, he used these alleyways in creative ways to extinguish occasional financial fires that arose. "I've tried to run my office like it was my own personal business, for profit, for the taxpayers of Orange County," said Citron in 1994.[6]

Citron acquired the reputation as one of the most capable county treasurers in the United States; yet, as his standing grew wider and more positive, Citron's tolerance for criticism grew shorter. He came to resent challenges to his authority in financial matters, and he took personal umbrage at any form of criticism. This disdain for confrontation and criticism was especially evident in 1994 when John Moorlach[7] ran for treasurer–tax collector against Citron just as Orange County's portfolio began to decline in value. Moorlach's election platform focused on the speculative risks Citron was taking with public funds, as well as the lack of supervision and oversight exercised by the Orange County Board of Supervisors.

From April until the election in June, Moorlach hammered relentlessly on themes of Orange County's declining portfolio value and shrinking profit margins. "This listing is junk," said Moorlach, as he railed against Citron's inventory of investment holdings on the grounds that it was impossible to determine their value or risks.[8] News stories of these criticisms were reported and embellished in national publications, such as *The Wall Street Journal*, and in more specialized business periodicals, such as *Derivatives Week* and *Bond Buyer*.

By contrast, Citron's re-election platform took the spotlight off risk and focused on return. Citron characterized Moorlach as a reckless proselytizer,

---

[5]James K. Glassman, "From Orange County, Eight Survival Lessons," *The Washington Post*, 1 January 1995. Found at http://global.factiva.com/en/arch/display.asp.

[6]Chris Knap, "O.C. Treasurer's Race Stirs Markets," *Orange County Register* (24 April 1994) B01.

[7]John Moorlach was a Costa Mesa newspaper columnist, member of the Republican Central Committee, as well as a Certified Public Accountant, Certified Financial Planner, and partner at the firm Basler, Horowitz, Frank & Wakeling.

[8]Anonymous, "County Official Lists Securities: Derivatives Attracted Criticism," *Wall Street Journal* (20 April 1994), p. C21.

whose slanderous statements could cost Orange County millions of dollars in added expenditures by raising borrowing costs. Regarding Moorlach's contention that profit margins were shrinking, Citron explained that, during the past 15 years, spreads between borrowing costs and reinvestments had been as low as 0.25% and as high as 3%; so, the current spread, about 1.5%, was still quite healthy.[9]

Citron assured the public that any losses pointed to by Moorlach were "paper losses" that never would be realized because the assets purchased were regulated by the state and by Orange County's charter. Only securities with the lowest default risk, like U.S. government securities, U.S. agency securities, and investment-grade corporate debt were approved. Citron explained that Orange County's portfolio bore almost no default risk, and so long as the securities could be held until maturity, their full value could always be recovered. A forced sale of assets was, of course, a remote possibility, but only if there were insufficient cash to meet the margin calls of brokers and dealers, as well as the day-to-day demands of investors; again, Citron reassured voters that Orange County had more than sufficient liquidity to meet any and all demands. In short, voters had nothing to worry about.

In the June election, Moorlach won nearly 40% of the Orange County votes, but it was not enough. Citron had won the confidence of voters, media, analysts, the investment community, state officials, city supervisors, and regulators. He seemed to be above suspicion and beyond reproach, which explains much of the reason why he was able to accumulate such massive speculative positions and carry them as long as he did.

The Orange County Investment Pool

The Orange County Investment Pool (OCIP) was a $7.6 billion portfolio that was managed by Robert Citron for the benefit of Orange County and about 200 other municipal entities, such as cities, school districts, special agencies, water works, a regional transportation agency, pension funds, and sanitation authorities (see Exhibit 6.2). OCIP was the portfolio into which these municipal entities deposited excess funds and the pool from which they made their operating and capital expenditures.

For many of these municipal investors, OCIP was the mandatory investment vehicle for their surplus funds,[10] but Citron's accomplishments attracted other participants (e.g., Orange County Transportation Agency,

---

[9]Anonymous, "Citron Defends his Financial Acumen," *Orange County Register* (24 April 1994), B02.
[10]California state law *required* school districts to invest 100% of their funds in the county treasury.

Exhibit 6.2 Investors in the Orange County Investment Pool 30 November 1994

Municipal Entity	Percent of OCIP Portfolio
Orange County	37
Orange County Transportation Authority	15
School districts (60)	14
Cities (37)	14
Water districts (11)	7
Orange County Sanitation District	6
Transportation corridor agencies	4.5
Orange County Employee Retirement System	2
Other	0.5
Total	**100%**

Source: Based on figures in Philippe Jorion with the assistance of Robert Roper, *Big Bets Gone Bad: Derivatives and Bankruptcy in Orange County*, Academic Press, 1995, p. 124.

Orange County Sanitation District, and Irvine Water District), who voluntarily invested funds to enjoy the benefits of his investment success.[11] A few of them (e.g., four school districts, like Irvine and Newport-Mesa, and water boards, like Irvine Ranch Water District) went even further and leveraged their positions by borrowing funds to invest in OCIP.

Centralizing the investments of these relatively small municipal groups made good investment sense. It enabled them to enjoy professional funds management, including all the cost-saving benefits that come from purchasing investments in bulk and the risk-reducing benefits that come from portfolio diversification. These municipal entities relied on Robert Citron to make wise investment decisions, and under normal circumstances, one would expect "wise investment decisions" to be those that put top priority on preserving investors' capital base and ensuring adequate liquidity to meet their needs for funds. By contrast, Citron put his highest priority on earning above-average returns because California municipalities, including Orange County, were feeling the pinch of insufficient tax revenues.

[11]Voluntary deposits constituted about 40% of OCIP's total deposits. Chris Knap, "O.C. Fund Down $1.5 Billion," *Orange County Register* (2 December 1994), A01.

A primary cause of the lack of tax revenue was Proposition 13, an act passed in 1978 and generally viewed as a visible manifestation of California taxpayers' revolt against high and rising property taxes. Due to the surge of inflation during the 1970s, California property values and the taxes on these properties soared. Unable to meet the rising tax demands, some voters were forced to sell their homes. Voters reacted by passing Proposition 13 with nearly a two-thirds majority, cutting California's notoriously high property taxes drastically by limiting them to no more than 1% of a property's assessed value or fair market value, and limiting the annual increase of a property's appraised value, unless the property was sold.[12] The resulting decreased tax revenues, in conjunction with a short recession in the early 1990s and growing public expenses, led to burgeoning deficits and drastic cutbacks of state funding to municipalities in 1993.

In this environment, Robert Citron became the source of desperately needed public funds and a hero to many Orange County residents. The average return on his portfolio was significantly above the return earned by many private portfolio managers and appreciably above the returns earned by the state of California. In 1993 (prior to the collapse), Citron could have boasted that, while he was treasurer–tax collector, his investment decisions had earned Orange County residents about three-quarters of a billon dollars more than they would have earned if their funds had been invested in the state government fund.[13]

In 1994 (the year of the election), 12% of Orange County's revenues came from interest income on investments, as compared to the average of 3% for all other California counties, and in his fiscal budget for 1995, Citron promised to increase the portion of Orange County's interest earnings to 35% of its revenues.[14] Citron's efforts to increase OCIP's portfolio returns were encouraged by the state, which decided in the early 1990s to relax restrictions on the types of investments municipal entities could make, thus allowing Citron to invest in some riskier assets that could bring higher returns.

The Major Risks Facing Assets in the OCIP Portfolio

Endemic to all investment portfolios are three major risks, namely, credit risk, market risk, and liquidity risk. Unfortunately, Citron, his supervisors,

---

[12]The average tax rate in California prior to Proposition 13 was less than 3% of market value, and there were no limits on the annual increase in appraised values.

[13]Philippe Jorion, "Lessons from the Orange County Bankruptcy," *Journal of Derivatives*, 4(4) (Summer 1997), p. 63.

[14]Mark Baldassare, *When Government Fails: The Orange County Bankruptcy*, Berkeley: Public Policy Institute of California and the University of California Press, 1998.

and state and federal regulators focused most of their attention on credit risk and trivialized OCIP's vulnerability to market risk and liquidity risk.

CREDIT RISK

Credit risk is the chance that the issuer of a security will be either unable or unwilling to repay its debts. The full benefits of owning investments with low credit risk are derived if these investments can be held to maturity. Under such circumstances, owners are ensured that they will receive back not only the principal of their investments but also the full investment yield. On these grounds, the OCIP portfolio was rock-solid safe because the assets Citron purchased were restricted to securities issued by the U.S. government, U.S. government agencies (e.g., Import-Export Bank), and high-quality companies (e.g., Bank of America and Ford Motor Company), all of which had a very low chance of declaring bankruptcy.

MARKET RISK

Market risk is the variation in the price of an asset (or liability) due to changes in market variables (e.g., interest rates, exchange rates, stock prices, and/or commodity prices). There is an inverse relationship between the price of a fixed-income security and its yield, and the longer an asset's maturity, the greater is its potential price variation for each percentage change in yield. Market risk has nothing to do with whether borrowers can or will repay their debts, but rather it captures the possible change in an asset's value if it is sold prior to maturity. The issuers of this debt (i.e., the borrowers) are under no obligation to repay their liabilities before maturity; so, if investors wanted their funds back early, they would have to sell their securities for what the market would bear. As interest rates rise, the price of fixed-income securities falls, and these investors incur capital losses. Likewise, if interest rates fall, the price of these securities rises and investors earn capital gains.

Exhibit 6.3 shows how the prices of four zero-coupon securities with different maturities vary when interest rates rise from 3.5% to 7% (as they did during 1994). Notice that the one-year bill changes in value by only −3.3%, but the five-, 10-, and 20-year securities change by about −15%, −28%, and −49%, respectively. In brief, the longer the maturity, the greater is the decline in the price of a fixed-rate note when interest rates rise. Portfolio managers, who are caught in a position where they have to sell fixed-income assets as interest rates rise, could lose a considerable amount of capital.

Orange County faced substantially more market risk than credit risk because OCIP was invested mainly in medium-term securities, and it was highly leveraged (i.e., large amounts were borrowed to finance the purchase of securities). As a result, the value of the OCIP portfolio varied significantly with changes in market yields.

Exhibit 6.3 Change in Price of Zero Coupon Securities with One-, Five-, 10-, and 20-Year Maturities When Yields Rise from 3.5% to 7.0% (*Face Value* = $1.000)

	One-Year Maturity	Five-Year Maturity	10-Year Maturity	20-Year Maturity
Price at 3.5%	966.2	842.0	708.9	502.6
Price at 7%	934.6	713.0	508.3	258.4
Change in Price	−31.6	−129.0	−200.6	−244.1
% Change in Price	−3.3%	−15.3%	−28.3%	−48.6%

LIQUIDITY RISK

Liquidity is the ability to turn an asset into cash quickly and without substantial loss of value. Liquidity risk for a fund manager is the chance of not having sufficient cash on hand to meet demand. With regard to liquidity risk, investment funds are like banks. If a large number of customers suddenly demanded back their deposits, no bank or fund would have enough cash on hand to meet the demand. This fact is important because it means even if a fund's assets were safe from credit risk, it could fail for lack of liquidity.

Liquidity risk can be tied directly to market risk because if interest rates rise and the value of a portfolio falls, investors could decide to withdraw their funds, thereby forcing portfolio managers to sell investment assets at their low current-market prices, resulting in losses that could threaten the fund's solvency. By outward appearances, OCIP had more than enough cash assets to meet normal demands by customers, brokers, dealers, and creditors; nevertheless, as we will see shortly, in a crisis, cash demands become amplified, thereby magnifying the degree of liquidity risk.

Although Citron and the board felt that OCIP was protected from credit risk due to the constraints on the types of investments Citron could make, it was, in fact, vulnerable to the confluence of all three risks. An overview of OCIP's assets and funding sources will demonstrate this vulnerability.

OCIP's Assets and Funding Sources

In December 1994, OCIP's portfolio consisted of 206 non-cash assets, most of which were high-quality (i.e., low credit risk), fixed-income securities and structured notes. Exhibit 6.4 separates the assets in OCIP's portfolio into two groups. The assets in Group 1 were the major causes of the Orange County

Exhibit 6.4 Balance Sheet of Orange County Investment Pool 1 December, 1994
(Millions of Dollars)

Assets		Liabilities and Equity	
GROUP 1: ASSETS THAT CAUSED THE FAILURE (83.8%)†		**Loans (63.2%)**	
		Reverse repurchase agreements (198)	$12,988.1
Structured notes			
Inverse floating-rate notes (62)*	$5,369.2 (26.1%)		
Fixed-income securities (116)	$11,857.3 (57.7%)		
GROUP 2: OTHER ASSETS IN OCIP'S PORTFOLIO (16.2%)		**Equity investment by investors (36.8%)**	
		Equity	$7,550.4
Cash	$646.5 (3.2%)		
Collateralized mortgage obligations (8)	$228.5 (1.1%)		
Structured notes			
Dual-index notes (2)	$150.0 (0.7%)		
Floating-rate notes (7)	$588.0 (2.9%)		
Index-amortizing notes (11)	$1,699.0 (8.3%)		
Total assets (206)	**$20,538.5 (100%)**	**Total liabilities and equity**	**$20,538.5 (100%)**

* Figures in parentheses represent the number of securities purchased in each asset and liability group.
† Percentage figures in parentheses represent the portion of assets or liabilities.

collapse; therefore, they are the focus of this section. The assets in Group 2 had a relatively small impact on OCIP's financial health and, therefore, are explained briefly in Risk Notepad 6.1: Other Assets in the OCIP Portfolio.

Two major asset types accounted for more than 80% of the OCIP portfolio: inverse floating-rate securities, which are a type of structured note, and fixed-income securities. They caused most of Orange County's losses when U.S. interest rates rose precipitously in 1994.

STRUCTURED NOTES

Almost 40% of the OCIP portfolio was invested in structured notes. Structured notes are customized investments with periodic payments that

Risk Notepad 6.1

Other Assets in the OCIP Portfolio

The assets listed in Exhibit 6.4 under the heading Group 2: Other Assets in OCIP's Portfolio were a relatively small portion of the total investment. For anyone interested in U.S. capital markets and derivatives, understanding these financial instruments is important.

CASH AND COLLATERALIZED MORTGAGE OBLIGATIONS

About 3% of the OCIP portfolio was invested in low-interest earning cash assets, which consisted mainly of overnight repurchase agreements and money market accounts, and about 1% was invested in collateralized mortgage obligations (CMOs). CMOs are investment-grade securities, which are backed by a pool of mortgages with fixed maturities. A CMO separates the monthly cash flows from its mortgage pool into future payments based on their interest, principal, or a combination of principal and interest. CMOs offer investors benefits, among which are an assortment of maturities (short-, medium-, or long-term), a broad secondary market that provides liquidity (which mortgages alone would not supply), and very high credit ratings (e.g., AAA) due to their collateral backing.

STRUCTURED NOTES

Besides inverse floaters, which are described elsewhere in the text, the OCIP portfolio was composed of three other types of structured notes: dual-index notes, floating-rate notes, and index-amortizing notes.

Dual-Index Notes

Less than 1% of OCIP's assets was invested in dual-index notes. Dual-index notes are securities with coupon rates that depend on the difference between two different indexes, such as the constant maturity rate on U.S. Treasury securities and LIBOR. The maturities of dual-index notes can vary, but typically they offer a fixed rate of return in the short term (e.g., the first two years) and a variable rate thereafter. For example, the coupon on a dual-rate note might begin with a fixed rate of 5% for the first two years and then change to a floating-rate equal to the 10-year U.S. Treasury bond rate minus the 6-month LIBOR. Dual-index notes are often used to bet on changes in the shape of the yield curve.

Floating-Rate Notes

Less than 3% of Orange County's assets were invested in floating-rate notes. Floating-rate notes (FRNs) are securities whose returns vary directly with a particular money market instrument or money market index. Because these rates vary frequently, FRNs have very low market risk (i.e., their values do not change substantially with time).

Index-Amortizing Notes

Slightly more than 8% of the OCIP portfolio was invested in index-amortizing notes (IANs). Similar in design to collateralized mortgage obligations, index-amortizing notes are debt instruments for which payments on the (notional) principal are tied to changes in a short-term money market rate, such as LIBOR, or a money market index. As interest rates rise, the maturities of IANs increase; as market interest rates fall, the maturities of IANs decline. Because IAN maturities are generally less volatile than the maturities of CMOs, IANs appeal to many risk-averse investors, who want to carry the type of risks inherent in CMOs

depend on future changes in market variables, such as interest rates, exchange rates, stock prices, and/or commodity prices. Brokers and dealers like structured notes because they are customized and, therefore, earn greater commissions and fees than straight bond issues or note issues; investors like them because they offer opportunities that are not readily available in the market. Robert Citron responded to the incentives of structured notes by investing almost $8 billion in these securities. Such investments would have posed no problems had Citron fully understood their risks, but herein was the problem.

Despite this lack of understanding, Citron invested heavily in four types of structured notes with varying degrees of risk. Of the four types, inverse floating-rate notes were, by far, the largest category and a major source of OCIP's losses.

Inverse Floating-Rate Notes

Most of OCIP's structured notes and more than 26% of its total assets were placed in inverse floating-rate notes (also called inverse floaters or reverse floaters). As the name suggests, inverse floaters are financial instruments whose return varies with market interest rates, but rather than vary directly (as would be the case with floating-rate notes), the return on these securities varies inversely with market interest rates. When market rates rise, inverse floaters earn lower returns; when rates fall, the return on inverse floaters rises.

An example might help demonstrate how the return on an inverse floater varies with market rates. Suppose on 1 January 1993 a portfolio manager purchased an inverse floater that earned an annual return equal to 7% minus the six-month LIBOR. If the six-month LIBOR rate on 1 January were 4%, then the inverse floater would earn a 3% annual return (i.e., 7% − LIBOR of 4% = 3%), which means it would earn just 1.5% for the six months from January to June (i.e., 6/12 × 3% = 1.5%). On 1 July six months later, the return would change. If LIBOR rose to 5%, the annual return on the inverse floater for the following six months would fall from a 3% to 2% (i.e., 7% − LIBOR of 5% = 2%), and if interest rates fell to 3%, the annual return on the floater would rise to 4% (i.e., 7% − LIBOR of 3% = 4%).

Robert Citron was betting on falling U.S. interest rates; so, it is easy to understand why inverse floaters were so appealing to him. Inverse floaters also could be tailored to fit his risk specifications, and Citron's inverse floaters were often structured to carry an extra wallop when interest rate changed. Some of his super-charged inverse floaters were designed to pay off at twice the change in LIBOR (e.g., 8% − 2 × LIBOR, rather than 8% − 1 × LIBOR), but there was a flip side. As interest rates rose, the earnings on these structured notes fell at twice the rate of a normal inverse floater.

FIXED-INCOME SECURITIES

Fixed-income securities were clearly the meat and potatoes of the OCIP portfolio. Constituting nearly 58% of the pool's assets, these securities paid either a fixed rate of interest or a rate that varied according to a predetermined schedule. They carried virtually no credit risk because the issuers were all high-quality borrowers, such as the U.S. government, U.S. agencies, and first-class corporations. The average maturity of the OCIP securities was under three years, but because these investments were leveraged (an issue that will be discussed shortly), the impact of changing market rates on their values was amplified. As U.S. interest rates rose, the value of these securities plunged.

OCIP's FUNDING SOURCES

In addition to concern about the composition of OCIP's assets, there was also concern about the structure of its funding sources. Investors contributed only $7.6 billion to OCIP, but, as Exhibits 6.4 and 6.5 show, the pool held assets equal to $20.5 billion. The difference between OCIP's total assets and investors' funds (i.e., almost $13 billion) was the amount Robert Citron borrowed to finance the additional assets. The ratio of OCIP's total assets to its equity, 2.7, was the leverage of OCIP's portfolio (see Exhibit 6.5).

Reverse Repurchase Agreements

To borrow such vast amounts, Citron made extensive use of reverse repurchase agreements (reverse repos, for short). To understand what went wrong at OCIP, it is crucial to understand what reverse repos are and how they can be used to leverage an investment portfolio. But before discussing reverse repos, it might be helpful to start with a short explanation of repurchase agreements (i.e., repos).[15]

---

[15]See Michael J. Fleming and Kenneth D. Garbade. "The Repurchase Agreement Refined: GCF Repo," *Current Issues in Economics and Finance*, Federal Reserve Bank of New York, Col. 9, Number 6 (June 2003), pp 1-7.

Exhibit 6.5 Orange County Investment Pool Portfolio: 1 December 1994
(Millions of Dollars)

	Book Value	Percent of Portfolio
OCIP assets purchased with investors' funds	7,550.4	37%
OCIP assets purchased with borrowed funds (i.e., reverse repurchase agreements)	12,988.1	63%
Total Assets	**20,538.5**	**100%**
Leverage factor = Total Assets ÷ Equity	20,538.5 ÷ 7,550.4 = 2.7	

Merton H. Miller and David J. Ross, "The Orange County Bankruptcy and Its Aftermath: Some New Evidence," *Journal of Derivatives*, 4(4) (Summer 1997), p. 53.

A repurchase agreement is the spot sale of an asset with a simultaneous agreement to buy it back at a fixed price in the future. Usually, the asset sold and repurchased is a fixed-income security, and when the term *repurchase agreement* is used, securities dealers are the borrowers (i.e., the security sellers) and their customers are the lenders.

On one hand, repos are just like collateralized loans, but on the other hand, they are like forward contracts. Repos are like collateralized loans because borrowers pledge assets (e.g., fixed-income securities) that back their promises to repay principal and interest in the future. For the counterparty who sells a bond and agrees to repurchase it in the future (i.e., the borrower), a repo transfers possession of the security in return for hard cash. When the security is repurchased, the difference between the original sale price and the higher repurchase price is the effective interest paid.

It is important to remember that when repo borrowers repay their debts (which is normally the case), they become, again, the owners of the pledged collateral; therefore, they receive all the interest and capital gains accruing to these assets. But if repo borrowers are unable or unwilling to meet their contractual obligations, lenders take possession of the pledged collateral, and they can sell it to extinguish the debts. Therefore, to lenders in a repo deal, credit risk depends more on the quality of the collateral than it does on the quality of the borrowers.

Repos are also like forward contracts because the repurchase prices of the pledged assets are identical to forward prices. The difference between the spot price (the current sale price of the security) and the forward (repurchase) price is like the capital gain earned on a derivative instrument. To borrowers,

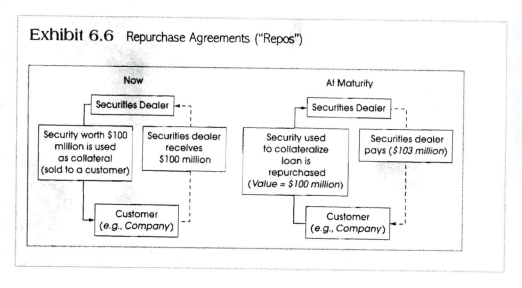

Exhibit 6.6   Repurchase Agreements ("Repos")

repos are like long forward contracts because they are agreeing to purchase assets in the future at prices agreed upon now. To the lenders, repos are like short forward contracts because they are agreeing to sell assets in the future at prices agreed upon now.

With the help of Exhibit 6.6, let's analyze the cash flows of a repurchase agreement. Suppose a dealer enters into a one-year repurchase agreement in which he pledges a fixed-income security in return for $100 million (see left side of Exhibit 6.6).[16] At maturity (i.e., one year later, in this case), the dealer would repurchase the security for its principal plus the repo interest rate. Assuming the repo rate was 3%, the dealer would pay $103 million (see right side of Exhibit 6.6).

A reverse repurchase agreement, which is how Citron borrowed most of his funds, is just like a repurchase agreement, except the roles of borrower and lender are reversed (see Exhibit 6.7). In a reverse repo deal, securities dealers are the lenders, who purchase securities from customers and agree to sell them back at a higher price in the future. Customers are the borrowers.

Leveraging the OCIP Portfolio

Repurchase agreements and reverse repurchase agreements are normally low-risk, conservative ways to borrow and lend, but Robert Citron used

---

[16]Normally, the amount the dealer receives would be less than the value of the security by a small amount (i.e., also called the "haircut" or "margin") so that the loan is overcollateralized and the lender is better protected. During the course of the repurchase agreement, if interest rate movements cause the value of the underlying securities to fall, repo borrowers could be required to post additional collateral (i.e., margin).

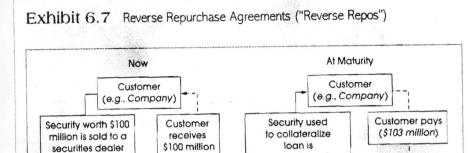

Exhibit 6.7 Reverse Repurchase Agreements ("Reverse Repos")

reverse repos to leverage the OCIP portfolio thereby increasing its assets from $7.6 billion to $20.5 billion. The assets he purchased carried almost no default risk. Nevertheless, due to their medium-term maturity and the leverage used to purchase them, the reduction in their market values due to rising interest rates was enough to cause the overwhelming majority (approximately $1 billion) of OCIP's $1.64 billion losses.

An example might help to clarify the risks Robert Citron took with Orange County's portfolio. Suppose the portfolio manager of an investment fund purchased $100 million of five-year U.S. government bonds earning a yearly coupon of 3.5%.[17] Not content with the return on these securities and willing to take a bit of risk with investors' funds, suppose the portfolio manager entered, subsequently, into a one-year reverse repurchase agreement with Merrill Lynch.

Under the terms of the reverse repo agreement, the investment fund would sell Merrill Lynch the five-year, U.S. government bonds for $100 million and agree to buy them back one year later at the prevailing one-year repo rate, which we will assume is 3%.[18] As a result of the reverse repo deal, the investment fund would now have a fresh $100 million to invest for one year, and it would also have the obligation to repay Merrill Lynch $103 million at the end of the year. Let's assume that the portfolio manager used the funds to purchase securities with the same maturity and yield as the ones he delivered to Merrill Lynch (i.e., $100 million worth of five-year bonds with 3.5% coupons).

[17]The funds from most of Citron's reverse repurchase deals were invested in government securities with five-year maturities.
[18]To simplify the example, assume that interest rates were 3.5% at the time, so the bond sold for its par value (i.e., $100 million).

At the end of the year, the reverse repo would mature, and the fund would honor its reverse repo commitment by paying $103 million to Merrill Lynch. The funds used to repay its repo loan would come from selling the securities that the portfolio manager purchased at the beginning of the year with the funds borrowed from Merrill Lynch. Assuming the newly acquired notes did not change in price, the investment fund would collect $103.5 million (i.e., $100 million in principal and $3.5 million from the 3.5% coupon on the securities). Because it needed only $103 million to repay Mer rill Lynch, the investment fund would be left with a net gain of $0.5 million.

But the story does not end here. Having settled its reverse repo obligations to Merrill Lynch, the investment fund would receive back the securities it used to collateralize the reverse repo loan, and from these securities, it would earn $3.5 million (i.e., a 3.5% coupon on the $100 million security). As Exhibit 6.8 shows, the reverse repurchase deal raises the investment fund's return from the 3.5%, which it would have earned had it simply held onto the original government securities, to 4.0%, the return on the original securities plus the (borrow and invest) reverse repo deal.

But why stop there? If the portfolio manager could guarantee investors a 0.5% return every time he entered into a repurchase agreement, then why not repeat the transaction multiple times and guarantee them even more? This is precisely what Robert Citron did, and so long as interest rates fell or remained constant, his profits soared.

Exhibit 6.8 Using Reverse Repos to Enhance Investment Returns: *An Example Assuming Unchanging Interest Yields*

Year-end Results	Earnings	Costs	Net
Original five-year note purchased with investors' funds	$3.5 million ($100 million × 3.5%)	0%	$3.5 million
Reverse repo transaction	$3.5 million ($100 million × 3.5%)	$3 million ($100 million × 3%)	$0.5 million
Total interest return			$4 million
Capital gains/losses on the securities	$0	$0	$0
Total return on investment	$4 million/$100 million = 4%		

Effects of Leverage on OCIP's Return

If you are asking yourself why falling or steady interest rates were crucial to Citron's reverse repurchase strategy, the answer can be most clearly understood by seeing what happens to OCIP's return when interest rates fall and comparing it to when interest rates rise.

OCIP's RISING RETURNS: EFFECTS OF FALLING INTEREST RATES

Even a cursory look at Exhibit 6.9 shows why Robert Citron, at one time, was considered a financial genius. From 1989 to 1992, U.S. Treasury security yields fell steadily, with only minor interruptions. For example, the one-year Treasury bill rate fell from (about) 9.0% to 3.7%, and the five-year Treasury note rate slipped from (about) 9% to 6%. As a result, Robert Citron's heavy concentration of fixed-income securities was rewarded handsomely with capital gains, and his inverse floaters earned increasingly higher returns.

An example might help clarify how the OCIP was able to profit from these falling interest rates. In 1994, OCIP's leverage factor was approximately 3:1 (see Exhibit 6.5), which means that for each $100 million worth

Exhibit 6.9 U.S. Yields on Five-Year Treasury Notes and One-Year Treasury Bills: 1989–1995

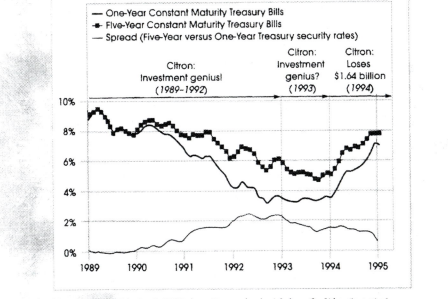

Source: Federal Reserve Bank of St. Louis FRED, http://research.stlouisfed.org/fred/data/irates/gs1

of securities purchased with investor funds, an additional $200 million worth of securities were purchased with borrowed funds (e.g., via reverse repurchase agreements). Suppose that, on the $200 million of borrowed funds, OCIP paid an annual (reverse) repo rate of 3%, and on the $200 million worth of additional five-year government bonds, it earned 3.5%. At the end of the year, the counterparties (e.g., Merrill Lynch) would expect OCIP to repay the principal of $200 million principal on the reverse repo plus $6 million of interest (i.e., 3% of $200 million).

Robert Citron was betting that interest rates would fall, and if they did, he positioned OCIP to earn even more attractive returns because, in addition to the interest income, his securities would earn capital gains. Suppose at the end of the year, interest rates declined from 3.5% to 2%. OCIP's original $100 million security would now be worth $107.07 million, a capital gain of $7.07 million.[19] As well, the $200 million of securities purchased with borrowed funds (i.e., the reverse repo funds) would now be worth $214.14.[20] With these funds, OCIP could repay its reverse repo debt amounting to $206 million (i.e., $200 million of principal and $6 million of interest). As Exhibit 6.10 shows, the effect of these capital gains raises OCIP's total return on its $100 million of equity from 3.5%, which it would have earned with no leverage, to 25.7%!

Exhibit 6.10 Results of Leveraging Reverse Repos to Enhance Investment Returns: *An Example Assuming Falling Interest Yields*

Year-end Results	Earnings	Costs	Net
Original five-year bond purchased with OCIP investors' funds	$3.5 million ($100 million × 3.5%)	0%	$3.5 million
Reverse repo transaction (Leverage factor = 3.0)	$7 million ($200 million × 3.5%)	$6 million ($200 million × 3.0%)	$1.0 million
Total interest return			$4.5 million
Capital gains/losses	+$ 7.07 million—securities purchased with OCIP funds +$14.14 million—securities purchased with borrowed funds		
	$21.21 million—total capital gains		
Return on investment = ($4.50 million + $21.21 million)/$100 million = 25.71%			

[19]This calculation assumes annual interest payments.
[20]2 × $107.07 million = $214.14 million.

In addition to the capital gains earned from falling interest rates, Citron also received another source of profits on his reverse repurchase agreements because from 1989 to 1992, the yield spread between medium-term and short-term interest rates rose. For example, Exhibit 6.9 shows that the spread between five-year U.S. interest rates and one-year rates grew from approximately 0% to more than 2%. As a result, Citron profited by borrowing, via reverse repos, from the short-term end of the yield curve and investing in assets on the medium-term and long-term sides.

OCIP's RETURN STABILIZES: 1993

During 1993, U.S. interest rates stopped their dramatic fall and stabilized. For example, one-year rates and five-year rates hovered around 3.4% and 5.1%, respectively (see Exhibit 6.9). As a result, Citron was deprived of the capital gains he had been earning on OCIP's fixed-income securities, and his inverse floaters no longer earned increasing returns. Profits fell, as well, because the spread between medium-term rates and short-term rates decreased, causing the net return on Citron's mountain of reverse repo-financed securities to decline. For instance, Exhibit 6.9 shows that that spread between five-year and one-year Treasury bills yields fell by nearly 1%. The combined effect of stabilized interest rates and declining interest rate spreads caused OCIP's profits to fall, but they remained relatively healthy—especially compared to other funds. As a result, Citron was still considered, by many, to be a cut above the typical portfolio manager.

OCIP's RETURNS PLUMMET: 1994—EFFECTS OF RISING INTEREST RATES

In the end, Robert Citron's bet on falling interest rates proved disastrously wrong. U.S. interest rates began to rise in February 1994, when the Federal Reserve tightened credit to reduce the threat of inflation and prevent the U.S. economy from overheating. During the span of 10 months, the Fed raised U.S. interest rates six times, causing the yield on one-year U.S. Treasury bills to rise from 3.54% to 7.14%—more than double! As a result, OCIP's heavily packed portfolio of fixed-income securities and inverse floaters began to spill red ink. The fixed-income securities incurred capital losses, and the spread between medium-term and short-term securities was rapidly approaching zero (see Exhibit 6.9).

Another example might help clarify how the effect of rising interest rates combined with leverage caused the returns to plummet. At the end of 1994, interest rates rose from about 3.5% to 7%. As a result, securities worth $300 million (i.e., the original $100 million bought with investors' funds plus the $200 million purchased with borrowed funds) at the beginning of the year were worth $256.95 million at the end of the year—a considerable difference.

At year's end, OCIP would still have to repay the $206 million in principal and interest on the reverse repo agreement; so, as Exhibit 6.11 shows, the effects of these capital losses would turn the safe 3.5% return on equity, which OCIP would have earned without leverage, into a loss amounting to 38.6%!

OCIP's profitability plunged in 1994 for another important reason. Like so many other derivative-related failures (e.g., Barings Bank), Robert Citron began using a doubling strategy. As interest rates rose and bond prices fell, Citron saw in each interest rate up-tick an opportunity to purchase (what he felt were) increasingly underpriced investment assets. To finance the purchases and profit from his expectations, he borrowed vast amounts, but interest rates continued to rise, causing his doubling strategy to lose even greater amounts than had already been lost.[21]

The dual effect of declining profitability and tumbling asset values attracted the attention of investors and creditors, who began to scrutinize carefully Citron's risk levels and match them with expected rates of return. The reaction of many to the bad news was to exit from the fund (or, at least, try to exit) as quickly as possible.

Exhibit 6.11   Results of Leveraging Reverse Repos to Enhance Investment Returns: An Example Assuming Rising Interest Yields

Year-end Results	Earnings	Costs	Net
Original five-year bond purchased with OCIP investors' funds	$3.5 million ($100 million × 3.5%)	0%	$3.5 million
Reverse repo transaction (Leverage factor = 3.0)	$7 million ($200 million × 3.5%)	$6 million ($200 million × 3%)	$1 million
Total interest return			$4.5 million
Capital gains/losses	−$14.35 million—security purchased with OCIP funds −$28.70 million—security purchased with borrowed funds		
	−$43.05 million—total capital losses		
Total return on investment	($4.50 million − $43.05 million)/$100 million = −38.55%		

---

[21]During the summer 1994, Orange County and the municipal entities in OCIP borrowed $1.2 billion to invest in additional securities and to meet the rising need for cash.

The main cause of Orange County's bankruptcy was the heavy concentration of structured notes and medium-term fixed-income securities in OCIP's portfolio, the risks of which Robert Citron did not fully understand. Citron made what amounted to an enormous one-sided bet that the U.S. yield curve would remain steeply upward sloping (i.e., short-term interest rates would remain considerably lower than medium-term and long-term rates) and that interest rates, on average, would fall. He lost his bet because the U.S. yield curve flattened, and interest rates rose in 1994. Rising interest rates led to a domino effect among the major risks facing OCIP. As the market value of fixed-income securities plummeted (market risk), demands by investors for their funds back forced OCIP to liquidate a large portion of its portfolio (liquidity risk), thereby turning paper losses into actual losses (credit risk).

The Consequences

In October 1994, Matthew Raabe, Orange County's assistant treasurer, went to Orange County's chief administrator, Ernie Schneider, and to Orange County's auditor-controller, Steve Lewis, to express his concerns about the losses OCIP was suffering. Raabe explained how OCIP's portfolio value had withered away by more than a half billion dollars. News of the losses shocked Schneider and Lewis. Quick action was called for, and one of the first priorities was getting an accurate external appraisal of OCIP's portfolio. For that, Orange County hired New York-based Capital Market Risk Advisers (CMRA). The analysis took about a week to complete, and the results were alarming. CMRA's analysis detailed the decimation of OCIP's portfolio. By CMRA estimates, the OCIP portfolio had lost approximately $1.5 billion in value.

MARKET RISK CAUSES LIQUIDITY RISK

Investors, already spooked by the effects that the Fed's tight credit policy and rising interest rates were having on earnings and portfolio values, began to fear for the solvency of OCIP. Capital flight resulted, beginning in mid-November 1994, when the Irvine Ranch Water District decided to withdraw $100 million from the OCIP portfolio. Citron and his staff (mainly, Matthew Raabe) spent the rest of the month trying to convince investors not to withdraw their funds and urging creditors not to pull their credit lines.

To stem the capital outflows and prevent a liquidity crisis, Citron tried to freeze the fund for 30 days and applied a 20% haircut (i.e., reduction in portfolio value) to investors wishing to withdraw their funds. The policy seemed to be fair. After all, these investors enjoyed the better years when OCIP was earning above-average returns; so, why should they not have to bear the burdens during more difficult times? Even though it is questionable whether Citron's 20% haircut would have survived a serious court challenge, it seemed to work. Investors realized that withdrawing their funds would immediately turn paper losses into actual (cash flow) losses that would have to be reported to the public.

Conversely, the haircut Citron used to stem the run by OCIP investors could not be used with creditors, and creditors were champing at the bit to get back their funds as soon as possible. As interest payments on Orange County's outstanding debts came due, most creditors refused to roll over their credits and others demanded back existing loans. Credit Suisse First Boston (CSFB), for instance, which had lent Orange County $2.6 billion in connection with reverse repurchase agreements, requested the repayment of $1.25 billion.[22] Orange County could not meet the rising demand for funds, and no one was willing to lend it such amounts. As a result, finding sources of liquidity to meet the investors' growing demands for cash became of paramount importance.

Attempts to gain the needed funds by selling OCIP's entire portfolio were unsuccessful, and appeals to the Securities and Exchange Commission, state treasurer's office, California attorney general, and Governor Pete Wilson all fell on deaf ears. Everywhere Orange County looked, pockets were empty, and the predominantly Democratic legislature in California had relatively little sympathy for the rich, Republican residents of Orange County.

GOVERNMENT PARALYSIS

The government of Orange County needed to act promptly, but swift action was hindered by the Brown Act, which was passed in 1953 to protect the community's right to attend and participate in public meetings. The act required 72-hour notification for regular meetings, 24-hour notice for special meetings, and one-hour notice for emergency meetings, but financial crises did not qualify as "emergencies." Criminal penalties were imposed on public officials who did not follow the rules. When news of the financial crisis first broke, Orange County's Board of Supervisors should have moved quickly, but they were caught on the horns of a dilemma. Due to the Brown Act, they had to provide the public with notification of any meetings, but if meeting announcements were made, they might fuel public fears and exacerbate the outflow of funds from OCIP.

---

[22]CSFB decided, as well, to exercise a 6 December 1994 put option on Orange County notes worth $110 million.

CITRON RESIGNS

When CMRA finished the audit of OCIP, it estimated the OCIP portfolio had lost approximately $1.5 billion. These losses were reported to the press on 1 December, and on 4 December, Robert Citron resigned as Orange County's treasurer–tax collector. News of the losses and Citron's resignation cast a dark shadow over financial markets nationwide, and capital flight from the fund became even more problematic. Municipalities tried to liquidate their deposits; counterparties to reverse repurchase agreements demanded additional collateral to back their outstanding transactions, and/or they seized billions of dollars of collateral to sell at market prices; creditors refused to roll over their loans or called them in early. State, county, and national bond prices fell (i.e., yields rose) as investors attached higher risk premiums to bond issues. Orange County housing prices fell, and residents braced themselves for the effects of emergency budget cuts, higher fees, and increased taxes.

LACK OF LIQUIDITY LEADS TO BANKRUPTCY

There was a run on OCIP in much the same way that depositors run on banks, and in an effort to meet the surging demand for cash, Robert Citron was forced to sell assets that were rapidly declining in value. OCIP was caught in a death spiral. As assets were liquidated, further losses were realized, stimulating even greater capital flight from the fund. With nowhere to turn, insufficient cash on hand, and no white knights in sight, Orange County filed for bankruptcy on 6 December 1994, citing the need for a "centralized forum within which to resolve any and all competing claims while assuring that nothing related to the problems of the fund interferes with the county's ability to provide any and all essential services that the residents of Orange County have come to expect from their government."[23]

FIRE SALE OF THE OCIP PORTFOLIO

Soon after bankruptcy was declared, Orange County appointed Tom Hayes, former California state treasurer, to reorganize the county's finances. After receiving permission from the U.S. Bankruptcy Court, Hayes set his sights on selling the portfolio with as little negative market disruption as possible and investing the recovered funds in safe, short term assets. Hayes hired Salomon Brothers to help, and, within six weeks, OCIP's assets were sold. Ironically, the sale of OCIP's assets received support from an unexpected source. In December 1994, the Mexican peso crisis led to the flight of international capital from developing nations to the safety of the U.S. dollar.

[23]Anonymous. "Repercussions: Riley's Statement on Chapter 9 Filing." *Orange County Register* (7 December 1994), A01.

The increase in the demand for U.S. financial assets raised security prices, adding to the earnings of Orange County.

Monday-Morning Quarterbacking

After the crisis subsided, analysts began to reconsider if the Orange County failure could truly be classified as a derivative-related failure, if a declaration of bankruptcy was really called for, if it was necessary to liquidate OCIP's portfolio at such a rapid pace, and if there was a way the failure could have been predicted.

WAS ORANGE COUNTY TRULY A DERIVATIVE-RELATED FAILURE?

Orange County's troubles are often referred to as a derivatives disaster. Nevertheless, even though derivative-related securities accounted for a significant portion of the decline in OCIP's portfolio value, Orange County's misfortune appears to be related more to leverage, bad management, and relatively large holdings of fixed-income securities than it was to mistakes from investing in derivative instruments. Exhibit 6.12 shows the composition of

Exhibit 6.12 Orange County Investment Pool Portfolio: 1 December 1994 *(Millions of Dollars)*

	Book Value	Market Value	Loss
Cash	646.5	646.5	$0.0
Collateralized mortgage obligations	228.5	222.8	$5.7
Structured notes	7,806.3	7,083.5	722.8
Dual-index notes	*150.0*	*137.4*	*12.6*
Floating-rate notes	*588.0*	*560.7*	*27.3*
Index-amortizing notes	*1,699.0*	*1,562.3*	*136.7*
Inverse floating-rate notes	*5,369.2*	*4,823.1*	*546.1*
Fixed-income securities	11,857.3	11,221.9	635.4
Total assets	20,538.5	19,174.7	1,363.8
Reverse repurchase agreements	−12,988.1	−13,055.2	67.1
Net value	7,550.6	6,119.5	1,431.0

Merton H. Miller and David J. Ross, "The Orange County Bankruptcy and Its Aftermath: Some New Evidence," *Journal of Derivatives*, 4(4) (Summer 1997), p. 53

OCIP's portfolio on 1 December 1994, the day it reported a $1.5 billion unrealized loss. OCIP held no forwards, futures, options, or swaps. The decline in its portfolio value was due to three main causes: structured notes ($722.8 million), fixed-income securities ($635.4 million), and reverse repurchase agreements ($67.1 million). Of these three sources, the losses on fixed-income securities and reverse repos were not derivatives related, but rather due to the rise in market interest rates and the reduction in spreads. Only if you considered reverse repurchase agreements to be a form of forward contract could you classify these losses as derivative-related, and even then, they would account for less than 5% of the total decline in OCIP's portfolio value.

Of the losses on structured notes, inverse floaters were the major culprits, accounting for more than three-quarters of the $722.8 million decline in portfolio value, but were all of these losses truly derivatives related? An inverse floater can be replicated by a floating-rate note (with a bullet repayment) and an interest rate swap that has double the notional principal. Therefore, rising interest rates caused both the floating-rate portion and the derivative portion of the structured note to change. To calculate the pure derivative-related losses from these structured notes, one would have to separate the value of the derivative from the floating rate note, and such an analysis would reduce the size of the derivative-related losses somewhat below the figures given in Exhibit 6.12. Regardless, the loss of anywhere near $700 million (for all structured notes) is substantial by virtually any comparative measure of derivative-related failure.

Another way to address whether Orange County's losses were mainly derivative-related is to rely on information provided by Robert Citron prior to the failure. When he was interviewed in April 1994, Citron revealed that only 20% of the OCIP portfolio was invested in derivative-related assets.[24] If that figure were accurate and if these derivative positions resulted in losses proportional to their share of the portfolio, then, at most, $328 million of the total $1.64 billion of losses were derivatives related. Losses of such magnitude would put Orange County into a special class of derivative-related failures, but it also would scale back dramatically the notoriety of the failure and weaken its relationship to derivative instruments.

WAS ORANGE COUNTY REALLY BANKRUPT?

The U.S. Bankruptcy Court ruled that Orange County's declaration of bankruptcy was valid, and, therefore, the county deserved Chapter 9 protection from creditors wanting immediate repayment, investors trying to cash out

---

[24]Anonymous, "County Official Lists Securities: Derivatives Attracted Criticism," *Wall Street Journal* (20 April 1994). p. C21.

their investments, reverse repo counterparties seeking additional collateral to back their loans, and other parties with whom Orange County had a long list of financial obligations.[25] Two financial measures that can give us insight into the economic health of Orange County when it declared bankruptcy are solvency (i.e., if the county's assets exceeded its liabilities) and liquidity (i.e., if the county had sufficient cash assets to meet demand).

Was Orange County Insolvent?

After careful analysis, the court decided that Orange County was insolvent; nevertheless, despite its thorough analysis, lingering doubts remain as to whether this decision was correct. Exhibit 6.12 (column 3) shows that on 1 December 1994, the market value of OCIP's assets was approximately $6.1 billion greater than the value of its reverse repurchase agreements, indicating that Orange County seemed far from insolvent. With a positive net value so large, it is hard to understand the basis on which the U.S. Bankruptcy Court made its determination.[26]

Was Orange County Really Illiquid?

On 1 December 1994, the day its catastrophic losses were reported, OCIP had almost $650 million of cash (i.e., highly liquid assets) at its disposal (see Exhibit 6.12). Clearly, these funds could not have satisfied all the cash demands from withdrawals, early pension fund redemptions, calls by counterparties for increased collateral, threats from banks to withdraw credit lines, and the payment of operating expenses (e.g., salaries); so, granting Orange County relief from its creditors was probably a reflection of justifiable liquidity needs. Nevertheless, OCIP had plenty of marketable securities it could have sold, along with approximately $32 million in monthly net interest earnings and its normal cash inflows of deposits from mandatory investors. As a result, the liquidity situation at OCIP may have been bad, but it may not have been as bad as it first appeared.[27] Again, the basis on which the U.S. Bankruptcy Court made its determination can be questioned.

WAS IT A MISTAKE TO LIQUIDATE THE OCIP PORTFOLIO?

Debate concerning the liquidation of OCIP's portfolio is moot because, to a large extent, liquidation was not a choice Orange County made on its own.

---

[25]The bankruptcy court ruling was made on 16 May 1996.

[26]See Merton H. Miller and David J. Ross. "The Orange County Bankruptcy and its Aftermath: Some New Evidence," *Journal of Derivatives*, 4(4) (Summer 1997), pp. 51–60.

[27]OCIP earned $94 million in monthly interest and paid $62 million on its outstanding reverse repurchase agreements. See Merton H. Miller and David J. Ross, "The Orange County Bankruptcy and Its Aftermath: Some New Evidence," *Journal of Derivatives*, 4(4) (Summer 1997), p. 54.

As the county defaulted on its debts, OCIP assets were confiscated by counterparties and sold at market prices. Of the total OCIP portfolio, more than half was liquidated in this manner.

But suppose investors and creditors were (somehow) convinced to wait. Exhibit 6.13 shows that the OCIP portfolio was liquidated at precisely the worst time possible. Interest rates in December 1994 peaked at just over 7%, and, during the next year, they declined by nearly 2%. After Orange County declared bankruptcy, OCIP's entire investment strategy changed. Previously, Robert Citron earned his profits by exploiting the upward-sloping yield curve (i.e., borrowing short term with reverse repurchase agreements and investing in higher-earning, medium-term assets), betting on declining interest rates, and leveraging the OCIP portfolio. The new strategy was to liquidate all existing positions, invest the funds in money market assets, and unlever the OCIP portfolio.

Clearly, if the administrators of OCIP had waited, slowly reduced the portfolio's leverage, and taken measured steps to liquidate the portfolio, results would have been remarkably different. By one estimate, if OCIP had pursued this hold-and-slowly-liquidate strategy from 1 December 1994 to 29 March 1996, the OCIP portfolio would have recovered approximately $1.8 billion of its value—an increase that would have eliminated all

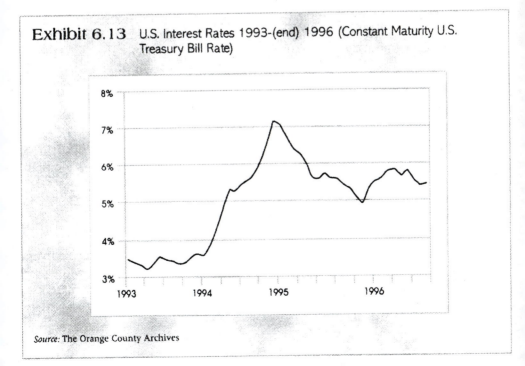

Exhibit 6.13 U.S. Interest Rates 1993-(end) 1996 (Constant Maturity U.S. Treasury Bill Rate)

Source: The Orange County Archives

the losses reported on 1 December 1994 and contributed a significant positive return.[28]

The problem was that no one knew in December 1994 how future interest rates would change. Had they risen, OCIP stood to lose considerably more than it already had, and further losses could have impoverished Orange County's already cash-strapped municipalities.

COULD THE DEBACLE HAVE BEEN PREDICTED?

Even though the future is unknown, reasonable estimates and efforts to moderate risk can still be made. For instance, Value at Risk (VaR) analysis might have been helpful to all the affected parties by clarifying the risks facing OCIP.[29] Based on OCIP's December 1994 portfolio, VaR analysis would have shown that OCIP faced a 5% chance of losing at least $1.1 billion (in addition to the existing losses) during the coming year. The same figures would also have shown that OCIP faced a 5% chance of earning at least $1.3 billion.[30] At a 5% level of confidence, a VaR of $1.1 billion means that once in 20 years there should be losses greater than or equal to $1.1 billion. Ironically, 20 years was about the tenure of Robert Citron as Orange County's treasurer–tax collector. Of course over the years, the size of OCIP's portfolio changed, as did the composition of its assets and liabilities, but still, one wonders if Orange County's Board of Supervisors and Administrative Officer would have challenged more critically the risks that Citron was taking if it knew OCIP's VaR and internalized its 20-to-1 meaning.

As it turned out, interest rates fell precipitously during 1995, thereby catapulting OCIP into the upper tail of the distribution, but OCIP administrators had no way of knowing this in December 1994. Faced with an emergency, the possibility of losing significantly more, and only the remote prospect of turning its losses into gains, the administrators decided that the risk of waiting and liquidating the portfolio slowly was too high.

Sentences, Blame, and Reform

For municipal bankruptcies, Orange County was in a class of its own. To put the Orange County bankruptcy into perspective, consider this. From 1937

---

[28]Merton H. Miller and David J. Ross, "The Orange County Bankruptcy and Its Aftermath: Some New Evidence," *Journal of Derivatives*, 4(4) (Summer 1997), pp. 54–57.

[29]Philippe Jorion, "Lessons from the Orange County Bankruptcy," *Journal of Derivatives*, 4(4) (Summer 1997), pp. 61–66.

[30]Ibid. As the basis for his analysis, Jorion used more than 40 years of historical data on fluctuations of one-year U.S. Treasury bill rates.

to 1994 (more than 55 years), a total of 362 municipal bankruptcies (i.e., under Chapter 9) in the United States had been filed with total debts amounting to $217 million.[31] Most of these bankruptcies involved relatively small municipalities and minor amounts of money; so, Orange County's colossal $1.64 billion loss was a paradigm-shifting event that set a new standard for municipal failures.

ROBERT CITRON

In large part, Orange County's bankruptcy was the result of a recklessly large bet by Robert Citron, but it was also caused by incompetence. After the dust settled, it became clear that Robert Citron was an inept manager of the leveraged portfolio he created. Despite 24 years of experience, Citron had not acquired the skills or staff needed to price, track, or hedge the speculative positions he took. In effect, Robert Citron ran an out-of-control hedge fund, but up until the end, Citron felt that it was the world, and not he, that had gone mad because Citron was convinced that Orange County had suffered only "paper losses" that never would have to be realized.

Court testimony added to the pile of evidence that Robert Citron was unable to manage the OCIP portfolio. Psychologists and Citron's attorney testified that Citron, the "financial wizard," had only seventh-grade-level math ability and performed so poorly on tests that he "bordered on brain-damaged."[32] Further testimony revealed that he suffered from a form of dementia and often relied on a mail-order astrologer and a psychic for his interest rate forecasts.[33] Chillingly, Ernie Schneider, Orange County chief administrator, rationalized Citron's behavior by saying, "Bob was always very unusual, eccentric, different, but I attributed it to, you know, brilliant psychics. Chess masters are not normal people."[34]

On 27 April 1995, after a 15-minute arraignment, Citron pleaded guilty to six felony counts and three special enhancements.[35] He was led away handcuffed, booked at the county jail, and then released on his own recognizance with bail set at $25,000. Under state sentencing guidelines, Citron faced a maximum prison stay of 14 years and a $10 million fine. The minimum penalty was six months in jail. Most of the charges against Citron

[31] Mark Baldassare, *When Government Fails: The Orange County Bankruptcy*, Berkeley: Public Policy Institute of California and the University of California Press, 1998.
[32] See Chris Knap, "Jail for Citron/O.C. Financial Crisis," *Orange County Register* (20 November 1996), p.A01.
[33] For the record, Citron's psychic told him that December 1994 would be a bad month. The psychic was correct, but, unfortunately, Citron did not listen.
[34] Ricky Young, "Blame Game: Testimony Painted Supervisors as Unwilling to Take Responsibility or Take Action," *Orange County Register* (29 December 1995), A01.
[35] Anonymous, "The 4/95 Plea/Sentencing Agreement of Bob Citron Re: His Criminal Role in the Orange County Bankruptcy," http://www.lectlaw.com/files/curl2.htm.

related to his misallocation of returns, misappropriation of funds, and misleading/false statements. Citron was not charged with embezzlement, conspiracy, collusion, fraud, or trading for personal gain.

In the end, he was sentenced to serve one year in the county jail, pay a $100,000 fine for his financial shenanigans (e.g., siphoning off the interest earnings from investments made by schools, cities, and some small agencies and placing them in the county-run investment account), serve five years of supervised probation, and perform 1,000 hours of community service. Citron ended up serving just nine months in a work-release program, which means the 71-year-old never spent a night in jail. Rather, he worked in the prison during the day but was allowed to go home in the evening. The light sentence was due largely to Citron's open remorse throughout the trial, his cooperation with investigating authorities, and his deteriorating health.

In the trial, Los Angeles Superior Court Judge J. Stephen Czuleger reprimanded Citron for "gambling with public money," and he chastised Citron for failing in his oath and obligations to the community. To Czuleger, the loss of public funds bothered him less than the damage Citron had done to the credibility of public officials.

OTHER PLAYERS: MATTHEW RAABE AND MERRILL LYNCH

In his three-page plea, Citron implicated Matthew Raabe, former Orange County assistant treasurer, claiming that Raabe assisted in falsifying OCIP's annual financial statements and lied about the fund's financial condition. In 1996 (19 months after the bankruptcy), Citron went further and testified that Raabe was responsible for conjuring up the scheme to divert funds from cities and special districts to Orange County's budget.

On 5 May 1997, Raabe was convicted on five counts of fraud and misappropriation of $88.5 million and sentenced to three years in the state prison. After serving only 41 days in jail, he was released, and in November 1997, his conviction was overturned on grounds that the former district attorney (Mike Capizzi) should not have prosecuted the case, due to his heavy involvement with the Orange County bankruptcy. In 2001, the California Supreme Court refused to review the overturned conviction. Raabe was free.[36]

Orange County filed a civil suit against Merrill Lynch, its major broker/dealer, on grounds that it sold improper and illegal securities to Citron and made false statements in its security sales. Orange County prosecutors even recruited Citron to help develop their case. Merrill Lynch claimed that its conduct with Orange County was proper and professional and accused Orange

---

[36]See Anonymous, "Ex-Orange County Official Is Convicted on Five Counts," *Wall Street Journal* (Eastern edition), New York, N.Y. (5 May 1997), B.12, and Deborah Finestone, "Calif. Supreme Court Won't Review Raabe Decision," *The Bond Buyer* 335 (31079) (6 February 2001), 4.

County of "letting the real culprit off because he's going to help you go after the deep pockets."[37] In 1998, the case was settled out of court.[38]

STEALTH SUPERVISION: SHARED BLAME

Even though Robert Citron was the chief protagonist in the Orange County bankruptcy, the lack of adequate supervision and control of the risks in OCIP's portfolio were significant contributing factors. Orange County's Board of Supervisors, the SEC, credit rating agencies, media, and residents of Orange County were all looking in the wrong direction when the fatal blow was struck.

Many people wondered why the Securities and Exchange Commission, which met with Citron in 1994, and multiple independent audits throughout 1994 found nothing unusual in the OCIP portfolio. They were also baffled about why the two largest U.S. credit rating agencies, Standard and Poor's and Moody's Investor Service, gave Orange County's portfolio in 1994 their next-to-the-highest ratings (AA and Aa1, respectively). The reason for Orange County being given a clean bill of heath appears to be, in large part, because, at each of the levels of overview, focus was put mainly on Citron's return and credit risk, rather than on the risks that brought on the Orange County collapse (i.e., market risk and liquidity risk).

Especially disappointing was the oversight role played by Orange County's Board of Supervisors. During the court proceedings, one Orange County supervisor admitted that his "knowledge of public finance matters was nil prior to the bankruptcy"; he never read any of Citron's reports and resolutions requesting approval for hundreds of millions of dollars in bond issues, and he rarely asked questions because "I wouldn't know the kinds of questions to ask."[39] In December 1995, the Orange County grand jury charged Board of Supervisors members Roger Stanton and William Steiner and auditor-controller Steven E. Lewis with willful misconduct, but these charges eventually were dismissed by the courts.

GOVERNANCE REFORMS

Having been burnt once and wanting to ensure it did not happen again, Orange County implemented a series of financial governance reforms. The bankruptcy spurred the establishment of a crisis management team, and the county appointed a chief executive officer and chief financial officer to make serious budget cuts and bring its financial house in order.

[37]Michael Utley, "Former Citron Assistant Is Implicated in Guilty Pleas," *The Bond Buyer,* 312 (29639) (1 May 1995), 1.
[38]For more on the legal proceedings after the Orange County bankruptcy, see Appendix 6.4, What Happened to the Mountain of Orange County Legal Cases?
[39]Ibid.

A package of state and local reforms was passed that mandated more transparent and timely reporting and oversight. An internal auditor was appointed, who reported directly to the Board of Supervisors. Public officials were required to make open disclosure of possible conflicts of interest. Prohibitions were imposed on oversight committee members from receiving gifts. Austere investment guidelines were introduced, which put top priority on acquiring assets with relatively low risk and high liquidity. Portfolio managers were constrained from leveraging investments (e.g., entering into reverse repurchase agreements), transacting derivative deals, and purchasing structured notes. The selection of brokers, dealers, and investment advisors also received greater scrutiny.[40]

Lessons Learned from Orange County

There is a lot to be learned from financial catastrophes, and two of the major lessons learned from the Orange County crisis are (1) safety, liquidity, *and* high yield are an impossible combination, and (2) if you can't explain it, then don't do it.

SAFETY, LIQUIDITY, *AND* HIGH YIELD ARE AN IMPOSSIBLE COMBINATION

One of the most basic relationships in finance is the direct relationship between risk and expected return. In markets where billions are invested, it is difficult to earn returns that consistently beat the market average, and investment funds that do are most likely carrying greater than average risks. For this reason, risk *and* return should be reported simultaneously to investors for rational choices to be made. To this end, portfolio managers should be required to communicate (and investors should demand) timely, transparent information on the risk and return profiles of their portfolios.

Value at Risk (VaR) analysis could have aided greatly in this effort because it communicates to investors the odds of losing a certain amount (or more) during a given period of time. So long as the investors understand these risks and are willing to bear their downside consequences, mistakes as well as the grounds for legal suits and crushed expectations are diminished.

IF YOU CAN'T EXPLAIN IT, THEN DON'T DO IT

As financial instruments become more complex, valuing them and tracking their risks requires financial sophistication that is beyond the abilities

---

[40]Rob Jameson, "Case Study: Orange County." *ERisk Learning,* June 2001. Available at http://www.erisk.com/Learning/CaseStudies/OrangeCounty.asp. Accessed 28 December 2007.

and/or time constraints of most investors. Even though investors in OCIP and regulators can be criticized for not demanding better explanations of Robert Citron's investment strategies, Citron is culpable for his inability to articulate them clearly. As intricate as investment strategies might be, there should always be a way of boiling them down to a short, informative overview. For instance, Citron might have explained his strategy like this:

> In the past, OCIP beat the average market return because medium-term interest rates remained above the short-term rates and because interest rates fell. During the coming year, we believe these conditions will continue, and therefore the OCIP portfolio is structured to profit from these two expectations. To capitalize on our outlook, we have leveraged the OCIP portfolio by borrowing about $2 for every $1 you have invested in the pool. More specifically, OCIP now has about $20.5 billion in total assets, of which $13 billion were purchased with borrowed funds, and the rest was financed with your (investor) funds. This (nearly) 3:1 leverage factor increases substantially the amount of risk you are facing.
>
> So far as risks are concerned, OCIP's assets have virtually no default risk because the portfolio contains only the best creditors (like the U.S. government), but OCIP does face a greater degree of market risk and liquidity risk. Market risk is the potential for OCIP's portfolio value to fall due to rising interest rates. Liquidity risk is the potential that we will not be able to meet the cash demands of investors, creditors, and/or investment counterparties.
>
> By our best estimates, there is a 5% chance that the currently structured portfolio could lose $1.1 billion or more during the next year and an equal chance that it could gain $1.3 billion or more during the same period. Seen another way, as of November 1994, the OCIP portfolio stands to win or lose about $550 million for every 1% change in market interest rates.

Conclusion

Orange County recovered quickly and maintained its position as a thriving community, with high-quality services and a per capita gross community product that was above the California average. Its credit ratings recovered lost ground, and Orange County's budget was in the black for the remainder of the 20th century. Nevertheless, progress came with a huge sacrifice in terms of increased debt levels and the loss of numerous municipal jobs. In the end, it was the combination of a healthy California economy and Orange County's willingness to make tough decisions that saved the day. Orange

County learned a valuable lesson, but the price tag on this lesson was higher than any community would want to pay.

The chances of a financial catastrophe like this happening again are remote because Orange County and the state of California made significant financial reforms focusing on transparency, overview, and timely reporting. Nevertheless, in any complex structure (e.g., a municipal government or company), there is always the chance of a catastrophe springing from a totally unexpected source. Risk management systems protect against the risks we see, but these systems also add an additional dimension of complexity to an already complex organization. The fear of many is that this increased complexity could, itself, be the source of the next disaster.

Review Questions

1. On what grounds can a case be made that the Orange County bankruptcy was *not* a derivative-related failure? On what grounds can a case be made that it was a derivative-related failure?

2. Explain how Robert Citron was able to earn above-average returns when U.S. interest rates fell.

3. Explain whether the Board of Supervisors was culpable for Orange County's bankruptcy. Given a second chance, what should the board have done differently?

4. Explain why credit risk alone is not a sufficient measure of a portfolio's overall risk and loss potential.

5. Why did Orange County recover so quickly after the default in December 1994? What internal changes took place and what external factors helped the county to recover?

6. What role did Proposition 13 play in the Orange County failure?

7. Explain how reverse repurchase agreements allowed Robert Citron to leverage the OCIP portfolio. Then explain how this leverage led to mammoth OCIP losses.

8. Explain the bet Robert Citron made with Orange County's funds and how it went bad.

9. Explain how Orange County's market risk led to liquidity risk and credit risk.

10. Was it a mistake to liquidate the bulk of OCIP's portfolio within six weeks of bankruptcy?

11. Was Orange County really bankrupt?

Further Reading

Please visit www.prenhall.com/marthinsen, where you can find the following embellishments on and extensions of this chapter.

- Appendix 6.1: Orange County's Recovery Plan
- Appendix 6.2: What Happened to Orange County's Public Services?
- Appendix 6.3: What Happened to Orange County's Debt Level and Credit Rating?
- Appendix 6.4: What Happened to the Mountain of Orange County Legal Cases?

Bibliography

Anonymous. "County Official Lists Securities: Derivatives Attracted Criticism." *Wall Street Journal* (20 April 1994), p. C21.

Anonymous. "OC Finance: Financial Issues, Restructuring." 20 May 1997. Orange County homepage available at: http://www.oc.ca.gov/. Accessed 19 December 2007.

Anonymous. "The 4/95 Plea/Sentencing Agreement of Bob Citron Re: His Criminal Role in the Orange County Bankruptcy." *Lectric Law Library*, Available at: http://www.lectlaw.com/files/cur12.htm. Accessed 19 December 2007.

Baldassare, Mark. *When Government Fails: The Orange County Bankruptcy*. Berkeley: Public Policy Institute of California and the University of California Press, 1998.

Fleming, Michael J., and Garbade, Kenneth D. "The Repurchase Agreement Refined: GCF Repo." *Current Issues in Economics and Finance*. Federal Reserve Bank of New York, 9(6) (June 2003), pp. 1–7. Available at http://www.newyorkfed.org/research/current issues/ci9-6.pdf. Accessed 19 December 2007.

Glassman, James K. "From Orange County, Eight Survival Lessons." *The Washington Post*. 1 January 1995. p. H1.

Jameson, Rob. "Case Study: Orange County." *ERisk Learning*, June 2001. Available at: http://www.erisk.com/Learning/CaseStudies/OrangeCounty.asp. Accessed 28 December 2007.

Jorion, Philippe. "Lessons from the Orange County Bankruptcy." *Journal of Derivatives* 4(4) (Summer 1997), pp. 61–66.

Jorion, Philippe. "Philippe Jorion's Internet Case Study: Orange County Case—Using Value at Risk to Control Financial Risk." Available at: http://www.gsm.uci.edu/~jorion/oc/case.html. Accessed 2 July 2003.

Miller, Merton H., and Ross, David J. "The Orange County Bankruptcy and its Aftermath: Some New Evidence." *Journal of Derivatives* 4(4) (Summer 1997), pp. 51–60.

Orange County Press Releases. Various. Orange County homepage. Available at: http://www.oc.ca.gov. Accessed 2 July 2003.

7

Barings Bank PLC

Leeson's Lessons

Introduction

Nicholas ("Nick") William Leeson was relaxing at a luxury resort in Malaysia, when he heard that Barings Bank PLC, London's oldest merchant bank, had lost $1.3 billion (£860 million), and the rogue trader responsible for these losses was fleeing from Singapore authorities. Though he was staggered by the size of the losses and stunned to learn that Barings Bank was in administration, Leeson was not at all surprised by the news because it was *his* massive speculative losses on the futures market over a brief two-and-a-half-year period that wiped out this venerable bank.

Leeson was chief trader and head of settlements for Barings' wholly owned subsidiary in Singapore, dealing mainly in futures contracts for Japanese stocks, government bonds, and euroyen deposits. Because of his huge trading profits, Leeson earned a reputation among Barings' management in London, Singapore, and Tokyo as a "star performer," and he was given virtually free rein. Many of Barings Bank's senior management believed that Leeson possessed an innate *feel* for the markets, but the story of this rogue trader reveals that he had nothing of the sort. How, one wonders, could

Barings' management have been so seriously mistaken and for so long?

This chapter addresses two main questions about the Barings collapse: why did the bank give Leeson so much discretionary authority to trade, allowing him to operate without any trading limits and with no effective oversight by mangers and internal control systems; and what trading strategy did Leeson employ to lose so much in such a short period of time?

Barings Bank PLC

Barings Bank PLC was the blue-blooded British merchant bank founded in 1762 by Sir Francis Baring.[1] The bank catered to royalty and was at the pinnacle of the London financial world. Among its many endeavors over the centuries, Barings financed the Louisiana Purchase in 1803, the Napoleonic Wars, and England's wars against rebellious America (1775–1783). The bank was also responsible for floating Guinness® stock in 1886, making it the first brewery to be incorporated on the London Stock Exchange. But the road to success was not always smooth. Barings survived wars and depressions but nearly went bankrupt in 1890 as a result of imprudent investments in Argentina, surviving only because of a last minute bailout organized by the Bank of England.[2] Despite occasional moments of turmoil, Barings was always one of the most well-placed and highly regarded players in London's financial hub. How ironic that this centuries-old bank would be toppled by one man operating out of Barings' remote Singapore office!

During the 1990s, Barings' operations focused on banking, asset management, and securities brokering, which created an internal culture clash that led to conflicts and back-office politics. Barings' bankers and asset managers stressed caution, deliberation, and long-term relationships over short-term gains. By contrast, its brokers were more adventuresome and spur-of-the-moment, with short-term gains uppermost in their minds. These two factions fought to allocate Barings' limited capital. The bank's decision to

[1]The bank was originally named the John and Francis Baring Company. In 1806, its name was changed to Baring Brothers & Co.
[2]The bailout cost the consortium £17,326,000, which was more than £1 billion when measured in terms of 1995 of pounds. Ironically, this amount is close to what was needed in February 1995 to purchase Barings Bank, recapitalize it, and absorb the bank's losses. See Stephen Fay, *The Collapse of Barings*, London: W.W. Norton, 1997, p. 11.

expand globally was divisive because its capital could not support equal expansion of all business lines. As a result, Barings decided in 1993 to merge its capital reserves to support all lines of business instead of allocating capital separately to each one. Unfortunately, this decision removed a major source of control over Leeson's activities.

Incessant bickering among Barings' senior managers in London and back-biting between executives in London and Singapore caused petty office politics to get in the way of good decision making and weakened traditional lines of authority. Leeson reported, in theory at least, to managers in London, Singapore, and Tokyo, but no one took responsibility for him. Internal discussions did not conclusively distinguish whether Leeson was in charge of settlements, compliance, arbitrage, proprietary trading, *or* just executing customer orders. In reality, he was doing *all* of these jobs, as well as taking unauthorized futures and option positions.

Nick Leeson: From London to Jakarta to Singapore

Nick Leeson (Exhibit 7.1) came from humble origins compared to most of Barings' officers. He had no family ties to the nobility, did not attend Eton, and did not serve in the Coldstream Guards. The son of a Watford plasterer, Leeson's first job at Barings (1989) was in the back office settling futures and option

Exhibit 7.1 Nick Leeson

trades, but he rose swiftly. His big break came in 1990 when he was sent to Barings' Indonesia office in Jakarta to sort out a tangled mess in the back office.

The Indonesia office had built a worrisome £100 million exposure in stocks and bonds that local operations could not reconcile. Trading volume on the Indonesian stock exchange had grown so fast that Barings' procedures for delivering stock and bond certificates could not keep up with the volume. The bank had hundreds of small discrepancies between the certificates it held and the certificates it was supposed to hold. As a result, Barings was in possession of securities worth millions of pounds that should have been paid for and delivered to customers. A team of four, including Leeson, was sent to sort out the problems in Indonesia. Within 10 months, the team had reduced the Jakarta exposure to a tenth of its original size. Leeson returned to London in 1991, and in the following year, was rewarded with the position of chief trader and head of settlements for Barings Futures (Singapore) (BFS). Later that same year, Leeson was promoted to Assistant Director and General Manager.

Barings Securities Singapore (BSS) was incorporated in 1986 and granted non-clearing membership on the Singapore International Monetary Exchange (SIMEX). At first, BSS' activities focused mainly on sock market transactions. But during the early 1990s, Barings decided to expand the bank's worldwide activities in Southeast Asia so it could take advantage of the region's relatively rapid growth and reduce its emphasis on Japan's waning stock and warrant markets. Therefore in 1992, Barings Bank applied for and received clearing membership for a newly established company called Barings Futures (Singapore).[3] Leeson's appointment to BFS was the ingredient needed to activate Barings' three seats on SIMEX.

What Was Leeson Supposed to Be Doing at BFS?

In a monumental lapse of good judgment, Barings Bank decided to make Leeson, who was only 25 years old and had no previous trading experience, the chief trader and floor manager for BFS on SIMEX, as well as the head of trade settlements.[4] You may ask, "What well-managed bank would allow its chief trader to be in charge of the back office?"

---

[3]BFS was a wholly owned subsidiary of Barings Securities (International) Ltd.

[4]In early 1992, Leeson applied to England's Securities and Futures Authority (SFA) for registration as a dealer. Shortly afterwards, Barings Bank withdrew his application when SFA found that Leeson had falsely stated that there were no civil judgments against him for unpaid debts. Leeson made the same false statement to SIMEX later in 1992 when he applied for dealer registration in Singapore. SIMEX did not catch Leeson's false statement, and Barings did not bring Leeson's civil judgments to the attention of SIMEX. See Bank of England, Board of Banking Supervision, *Report of the Board of Banking Supervision Inquiry into the Circumstances of the Collapse of Barings London* (ordered by the House of Commons), (July 1995).

The answer is easier to understand once you realize that, initially, BFS was supposed to be executing orders placed exclusively by Barings' affiliates worldwide on behalf of their customers, an activity called "agency trading." As a result, supervisors reasoned that any loss of control resulting from putting Leeson in charge of both the front and back offices would be insignificant compared to the cost savings from having one person perform both jobs.

But as competition became keener, Leeson's (and BFS') responsibilities expanded. By 1993, Leeson was allowed to trade options for clients and to conduct inter-exchange arbitrage (also called "switching"). Most of his arbitrage activities involved simultaneously buying and selling financially identical futures contracts that were offered at different prices on two exchanges, a practice called "futures arbitrage." But he also engaged in "cash-futures arbitrage," which involved trading large baskets of stocks sold in the cash markets and contracts in the futures markets.

Even though these arbitrage transactions exposed Barings' equity to a potential risk, the threat was considered to be minimal because the time gap between buy and sell orders could be measured in seconds (or fractions of a second). Therefore, Barings would have an almost continuous stream of offsetting contracts that were traded simultaneously on two exchanges.

In 1994, Leeson landed a very large customer (Philippe Bonnefoy) and was given permission by senior management to trade for his account.[5] Bonnefoy worked for the Bahamas-based European Trust and Banking Company and was known to trade in excess of 5,000 contracts per day. In a good month, Leeson could earn commissions of $100,000 or more from this business. To Leeson's supervisors, trading for Bonnefoy's account posed no major security breach because the bank's equity was not at risk. Only if BFS took independent positions would Barings be exposed, and such positions were prohibited by the bank's internal rules.

Leeson focused his arbitrage activities on three futures contracts: the Japanese Nikkei 225 stock index,[6] 10- year Japanese government bonds (JGB),[7] and three-month euroyen deposits.[8] The Nikkei 225 futures contract was traded simultaneously on SIMEX and the Osaka Stock Exchange

---

[5] See Nick Leeson (with Edward Whitley), *Rogue Trader: How I Brought Down Barings Banks and Shook the Financial World*. Boston: Little, Brown, 1996, 50.

[6] A full description of the Nikkei 225 Index can be found at Nikkei Net Interactive. http://www .nni.nikkei.co.jp/. Accessed 24 December 2007. A full description of the Nikkei 225 futures contract can be found at http://www.sgx.com/psv/derivatives/futures_options/equity_index/index.shtml. Accessed 24 December 2007.

[7] A full description of the futures market for 10-year Japanese government bonds can be found at http://www.mizuho-sc.com/english/ebond/bonds/jgb.html. Accessed 24 December 2007.

[8] A full description of the three-month euroyen futures market can be found at http://www.sgx.com/psv/ derivatives/futures_options/interest_rates/SGX_Euroyen_TIBOR.shtml. Accessed 24 December 2007.

(OSE); the JGB futures contract was traded simultaneously on SIMEX and the Tokyo Stock Exchange (TSE), and the three-month euroyen futures contract was traded simultaneously on SIMEX and the Tokyo International Financial Futures Exchange (TIFFE).[9]

Throughout the day, Leeson would communicate the futures prices quoted on SIMEX to Barings' traders on the Japanese exchanges. For example, if the Nikkei 225 futures contract was trading at 18,<u>000</u> on SIMEX and 18,<u>100</u> on OSE, Leeson would buy in Singapore and the OSE trader would simultaneously sell in Osaka to lock in a profit. These deals were simple, safe, and, therefore, the profit from each one was small. If Leeson had only been doing arbitrage trades of that sort, he would probably never have caused any disturbance. But he was also engaging in outright "naked" speculation, and that was how he lost more than $1 billion. How was he able to evade his managers, as well as internal and external auditors for so long?

Five Eights Account

Barings' internal guidelines required affiliates to post discrepancies and trading mistakes to an Errors Account that was linked to headquarters. That way, the bank's books would balance, discrepancies would be isolated and dealt with separately, and the bank could make its regulatory filings without delay. Any open positions resulting from trading mistakes and separated in this way were expected to be closed and the resulting losses (or profits) charged to Barings' earnings. The bank intended for these discrepancies to be handled within a short period of time (e.g., a day).

Brokers, like BFS, and banks, like Barings, normally have error accounts because traders make mistakes, back-office settlements are not always synchronous, and some trades are disputed. In the melee of SIMEX's open-outcry trading sessions, it is easy for traders to occasionally buy when they should have sold, execute trades at incorrect prices or maturities, and make mistakes recording transactions.

When BFS began trading SIMEX contracts on 1 July 1992, it already had an errors account called the "99905 Account," which was linked directly to Barings London. During the first two days of trading, Leeson's team made a bevy of small errors and unreconciled trades, which were dutifully recorded in the errors account and reported to headquarters. Inundated with the

---

[9]SIMEX's Nikkei 225 futures contract is half the size of the OSE contract, and SIMEX's JGB futures contract is half the size of the TSE contract; therefore, two SIMEX contracts are *financially identical* to the contracts sold on OSE or TSE. The three-month euroyen contracts on SIMEX and TIFFE are the same size.

Risk Notepad 7.1

Errors Accounts

In addition to correcting trading mistakes and resolving disputed trades, errors accounts are used to reconcile many types of financial transactions for which there are temporary imbalances. Cash management systems often allow intra-day overdrafts and these overdrafts can be large. For instance, a client may send out wire transfers every morning and receive incoming wire transfers every afternoon or may make transfers from different time zones. Every cash management account is supposed to balance at the end of the business day, and if there is an account overdraft, the overdraft amount is supposed to be less than the customer's credit limit.

In that same spirit, securities trading systems customarily allow overdrafts that match the delivery period for securities. For example, stockbrokers allow their customers to sell a stock and then immediately use the proceeds to buy a different one even though the proceeds from the sale will not arrive until several days later. The customer's account is potentially in overdraft because, if the proceeds from the sale do not arrive, the customer still has to pay for the purchased shares.

Big discrepancies can arise between what clients have and what they owe, and these temporary imbalances pose risks. Even if these imbalances arise in the regular course of business and seem innocuous, they can still do harm. One reason is that discrepancies introduce delays in recognizing exposures, but another reason is that they create opportunities for clever and unscrupulous employees to take improper advantage of the permissive treatment of temporary imbalances. Nick Leeson was certainly both clever and unscrupulous.

workload caused by BFS' tiny mistakes and perhaps concerned about attracting greater regulatory scrutiny, headquarters asked Leeson (on 3 July 1992) to set up a second errors account that was not linked directly to London. In this way, BFS' mistakes could be reconciled in Singapore, instead of in London. The Chinese consider the number "8" to be lucky; so Leeson named the new errors account the "88888 Account" (the "Five Eights Account.")[10]

Leeson put himself into the role of guardian and proprietor of his newly discovered door to fortune and fame. During the first week of trading, he had the computer software (i.e., the CONTAC system) changed so that transactions booked to 88888 Account almost vanished from the daily reports sent to London. Specifically, Leeson deleted the system's daily trade

[10]During the investigation that was authorized by Singapore's Minister of Finance, Barings' senior managers denied having any knowledge of the 88888 Account. The inspectors' findings, however, expressed a lack of belief in these assertions. See Lim, Michael Choo San, *Barings Futures (Singapore) Pte Ltd: investigation pursuant to section 231 of the Companies Act (Chapter 50); the report of the Inspectors appointed by the Minister for Finance* Michael Lim Choo San, Nicky Tan Ng Kuang. Singapore: Singapore Ministry of Finance, 1995.

feed, which listed all the trades that BFS executed on behalf of its customers. He did not, however, delete a crucial report that was created from BFS' daily margin feed. This report listed the margin calls for all of BFS' customers, and it included the 88888 Account as a line item. From his experiences working in Jakarta and in Barings' London back office, crafty Leeson knew that the margin feed report posed no problem because it was neither reviewed by Barings' senior managers nor merged into London's broadly used reporting system (called First Futures).

Shortly after Leeson created the 88888 Account, headquarters informed him that it had installed a new computer system, which was capable of handling any and all of BFS' errors. He was instructed to close the 88888 Account and book all future errors in the 99905 Account. But Leeson did not follow orders, and no one in the Barings organization checked to ensure that he had.

The 88888 Account was the keystone of Leeson's financial fraud and deception. Without it, his reckless trades could not have been executed, and this ignominious financial disaster would have been avoided. He used the account to make unauthorized trades in futures and options, falsify reports to headquarters, misstate BFS' profits, record invented trades, and create fictitious accounting entries. Barings had strict trading limits and *believed* that it was diligently monitoring all its traders to make sure they did not exceed their limits, but the bank's systems were not good enough to catch the deception and misrepresentation that Leeson committed.

Leeson's turbocharged use of the 88888 Account began soon after it was created.[11] Between July 1992 and the end of the year, he booked numerous transactions to this account, causing BFS' *hidden* losses to grow from £20,000 to £2 million. When his arbitrage activities began in 1993, Leeson was able to report strikingly large profits, and a major source of these profits came from *cross-trades* he booked in the 88888 Account. Cross-trades occur when a broker matches customers' buy and sell orders internally rather than using the exchange floor. These trades must be for financially identical contracts that have the same total value.[12] Leeson increased his reported profits by recording fictitious buy *and* sell orders in his 88888 Account at prices that

[11]Leeson claims that his unauthorized use of the 88888 Account began about 10 weeks after it was opened. He used the account to cover up a £20,000 trading mistake made by an inexperienced employee who earned £4,000 per year and had just begun working for BFS. The mistake could have been grounds for her dismissal. There is skepticism about Leeson's claim, as records indicate that he used this account improperly from the day it was created. See Nick Leeson (with Edward Whitley), *Rogue Trader: How I Brought Down Barings Banks and Shook the Financial World.* Boston: Little, Brown, 1996, pp. 39–42 and Stephen Fay, *The Collapse of Barings*, London: W.W. Norton, 1997, p. 97.
[12]On SIMEX, a trader must first call out prices for these contracts three times on the exchange floor. Only if the orders are not filled on the floor can the trader execute a cross-trade. Obviously, Leeson did not obey this rule.

guaranteed him profits. He also transacted legitimate business for Barings' worldwide affiliates and then crossed these transactions with fictitious trades in the 88888 Account. As a result, it seemed as if he were making arbitrage profits, but many of these profits were fabricated and were only a small part of the trades he was posting to the 88888 Account. The unreported losses in that account exceeded the arbitrage gains he was reporting.

To protect himself from being caught, Leeson often requested BFS' back office to divide his large cross-trades into a number of smaller deals to make it seem as if they had been transacted in different amounts and at different times throughout the day. In this way, his trades and positions would not arouse the suspicions of Barings' supervisors and auditors. Because he controlled the 88888 Account, Leeson was able to assign any trades he desired to it—and he did. As a result, an inspection of Leeson's normal trading showed robust profits and moderate amounts of futures contracts with positions and activity within authorized trading limits.

Leeson's Trading Strategy: Doubling

Leeson quickly acquired a reputation as a hotshot trader, and success gave him credibility with his managers and colleagues. As a result, his trades were not scrutinized the way they should have been. He made enormous bets on the movement of Japanese stock prices and interest rates. Instead of neutralizing or closing his position when the market turned against him, Leeson viewed every disadvantageous move in the market as an opportunity to recoup his losses. This led him to the fatal strategy of doubling. Doubling requires a trader to double his bets each time he loses. It is a do-or-die strategy that required Leeson to multiply the size of his bets in the 88888 Account so that any favorable movement in Japanese stock prices or interest rates would bring him back to even.

Leeson used his doubling strategy in an attempt to recoup significant losses in the 88888 Account. Meanwhile, he continued to report profits in his regular trading account. After one brush with disaster during the summer of 1993, when the 88888 Account was £6 million in the red, Leeson managed to bring it back to about zero and swore to himself (and to his wife) that he would never use the account again. But like a moth attracted to a flame, Leeson could not resist the twin lures of temptation and access to a seeming limitless supply of funding. After only a weekend's hiatus, he was back at it, with transactions on a larger and grander scale. Leeson had become addicted to fame, which meant he needed to keep his reputation as a brilliant trader. To accomplish that, he had to earn large profits for the bank, which translated into higher bonuses for everyone at Barings, including Leeson and his supervisors.[13]

In 1993, Leeson's Singapore operations reported earnings equal to £8.8 million, but actually, his losses amounted to more than £21 million.[14] During 1994 and the first two months of 1995, his losses increased exponentially. For Leeson, it became an all-or-nothing game. Determined to trade his way out of this predicament, he doubled, redoubled, and then doubled again his positions. But time and time again, the market turned against him. By year-end 1994, BFS' reported profits equaled £28.5 million, but Leeson's actual losses were £185 million, and cumulative losses (i.e., since operations began in 1992) had reached £208 million.[15]

In 1995, the situation got worse—much worse. By February 24, Leeson had lost £600 million, and on February 27 (just three days later), when Barings Bank filed for bankruptcy, his estimated losses had reached £830 million.[16] As for the power of doubling, had Leeson's activities been identified and stopped just one month prior to the Barings collapse (i.e., stopped at the end of January 1995 rather than the end of February 1995), total losses would have been less than one quarter as large, and the bank would have survived. Had he been stopped just one week prior to the end, losses would have been approximately half.

Funding Margin Calls

As the losses in Leeson's 88888 Account grew, he faced a major problem. The purchase or sale of futures contracts required him to deposit funds in margin accounts with the exchanges on which he was placing his trades. Adverse movements in prices often required Leeson to deposit additional variation margin payments because his positions were marked to market on a daily basis. Leeson had to be careful because, if his positions got too large, he would not be able to raise the cash needed to meet the margin calls.

At first, losses in the 88888 Account were small enough for Leeson to fund by diverting BFS' commissions and using client deposits. But as the required payments grew larger, he searched in desperation for other funding alternatives and found four: increasing commission income by offering

[13]For his performance in 1992 and 1993, Leeson received bonuses of £35,746 and £130,000, respectively.
[14]Leeson was able to report these profits because he sold about £30 million of options. See Bank of England, Board of Banking Supervision, *Report of the Board of Banking Supervision Inquiry into the Circumstances of the Collapse of Barings London* (ordered by the House of Commons), (July 1995).
[15]Ibid. For his *stellar* performance in 1994, Leeson was scheduled in February 1995 to receive a bonus of £450,000.
[16]Ibid.

Risk Notepad 7.2

Doubling

To understand Leeson's *doubling strategy*, let's experiment with a fair coin. Suppose we want to win $1; so we flip a coin and bet $1 that it would come up heads. If it comes up tails, we lose $1; so to win the $1 we want, we try again, but this time, we bet $2 that the coin would come up heads on the next toss. If we lose again, we would be out a total of $3, so to win our elusive dollar, the next bet is for $4, and so on it would go. If we lose three consecutive times, our bet on the fourth try (just to win $1) would grow to $8, and after the seventh consecutive loss, we would be betting $128 for the chance of gaining just $1 (see Exhibit RB.7.2.1). Statisticians call it the *gambler's ruin*, and the term accurately describes what happened as Leeson compulsively took bigger and bigger risks.

Doubling strategies are dangerous for two major reasons. First, they can quickly result in gigantic loses, which have to be doubled once again just to break even or to make a small gain. Betting wrong at such high speculative altitudes can threaten the solvency of even the most well-capitalized institutions. The second, and perhaps most frightening, reason the doubling strategy is so dangerous is because, up until the end, individuals who use it often *appear* to be conservative, talented traders who earn rather stable investment returns.[17] As a result, they are relatively unsupervised, which means that, when this strategy goes wrong (i.e., when there are repeated losses), the financial roof falls in virtually overnight and the common reaction of supervisors is one of shock and utter surprise.

A frequently quoted riddle concerning ecological catastrophes can help to show how quickly the doubling strategy can result in catastrophe.

Exhibit RN 7.2.1 Losses from Consecutive Gambles with 50-50 Odds to Win $1

Bet Number	Amount Paid for a Bet to Win $1	Win/Lose	Cumulative Loses from Betting
1	$1	Lose	$1
2	$2	Lose	$1 + $2 = $3
3	$4	Lose	$1 + $2 + $4 = $7
4	$8	Lose	$1 + $2 + $4 + $8 = $15
5	$16	Lose	$1 + $2 + $4 + $8 + $16 = $31
6	$32	Lose	$1 + $2 + $4 + $8 + $16 + $32 = $63
7	$64	Lose	$1 + $2 + $4 + $8 + $16 + $32 + $64 = $127
8	$128	Win?/lose?	Either a loss of $255 or a gain of $1

[17]This is a fact about the strategy and not the people who use it. See, Stephen J. Brown and Onno W. Steenbeek, "Doubling: Nick Leeson's Trading Strategy," *Pacific-Basin Finance Journal* 9 (2001), 83–99.

A lily pad is placed in a pond. Each day thereafter the number of lily pads doubles (i.e., two lily pads on the second day, four on the third day, eight on the fourth, etc.). On the thirtieth day, the pond is covered completely by lily pads, and all life is choked off. A warning bell sounds when the pond is half full. On what day will the warning bell ring? (See footnote for the answer.)[18]

deals at non-market prices, using the financial resources of Barings as his cash cow, booking fictitious trades and falsifying records, and finally, selling options.

INCREASING COMMISSION INCOME BY OFFERING DEALS AT NON-MARKET PRICES

Leeson increased his commission income by making deals with customers at prices that were highly disadvantageous for Barings. At times, winning the business meant taking uncovered positions and then hoping that his newly created exposures would turn favorable, thereby earning him both commissions on the increased business *and* gains on the unhedged positions. For example in July 1993, Leeson swapped 6,000 long calls with Philippe Bonnefoy, his major customer. Bonnefoy sold Leeson 6,000 September 1994 calls on the Nikkei 225 Index with a *strike price* of 19,220 and purchased 6,000 December 1994 calls with a strike price of 19,200. Leeson gave Bonnefoy an exceptionally favorable deal for the options and earned an attractive commission, but the transaction exposed Barings to a serious risk. Leeson tried to hedge the risk but was unable to do so without incurring losses. The end result was that Leeson's immediate need for commission income was solved, but Barings suffered considerable losses later, which were greater than his commissions. To put this deal into perspective, for most traders, taking an unhedged position of 100 contracts would have been considered *large*. Leeson's 6,000 contract deal was over the top.

USING THE FINANCIAL RESOURCES OF BARINGS AS HIS CASH COW

Leeson also tapped Barings' offices in London and Tokyo for needed funds. He fabricated a story that the transfers were needed, in part, to meet the margin calls of Barings' customers, many of whom lived in different time zones and had trouble clearing checks in time. He also convinced his supervisors that

---

[18]Answer: *It will ring on the twenty-ninth day—just one day before life in the pond ceases.* This riddle can be found in Lester Russell Brown, *The Twenty-Ninth Day: Accommodating Human Needs and Numbers to the Earth's Resources.* London: W. W. Norton, 1978.

large margin calls were a natural counterpart of his profitable arbitrage trading activities. Leeson argued that arbitrage transactions, in general, earn so little profit per transaction that he needed large gross positions to conduct his deals.

Because these positions were on two separate exchanges, each with its own margin requirements and, therefore, having no mutual netting provisions, he had to pay margins on the gross positions in both markets. As a result, Leeson persuaded his supervisors that the cash flow difficulties were more apparent than real—basically, an illusion. None of his supervisors at Barings seemed to question Leeson's explanation even though it should have been obvious that, if he were meeting margin calls on one exchange, he should have been receiving margin funds on the other. After all, he was supposed to be arbitraging.

Many of the remittances made by Barings London to BFS were "top up" payments, which means they were made without the settlements department in London knowing which specific clients' accounts should be debited. Barings London recorded these transfers generically as *loans to clients*, which implied that someone inside the bank was supposed to be checking these customers' creditworthiness and levels of exposure to see if they posed any risks to the bank. Matching customers' transactions with specific transfers also would have been important if Barings intended to charge interest on these loans.

Leeson's supervisors in London and Singapore were fully aware that customer accounts should be reconciled with margin payments and that this reconciliation duty should be separated from Leeson. Therefore, they should have known that there were serious problems at BFS. How could they not have known? Internal audits as early as 1992 (the year Leeson started at BFS) and 1993 recommended reconciliations at BFS and strongly advised that Leeson's responsibilities be separated and more broadly delegated. Hard evidence came in 1993 when a £15-million discrepancy was identified between the margin deposited by Barings' customers and the amount of funding requested by Leeson. By the second half of 1994, this funding discrepancy had grown to £100 million!

Looking back, it is clear that Barings had weak internal checks and balances in its accounting and reporting system, but perhaps more important was the failure by Barings' supervisors to act when problems were identified and warning bells sounded. Barings' first serious attempt at reconciliation started just two weeks before the bank was bankrupt. Within a few days after the audit began, the 88888 Account was discovered and a ¥14-billion discrepancy revealed, but the auditor stalled (and was stalled by Leeson) for a week, and by then, Barings could not be saved. Anything the bank did at that point would have been too little and too late.

There was a pervasive and mystifying lack of urgency at Barings to rein in Leeson. One reason might have been because his margin requests were internal (e.g., from Barings London to BFS); therefore, Barings was not required to report these transactions to the Bank of England as a large *external* exposure. Another reason for procrastinating might have been because Leeson was making sizeable profits, which increased the bonuses of his bosses. Finally, Barings delayed because Leeson was also able to convince his supervisors that reconciliations, even weekly, were too much work and not needed. Management believed him! Therefore, top-up transfers were not reconciled; customers' credit worthiness was not assessed, and interest was not charged to clients' accounts. Only SIMEX seemed to be worried because it suspected that Barings' top-up payments were financing customers' variation margins, which was against exchange rules. To gain perspective into how glaring Barings' lack of oversight was, consider this: when Barings failed in February 1995, more than £300 million had been paid to BFS without identifying the specific customers who were responsible for the trading losses.[19]

BOOKING FICTITIOUS TRADES AND FALSIFYING RECORDS

The need for cash to meet margin calls drove Leeson to desperation. He began to record fictitious trades and falsify internal transfer records. Leeson's fictitious trades were blatant and illegal deceptions. Often, he booked trades late in the day to make it seem as if his net position was zero. Then, he would adjust the prices of these trades during the evening to increase his profits and/or reversed them early the next morning.

In one of Leeson's financial shell games, he pretended to transfer and trade large blocks of stocks between the accounts of the various Barings affiliates and the 88888 Account. By doing so, Leeson gave the impression that his profits were high and net exposures were small, thereby duping exchanges into charging him less margin than he should have paid. He entered false trades into the accounting system almost every day during the two months before Barings' failure, providing him with margin relief on some days by as much as $160 million. All of these shenanigans had the effect of temporarily postponing Leeson's day of reckoning. Meanwhile, Leeson continued to hope that the Japanese stock market would rise, bringing him enough profit to put everything right.

Selling Options and Straddles

Leeson's final source of funding came from selling options, a practice that was in strict violation of Barings' internal rules. He began selling options in 1992, but this unauthorized activity increased dramatically during the final

---

[19]Bank of England, Board of Banking Supervision, *Report of the Board of Banking Supervision Inquiry into the Circumstances of the Collapse of Barings London* (ordered by the House of Commons), (July 1995). Sections 13.22 and 13.23.

Risk Notepad 7.3

Leeson's Most Flagrant Falsification Scheme

The most flagrant of Leeson's falsification schemes occurred in January 1995, one month before the end. Coopers and Lybrand (C&L), Barings' external auditor, caught a ¥7.78 billion (about $77.8 million) hole in Barings Bank's balance sheet while auditing BFS's year-end accounts. Leeson had used the ¥7.78 billion to pay for his losses in the 88888 Account, and he covered his tracks by booking a fictitious sale of options to bring the 88888 Account back to zero. Because the transaction was fictitious and no cash inflows resulted from the transaction, Leeson simply fabricated a journal entry to make it seem that Barings had a ¥7.78 billion deposit in Citibank (Tokyo). C&L was not able to reconcile the deposit with the transaction, which means C&L looked, but the funds were not in Citibank.

Barings supervisors were in a panic, but Leeson was able to ease their worries by manufacturing a story. His fairy-tale varied depending on who he was talking to (there were at least six versions in all), but the one that stuck was both clever and diabolical. Leeson explained that the missing funds were the result of an erroneous payment on an over-the-counter trade that he brokered between Banque Nationale de Paris (BNP) and Spear, Leeds, and Kellogg (SLK), a New York-based brokerage house that specialized in futures and options. He assured everyone that Barings had paid BNP by accident and that SLK would deposit the missing funds in Barings' Citicorp account.

To pull off this incredible lie, Leeson forged three letters and performed an act of Harry-Potter-like accounting wizardry. First, he forged the signature of Richard Hogan, Managing Director of SLK, on a letter that confirmed SLK's side of the (1 October 1994) deal. The other two forgeries were created by Leeson (using scissors, paste, and a copy machine) and then faxed to BFS from his home. The first of these two forged letters was, again, from Richard Hogan at SLK, but this time it confirmed that payment would be made to BFS (on 2 February 1995). The second forgery was a letter from Ron Baker, Leeson's boss and Head of Barings' Financial Products Group, confirming his knowledge and prior approval of the deal.

Leeson's final deed was a brazen act of financial legerdemain. Needing to show that ¥7.78 billion had actually been deposited in Barings' account at Citibank (Tokyo), he ordered the BFS back office to transfer these funds from the accounts of Barings' customers. What made this order so absurd and preposterous was that the accounts of Barings' customers amounted to only ¥3.45 billion—barely half the amount needed. Leeson knew the transaction would bounce, but before reversing it, he asked Citibank to send him a fax showing that the funds had been deposited. Citibank's fax (which Leeson doctored to his needs) and the forged letters were enough to get Leeson a clean bill of health from the C&L audit team.

Leeson's managers in London and Singapore were jubilant! The missing ¥7.78 billion had been found, and their year-end bonuses were no longer in jeopardy. Very few at Barings seemed interested in finding answers to important questions, such as:

- Who authorized Leeson to broker an over-the-counter trade?
- Who authorized him to make payments to *anyone* as large as ¥7.78 billion?

- Who gave credit authorization for the payment of ¥7.78 billion to SLK when the company's line of credit with Barings was only ¥500 million (about $5 million)?
- Why was ¥7.78 billion taken out of another Barings account on the same day that ¥7.78 billion was deposited in Citibank?
- Why were there inaccuracies and inconsistencies in the documents Leeson provided? For example on the (forged) transfer confirmation, why was the amount paid (i.e., ¥7.778 billion) different from the amount returned ¥7.878 billion, and why was the deal listed as a SIMEX trade rather than OTC trade?
- Finally, why was the greeting *From Nick and Lisa* printed on the top of the (forged) payment confirmation from Richard Hogan and (forged) deal confirmation letter from Ron Baker?[20]

two months of 1994. During January 1995 (the month before the end) Leeson's option sales diminished because his cumulative losses had reached a whopping £208 million and option prices had fallen dramatically. In February, however, he was back in the market, again, trying to sell options as a way of getting cash to meet margin calls on his existing positions, which were still going against him. One of Leeson's favorite option contracts was a short straddle, which is the simultaneous sale of both a call option and put option at the same strike price and maturity.

One way to better understand the corner into which Leeson painted himself and the bets he was making is by diagramming the profit/loss profile of his *combined* positions. The graphic explanation in the next section illustrates what really went wrong at Barings. We will use his futures and options positions in the Nikkei 225 as the basis for this explanation.

Net Profit/Loss Profile of Leeson's Exposures

LEESON'S LONG FUTURES POSITIONS

From mid-1992 (when Leeson began at BFS) to mid-1994, the Nikkei 225 Index rose and fell with market forces (see Exhibit 7.2). During this period, Leeson varied his positions in Nikkei 225 futures contracts from long to short and back again. For example, if he was long and the market moved persistently against him, he would occasionally reverse his entire position and, out of desperation, go short. Exhibit 7.2 shows how it was possible for Leeson to have been on the wrong side of rising and falling markets. Our analysis begins in mid-1994 because that was the fatal time period before the Barings collapse.

---

[20] The greeting "From Nick and Lisa" was automatically stamped on all messages sent from Leeson's home fax machine. In his haste to send the two forged letters, he forgot to turn off the automatic stamp.

Exhibit 7.2 Nikkei Index Closing Quotes: 1 July 1992 to 27 February 1995

In June 1994, Leeson was betting the Nikkei 225 Index would rise; so, he built a sizeable long position in Nikkei 225 futures contracts. As Exhibit 7.2 shows, Leeson totally missed the market trend. Rather than rise, the Nikkei 225 Index fell strongly from mid-June 1994 to the end of February 1995—and beyond.

The payoff profile of a long futures position is upward-sloping, and as Exhibit 7.3 shows, any decline in the underlier's price (in this case, the Nikkei 225 Index) causes losses. Leeson was long on both OSE *and* SIMEX. As a result, a falling Nikkei 225 Index forced him to pay variation margin to both exchanges. At first, he tapped BFS's commission income, customer deposits, and the financial resources of Barings' London and Tokyo offices, but as his margin calls grew in size, he relied increasingly on the sale of options, in general, and on the sale of straddles, in particular.

LEESON'S SHORT STRADDLES

From November to December 1994, Leeson financed a large portion of his margin calls with unauthorized short straddles, and he hid these transactions in the 88888 Account. A short straddle is the hybrid derivative created when a put option and a call option with the same strike price are simultaneously sold (Exhibit 7.4). The only way a short straddle can earn profits is if the price of the underlier does not move substantially in either direction. A short

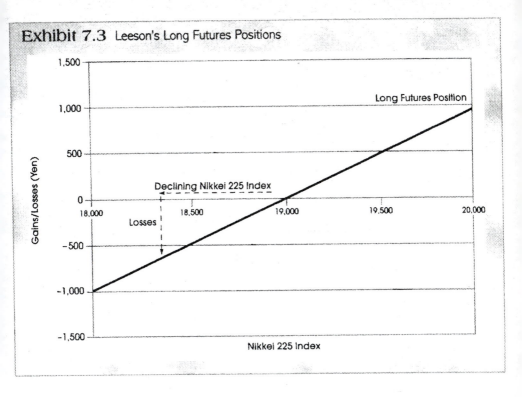

Exhibit 7.3   Leeson's Long Futures Positions

straddle looks like an iceberg, with most of its mass underwater (i.e., below zero). Notice how little of the straddle is above zero, compared to the total profit/loss profile. The portion of the short straddle that is above zero depends on the size of the premium relative to the total exposure.

PROFIT/LOSS PROFILE: COMBINING *ONE* SHORT STRADDLE AND *ONE* LONG FUTURES CONTRACT

We must remember that the short straddle positions taken by Leeson were not in isolation. As Exhibit 7.5 shows, he combined his short straddles with long futures positions.

For every straddle he sold, Barings got cash, which Leeson used to pay the required initial margin deposits on new trades and to meet the escalating margin calls on his existing futures positions. Exhibit 7.5 shows that, to profit from his long futures position, the Nikkei 225 Index had to rise above the futures price.[21] But if it rose too much, every yen gained on his futures position would be offset by losses on his short straddle (or more specifically, on the short call portion of the straddle).

---

[21] To simplify the explanation in this example, the futures price is equal to the strike price. Of course, this equality did not have to be the case. For example, if the strike price were greater than the futures price, the short straddle *and* long futures would profit until the strike price was reached. Only afterwards would they offset each other.

Exhibit 7.4 Profit/Loss Profiles of a Short Put, Short Call, & Short Straddle Hybrid

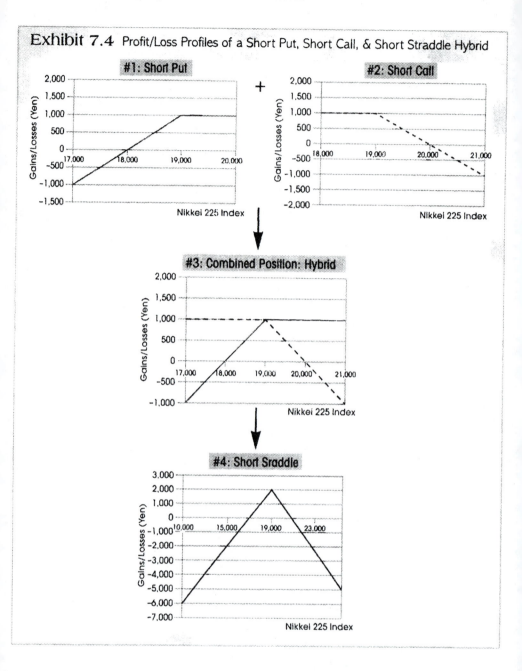

On the down side, the situation was much riskier. A drop in the Nikkei 225 Index caused simultaneous losses on his futures position *and* on his straddle position (or more specifically, on the short put portion of the straddle). The only thing standing in the way of losses at every lower price level was the premium Leeson collected up front, at the time he sold the straddle.

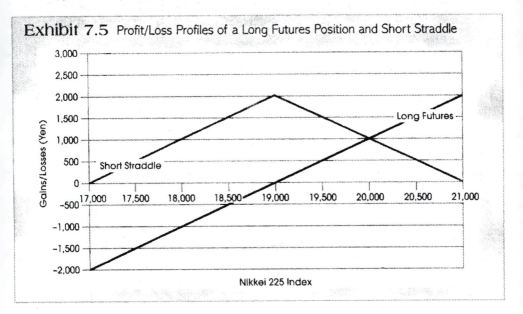

Exhibit 7.5 Profit/Loss Profiles of a Long Futures Position and Short Straddle

Exhibit 7.6 shows the profit/loss profile created when *one* short straddle and *one* long futures position are combined. It looks like a short put, except the downward-sloping portion of the profit/loss curve is even steeper than usual because the long futures contract incurs losses as the price falls below the futures price, and the short straddle incurs losses as the price falls below the strike price. Notice in Exhibit 7.6 that the gains from a short put position are capped. By contrast, the potential losses could be enormous if the Nikkei 225 Index fell—and it did.

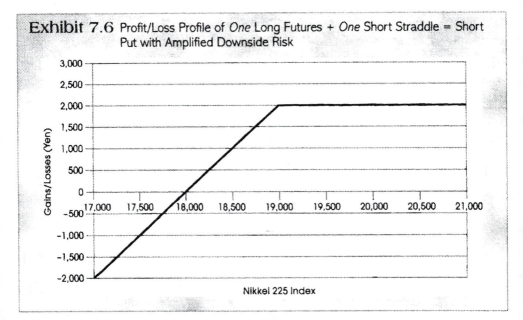

Exhibit 7.6 Profit/Loss Profile of *One* Long Futures + *One* Short Straddle = Short Put with Amplified Downside Risk

PROFIT/LOSS PROFILE: COMBINING A LONG FUTURES POSITION AND "NUMEROUS" SHORT STRADDLES

The profit/loss profile from combining one short straddle and one long futures position gives the illusion that Leeson had a viable trading strategy, and he just guessed wrong in terms of the price movement. Exhibit 7.6 shows a large span of prices to the right of the strike price, which offers, at least, a glimmer of hope that profits could be earned. Unfortunately, we will find that this was not the case. In fact, Barings would have been lucky if Leeson had put the bank in such a position. The illusion is revealed once you understand that Leeson's need for large sums of cash to fund his margin calls forced him to sell disproportionate numbers of short straddles for each long futures position he took. Exhibit 7.6 shows the results if _one long futures_ contract were combined with _one short straddle_, but this one-for-one combination was not what Leeson did. Rather, he combined numerous short straddles with each long futures position.

Exhibit 7.7 shows the profit/loss profile when numerous short straddles are combined with a long forward contract. The hybrid profit/loss profile looks, again, like an iceberg ("Leeson's Iceberg") because 90% or more is underwater (i.e., in the red). The only outcome that could have been even slightly profitable were if the Nikkei 225 Index hovered within a narrow range. For example, if the Nikkei 225 Index rose slightly, Leeson's long futures contracts would have generated small gains, and his put and call options would have expired _out-of-the-money_, thereby leaving him with the

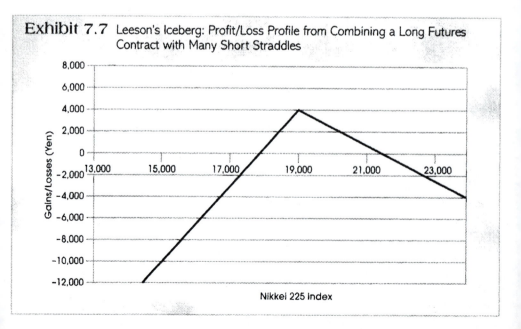

Exhibit 7.7 Leeson's Iceberg: Profit/Loss Profile from Combining a Long Futures Contract with Many Short Straddles

premiums. But if stock prices rose too much, the losses on Leeson's mountain of short calls would have overwhelmed the gains on his futures contracts. By contrast, if stock prices fell, losses on Leeson's long futures would have been amplified by the losses on his mountain of short puts.

MASSIVE PURCHASES OF NIKKEI 225 FUTURES CONTRACTS

By 31 December 1994, Leeson had accumulated losses of £208 million. Most of his short straddles had strike prices between 18,500 and 20,000. Leeson figured that to keep earnings positive, he needed the Nikkei 225 Index to remain between 19,000 and 20,000. Luckily, during the first two weeks of January 1995, this index averaged 19,507, which was solidly within his desired range. Unfortunately, any sparkle of hope Leeson had that he might survive was extinguished on January 17 when Japan suffered the Kobe earthquake, one of its worst disasters of the twentieth century. Registering 7.3 on the Richter scale, this earthquake killed almost 6,500 people, and caused an estimated ¥10 trillion worth of damage to the Japanese economy. As a result of the devastation, the Nikkei 225 Index plummeted during the following weeks.

Exhibit 7.2 shows the daily closing quotes for the Nikkei 225 Index and their death-spiral fall that took Leeson and Barings to ruin. By 20 January 1994, the index had fallen to 18,840. Leeson was in real trouble, and his anguish was intensified by managers at Barings London, who were pressuring him to reduce drastically (and at almost any cost) his positions. But Leeson did not obey the directive;[22] in fact, his positions grew explosively. Had Leeson wished to hedge, he would have *sold* futures contracts, but he did just the opposite and bought them (i.e., doubled) with every drop in the market, hoping to recover his losses when the market rose. In retrospect, his frantic and massive purchases looked like a single-handed effort to hold the Nikkei 225 Index at the 19,000 level. But the wave of selling was too great, and Leeson's efforts were as unsuccessful as a child trying to hold back a rising tide. By 23 February 1995, he owned more than 61,000 Nikkei 225 futures contracts, and despite his frantic buying efforts, the Nikkei 225 Index fell sharply to 17,830.

For Leeson, the end was near. Barings' supervisors and internal auditors, external auditors, and SIMEX officials were at his doorstep. By 27 February 1995, his position had deteriorated further, increasing Leeson's losses to an astounding £860 million (approximately $1.3 billion),[23] which was

---

[22]Ironically, the order from London to reduce Leeson's position seemed to be based more on the desire to quell negative market rumors that Barings was losing its conservative reputation than on any negative reaction to Leeson's activities. After all, he was arbitraging, wasn't he?

[23]Bank of England, Board of Banking Supervision, *Report of the Board of Banking Supervision Inquiry into the Circumstances of the Collapse of Barings London* (ordered by the House of Commons), (July 1995).

considerably more than Barings Bank's equity base of £440 million. Knowing there was no way out, Leeson fled with his wife, Lisa, to Kota Kinabalu, Malaysia, stopping in Kuala Lumpur to fax Barings his resignation, in which he offered "sincere apologies for the predicament that I have left you in."

Beyond Irony: The Barings Failure in a Broader Time Frame

As enormous as his losses were after the stunning drop in Japanese stock prices, Leeson's strategy still could have earned considerable profits if Barings had been able to hold his positions until the end of the year. Exhibit 7.8 shows that, between 27 February 1995 (when Barings failed) and the end of December 1995, the Nikkei 225 stock index rose by more than 3,000 points. Due to the colossal number of Nikkei 225 futures contracts he had purchased during January and February 1995 trying to keep the Nikkei 225 Index at 19,000, *Leeson's Iceberg* (Exhibit 7.7) had been transformed into *Leeson's Hockey Stick* (Exhibit 7.9). His new position had a sharply sloping downside, reflecting the losses he would incur on his short straddle and long futures positions if the Nikkei 225 Index fell. But if prices rose, he would have earned profits because the earnings from his mountain of long futures positions would now have overpowered the losses on his short straddles.

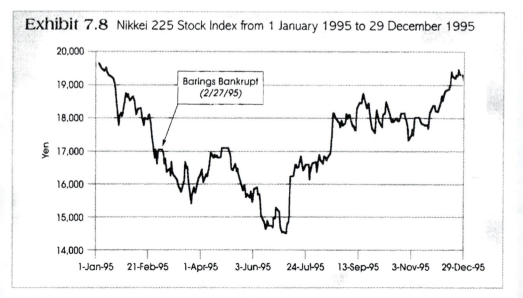

Exhibit 7.8 Nikkei 225 Stock Index from 1 January 1995 to 29 December 1995

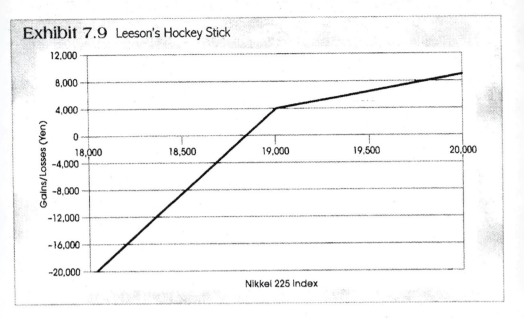

Exhibit 7.9   Leeson's Hockey Stick

A Bank for a Pound

It was not until SIMEX issued its mega-margins calls in January and February 1995 that Barings' directors in London suspected that Leeson's trading was not arbitrage and that he was not a star trader. Barings sent auditors to Singapore, but by the time the team exposed the reckless trader, it was too late. Losses had mounted and exceeded the bank's net worth. Barings had no way to recover, and efforts to extricate itself from financial ruin failed. Unlike the near bankruptcy of 1890, no white knight came to the rescue. The choice for Barings was simple: bankruptcy or sale. In the end, a Dutch bank, Internationale Nederlanden Groep (ING), purchased Barings for £1 (about $1.50) and assumed all of the bank's liabilities.[24] SIMEX immediately liquidated all of Barings' positions, using the deposited margin to repay all counterparties.[25]

Leeson tried desperately to get back to England so he could be tried in an English court. If he were imprisoned, Leeson wanted to be close to his family and not in a foreign jail. From Singapore, he and his wife fled to

[24]The cost to ING for Barings was closer to £660 million, which can be calculated by subtracting from Barings' equity, which equaled £440 million, BFS' losses of £860 million and the infusion of £240 million needed to recapitalize Barings. If we also included estimated foreign exchange losses, which were equal to about $60 million, Barings' price would have increased to about £720 million. Why would ING pay such a price for Barings? Remember that, even though BFS had lost £860 million, ING also purchased Barings' profitable banking and asset management businesses. See Stephen Fay, *The Collapse of Barings*, London: W. W. Norton, 1997, 231–232.

[25]Actually, $86 million in margin payments were returned to BFS.

Malaysia, and from there to Brunei, Bangkok, Abu Dhabi, and finally Frankfurt, where Leeson was apprehended by the police as he disembarked from a plane. London's Serious Fraud Office (SFO) was not interested in extraditing Leeson to England to stand trial. Even though Leeson's crimes had been against an English bank, they had occurred in Singapore, and it was difficult for British lawyers to find charges on which to build their case. SFO could have tried Leeson for theft, but this charge was considered to be trivial compared to his reprehensible deeds; therefore, SFO was happy to have Leeson stand trial in Singapore.

After losing a seven-month battle to be tried in an English court, Leeson accepted extradition to Singapore, where he pleaded guilty to two charges of fraud.[26] His penalty for misreporting contracts worth £300 million (1 February 1995) was a six-year sentence in Singapore's Changi jail, and his penalty for forgery was six months in the same jail. Leeson's imprisonment was backdated to account for the time he spent in Germany's Hoechst Prison. While in prison, he was diagnosed with colon cancer that had spread to his lymph nodes, and his marriage dissolved. In July 1999, Leeson was released from prison on good behavior after serving about four and a half years of his six-and-a-half year sentence.

Aftermath of the Barings Failure

Peter Baring, Chairman of Barings PLC, was convinced that the failure of his bank was the work of a conspiracy, which was much broader than Nick Leeson's involvement alone. After all, if Leeson bought so many Nikkei 225 futures contracts, someone must have sold them. Leeson was certain that his phone had been tapped, and he was the victim of competitors who unfairly beat him to the market and robbed him of profitable trades. Still others were sure that Leeson had a "pot of gold" hidden away for after he was released from jail. When the smoke cleared, virtually all of the conspiracy theories were either disproved or carried little credibility. The failure of Barings Bank PLC shocked the financial industry into realizing just how powerful one trader's undiscovered and unsupervised transactions could be. As a result of this catastrophe and others that occurred in the 1990s, the financial industry set its sights on the target of implementing

---

[26]Leeson was extradited on 11 charges: three related to fraud, two related to amending prices, and six related to reducing his margins with cross trades. Nine of the charges were dropped in the judicial proceedings, but they were used in determining Leeson's sentence. Under Singapore law, it was difficult to charge Leeson with many of his unauthorized activities. That was one of the main reasons why all of the charges against him were for activities he performed after 6 January 1995.

new and improved risk management measures. Today, financial tools and approaches to risk management, such as value at risk and enterprise risk management, have grown in popularity due to the lessons learned in the 1990s.

Because ING purchased Barings and assumed all its losses, none of Barings' depositors, bank creditors, or customers was hurt by the collapse, and only a minority (about 1,200) of Barings' employees lost their jobs. Nevertheless, shareholders and bondholders suffered terribly.[27] As for the financial markets, the Barings failure turned out to be little more than a speed bump on the global financial turnpike. For a short time, market volatility and transaction costs (i.e., bid-ask spreads) increased marginally, but they returned to normal after a few months as the markets shrugged off this financial debacle.[28]

How Could Barings Have Caught Leeson Sooner?

It is difficult to understand why Barings London did not discover and stop Leeson's reckless trading far sooner than it did, but then everything seems simple with 20:20 hindsight. A large part of the problem was that Barings' control systems were ineffective and toothless, but equally important was management's inability or unwillingness to act on the information and warning signs it had. In July and August 1994, a Barings auditor spent two weeks in Singapore and occupied the chair right next to Leeson but did not discover the unauthorized positions in his 88888 Account.

There were also plenty of advance warnings, but they were either disregarded or not taken seriously. Leeson's excessive margin calls were not challenged, when they should have been. Warning bells should have rung loudly when his daily requests for funds were evenly split between Barings' house account and customers' accounts—an occurrence that probabilistically should not have occurred even once, let alone almost every day. How difficult should it have been to expose this rogue trader? Regrettably, the answer is "not very difficult."

---

[27]In 1993, Barings issued £100 million worth of perpetual bonds. After the bankruptcy, ING offered to repay the owners of these bonds only about 5% of their value. See Bank of England, Board of Banking Supervision, *Report of the Board of Banking Supervision Inquiry into the Circumstances of the Collapse of Barings London* (ordered by the House of Commons), (July 1995).

[28]See David M. Walsh and Jinwei Quek, "An Empirical Examination of the SIMEX Nikkei 225 Futures Contract Around the Kobe Earthquake and the Barings Bank Collapse," *The Journal of Futures Markets*, Vol. 19, No. 1 (1999) 1–29.

- Barings could have looked (just once) at the simple, but informative, one page margin statement that was sent to Barings managers by SIMEX every working day from July 1992 (when Leeson began trading at BFS) until February 1995 (when Barings failed). Just adding together customers' margins calls for the day and comparing this total to the amount requested by Leeson would have revealed an eye-popping difference. This difference would have proved immediately that Barings' customers were not the cause of the large payments that Barings London was sending to BFS.

- To separate customers' business from its own and reconcile the difference, Barings London could have asked Leeson to prepare a report that showed cash balances with banks, loan positions, and margin balances for its agency and proprietary businesses.[29]

- The 88888 Account was hidden from Barings London, but it was not hidden from SIMEX. To expose Leeson's fraud, Barings' managers needed only to ask SIMEX for its daily position statement and then compare it with its own position statement. This comparison would have shown that Barings Bank (itself) had an enormous and unauthorized exposure to the exchange.

- Barings could have compared its positions on SIMEX and OSE to see that Leeson's trades were not offsetting. When Barings failed, he was long in both markets, which meant that Leeson was speculating and not arbitraging.

- Barings' internal and external auditors could have asked for a list of all BFS accounts. The 88888 Account was in BFS' computer system and would have been printed (along with all of BFS' other positions) for anyone to see.

- Barings' external auditors could have examined the yearly activity the 88888 Account instead of focusing exclusively on the ending balance. Before each audit, Leeson reduced the 88888 Account to a trivial balance; therefore, auditors saw no need (from 1992 to 1994) to inspect this *immaterial* (sic) account. As well, auditors could have (should have) relied on original sources to verify audit information, rather than ask Leeson to provide it.

- SIMEX wrote three important letters to Barings' senior management. One was written as early as 1993, and the other two were written during the two months before Barings went bankrupt. The 1993 letter informed Barings of a minor fine imposed on Leeson because of trading violations, and it specifically mentioned the 88888 Account. The second letter (11 January 1995) also mentioned the 88888 Account and went on to complain about the lack of information coming from BFS. Moreover, it cautioned Barings that the bank might be violating a SIMEX rule that forbade clearing members from funding customers' variation margin payments. This letter was never sent to London by Leeson's Singapore manager, and to make matters worse, the same manager asked *Leeson* to draft Barings' reply to SIMEX. The final letter from SIMEX (27 January 1995) asked for Barings' assurances that it could meet future variation margin requirements. This letter was sent to London, and astonishingly, Barings responded to SIMEX (on 10 February 1995) with a resounding confirmation of its funding abilities. It was obvious afterwards that Barings' managers spent no time researching the accuracy of their misleading response to SIMEX.

To gain an understanding of the degree to which Leeson's trades took him outside Barings' internal rules, consider Exhibit 7.10, which

Exhibit 7.10 Reported and Actual Trades of Barings Futures (Singapore) on 27 February 1995

Contract	Reported to Barings London Number of Contracts[a]	Trades Booked in 88888 Account Number of Contracts[a]
Total Futures	**46,653**	**95,918**
Nikkei 225	30,112	Long 61,039
JGB	15,940	Short 28,034
Euroyen	601	Short 6,845
Total Options	**0**	**70,892**
Short Calls	0	37,925
Short Puts	0	32,967

[a] Contracts are measured in terms of SIMEX contracts, which are half the size of OSE and TSE contracts.

Source: Bank of England, Board of Banking Supervision, Report of the Board of Banking Supervision Inquiry into the Circumstances of the Collapse of Barings London (ordered by the House of Commons), (July 1995).

compares the trades Leeson reported to London at the end of February, 1995 with the actual trades booked in the 88888 Account. Barings London assumed that the SIMEX trades Leeson was reporting were offset by equally valued trades on OSE. Moreover, the bank's internal rules limited traders' intraday positions in the Nikkei 225, Japanese government bonds, and three-month euroyen contracts to 200, 100, and 500 contracts, respectively. These same internal rules also prohibited traders from taking proprietary positions (i.e., positions using Barings as a counterparty), such as selling options or holding unauthorized positions overnight.

Leeson was in gross violation of all these limits. At the end of February 1995, he stood to gain or lose more than $30.5 million with each 100-point movement of the Nikkei index[30] and more than $28 million for each 100-point change in Japanese government bond prices.[31] His positions were so large that they caused Barings to run afoul of Bank of England protocols. To control credit risk, English banks were required to report to the Bank of England all customer exposures that exceeded 10% of the bank's shareholders' equity and to notify the central bank *before* an exposure would exceed 25%. Yet during 1994 and 1995, Barings had persistent exposures to SIMEX, OSE, and TSE that were each in excess of 25%. In February 1995, when Barings failed, its exposures to OSE and SIMEX were 73% and 40%, respectively.[32]

Conclusions: Leeson's Lessons

The Barings failure was a spectacular calamity that provided some valuable lessons. Effective risk management requires a clear line of demarcation between the responsibilities of front-office and back-office managers and staff. Otherwise, there will always be temptation to fix the books to

---

[30] 61,039 Nikkei 225 contracts $\times$ ¥500/tick $\times$ 100 ticks $\times$ $0.01/¥ = $30,519,500.

[31] 28,034 JGB contracts $\times$ ¥1,000/tick $\times$ 100 ticks $\times$ $0.01/¥ = $28,034,000.

[32] In 1993, the Bank of England made an *informal concession* to Barings that granted a temporary right to exceed the 25% equity limit. Barings inquired whether this rule applied to banks when the foreign counterparty was an exchange rather than a private entity, such as an individual or company. Barings must have interpreted the Bank of England's tacit approval as a perpetual right because it did not report its rising SIMEX and OSE exposures during 1994 and 1995. At the same time, the Bank of England delayed for almost two years before ruling that a bank's exposure to a foreign exchange cannot exceed the 25% equity limit. Bank of England, Board of Banking Supervision, *Report of the Board of Banking Supervision Inquiry into the Circumstances of the Collapse of Barings London* (ordered by the House of Commons), (July 1995), Section 13.63.

enhance performance. Without this separation, control systems that monitor risks, such as trading limits, creditworthiness, liquidity, and cash flow, lose most of their significance. Barings allowed Nick Leeson to settle his own trades, by giving him authority over both the front and back offices. As a result, he could manipulate accounts at the Singapore branch, while reporting fraudulent totals that appeared accurate. Giving Leeson authority over front- and back-office functions was equivalent to giving the fox responsibility for counting the chickens in the chicken coop.

Perhaps the most embarrassing aspect of the Leeson-Barings catastrophe was the role played by senior management (i.e., Leeson's direct supervisors, the bank's management committee, and the Board of Directors), whose errors were ones of omission rather than commission. Barings management gave too much autonomy to Leeson, who was, in more ways than one, far beyond the scrutiny of his supervisors. From the start, there were no clear reporting lines in Barings' highly political matrix organization. As a result, there was a gaping lack of understanding throughout Barings of exactly what Leeson was doing.

Barings' controls proved to be pathetically ineffective. No one in the bank seems to have fully understood the risks that Leeson was taking. He was thought to have the Midas touch, and too much restraint would cramp his trading style. Therefore, no one posed the hard questions that should have been asked. Even routine tasks, such as reconciling margin payments with customers' accounts and verifying information sent from BFS to headquarters, were not performed in a professional way. Barings' management committee should have set up reporting systems to ensure that important information on operational risks reached it, and the Board of Directors should have put the management committee under constant pressure to formulate these risk-reporting systems.

Barings management thought Leeson was hedging and, therefore, it funded his margin calls without demanding a full explanation. Had Leeson been fully hedged, then the margin calls on one exchange should have been offset by gains in the other. When he earned 20% to 50% of Barings' worldwide annual profits on *riskless* trades, alarm bells should have sounded immediately.[33] Yet no one from Barings investigated the source of these profits. Instead of scrutinizing these absurd profits, Barings management

[33]See BBC Online Network, *Business, The Economy How Leeson Broke the Bank* (Tuesday, June 22, 1999). Also see, Stephen J. Brown and Onno W. Steenbeek, "Doubling: Nick Leeson's Trading Strategy," *Pacific-Basin Finance Journal* 9 (2001), 83–99.

convinced itself that the source of the BFS' competitive advantage over rivals came from its large customer base, ability to arbitrage the Japanese and Singapore exchanges, and having the *wisdom* to hire Leeson, the golden boy of arbitrage trading.

Senior Barings managers ignored internal audit reports, as well as inquiries from the Bank of England and Bank for International Settlements. They even ignored (for a while) the cold reality of Leeson's call for cash, when trading losses required Barings to borrow the needed funds and wire them to Singapore. The bank had rules and regulations in place that were supposed to stop traders (including Leeson) from activities such as exceeding intraday trading limits, carrying open overnight positions, and exposing the bank to excessive customer risk, but rules are useless if they are not obeyed or enforced.

From all their years of trading and security dealing, one would expect banks, like Barings, to have learned from their successes and failures how to control the positions of their employees. But control is an elusive goal when banking activities have so many dimensions and when each trading operation and each new instrument offers its own secret passageways to the bank vault. Derivatives can involve huge amounts of *leverage*, and their net risks can be masked by joining them in countless combinations, permutations, and variations. Nevertheless, almost no twisting and turning can reverse the fact that many levels of management above and around Leeson failed to function properly. Whatever arguments Leeson's supervisors concocted to absolve themselves were invalid and shallow. Leeson was only 25 years old and had no previous trading experience when he became BFS' chief trader and head of settlements. It is sobering to think how many individuals with brilliant minds and the opportunity to study at prestigious universities, like Oxford and Cambridge, were duped by a lone rogue trader in Singapore.

Epilogue

What Happened to the Key Players in the Barings Financial Fiasco?

The Barings fiasco was a story meant for the movie screen. If Leeson, himself, was not colorful enough, Barings' highly educated managers came out looking like the banking industry's equivalent of the Keystone cops. What happened to these individuals who peppered the landscape during Nick Leeson's brief stint with the 233-year-old Barings Bank?

Exhibit E 7.1 What Happened to the List of Characters After Barings' Financial Fiasco?

No.	Name	Position and/or Relationship to Leeson	What Happened to Him/Her?
1	Ron Baker	• Head of Financial Products Group, Barings Investment Bank (London) • Leeson's direct boss in Singapore	• Censured by the Department of Trade and Industry's inquiry. Prohibited from serving as a company director. • Found by England's Securities and Futures Authority to have breached securities industry rules.
2	Peter Baring	Chairman, Barings PLC	• Had planned to retire, anyway, in 1995 due to his age. Resigned from ING in April 1995 and decided to retire from finance to live in his country estate. • Absolved of any responsibility for the failure.
3	James Bax	• Managing Director, Barings Securities (Singapore) • Leeson's main boss in Singapore	• Found by the Securities and Futures Authority to have breached securities industry rules. • Censured by the Department of Trade and Industry's inquiry. Prohibited from serving as a company director for four years. • Returned to Scotland, his native country.
4	Geoffrey Broadhurst	Group Finance Director, Barings Investment Bank. (London)	• Found by the Securities and Futures Authority to have breached securities industry rules. • Censured by the Department of Trade and Industry's inquiry. Prohibited from serving as a company director for four years.
5	Tony Gamby	Director of Settlements, Barings InvestmentBank (London)	• Found by the Securities and Futures Authority to have breached securities industry rules. • Censured by the Department of Trade and Industry's inquiry. Prohibited from serving as a company director.

(Continued)

Exhibit E 7.1 (Continued)

No.	Name	Position and/or Relationship to Leeson	What Happened to Him/Her?
7	Tony Hawes	Group Treasurer, Barings Investment Bank (London)	• Found by the Securities and Futures Authority to have breached securities industry rules. • Censured by the Department of Trade and Industry's inquiry. Prohibited from serving as a company director. • Retired from ING.
8	Ian Hopkins	Director and Head of Group Treasury and Risk, Barings Investment Bank (London)	• Found by the Securities and Futures Authority to have breached securities industry rules. • Censured by the Department of Trade and Industry's inquiry. Prohibited from serving as a company director for five years and received a reprimand from the Securities and Futures Authority.
9	Simon Jones	• Director, Barings Futures (Singapore) and Finance Director of Barings Securities (Singapore) • One of Leeson's bosses in Singapore	Found by the Securities and Futures Authority to have breached securities industry rules.
11	Lisa Sims Leeson	Nick Leeson's former wife	• Became an airline stewardess for Virgin Airlines. • Divorced Nick Leeson in 1997. • Postponed her August 1998 marriage to Keith Horlock, a London trader, when she learned of Nick Leeson's cancer, but in December 1998 married Horlock in a private ceremony.

(Continued)

Exhibit E 7.1 (Continued)

12	Nick Leeson	• General Manager and Assistant Director of Barings Futures (Singapore)
		• His own best friend and his own worst enemy

• Sentenced to six and a half years in prison in the Changi Prison, Singapore (December 1995).
• While in prison:
  • Worked in the prison library and later worked on accounts in the prison sewing room.
  • Wrote *Rogue Trader: How I Brought Down Barings Bank* (1996), the rights to which Little, Brown, and Company paid more than £450,000. The book was later turned into a popular movie (1999) staring Ewan McGregor and Anna Friel.
  • Divorced his wife, Lisa Sims Leeson (1997).
  • Diagnosed with colon cancer that had spread to his lymph nodes (early 1998).
  • Had colon surgery in Changi General Hospital, Singapore (August 1998), a civilian hospital, and afterwards, transferred to the high-security Tanah Merah Prison, Changi, Singapore (August 1998).
  • Underwent six months of chemotherapy (five days on and three weeks off).
• Released from prison in early July 1999.
• After his release from prison:
  • His cancer went into remission, and five years after his operation, Leeson received a clean bill of health.
  • Married Leona Tormay, an Irish beautician (2003).
  • Earned a psychology degree from Middlesex University.
  • Wrote a second book entitled *From the Brink: Coping with Stress* (2005).
  • Was named Commercial Manager (April 2005) and then General Manager (November 2005) of the Galway United Football Club in Galway, Ireland.
  • In 2007, Leeson lived in Galway, Ireland with Leona, his wife, a son he conceived with Leona (2004), and two sons from Leona's prior marriage. Leeson does charity work and gives occasional after-dinner and conference speeches on topics such as risk management, stress, and the Barings failure.
  • Leeson's official website is http://www.nickleeson.com/index.html.

(Continued)

Exhibit E 7.1 (Continued)

No.	Name	Position and/or Relationship to Leeson	What Happened to Him/Her?
13	Peter Norris	Chief Executive Office, Barings Securities Limited	• Found by the Securities and Futures Authority to have breached securities industry rules. • Censured by the Department of Trade and Industry's inquiry. Prohibited from serving as a company director for four years. • Worked subsequently for John Brown Enterprises and the private equity firm New Boathouse Capital. • Norris also served as a financial advisor to Sir Richard Branson and Virgin.
15	Andrew Tuckey	Deputy Chairman, Barings PLC	• Absolved of any responsibility for the failure. • Censured by the Department of Trade and Industry's inquiry. Prohibited from serving as a company director. • Resigned from ING in April 1995 and almost immediately became a consultant for ING. • Was responsible for administering the resignations and firing of the key players in the Leeson fiasco. • Also worked as an advisor to prestigious financial institutions such as Bridgewell Capital, Credit Suisse First Boston, DLJ, Lloyds, and Bridgewell Capital
16	Mary Walz	Global Head of Equity Financial Products, Barings Investment Bank (London)	• Censured by the Department of Trade and Industry's inquiry. Prohibited from serving as a company director, but she was not disciplined by the SFA. • Found by the Securities and Futures Authority to have breached securities industry rules. • Believed to have returned to the United States, her native country.

Sources: Anonymous, "Ten Years Later: Barings Survivors", *The Guardian*, London (21 Feb. 2005) 11 (reproduced by Taipei Times, http://www.taipeitimes.com/News/biz/archives/2005/02/21/2003224023, accessed 28 July 2007); and see Stephen Fay, The Collapse of Barings, London: W.W. Norton, 1997, Ch. 17 and Postscript.

Review Questions

1. Explain the difference in risk between "agency trading" and "proprietary trading," and why it is important to the Barings fiasco.

2. Explain "futures arbitrage (i.e., switching)" and how Leeson used it to increase his reported profits.

3. Plot the net shape of BFS' profit/loss profile after Leeson's 1993 swap with Philippe Bonnefoy. To answer this question, you must explain whether the premium he paid was greater than, less than, or equal to the premium he received.

4. What was the 88888 Account, and how did Leeson use it to deceive senior management at Barings?

5. What are cross-trades, and how did Leeson use them to increase his reported profits?

6. Explain Nick Leeson's doubling strategy.

7. Explain the major ways that Leeson funded his margin calls.

8. Explain how Barings' "top up" payments contributed to the bank's eventual downfall.

9. Explain how Barings could have caught Leeson earlier if it had reconciled its customers' accounts with the margin transfers sent by Barings London to BFS.

10. Was senior management at Barings aware that there was a problem at BFS? Explain.

11. Explain the SLK-BNP deal and why it was important to Nick Leeson.

12. Why did Nick Leeson sell numerous short straddles for each long futures contract he bought?

13. Plot the profit/loss profile of the derivative hybrid created when you combine one long futures position with a futures price of 19,000 and three short straddles with a strike price of 19,000. Assume the put and call premiums are ¥1,000 each.

14. Plot the profit/loss profile of the derivative hybrid created when you combine three long futures positions with a futures price of 19,000 and one short straddle with a strike price of 19,000. Assume the put and call premiums are ¥1,000 each.

15. Why was the Kobe earthquake important to the failure of Barings Bank?

16. Has Nick Leeson drawn too much of the blame for what went wrong at Barings Bank? Who else bears some of the responsibility? Why?

17. Was the Barings Board of Directors culpable for the losses of Nick Leeson?

18. Nick Leeson traded simultaneously on two exchanges in two different time zones. Does the fact that he was trading on two exchanges simultaneously automatically mean he was speculating, or is it what he was doing that makes the trades speculative?

19. Nick Leeson sold short straddles and combined them with long futures contracts. Why did he sell straddles instead of buying them?

20. Was the existence of the 88888 Account one of the fundamental problems at Barings Bank PLC or was the problem with its use? Explain.

Bibliography

Bank of England. Board of Banking Supervision. *Report of the Board of Banking Supervision Inquiry into the Circumstances of the Collapse of Barings London* (ordered by the House of Commons), (July 1995).

BBC Online Network. *Business: The Economy How Leeson Broke the Bank.* Tuesday, 22 June 1999. Available at http://news.bbc.co.UK/2/hi/business/375259.stm. Accessed 24 December 2007.

Brown, Stephen J. and Steenbeck, Onno W. "Doubling: Nick Leeson's Trading Strategy." *Pacific-Basin Finance Journal* 9 (2001), 83–99.

Chin, Yee Wah. "Risk Management Lessons From the Collapse of Barings Bank." *Japan Insurance News* (March-April 2002), 12–17.

Fay, Stephen. *The Collapse of Barings.* New York: W.W. Norton, 1997.

Greener, Ian. "Nick Leeson and the Collapse of Barings Bank: Socio-Technical Networks and the 'Rogue Trader.'" *Organization* 13(3) (London: May 2006), 421–441.

Leeson, Nick with Whitley, Edward. *Rogue Trader: How I Brought Down Barings Bank and Shook the Financial World.* Boston: Little, Brown, 1996.

Lim, Michael Choo San and Tan, Nicky Ng Kuang. "Barings Futures (Singapore) Pte Ltd: Investigation Pursuant to Section 231 of the Companies Act (Chapter 50): The Report of the Inspectors Appointed by the Minister for Finance." Singapore: Singapore Ministry of Finance, 1995, xi, p. 183.

Walsh, David M. and Quek, Jinwei. "An Empirical Examination of the SIMEX Nikkei 225 Futures Contract Around the Kobe Earthquake and the Barings Bank Collapse." *The Journal of Futures Markets* 19(1) (1999), 1–29.

8

Long-Term Capital Mismanagement

"JM and the Arb Boys"

Introduction

Long-Term Capital Management (LTCM) began operations in 1994 with more than $1 billion in capital and what looked like an unbridled potential to succeed. Among its principals was a virtual who's who of world-class academics and seasoned Wall Street practitioners. A string of outstanding successes[1] built LTCM's equity position in three short years to $7.1 billion. In 1996 alone, the company cleared more than $2 billion. LTCM's principals, who had invested $146 million in 1994, watched as their share of the pie grew to $1.9 billion. They were all multimillionaires, and so was everyone lucky enough to have a piece of the action. In fact, one LTCM principal was already half way to becoming a billionaire.

Who would have guessed that, by 1998, LTCM would be bankrupt, its principals heavily in debt, and the world's financial system would have barely escaped a financial meltdown? The story of LTCM's precipitous decline is told with a smile, a tear, and a smirk. After all, it's not every day

---

[1]Profits for the first 10 months of operation in 1994 were 20%, and for the three years thereafter, they were 43%, 41%, and 17%.

that the best, the brightest, and the most arrogant fail so astoundingly and so visibly.

This chapter is divided into seven major parts. It begins by describing LTCM—the company, its business, and who ran it. The second part of the chapter explains LTCM's investment strategy. It clarifies how a hedge fund,[2] like LTCM, can structure an investment portfolio that earns profits regardless of whether the market moves up or down (i.e., a market-neutral portfolio). Spreads, convergence and relative value trades, volatility plays, and leverage enter heavily into this explanation. The discussion then turns to LTCM's rise to stardom from 1994 to 1997, followed by an explanation of the considerable value this company added, for three years, to the global financial markets. The next part focuses on why LTCM failed and how it managed to lose $4.5 billion in less than two months without the complicity of rogue traders, deception, or market manipulation. Part six describes how LTCM was rescued, and the final section suggests some conclusions and lessons to be learned from this very unfortunate financial debacle.

Risk Notepad 8.1

What Is a Hedge Fund?

The term *hedge fund* is an oxymoron because these funds often take positions—large positions—that are anything but hedged. In fact, the name has little or nothing to do with the functions these funds perform. Hedge funds are mostly unregulated,[3] highly diversified portfolios of assets that may or may not specialize in opportunities associated with specific risks.

They are usually privately organized limited partnerships or limited liability companies that professionally manage investment funds for *qualified purchasers* (e.g., wealthy individuals

---

[2]See Risk Notepad 8.1: What Is a Hedge Fund?
[3]In the United States, hedge funds are not regulated by the Securities and Exchange Commission, but they do come under the supervisory powers of the Commodity Futures Trading Commission and National Futures Association.

and institutional investors), who do not need all the regulatory protections from risk-taking that many of us find helpful. Hedge funds often employ aggressive, short-term trading strategies and have high leverage ratios compared to other financial intermediaries. They earn revenues from fees that are based partly on the amount of assets under management and partly on performance. To remain unregulated in the United States, they limit the number of beneficial owners, abstain from raising funds via public offerings, and refrain from advertising or soliciting widely. Hedge funds compete directly with the trading desks of banks, security firms, insurance companies, mutual funds, and other managed funds.

When LTCM failed in 1998, there were between 2,500 and 3,500 hedge funds in the United States combined with capital between $200 billion and $350 billion and assets ranging from $800 billion to $1 trillion. Compared to other broad types of financial intermediaries, hedge funds were relatively small, ranging from 20% to 40% the size of mutual funds, pension funds, commercial banks, insurance companies, and retirement funds.[4]

There is no "typical" hedge fund. They vary enormously and take a variety of positions, ranging from outright purchases and sales of assets to arbitrage transactions, spread trades, and derivative positions (e.g., options, futures, forwards, and swaps). In short, they can do almost anything their investors, creditors, counterparties, and management allow them to do. To the typical investor, these funds bring value because they provide wide diversification, economies of scale in purchasing, and professional investment expertise.

It is a misconception to think that all hedge funds are highly volatile, speculative ventures, but it is equally misguided to think that they are safe, just because the word "hedge" is in the name. The rule of thumb is *buyer beware*; remember that you must not underestimate the danger of a rattlesnake just because the word "rattle" is in its name. Investments in hedge funds may or may not be hedged. Hedge funds can pursue a wide range of investment strategies, including highly leveraged speculative positions. Depending on your age, as well as family and financial status, you can choose among hedge funds with larger or smaller risks.

Normally, hedge fund portfolios are revalued (i.e., marked-to-market) daily. They differentiate themselves by the strategies they use to select investments and by how much risk they take with clients' funds. Many use proprietary strategies, analytical methods, and trading models. They achieve economies of scale by making large transactions, and then distribute the benefits to their clients.

Just as animals can be classified into major species, hedge funds can also be classified into a few broad categories. The major categories of hedge funds are aggressive growth, convergence, distressed-security, emerging-market, equity, income-generating, macro, market-neutral, pooled, relative-value, and risk-management.

Over the years, some hedge fund managers have gained almost celebrity status and their generous salaries have made them among the richest people in the world. People like George Soros (Soros Fund), Stanley Druckenmiller (Soros Fund), Henry Kravis (Kohlberg Kravis Roberts), Thomas Lee (Thomas H. Lee Co.), and Julian Robertson (Tiger Management) have become familiar names both for their brilliant performance and sometimes self-aggrandizing behavior.

---

[4]President's Working Group on Financial Markets. *Hedge Funds, Leverage, and the Lessons of Long-Term Capital Management: Report of the President's Working Group on Financial Markets.* Washington, DC: Department of Treasury, 28 April 1999.

LTCM: The Company

LTCM opened its doors for business at the end of February 1994. Its capital was about half the $2.5 billion that John Meriwether, its founder, had set as a goal for beginning equity when he left Salomon Brothers, but then, not many hedge funds start operations so well endowed. Long-Term Capital Portfolio L.P. (LTCP) was the actual "Fund," and this Cayman Islands limited partnership was managed by Long-Term Capital Management L.P., which was a Delaware-chartered limited partnership that was operated from Greenwich, Connecticut and owned by John Meriwether and the 11 other principals.[5]

Investors did not invest directly in LTCP. Rather, the Fund had a hub-and-spoke-type structure, with a network of global conduits collecting funds and investing in LTCP. Each conduit tailored its investment terms to the regulatory, tax, and accounting idiosyncrasies of a particular nation or region. By 1997, all of LTCM's investors were multimillionaires, but that was not a high hurdle to clear because they were all millionaires in 1994, when LTCM began. The minimum investment needed to claim a piece of LTCM's action was $10 million; so, it was an exclusive club, with only the rich and a host of domestic and foreign financial intermediaries as members.

THE LTCM BUSINESS

The company's initial trades were primarily arbitraging the global bond markets; though, by 1995, it had already diversified its portfolio by entering into domestic and foreign equity arbitrage trades. And why not? LTCM's strategy, after all, did not require an in-depth knowledge of any particular underlier (e.g., Microsoft stock), but rather it required a keen understanding of the *spreads between the yields or prices of underliers*—and that was largely the domain of statistical modeling and security market wisdom that came from years of experience—or at least they thought.

THE PRINCIPALS

One of the exceptional features of LTCM was the cast of characters who founded and ran the company. It was a distinguished and impressive group, among whom were two Nobel laureates, a vice chairman of the Federal Reserve System, and some of the brightest, most successful bond arbitragers

---

[5]LTCM's *limited partners* presented themselves as *principals* and *not as partners* because they felt it might be viewed as deceptive to have titles that implied unlimited liability. The LTCM principals also did not want a hierarchy of corporate titles; so they chose the title "principal" for all limited-partner-type people at LTCM. Unless otherwise noted, the management company (LTCM) and Fund (LTCP) are treated as one in this chapter and generically called Long-Term Capital Management (LTCM).

on Wall Street (known as the "arb boys"). Initially, LTCM had 12 principals, but four of them deserve special mention.

John Meriwether

John Meriwether ("JM," as he was called), the founder of LTCM, was clearly the company's guiding light. He was a tough, respected, nice guy, who started LTCM after leaving his former job at Salomon Brothers. In the late 1970s and 1980s, Meriwether built a highly profitable bond arbitrage group at Salomon Brothers and went on to become vice chairman in charge of Salomon's global fixed-income trading, arbitrage, and foreign exchange businesses.

His trading operation at Salomon Brothers was so successful that, by 1986, the company was devoting half its equity to JM and his team, but in 1991, one of his traders, Paul Mozer, confessed to making false bids at U.S. government security auctions. Meriwether knew the violations were significant and reported them to his bosses, Thomas (Tommy) Strauss and CEO John Gutfreund. All three men understood the infractions were serious and should have been reported immediately to the Federal Reserve and U.S. Treasury; Mozer should have been dealt with deliberately—perhaps fired.

Astonishingly, Mozer was not reprimanded; in fact, he was kept as the head of Salomon Brothers' government bond trading desk, and Salomon delayed too long before disclosing the infractions to the Federal Reserve and U.S. Treasury. The scandal blossomed and resulted in the 1991 resignations of both Gutfreund and Strauss. Leaderless, Salomon Brothers convinced Warren Buffett, a premier investor, head of Berkshire Hathaway Holding Company, and major shareholder in Salomon Brothers, to become its temporary CEO, saving Salomon from a potentially worse situation.

Meriwether's resignation came just a few days after Buffett took the helm at Salomon Brothers. As part of a Securities and Exchange Commission administrative proceeding, Meriwether agreed to pay a $50,000 fine and suffered a three-month suspension.[6] After a brief hiatus, Meriwether founded LTCM in 1994, and, by 1995, he plucked from Salomon Brothers eight members of his old team, who were responsible for almost 90% of Salomon's trading profits.

Robert C. Merton shared the 1997 Nobel Prize in Economics with Myron Scholes for their trailblazing work on option pricing. Merton was a brilliant mathematician, who earned an undergraduate degree in engineering at Columbia University, a Ph.D. in applied mathematics at the California

---

[6]Meriwether neither admitted nor denied culpability. As for the fine, it did not hit his bank account too hard. In December 1992, Meriwether and Thomas Strauss settled a suit for back pay against Salomon Brothers. Meriwether's share of the compensation settlement was $18 million. Kevin Muehring, "John Meriwether by the Numbers," *Institutional Investor* 30 (11) (November 1996), 68–81.

Institute of Technology, and a Ph.D. in economics from the Massachusetts Institute of Technology (MIT). While teaching at MIT's Sloan School of Management and later at the Harvard Business School, Merton made significant contributions to finance in the area of option pricing models. His research linked continuous-time stochastic processes with continuous-decision-making by agents, and this led him into pricing contingent contracts, like options.

Myron S. Scholes, a native Canadian, was one of the most creative dreamers in the LTCM group. He graduated from McMaster University in Canada with a degree in economics and went on to receive a Ph.D. from the University of Chicago. Afterwards, Scholes taught at prestigious academic institutions, such as MIT's Sloan School of Management, the University of Chicago's Graduate School of Business, and Stanford University's Business School and Law School. From the start, Scholes was interested in factors determining the demand for traded securities and the characteristics that differentiated one security's risk/return profile from another. Scholes met Robert Merton while they were both teaching at MIT and began collaborating on the work that won them the Nobel Prize. Later, they renewed contact when they were hired by Salomon Brothers as consultants.

David W. Mullins, Jr., became a professor at Harvard University's Graduate School of Business Administration after completing his undergraduate work at Yale University, receiving his M.S. degree in finance from MIT's Sloan School of Management, and earning a Ph.D. in finance and economics at MIT. In March 1989, Mullins was selected by President George H. W. Bush to be Assistant Secretary for Domestic Finance, and in December of the same year, he became one of the seven members of the Federal Reserve System's Board of Governors. Highly regarded and well connected, especially in international circles, some thought that Mullins might one day replace Alan Greenspan as Chairman of the Federal Reserve.

These four principals joined a handful of others from academia and practice to form LTCM. Together they helped to develop trading strategies, which they were confident would bring them all unheard-of profits.

LTCM'S Strategy

The principles guiding LTCM's strategy were focused and clear: identify small imperfections in the market; exploit these imperfections mercilessly, using as little equity capital as possible by taking leveraged positions that elevate risks to relatively high, but controlled, levels; secure long-term funding to be able to ride out aberrations in price movements; and charge hefty fees for the world-class talent employed to develop and implement trading strategies.

IDENTIFYING SMALL MARKET IMPERFECTIONS

LTCM earned its profits during the transition periods when markets were out of equilibrium (i.e., moving from one equilibrium to another). The company was not trying to find a needle in the haystack; rather, it was trying to find a haystack of needles. In other words, LTCM did not devote research time and effort trying to discover rising stars, like Microsoft or IBM. Rather, it searched for a multitude of low-risk arbitrage deals, each earning relatively miniscule returns, but, using its billions of dollars of investment funds, LTCM was able to accumulate substantial earnings. Relatively few of LTCM's trades were outright bets on the direction of individual assets' prices, but rather they were wagers on the spread between asset prices and the spread between yields. The goal was to construct a market-neutral portfolio that gained value in rising and falling markets.

To execute its strategies and attain the desired risk-return goals, LTCM needed abundant sources of credit and substantial market liquidity to reverse positions quickly and at firm prices. Therefore, maintaining a high credit rating was essential because, without it, LTCM's sources of finance and trade counterparties would surely disappear.

LTCM used its high-powered research team and expert understanding of security markets to study relationships between the prices of different investment assets, assorted maturities of the same asset, assets and their derivative counterparts, as well as various types of derivatives. Whenever two assets' *relative values* looked out of whack and a rational explanation could be given for why they should converge to the historic norm, LTCM traders exploited the opportunity with as much financial firepower as they could muster, purchasing the relatively underpriced asset and simultaneously selling the relatively overpriced asset.

USING A MINIMUM OF EQUITY CAPITAL

The second facet of LTCM's strategy was to exploit market imperfections, using as little equity capital as possible. Equity was conserved to pay for necessities, like margin requirements on LTCM's leveraged (equity and derivative) positions and *haircuts* on its reverse repurchase agreements.[7] The company also earmarked risk capital in case unfavorable price movements caused cash outflows on contracts that were marked to market. Exhibit 8.1

---

[7]This leverage ratio put LTCM nearly on par with the top five investment banks and approximately double the ratio of the top five banks. See President's Working Group on Financial Markets. *Hedge Funds, Leverage, and the Lessons of Long-Term Capital Management: Report of the President's Working Group on Financial Markets*. Washington, DC: Department of Treasury, 28 April 1999, 29.

Exhibit 8.1   LTCM's Asset-to-Equity Ratio: March 1994 to July 1998

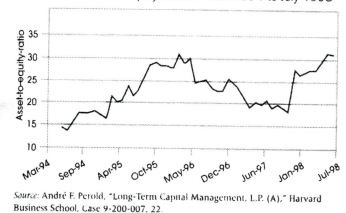

Source: André F. Perold, "Long-Term Capital Management, L.P. (A)," Harvard Business School, Case 9-200-007, 22.

shows LTCM's asset-to-equity ratio from March 1994 to July 1998. At times during this period, LTCM's leverage exceeded 30-to-1.

In the absence of equity, LTCM financed most of its security purchases with reverse repurchase agreements (reverse repos) having six-month to 12-month maturities.[8] Under a reverse repo agreement, LTCM bought a bond, and then used it as collateral for a loan, the proceeds from which LTCM used to pay for a new bond. So long as LTCM's interest costs were less than the return on its securities, profits could be earned.[9]

With limited equity at its disposal, LTCM also leveraged its positions by entering into over-the-counter total return swaps. In exchange for paying a fixed or floating rate of interest, these financial instruments gave LTCM the financial benefits of owning the underliers (e.g., equity indices, bundles of loans, or portfolios of bonds) but at a fraction of the cost in terms of equity expended. For example, with a total return swap on a share index, LTCM could acquire the risk-return profile of a diversified stock portfolio, finance it with fixed-rate or floating-rate borrowings, and use a relatively small portion of its own capital to meet any collateral requirements and/or mark-to-market obligations.[10] The U.S. margin requirement on stocks is 50%; so, the savings, in terms of capital conservation, can be considerable.

---

[8]Under a *reverse repurchase agreement*, an individual sells securities at a specified price to a securities dealer with a simultaneous commitment to repurchase the same or similar securities at a fixed price on a specific date in the future. Usually, reverse repos have very short-term maturities (e.g. overnight), but term repos are also available. The yields on repo loans are among the lowest, because they are colateralized with securities.

[9]LTCM had about 75 counterparties for its repurchase and reverse repurchase agreements.

[10]Collateral requirements are negotiated based on a hedge fund's overall level of perceived risk.

An example might help to clarify these swaps. Suppose LTCM entered into a total return swap on the S&P Stock Index with no collateral or mark-to-market provisions. The swap had a maturity of two years and a $100 million notional principal.[11] LTCM was required to pay the London interbank offered rate (LIBOR) plus 1.5%, and LTCM received the total return earned on the S&P Stock Index. At the end of Year 1, if dividends equaled 2%, and the S&P Stock Index *appreciated* by 10%, then LTCM would receive 12% of the notional principal and have to pay LIBOR plus 1.5%. If LIBOR were 5%, then LTCM would receive a net payment equal to 5.5% (i.e., $5.5 million) from its swap counterparty.[12] By contrast at the end of Year 2, if dividends equaled 1%, the S&P Index *fell* by 8%, and LIBOR were 6%, then LTCM would pay its swap counterparty 14.5% (i.e., $14.5 million).[13]

The Effects of Leverage on Risk and Return

LTCM's leveraged positions elevated both risk and potential return. Leverage created an enormous difference between the company's return on total assets and its return on equity. To understand why there was such a large difference, let's round off LTCM's 1997 equity at $5 billion and see what difference leverage has on the company's return on equity.

If LTCM started with $5 billion of equity and invested only these funds (i.e., it borrowed nothing) in assets earning 5%, at year's end, it would have earned $250 million, which would be a 5% return on both its assets and its equity (see Exhibit 8.2). By contrast, assume that LTCM leveraged its $5 billion equity by borrowing $120 billion and earning a net return on these assets of 5%. At year's end, the $5 billion of equity-financed assets would have earned $250 million (just as before) and its $120 billion of debt-financed assets would have earned $6 billion. The total return on assets would be 5% (i.e., [$250 million + 6 billion]/[$5 billion + $120 billion] = 5%), but the return on equity would be 125% (i.e., [$250 million + $6 billion]/[$5 billion] = 125%); see Exhibit 8.2. In other words, the return on assets was exactly the same as before, but borrowed funds increased the return on equity 25 times.

For highly leveraged firms like LTCM, any profits on the mountain of debt-financed assets causes the return on equity to skyrocket, but at the same time, losses could quickly wipe out the skimpy equity backing these

---

[11]The $100 million principal is *notional* because it is in the background from the beginning to the end of the swap. Neither counterparty is required to pay or expects to receive it. The $100 million principal is used only to figure out the counterparties' net payment/receipt each period.

[12]LTCM would earn 2% in dividends, plus 10% in capital gains, and be required to pay LIBOR plus 1.5% (i.e., 6.5%), which yields a *net return* of 5.5% (i.e., 10% + 2% − 6.5% = 5.5%).

[13]LTCM would earn 1% in dividends, lose 8% on the S&P Stock Index, and be required to pay a LIBOR plus 1.5% (i.e., 7.5%), which yields a *net loss* of 14.5% (i.e., 1% − 8% − 7.5% = −14.5%).

Exhibit 8.2 Is Return on Equity Meaningful for Highly Leveraged Companies?

	Equity (Millions $)	Assets (Millions $)	Dollar Returnn on Assets (Millions $)	Return on Equity	Return on Assets
Case 1	5,000	5,000	250	250/5,000 = 5%	250/5,000 = 5%
Case 2	5,000	125,000	250 +6.000 6,250	6,250/5,000 = 125%	6,250/125,000 = 5%

assets. At the beginning of 1998, LTCM had assets equal to approximately $125 billion and equity equal to $4.7 billion, so a mere 3.8% decline in asset value would have eliminated all of the firm's equity.

Elevate Risks to Relatively High, but Controlled, Levels

LTCM increased the risk of its portfolio because the company understood full well that greater risk brought the potential for greater returns. To control these risks, LTCM diversified its portfolio and used a statistical tool called Value at Risk. LTCM also employed an extensive and detailed working capital model that gave incentives to traders to finance their positions using term agreements, rather than use overnight financing to manage liquidity risks.

Diversification LTCM's managers tried to acquire a portfolio that was diversified by geographic region, security market, and currency. By owning positions with uncorrelated returns, unexpected negative shocks were expected to offset (fully or partially) unexpected positive shocks, thereby smoothing the portfolio's average return. For example, if LTCM was long European swaps but short U.K. swaps, the unanticipated gains (or losses) on the U.K. swaps might offset (fully or partially) the unanticipated losses (or gains) on the European swaps. Similarly by making diversified currency bets, LTCM's returns could be stabilized because the depreciation of one currency might be offset by the appreciation of another.

Value at Risk (VaR) To determine the appropriate level of risk, LTCM relied heavily on Value at Risk (VaR) analysis to quantify the vulnerability of its portfolio to changes in market prices and returns. VaR is a statistical measure, which is used mainly by institutions that want to determine the downside vulnerability of their actively traded portfolios. With VaR, a company can make statements like: "We are 99% certain that our portfolio will lose no more than $105 million during any one day" or "For 99 of the next 100 days, we should lose no more than $105 million."[14]

VaR analyses are based on estimates of volatility, and typically the historical standard deviation of the asset returns in a portfolio is used as a proxy for this volatility. The academic superstars at LTCM were skilled in advanced econometric and computer techniques; so, they could interpret past data in very sophisticated and meaningful ways. But for all their sophistication, the results of these analyses were meaningless if the future turned out to be significantly different from the past.[15]

The operational goal at LTCM was to lift the risk of its portfolio to 20% of net asset value (NAV)[16] per year (i.e., it wanted its portfolio to have a yearly range of fluctuation equal to 20% of its value),[17] but the company found this goal was almost impossible to achieve. Despite the leverage it maintained, LTCM could not raise its portfolio's risk level to the desired height. One reason LTCM found this task to be so difficult was because it was engaged mainly in spread trades, which are inherently less risky than outright positions.

Another reason for LTCM's inability to increase its level of portfolio risk can be traced to the fund's size. LTCM was so large that, when an opportunity presented itself, the fund would quickly try to build a position, but in doing so, LTCM would buy and sell in such volumes that market prices would change and erode the potential profits. As a result, LTCM's ability to make large trades was curtailed. Similarly, when LTCM tried to liquidate its positions, the size of its transactions and the illiquidity of the assets in its portfolio caused prices to move adversely and erode the company's gains. As a result, LTCM had to take smaller positions than desired because it was not sure that they could be liquidated at profitable rates.

Finally, LTCM had difficulty increasing its level of risk because success breeds imitators. Try as LTCM did to keep its strategies, positions, and transactions secret, the financial world was not blind to the sources of this company's success. Imitators with similar strategies and portfolios began to dot the financial landscape like dandelions in spring. Competition made the markets more competitive, which reduced the opportunity to earn returns on mispriced assets.

---

[14]VaR estimates could be made for any desired time period (e.g., day, week, month, or year), as long as sufficient information was available.

[15]See Appendix 8.2: What Are the Problems With Value at Risk, which can be found at http://www.prenhall.com/marthinsen.

[16]"Net asset value" is the dollar value of a fund's assets minus its liabilities divided by the number of shares outstanding. Net asset values are closely watched statistics and usually updated every day.

[17]See André F. Perold, "Long-Term Capital Management, L.P. (A)," Harvard Business School, Product number: 9-200-007 (5 November 1999), 11–12.

SECURING LONG-TERM FUNDING

In developing its strategy, LTCM knew that some of its positions could take as long as six months to two years before they earned profits, and, therefore the company needed well-developed and extensive financial backing (liquidity) from banks and other financial institutions to be able to wait it out. LTCM arranged credit lines ($900 million),[18] a three-year, unsecured loan ($230 million), and financed most of its security purchases in the six-month to one-year (reverse) repo market, which gave the company a buffer that would not have been present if it had used the *short-term* reverse repo market. LTCM also stabilized its equity financing by writing a covenant into the investment contract that limited investors' ability to withdraw capital from the fund. At first, this covenant stipulated that equity remain invested for at least three years, but in 1996 this restriction was eased, allowing investors to cash out one third of their capital at the end of each year after the first one. Therefore, someone who invested $12 million at the end of 1996 could withdraw nothing in 1997, but thereafter could withdraw $4 million at the end of 1998, 1999, and 2000.

It is fair to say that without these immense and, at times, unquestioned funding sources, LTCM could never have pyramided its positions to the towering levels it achieved. Brimming with funds during the boom years of the 1990s and eager to do business with the best and the brightest, many banks and dealers ignored time-tested banking principles, like demanding collateral for loans, ensuring that charges were sufficient for the risks taken, properly accounting for (off-balance-sheet) derivative positions that increased their exposures to LTCM, and demanding business relationships that were transparent instead of obfuscated with crafty legerdemain. LTCM's secretive practices created a shield behind which the fund could conceal the extent to which it was indebted. As a result, each counterparty saw only its piece of the business and not the total structure of risks and returns that LTCM had built.

Long-term funding was crucial to LTCM's strategy because it allowed the company to take positions and then hold them, if necessary, for extended periods. LTCM was a risk taker and often took positions that few others would touch. Of course, LTCM took these positions because it felt the expected rewards were adequate for the risks being assumed. As the company's portfolio grew and became more diversified, additional risk became easier to take on because most of the nonsystematic risks associated with the new positions dissolved in the vast melting pot of LTCM's other assets.

---

[18]This credit facility was syndicated by Chase Manhattan Bank with about 24 other financial institutions. In general, credit lines are relatively expensive sources of financing for hedge funds. Therefore, they usually increase their leverage with reverse repurchase agreements and derivatives.

To ensure that LTCM had sufficient liquidity, long-term sources of financing were crucial, but equally important were the roles of LTCM's back office and Bear Stearns, LTCM's agent for clearing, settling, and keeping track of trades. At times, LTCM had thousands of open derivative positions with a total notional value of about $1.25 trillion. Many of LTCM's contracts were marked to market, which meant that the company had to pay out funds daily to settle its losing trades and, of course, it had to make sure payments were received on its winning trades. Tracking the cash flows connected to LTCM's numerous positions was a sophisticated operation. What made this task even harder was LTCM's custom of hiding its positions by transacting complicated deals using multiple counterparties for different legs of the transactions. As a result, netting margin payments was often impossible.

CHARGING HEFTY FEES

LTCM's fees were head-and-shoulders above the industry average (some would say excessive), charging an annual 2% base fee on the fund's NAV. Most other hedge funds charged 1%. In addition, an incentive fee amounting to 25% of the increase in the company's NAV was charged. Most other funds charged 20%, but if LTCM's NAV fell, the 25% charge did not kick in until the fund's all-time high was surpassed.

How could LTCM charge fees that were so much above the industry standards? What would *you* pay to have the intellectual power this company brought to the table? An article in *Institutional Investor* characterized LTCM as having "...in effect the best finance faculty in the world."[19] Seven of its 12 founding principals were connected, in some way, to Harvard University or MIT, either as graduates, faculty members, or both. Clearly, the LTCM principals were able to convince investors that their strategy would work; for a while, it seemed they were right.

LTCM'S Impressive Performance: 1994–1997

In the early years, LTCM's record spoke for itself. From 1994 to 1997, LTCM's total assets increased from approximately $20 billion to $130 billion (Exhibit 8.3).

One of the main reasons for the rapid increase in LTCM's assets was because of the company's outstanding earnings record. Exhibit 8.4 shows

[19]Comment by Douglas Breeden, professor at Duke University and principal at Smith Breeden Associates. See Kevin Muehring, "John Meriwether by the Numbers," *Institutional Investor* 30 (11) (November 1996), 68–81.

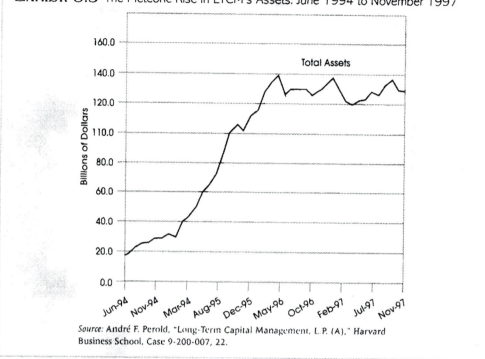

Exhibit 8.3 The Meteoric Rise in LTCM's Assets: June 1994 to November 1997

Source: André F. Perold, "Long-Term Capital Management, L.P. (A)," Harvard Business School, Case 9-200-007, 22.

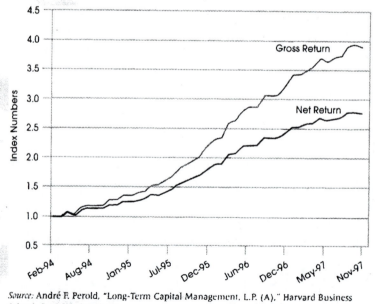

Exhibit 8.4 Index of LTCM's Gross and Net Returns: February 1994 to November 1997 *(February 1994 = 1.0)*

Source: André F. Perold, "Long-Term Capital Management, L.P. (A)," Harvard Business School, Case 9-200-007, 19.

the gravity-defying increase in LTCM's earnings from February 1994 to November 1997, as LTCM's gross returns and net returns (i.e., returns net of LTCM fees) increased by approximately 290% and 180%, respectively. Not only were these returns high, they were also stable, with only occasional monthly declines, which were quickly offset the following months by gains.

From 1994 to the end of 1997, LTCM's investors, along with its principals and hundred-fifty or so employees, were elated with the fund's performance. The principals were especially happy. Between March 1994 and November 1997, LTCM built its equity base from $1.25 billion to $7.1 billion (Exhibit 8.5). Principals, who invested $146 million, had their LTCM equity grow in three short years to $1.9 billion.

"Phenomenal" and "sensational" were adjectives attached to LTCM's performance. During the first three years of its life, the annual return on equity exceeded 40%. But can success be judged only by looking at the growth of assets and equity and the return on equity? Shouldn't risk also be considered? Most of LTCM's return on equity was due to the stratospheric levels to which the company leveraged itself. Despite LTCM's exceptional returns from 1994 to 1997, estimates indicate that the company's gross return on assets was mediocre, between 0.67% and 2.45%, and when its off-balance-sheet

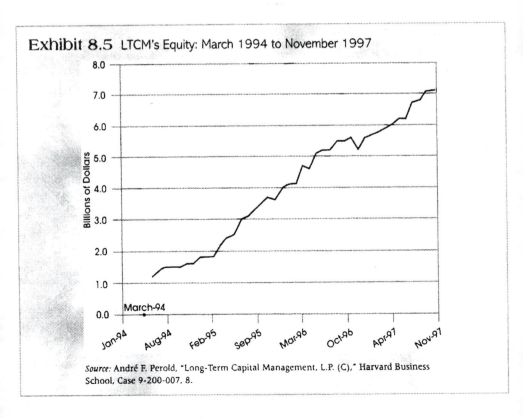

Exhibit 8.5 LTCM's Equity: March 1994 to November 1997

Source: André F. Perold, "Long-Term Capital Management, L.P. (C)," Harvard Business School, Case 9-200-007, 8.

positions were considered, the return was 1% or lower.[20] But even at a paltry 1%, when leveraged by a 30-to-1 ratio, translated into a 30% return on equity.

Evaluating LTCM based on its risk-adjusted rate of return is an even-handed way of assessing the company's performance relative to other hedge funds and investments. At the same time, any overall evaluation of LTCM should recognize the company's positive impact on the development and functioning of the global financial system.

LTCM'S Contributions to Efficient Markets

LTCM's contributions go beyond the return on equity it gave to its principals and investors during the three-year period of extraordinary growth. For a brief while, LTCM contributed significantly to the functioning and efficiency of the national and international capital markets. LTCM provided liquidity to markets that needed buyers *and* sellers. Many of its positions were illiquid because no one else dared to accept the risks at quoted market prices. LTCM was willing to do so only because its expertise (and there was enormous expertise in the company) in finding mispriced opportunities led it to accept such risks. LTCM was the willing counterparty to which numerous market participants could transfer risks, and its profits came from valuing the risks more accurately than other market participants.

LTCM's return on assets was small, but it made extraordinary profits by borrowing a mountain of funds and using them to sweep up money that was left sitting on the table due to capital market inefficiencies. As a result of its buying and selling (and LTCM was willing to take either side of a misaligned market), the markets came closer into alignment, which ensured that thousands of other participants got fairer prices for their transactions.

Despite its contributions to market efficiency and its initial successes, in the end, LTCM failed—and in spectacular fashion. Understanding the causes of this collapse provides insight into why no strategy is bulletproof and no bet is a sure thing when global financial markets are involved.

Why and How LTCM Failed

LTCM was an extraordinary company that failed because of extraordinary circumstances. Just as a well-built house can collapse if it is constructed

---

[20]See Roger Lowenstein, *When Genius Failed: The Rise and Fall of Long-Term Capital Management*. New York: Random House, 2000, 78, and Carol Loomis, "A House Built on Sand," *Fortune* 138 (8) (26 October 1998), 110–118.

on a geological fault line, a well-built hedge fund can crumble if it is constructed on faulty assumptions about the market and the inherent risks in its portfolio. The risks associated with LTCM's enormous size and high leverage ratios were supposed to be controlled by a diversified portfolio and state-of-the-art risk management tools. The company was supposed to earn stable returns regardless of whether the markets were rising or falling. What happened?

LTCM's failure was the result of a chain reaction involving three major catalysts. The first was a series of *exogenous macroeconomic shocks* that acted like economic lightening bolts to shake the entire hedge fund industry. Once shaken, the hedge fund industry attacked itself, causing many self-inflicted wounds. These *endogenous, hedge-fund-related reactions* undermined many of LTCM's basic risk-management assumptions and called into question the company's risk-management measures. The final catalyst in this chain reaction of events involved *feedback effects* that jeopardized LTCM's creditworthiness and, therefore, threatened its sources of financing and its clearing arrangements. Even though LTCM was able to meet every margin and collateral call, there was considerable fear (especially in September 1998) that it would not be able to do so.

EXOGENOUS MACROECONOMIC SHOCKS: U.S. AND GLOBAL SPREADS WIDEN

LTCM and its many imitators placed major bets on spreads narrowing in worldwide markets. But because of a series of major economic catastrophes, spreads widened in almost every market, and everywhere you looked (i.e., domestically, internationally, and cross-border) these bets began to hemorrhage cash.

U.S. Yield Spreads Widen

During 1998, U.S. spreads skyrocketed. For example, relative to U.S. Treasury bonds, the spread on mortgage rates surged from 95 basis points to 120 basis points; the spread on corporate bonds rose from 99 to 105 basis points; junk bond spreads rose from 224 to 276 basis points; swaps rose from 35 to nearly 100 basis points, and the spread on B-rated bonds relative to triple-A-rated bonds rose from 200 to 570 basis points. Emerging country debt rose from 300 to 1,700 basis points above the U.S. Treasury bond rate. The same pattern appeared throughout the world. Remember, LTCM's strategy was to bet that spreads would return to a normal range. As spreads continued to widen, LTCM began to record deep losses.

Yield Spreads Widen Globally

Numerous events converged on LTCM (and the world at large) in 1997 and 1998 to widen the spreads on virtually all financial assets. A statistician, trying to estimate the probability of *all* these events happening at once, would probably have calculated the odds at about the same level as someone being struck multiple times by lightning or being killed by falling space debris.

Asian Tiger Crisis of 1997 One of the first significant events to hit LTCM was the Asian Tiger crisis, which started in Thailand during the summer of 1997, spread to other East Asian countries (the Philippines, Malaysia, South Korea, Indonesia, and Hong Kong), and went on to affect countries as far away as Argentina, Brazil, and (yes) the United States. The source of the 1997 problem was the Asian countries had long pegged their currencies to the U.S. dollar, but their exchange rates had become unsustainably overvalued. Speculators, sensing devaluations were imminent, pounded the markets tenaciously by selling baht, rupiahs, ringitts, and pesos. The central banks of these Asian nations supported their fixed exchange rates until they ran out of international reserves. When they did, their currencies were cut loose to float untethered to the moorings of the U.S. dollar.

When currency crises like these happen, investors typically respond by investing heavily in safe assets and sound currencies. As a result, they bought dollar-denominated U.S. government bonds and invested deeply in stable assets denominated in European currencies, such as German marks and Swiss francs. This flight to quality pushed down the yields on financial assets in the developed nations and pushed up the return on assets in the emerging markets, causing spreads to widen. LTCM had bet continuously that the spreads would narrow, so when they widened, the company lost on both sides of its spread positions. But in the stormy clouds of this international crisis, LTCM saw a glimmer of light because wider spreads meant new opportunities to increase its positions and to benefit later when the spreads converged to their historically normal ranges. The problem was finding ways to finance these new opportunities in a stressed economic environment.

Because its Asian investments were concentrated mainly in Japan, LTCM weathered the Asian storm and managed to end 1997 with a respectable, albeit diminished, return. Even after refunding $2.7 billion[21] to investors at the end of 1997, LTCM's equity capital was still at a healthy $4.7 billion

---

[21] At the end of 1997, LTCM forced investors to take back $2.7 billion of their investment funds, but the company did not reduce its investment positions. This forced refund is discussed later in this chapter and also in the Epilogue: What Happened to the Partners, Creditors, Investors, and Consortium? at the end of the chapter.

level. *What doesn't kill you, makes you stronger* might have been the credo at LTCM as 1998 began.

Russian Default No sooner had the Asian crisis left the front pages of the press than the financial crisis in Russia began. Like the Asian Tigers' currencies, capital flight put enormous pressure on the international value of the ruble; to complicate matters, the price of oil (a major Russian export) was falling. Russia tripled its interest rates to encourage investors to stay in rubles, but these efforts only served to undermine the ability of domestic businesses to borrow at reasonable rates in order to finance normal business activities (e.g., working capital, capital expenditures, and expansion). Who can afford to borrow when interest rates are more than 200%?

Bankruptcies soared, unemployment rose, government budget deficits grew, many banks were threatened with insolvency, and the central bank's international reserves were depleted. With Russia's economic and financial systems staggering on the brink of collapse, the IMF arranged a $22.6 billion bailout in July 1998; unfortunately, the bailout was not enough to stave off the crisis. The ruble continued to fall. On 17 August, Russia devalued the ruble and announced a debt moratorium on $13.5 billion of *local currency* debt.[22]

LTCM lost on its Russian bond positions, but the company's exposures were limited relative to other hedge funds and securities firms. What was important about the Russian ruble crisis was that it triggered contagion,[23] which spread to other parts of the world (e.g., Brazil, Turkey, and Venezuela), to many other investment markets and, thereby, affected many other hedge funds in a similar way.

Volatile Political and Economic Climate

Bad economic and political news continued during late 1997 and 1998 and hit LTCM like relentless sledgehammers. In August 1997, Tellabs, Inc., a company in which LTCM held positions, announced that the shareholder vote for its acquisition of Ciena Corp. would be canceled. Spreads widened and LTCM incurred heavy cash outflows to meet compulsory margin requirements. In the end, losses amounted to about $150 million. LTCM's profits were further eroded when an International Monetary Fund (IMF)–led bailout of Indonesia ran into problems, and rioting forced President Mohamed Suharto to resign after 32 years of authoritarian rule; China threatened to devalue the yuan because the Japanese yen's depreciation had hurt China's export trade; Iraq was stirring Middle East tensions as it

---

[22]Russia had made a $3.5 billion Eurobond issue less than a month before the default, causing widespread speculation that Russia would default, as well, on these dollar-denominated securities.
[23]See Risk Notepad 8.2: What Is Contagion?

Risk Notepad 8.2

What Is Contagion?

Contagion occurs when events in one nation or region spill over to other nations or regions. The more closely linked the economies, the more likely changes in one will influence the other, and the more similar are countries' circumstances (e.g., in terms of current account and budget deficits, and rates of inflation, real GDP growth, and unemployment), the more likely currency speculators will select those countries as potential targets.

Contagion has been responsible for transmitting considerable economic hardship to many countries. For instance, when the Mexican peso (*Tequila*) crisis occurred in December 1994, investors panicked and tried to pull their funds out of countries like Argentina, Brazil, and Venezuela, which had similar economic characteristics (e.g. unsustainable fiscal and current account imbalances) as Mexico. Similarly, the Asian crisis in 1997 and 1998 had a significant impact on nearby countries as the core of the crisis spread from Thailand to the Philippines, Malaysia, South Korea, Indonesia, and Hong Kong, but it also spread as far as Latin America, where countries like Argentina and Brazil were impacted.

Contagion is herd behavior at its worst, and its cold, cruel touch can disrupt trade flows, capital markets, investment decisions, government and central bank policies, bank lending, inflation rates, and the size of government budget deficits.

thwarted U.N. weapon inspection teams. All of these events converged and drove a larger wedge between developing nations' yields and the yields of developed nations. As yield spreads widened, LTCM's losses mounted.

ENDOGENOUS SHOCKS: SPREADS GO HELTER SKELTER AND VAR GETS TWISTED

By 1998, many hedge funds were built to imitate the past successes of LTCM. As a result, the diversified portfolio that LTCM spent so much time constructing was duplicated many times over. Wider margins put these similarly structured hedge funds under pressure to cover their losses, as well as meet the collateral obligations, haircuts, and margin requirements on both new trades and existing positions. Investors fled to safer investments, and hedge fund managers tried, simultaneously, to reduce their exposures.[24]

The mass exodus of hedge funds from existing positions caused market spreads to change in predictable but bizarre ways. Relative value trades

[24]The importance of these endogenous reactions is highlighted in Donald MacKenzie, "Long-Term Capital Management and the Sociology of Arbitrage," *Economy and Society* 32(3) (August 2003), 349–380. A relatively recent empirical study casts some doubt on the importance of the endogenous effects. See Tobias Adrian, "Measuring Risk in the Hedge Fund Sector," *Federal Reserve Bank of New York Current Issues in Economics and Finance* 13(3) (March/April 2007), 1–7. This study is also available at: http://www.newyorkfed.org/research/current_issues. Accessed 28 December 2007

that were bets on wider spreads narrowed, and relative value trades that were bets on narrower spreads widened. It was as if all the care and thought that talented hedge fund managers had put into analyzing and then taking positions were suddenly thrown out the window.[25] In June and July of 1998, the situation got worse as Salomon Brothers began to liquidate its proprietary bond arbitrage business. Salomon's decision to exit resulted in a flood of security sales that coincided with LTCM's largest pre-crisis withdrawals and helped set the stage for even greater losses for LTCM later.

LTCM built *what it thought* was a portfolio of economically unrelated positions. What it missed seeing was that many of these positions were linked by similar investment fund owners with similar strategies. As a result, the price volatility of these positions was connected by parallel risk tolerances, funding needs, and liquidity requirements. Rather than being highly uncorrelated, the positions in LTCM's portfolio turned out to be highly correlated with the portfolios of other hedge funds. This misperception caused LTCM to underestimate its true level of risk, causing the company to move with abandon in the wrong direction. Under normal conditions, LTCM's asset distribution would have been fine, but when the correlations among returns converged to one (i.e., perfect correlation), the normal protections afforded by diversification were eliminated. Losses on one position were just as likely to be matched, rather than offset, by other positions.[26]

The situation was made even worse by hedge funds and proprietary shops selling positions in anticipation of LTCM liquidating its portfolio. In many cases, these trades were highly speculative because the sellers did not have accurate information about the composition of LTCM's portfolio.

Value at Risk Analysis Gone Awry

How could LTCM have suffered such heavy losses when it systematically used VaR analysis as a navigation tool for estimating its vulnerability to short-term changes in market prices? The fund had never lost more than 2% of its value (i.e., $100 million) in any month since operations began in 1994. At the 99% level of confidence, LTCM's econometricians assured the

---

[25]This result was anticipated in a research article published in 1997. The authors showed that even trades that will eventually be profitable may have to be abandoned early due to adverse price movements. Therefore, arbitrage may not be able to completely eliminate price anomalies. See Andrei Shleifer and Robert W. Vishney, "The Limits of Arbitrage," *Journal of Finance* LII(1) (March 1997), 35–55.

[26]Based on five-year historical data, the correlation among the asset returns in LTCM's portfolio was approximately 0.1 (or lower). LTCM used a more conservative correlation of 0.3 in its VaR analyses, but even that was not enough. Richard Leahy, a LTCM principal, felt that the true correlation in 1998 was seven times the historic level. See Donald MacKenzie, "Long-Term Capital Management and the Sociology of Arbitrage," *Economy and Society* 32(3) (August 2003), 358, 364.

principals and investors that the company should lose no more than $105 million per day.[27] With LTCM's sizeable equity, there seemed to be more than enough cushion to endure any major hit.

Model Risk

On two important levels, LTCM suffered from high model risk. First, the company adopted the risk-management system of Salomon Brothers, where JM and many of his traders had worked previously. But investment banks are different from hedge funds, and their risk-management systems should also be different. Investment banks usually have a larger number of independent income sources and better access to liquidity than hedge funds. These differences are significant because they influence these financial institutions' exposures to risk and their ability to sustain losses until positions become profitable.

A second source of model risk came from LTCM's use of VaR as its principal measure of portfolio risk. VaR assumes that the future will be like the past, and the world can be summarized by assuming all possible future events fit neatly into a normally distributed, bell-shaped distribution function.[28] Both of these assumptions may be true most of the time, but they are not true all the time.

Exhibit 8.6 summarizes the losses sustained by LTCM in 1998, which amounted to approximately $4.5 billion. Based on VaR, with 99% probability, this company's *yearly* returns should have varied by no more than about $714 million, which was only 10.5% of LTCM's $6.8 billion equity.[29] Otherwise stated, a yearly reduction in returns by an amount greater than $714 million should have occurred roughly *once every hundred years*. Nevertheless, just for the month of August, LTCM's performance was down 44%, and it was down 52% from the previous year.[30] On one day (Friday, 21 August) alone, LTCM lost $553 million, and four trading days later (Thursday, 27 August), it lost an additional $277 million. During the five trading

---

[27]This $105 million figure is an overestimate. Assuming a highly diversified portfolio, the daily standard deviation of LTCM's portfolio in September 1997 was $45 million/day; which means that a 99% level of confidence would be 2.33 standard deviations (2.33 × $45 million/day = $105 million/day) from the *average* return. See André F. Perold, "Long-Term Capital Management, L.P. (A)," Harvard Business School, Product number: 9-200-007 (5 November 1999), 11–12.

[28]See Appendix 8.2: What Are the Problems With Value at Risk, which explains in more detail some of the deficiencies of VaR analysis. Available at http://www.prenhall.com/marthinsen.

[29]This $714 million figure was derived as follows: (Standard deviation per year) = (Standard deviation per day) × (Square root of 252 trading days per year). Therefore, $45 million/day × (252 working days/year)$^{0.5}$ = $714.4 million/year.

[30]John Meriwether, "Letter to Investors of LTCM" (2 September 1998). See André F. Perold, "Long-Term Capital Management, L.P. (D)," Harvard Business School, Product number: 9-200-010 (28 October 1999).

Exhibit 8.6 Trades That Caused LTCM's Losses in 1998

Activity	Losses
Stock market volatility	$1,300 million
Swaps	$1,600 million
Emerging markets: Russia	$430 million
Directional trades	$371 million
Equity pairs (e.g., Volkswagen and Shell)	$286 million
Yield curve	$215 million
S&P stocks	$203 million
Junk bond arbitrage	$100 million
Risk arbitrage	Broke even
Total	**$4,505 million**

Source: Roger Lowenstein, *When Genius Failed: The Rise and Fall of Long-Term Capital Management.* New York: Random House, 2000, 234.

days from Thursday, 10 September to Wednesday, 16 September, LTCM lost $145 million, $120 million, $55 million, $87 million, and $122 million, respectively—accumulated losses of $529 million![31] On Monday, 21 September, LTCM again lost $553 million, and the following day racked up losses of $152 million.[32] According to VaR, losses of such magnitude should happen perhaps once every few millennia, but not during the course of one month.[33]

FEEDBACK SHOCKS

As LTCM's position worsened, liquidity dried up, its counterparties sought to protect themselves, and the services of LTCM's clearing agent became problematic. LTCM was desperate for funds and wanted to reduce its exposures, but many of these positions were illiquid. The company knew from the beginning that its positions might be hard to liquidate; so the company

---

[31] Roger Lowenstein, *When Genius Failed: The Rise and Fall of Long-Term Capital Management.* New York: Random House, 2000, 180.
[32] Ibid., pp. 191 and 197.
[33] Almost half of LTCM's cash outflows in September 1998 (about $1 billion) were from its index option positions. Swaps also accounted for a large portion of the losses. See Donald MacKenzie. "Long-Term Capital Management and the Sociology of Arbitrage," *Economy and Society* 32(3) (August 2003), 349–380.

positioned itself to have enough funding if things went wrong. Now, LTCM found itself with a portfolio of assets that few individuals wanted, and potential buyers, like Salomon Dean Whitter, Société Générale, Bankers Trust, and Morgan Stanley Smith Barney, were driving hard bargains because they knew how distressed LTCM had become.

Aggressive Marking to Market

LTCM always negotiated two-way (i.e., LTCM and its counterparty) collateral and mark-to-market covenants in order to conserve and stabilize its supply of working capital. The company also negotiated term agreements for posting collateral; therefore, when LTCM ran into trouble, dealers could not change the haircuts or other financing terms on LTCM's existing positions. Without such recourse, dealers tried to collect as much as they could by aggressively marking to market LTCM's positions in favor of themselves. This aggressive mark-to-market pricing caused a systematic decline in LTCM's net asset value for virtually every position in its portfolio.

The problem was that, during the 1990s, competition for hedge fund business caused many banks and security firms to relax or discard parts of their internal risk-management policies. Rather than impose collateral requirements that accounted for a hedge fund's *potential* exposures, these financial institutions were satisfied if they covered just *current* exposures. Instead of analyzing the joint effects of credit, liquidity, and market risks, they analyzed each risk as if it were independent. Now, the tide had turned, and these counterparties were scurrying to protect themselves from these highly interdependent risks.

LTCM's penchant for secrecy and opaqueness exacerbated the problem. In an effort to conceal its profitable positions and trading strategies from the market, LTCM often used different counterparties for each leg of a complex deal. For example, it might take a long position in Royal Dutch Shell (RDS) and a short position in Shell Transport (ST), which as a pair has very little risk, but then use RDS as collateral for a margin loan from JP Morgan and borrow ST from Union Bank of Switzerland. Counterparties knew, at best, their own (bilateral) exposures to LTCM, but they had no idea of LTCM's overall level of risk. When LTCM came under financial pressure, these counterparties assumed the worst and panicked. En masse, they considered just their own unhedged legs of LTCM's deals and, therefore, overestimated the company's true level of risk. If they had access to LTCM's records, they would have seen that it had a closely related short position for almost every long instrument and a closely related long position for almost every short instrument. Therefore, the net risk on LTCM's deals was much smaller than the sum of their parts.

Clearing Services and Legal Uncertainties

LTCM was also in danger of losing the services of Bear Stearns, its agent for clearing, settling, and recording trades.[34] Bear Stearns was adamant that it would stop performing these functions the minute LTCM's deposits fell below $500 million, and LTCM was rapidly approaching this critical threshold level. As conditions worsened, the noose got tighter.

Another problem was that rumors of LTCM's possible demise began to circulate with reports that the company might file for bankruptcy protection in the Cayman Islands. Creditors and counterparties were uncertain of their rights under Cayman law—especially, concerning their ability to net positions, close-out (i.e., terminate) contracts, and sell collateral. This added risk further reduced the willingness of market participants to deal with LTCM.

A Ray of Sunshine: LTCM's Credit Line

Fortunately for LTCM, one source of liquidity not threatened was its $900 million revolving credit line with a syndicate of banks led by Chase. When this credit line was negotiated in 1996, LTCM paid dearly to exclude the *material adverse change* (MAC) provision, which would have allowed the bank syndicate to cut or cancel LTCM's line of credit. LTCM figured (correctly) that, if these funds were ever needed, the MAC provision would probably be in effect. The credit-line agreement stipulated that only if LTCM's equity fell by 50% or more at the end of any accounting period could the facility be canceled.[35] But LTCM's accounting period ended 31 July 1998, and at that point, it had more than enough equity to meet this capital threshold.

The Beginning of the End

In May and June 1998, LTCM posted losses of approximately 7% and 10%, respectively, then, during July (the lull before the storm), the company almost broke even. The floodgates opened in August 1998, when LTCM's performance was down 44% with 82% of the losses coming from relative trades and 18% from directional trades.[36] Losses of $1.8 billion in August 1998 reduced LTCM's capital base to $2.3 billion, which was about 50%

---

[34]Bear Sterns was also responsible for financing LTCM's intraday foreign exchange and security transactions, providing margin to purchase securities, and borrowing securities for LTCM's short positions. Bear Sterns eventually stopped providing LTCM with intraday clearing credit and required it to collateralize *potential* settlement exposures.

[35]Covenants on the $900 million term credit prohibited LTCM from drawing down, from one accounting period to the next, more than 50% of the amount by which its equity exceeded $1 billion. See André F. Perold, "Long-Term Capital Management, L.P (C)." Harvard Business School, Product number: 9-200-009 (5 November 1999), 4.

[36]John Meriwether, "Letter to Investors of LTCM" (2 September 1998). See Perold, André F. "Long Term Capital Management, L.P. (D)." Harvard Business School, Product number: 9-200-010 (28 October 1999). See Appendix 8.1: LTCM's Major Trades, which can be found at http://www.prenhall.com/marthinsen.

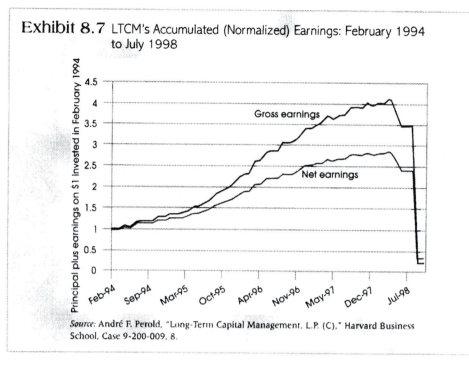

Exhibit 8.7 LTCM's Accumulated (Normalized) Earnings: February 1994 to July 1998

Source: André F. Perold, "Long-Term Capital Management, L.P. (C)," Harvard Business School, Case 9-200-009, 8.

below its year-earlier level. Of these losses, 16% were from LTCM's positions in emerging markets. Despite the illiquidity of its portfolio and its size, LTCM still felt that its funding sources were more than adequate to ride out any storm, but it soon became apparent that the company's funding sources would be exhausted long before the profits on healthy trades could be realized.

Exhibit 8.7 shows the rise and fall of LTCM's earnings from 1994 to 1998. Between 1994 and the end of 1997, LTCM turned each dollar of invested funds into more than $4 of accumulated capital, but in 1998, investors watched in shock as their accumulated earnings fell from $4 to about 33 cents.[37]

The Fed, Warren Buffett, and the Rescue of LTCM

Banks and securities firms that had been funding LTCM and providing necessary services during the company's meteoric rise wanted nothing to do with it once losses started accumulating. No one at the Fed felt any particular responsibility to save LTCM's wealthy principals or its sophisticated investors. Nevertheless, there was fear that LTCM had grown so large and its tentacles had penetrated so deeply into such a wide cross section of the global financial markets that its bankruptcy could result in a financial meltdown of the

[37]Investors who were not principals or in the core investor group did not lose that much when LTCM failed because the company *forced them* in 1997 to take back $2.7 billion of their invested capital. Because LTCM had been so successful up until that point, investors resisted taking back these funds, but in the end, the forced refund saved them billions in losses.

U.S. and worldwide capital markets. If the markets began to question the solvency of all their counterparties, liquidity in the market could dry up quickly. Globally, Germany's Dresdner Bank AG was facing LTCM-related losses of $144 million; Switzerland's UBS and Credit Suisse reported losses of $678.5 million and $55 million, respectively. Financial institutions in the United States also faced substantial write-offs.

At first, it looked as though LTCM's positions were distributed broadly enough among banks so that, for the most part, losses would not result in any large bank failure or systemic damage (i.e., a domino effect among banks and other financial institutions). Nevertheless, there were still too many hidden cards for the Fed to know how much to wager on this assumption. With LTCM's $80 billion in assets on the line, massive collateral sales could have led to horrific reductions in asset prices and resulted in complicated financial problems, such as the deterioration in bank assets and the withering of credit.

Until 1998, LTCM's records were closely guarded secrets,[38] but by mid-1998, the word was out that it was actively seeking a white knight. No suitors would buy a portfolio sight unseen; so, to convince them that its positions had long-term potential, LTCM had to open its books to Wall Street. The problem was that many of these suitors were LTCM's major competitors, and if they were allowed more than a peek at these records, they could have relayed LTCM's positions to their trading desks and fleeced LTCM like a lamb.

In September 1998, William (Bill) J. McDonough, President of the New York Federal Reserve Bank, called together a consortium of major banks to see if a rescue could be negotiated. Technically, the Fed was sailing in uncharted waters because it did not have jurisdiction over hedge funds like LTCM, but time was running out. On Friday, 18 September, when William McDonough convened the prestigious financial institutions, LTCM's equity stood at $1.5 billion. By the following Wednesday, it was already down to about $600 million. Something needed to be done quickly.[39]

On Wednesday (23 September), just a few days before a deal was struck, Warren Buffett, head of Berkshire Hathaway, along with American International Group Inc. (AIG), and Goldman, Sachs & Co. (GS) made an offer for the assets, liabilities (financing), and contractual positions of Long-Term Capital Portfolio L.P.(LTCP), which was the Cayman Islands–based fund that was managed by LTCM. Buffett wanted to purchase LTCP, keep the financing in place, buy off any net asset value of third-party investors, boot out LTCM's

---

[38]LTCM was so secretive that it kept its trades confidential even *after* the positions were closed.

[39]The negotiations among LTCM, consortium members, and the Federal Reserve can be analyzed in the context of a classic *prisoner's dilemma* game. This framework illuminates the tradeoffs between private and public incentives as well as the differences between one-time static games and repeated games. See Beth Seely, "Long-Term Capital Management: An Analysis of Intervention as a Prisoners' Dilemma," *Working Paper No. 99–01*, Division of Economic Analysis: Commodity Futures Trading Commission (Washington D.C., 24 February 1999), 1–20.

madcap traders, and take control of the board of directors. The $250 million offer would have gone to LTCM's shareholders with the promise of an additional $3.75 billion, if needed, to stem future losses. Most of the funds ($3 billion) were to come from Berkshire Hathaway.[40] Buffett made his offer at about 11:00 A.M. and gave LTCM an hour to respond. Given the strict time limit, JM was unable to secure the needed approvals.[41] As a result, Buffett's offer went unanswered and lapsed after one hour.

Risk Notepad 8.3

Another Look at Warren Buffett's Offer for LTCM

LTCM might have accepted Warren Buffett's offer, but there was a major technical problem. JM and his management team had only one hour to respond. Many financial agreements (e.g., swaps) require counterparty approval before they can be assigned. Cleary, most of LTCM's counterparties would have been delighted to transfer their positions to BH-AIG-GS, but LTCM had more than 240 major counterparties and thousands of complicated deals to consider.[42] Under normal conditions, it would have taken more than an hour to get the necessary approvals. Accomplishing this feat under the threat of bankruptcy and while making sure to avoid claims of fraud or deception proved to be an impossible task in the space of 60 minutes. As a result, Buffett's offer was not rejected by JM. It simply lapsed without an answer.

To this day, the one-hour time limit imposed on JM is confusing. It makes sense from the perspective that LTCM's asset prices were changing dramatically, and any bid faced considerable risk. The short time fuse was also a precaution against having the bid shopped around. Still, Warren Buffett was one of the premier investors of the twentieth century and must have known (or been advised) that LTCM needed counterparty approval before positions could be transferred. Therefore, it is unclear why Buffett, the Sage from Omaha, structured this offer the way he did.

Ultimately, the consortium's $3.65 billion offer was accepted. It did not require counterparty approval because the offer was an investment in LTCM's equity, rather than the transfer of positions. The economic difference was subtle, but the legal difference was crucial. The consortium deal was head and shoulders better than the BH-AIG-GS offer, and this is important. The LTCM principals had a fiduciary responsibility to act with undivided loyalty and transparency, to avoid conflicts of interest and fraud, and to negotiate the best deal possible for its owners. The difference between the BH-AIG-GS offer and the consortium offer was unquestionably material.

---

[40] Goldman Sachs agreed to invest $300 million and manage LTCM's portfolio. Berkshire Hathaway Inc., agreed to contribute $3 billion, and AIG was willing to contribute $700 million. See Mitchell Pacelle, Leslie Scism, and Steven Lipin, "How Buffett, AIG and Goldman Sought Long-Term Capital, but Were Rejected," *Wall Street Journal* (30 September 1998), C1.

[41] See Risk Notepad 8.3: Another Look at Warren Buffett's Offer for LTCM.

[42] About 90% of LTCM's trades were with 15 counterparties, but in some cases, the counterparties were affiliates (e.g., JP Morgan, JP Morgan Tokyo, and JP Morgan London). Negotiating with 40 counterparties each having six affiliates meant involving 240 counterparties. The President's Working Group on Financial Markets reported that LTCM had more than 60,000 trades on its books. See President's Working Group on Financial Markets, *Hedge Funds, Leverage, and the Lessons of Long-Term Capital Management: Report of the President's Working Group on Financial Markets*, Washington, DC: Department of Treasury, 28 April 1999, 11

The recapitalization agreement for LTCM was finalized on 28 September, when 14 banks and brokerage houses contributed $3.65 billion to the rescue effort.[43] Contrary to some published reports, the Federal Reserve System did not advance a penny of the funds; its role was purely as a facilitator and a forum provider (and perhaps, as an arm-twisting persuader for the reluctant). Together with LTCM's $400 million in remaining equity, the cash infusion looked to be enough to get LTCM through this financial crisis. The consortium was expected to last for three years while LTCM was liquidated.

For most of the participants, rescuing LTCM was a bitter pill to swallow because they were being asked for help at a time when their own income statements, balance sheets, and credit ratings were being decimated by the slumping markets.[44] Shares of these financial institutions had been pummeled in the market; Goldman Sachs, a private company, had to postpone its IPO due to poor market conditions.[45] Now, these financial institutions were being asked to save a group whose arrogance, secrecy, and overbearing style of trading were of epic dimensions, which just added to the consortium members' chagrin. Nevertheless, the liquidation went smoothly, and by early 2000, LTCM's portfolio had been sold. In the end, none of the top six security firms incurred any realized or unrealized losses during the third quarter of 1998 as a result of the failure. LTCM's mark-to-market exposures in August and September were fully collateralized. Even in September 1998, when margin calls ran into tens of millions of dollars, LTCM had more than 300% of the needed funds in its margin account.[46]

Under the recapitalization plan, the consortium gained 90% ownership of the fund (i.e., LTCP) and operational control as general partner. The original owners' (i.e., LTCM's principals' and investors') claim on the company was written down to 10%, with the provision that the principals stay with LTCM for one year and help liquidate its trades in an orderly manner. By accepting 10% of a company that now had at least $3.65 billion in

---

[43]The banks were: 1. Bankers Trust ($300 million), 2. Barclays ($300 million), 3. Chase Manhattan ($300 million), 4. Deutsche Bank ($300 million), 5. Union Bank of Switzerland ($300 million), 6. Travelers/Salomon Smith Barney ($300 million), 7. J.P. Morgan ($300 million), 8. Goldman Sachs ($300 million), 9. Merrill Lynch ($300 million), 10. Crédit Suisse-First Boston ($300 million), 11. Morgan Stanley Dean Witter ($300 million), 12. Société Générale ($125 million), 13. Bank Paribas ($100 million), and 14. Lehman Brothers ($100 million). Steven Lipin, Matt Murray, and Jacob M. Schlesinger, "Bailout Blues: How a Big Hedge Fund Marketed Its Expertise and Shrouded Its Risks—Regulators and Lenders Knew Little About the Gambles at Long-Term Capital—'Stardust' in Investors' Eyes," *Wall Street Journal* (25 September 1998), A1.

[44]Credit rating agencies, like Standard and Poor's, were threatening to downgrade the debt of investment banks, such as Lehman Brothers, Goldman Sachs, and Merrill Lynch.

[45]Goldman Sachs waited until May 1999 to go public.

[46]President's Working Group on Financial Markets. *Hedge Funds, Leverage, and the Lessons of Long-Term Capital Management: Report of the President's Working Group on Financial Markets.* Washington, DC: Department of Treasury, 28 April 1999, B-7 and C-12.

consortium-supplemented equity, the LTCM's shareholders had increased their take by $150 million more than the Buffett et. al proposal, but it was still only one-tenth of their positions one year earlier. The deal also came with an implied call option because, if LTCM recovered, the principals' interests would rise and, conceivably, they could repurchase LTCM from the consortium.

Reaction to the Fed-sponsored rescue was mixed. Those who favored it lauded the Fed and the consortium for saving the global financial system from immeasurable damage. At the same time, critics protested that the rescue was just another example of capitalist hypocrisy.[47] Why was the Fed willing to intervene on the behalf of rich investors, about 150 employees, and a handful of principals? Why should the LTCM principals be allowed to keep anything after inflicting such losses? Wasn't this the fund that was incorporated in the Cayman Islands to avoid paying U.S. taxes? Why was the Fed not giving such limousine service to countries like Russia, Brazil, and Argentina? Frustrations and anger ran deep.

One of the central issues involved *moral hazard,* a major cause of market failure.[48] For the Fed, the moral hazard issue boiled down to a simple question: If it bailed out LTCM, might the Fed be signaling to other hedge funds and financial institutions that there would always be a safety net for those companies deemed "too big to fail," resulting in an even greater number of failures in the future? In other words, would the Fed be granting LTCM a free put option on its own portfolio, thereby providing an incentive for other companies to take greater financial risks in the future?[49] Although the Fed did not contribute a penny to the recapitalization, its presence might have raised the value of the implied protection (the put option) given to LTCM.

Conclusions and Lessons to Be Learned

LTCM was a creature of turmoil, structured to thrive in turbulence, regardless of whether the markets went up or down. The greater the volatility (and it made no difference whether this instability was company, industry, domestically, or globally based), the greater the opportunities. How ironic, then, that in the end, turbulence was a major cause of the company's undoing. The LTCM failure was like a huge plane crash in which all the passengers, crew, and crash site residents walked away with relatively minor

---

[47]Michael Schroeder and Jacob M. Schlesinger. "Fed May Face Recrimination over Handling of Fund Bailout," *Wall Street Journal* (25 September 1998), A8.
[48]Moral hazard occurs when individuals with insurance take greater risks (because they are protected) than they would have taken without insurance.
[49]See, Anonymous (editorial), "Decade of Moral Hazard," *Wall Street Journal* (25 September 1998), A14.

injuries. Despite the lack of extensive damage, there are many lessons to be learned from this episode.

BE CAREFUL WHAT YOU WISH FOR

LTCM tried to profit from mispriced spreads. When spreads facing the hedge fund industry widened and then went topsy-turvy, they undermined historically based risk management measures. Greater economic and financial turbulence gave rise to an abundance of new opportunities, but the market's *flight to quality, flight to liquidity,* and *flight from arbitrage* threatened LTCM's sources of credit as well as the willingness and ability of its counterparties to engage in new trades and to hold open positions.

BEWARE OF MODEL RISK

LTCM placed large bets using considerable practical experience and sophisticated statistical analyses, but its conclusions were based on a risk management model that ultimately proved to be faulty for two major reasons. First, it used risk management parameters that may have been better suited to an investment bank than a hedge fund; second, it did not account for those occasions when markets react and move in ways that are inconsistent with historical precedent.

LTCM made and deeply believed in four major assumptions that proved wrong. First, it assumed that prices would move continuously, which means large discrete price changes would not occur. It was wrong. Secondly, it assumed that price volatility would return quickly to its historic average. Again, it was wrong. Thirdly, LTCM assumed that asset returns were normally distributed, so that, with 99% accuracy, the company could calculate and control its risk levels. Again, it was wrong—the real world seems to have fat tails, which means extreme events have much larger probabilities of occurring than the normal distribution indicates (i.e., very bad and very good things happen more often than expected). Finally, LTCM assumed that investors' decisions were independent of one another in the sense that what someone decides today will not influence what he decides tomorrow, and what someone decides today will not influence anyone else. Again, LTCM was wrong. Momentum in the global financial markets kept spreads moving against LTCM, indicating that decisions are not independent.

ALL FOR ONE AND "1" FOR ALL

LTCM was not the only financial intermediary to experience profitability and cash flow problems. Losses were endemic to the industry. In part, the industry-wide losses were due to hedge funds that emulated LTCM's successes and adopted similar strategies. When these imitator funds tried to liquidate their positions all at once, market prices turned sharply against them. Correlations among the prices of otherwise unrelated assets suddenly converged to one, their highest level. Portfolios that were once very diversified looked increasingly like a common, industry-wide portfolio. The new correlations made LTCM's VaR estimates virtually useless indicators of the true risks facing the company.

LEVERAGE IS A FAIR-WEATHER FRIEND

In its final report in 1999, the President's Working Group on Financial Markets concluded that the principal policy issue emerging from the LTCM collapse was excessive leverage.[50] At times, LTCM's leverage ratio rose above 30:1, which meant if investment returns increased assets by a little less than 3.5%, the company earned 100% on its equity, and if they fell by the same amount, the company was insolvent.[51] Leverage adds to risk and, therefore, gives companies more opportunities to succeed and also more opportunities to fail. It is for this reason that the credit risk of leveraged hedge funds, even those with market-neutral strategies and stellar past performances, must be objectively assessed and constantly monitored.

FINANCIAL TRANSPARENCY IS THE FIRST STEP IN MEANINGFUL REFORM

The lack of financial transparency was a major source of this debacle. LTCM hid its positions by dividing trades among half dozen or more counterparties, each having only a partial understanding of LTCM's overall position. Only part of these chain-linked trades surfaced to the balance sheets of these financial intermediaries because they were derivative positions, many of them highly leveraged. In the end, these positions increased substantially the systemic risks from LTCM's failure, and the contagion from LTCM's failure threatened to spill over into the global financial markets. Because hedge funds are here to stay, financial regulators (e.g., the Federal Reserve System, Securities and Exchange Commission, Japanese Ministry of Finance, and European Central Bank) are seeking efficient ways to balance regulation with open competition. Central banks worldwide are also searching for more effective methods to supervise the network of regulated banks that deal on a regular basis with hedge funds.

---

[50]President's Working Group on Financial Markets. *Hedge Funds, Leverage, and the Lessons of Long-Term Capital Management: Report of the President's Working Group on Financial Markets.* Washington, DC: Department of Treasury. 28 April 1999.
[51]Near the end, in the summer of 1998, LTCM's leverage rose above 100:1 because of the rapid decline in its equity and the more sluggish relative decline in its assets.

IN THE LONG RUN, BET ON GLOBAL FINANCIAL MARKETS BEING EFFICIENT

In competitive markets, excess profits are difficult to achieve because success invites imitation, and imitation reduces the margins on which the original profits were made. Some markets may be slow to react, but over time, profiting from inefficient markets is like picking low-hanging fruit or sweeping money off a table. If it is that easy, then others will be sure to follow. LTCM soon had many imitators, and as a result, its proprietary techniques lost their distinctive edge, which meant the company fell victim, increasingly, to its own success.

YOU CAN'T FLOAT WITHOUT LIQUIDITY

If the first rule of mountain climbing is *Don't let go of one thing until you have a hold of something else*, then the first rule of hedge funds is *Don't buy what you can't sell*. When the going gets rough, liquidity is crucial, and if you do not have a ready market into which you can sell your assets, then maybe a second (or third) look at your assets is needed. Had LTCM not leveraged itself to such extreme levels, illiquidity would not have been such a problem, but when economic conditions in 1997 and 1998 unexpectedly went helter skelter, LTCM had to liquidate portions of its portfolio at fire sale prices just to meet its ever-increasing margin calls and collateral requirements.

The problem was that many financial intermediaries had very similar portfolios and risk management systems. As well, they were forced by the market to focus on short-term financial results because their portfolios were marked-to-market daily. In a liquidity crunch, these institutions acted in the same way. Their flight to liquidity depressed asset prices and threatened the solvency of these highly leveraged companies.

SOME THINGS ARE WORTH DOING FOR THE *GREATER GOOD*

By mere size alone, LTCM dominated the hedge fund landscape. When it was rescued in 1998, LTCM was the biggest and the most highly leveraged large hedge fund reporting to the U.S. Commodity Futures Trading Commission (CFTC). Its $125 billion of assets were nearly four times greater than the next largest fund.[52] By comparison, the 10 largest U.S. hedge funds had an average size of only about $36 billion.

LTCM's failure could have caused widespread contagion, which would have brought significant financial pressures on its large, direct counterparties, many of whom were losing considerable amounts because of

---

[52]See President's Working Group on Financial Markets. *Hedge Funds, Leverage, and the Lessons of Long-Term Capital Management: Report of the President's Working Group on Financial Markets.* Washington, DC: Department of Treasury. 28 April 1999, 14 and C-13.

their comparable portfolio positions.[53] The financial crisis could have also caused pressure on international exchanges where LTCM represented 5% to 10% of the open interest and an even greater percent of the daily turnover. But over and above this, if LTCM's counterparties were hedged beforehand, the failure of this fund could have caused a mass scramble to shore up the newly exposed positions. As a result, market prices could have moved even more unfavorably, causing wider and deeper consequences. Credit risks would have been reevaluated, which could have led to a credit squeeze, and the greater uncertainty could have increased the risk premium embedded in nominal yields.

When the greater good is larger than the sum of benefits accruing to the individual vested interests (i.e., in this case, the counterparties to LTCM's trades and its creditors), there needs to be a way to communicate fully and clearly what is at stake. If private parties have no incentive to limit their bilateral risks to reduce contagion effects, then perhaps, it is up to central banks, securities regulators, and private associations to open the eyes of key players about the externalities. The trick is doing this without rewarding irresponsibility or encouraging bad behavior in the future.

Epilogue

What Happened to the Principals, Creditors, Investors, and Consortium?

LTCM's management company, Long-Term Capital Management L.P., was transferred to the consortium. The recapitalization saved most of the parties involved in this debacle from serious collateral damage. Because the destruction seemed so small, after the dust settled, Myron Scholes called LTCM's failure the "non-fault bankruptcy of his hedge fund," but he was probably not considering the damaged reputations and lost jobs at hedge funds and financial institutions around the world.[54]

THE PRINCIPALS AND EMPLOYEES

Myron S. Scholes retired four months after LTCM collapsed, planning to return to California, where he would lecture and write at Stanford University.[55] In August 2000, Scholes began working for Oak Hill Platinum Partners

---

[53]LTCM estimated that its top 17 counterparties would have lost between $3 billion to $5 billion if it defaulted. Ibid. p. 17.

[54]This quote comes from a speech by Myron Scholes at an *Economist* magazine–sponsored symposium on the first anniversary of LTCM's failure. Cited in Anonymous, "Finance and Economics: Economics Focus: When the Sea Dries Up," *The Economist* 352 (8134) (25 September 1999), 93.

[55]Anita Raghavan and Mitchell Pacelle, "Key Figures Set to Leave Hedge Fund—Long-Term Capital Losing Two Partners," *Wall Street Journal* (3 February 1999), C1.

Fund, a hedge fund backed by Robert M. Bass.[56] Robert C. Merton, who held a full-time professorship at Harvard University since 1988, continued his heavy schedule of lecturing, researching, and consulting. David W. Mullins, Jr., left LTCM to become chairman of vSimplify, a portal company.

Since the fund's inception, LTCM's staff members had been the servants of the arbitrage lords and routinely invested all their bonuses back into the company. Those invested bonuses were now gone, and by the end of October 1998, many of these employees (about 20%) were laid off. John Meriwether and the other principals lost most of their autonomy to make trading decisions, and their exorbitant management fees were slashed, sliced, and diced. Nevertheless, as part of the deal, LTCM's principals got to keep their homes[57] and received bonuses of $250,000 for the year they stayed with the company. Many of the principals still faced bitter financial set backs, but that should be expected because they caused the fiasco and deserved some downside consequences. Some of them were permitted to leave before year's end for lucrative jobs on Wall Street. Just over a year after the collapse, John Meriwether, along with five of his colleagues[58] at LTCM, had already started a new hedge fund.

CREDITORS AND INVESTORS

Because of the rescue, virtually all of LTCM creditors were paid in full; in an ironic twist of fate, investors who were not principals or part of LTCM's core group made out much better than you might at first expect. After trying unsuccessfully to amplify its risk to the desired 20% per year level, the LTCM principals decided that, for the level of risk it was taking, the company did not need such a large capital base. As a result, it took the bold step in December 1997 of *forcing* investors to take back $2.7 billion of their equity capital, but the company did not reduce its investment positions. As a result, LTCM began 1998 with approximately $4.7 billion in equity capital rather than over $7 billion, which it would have had.

Investors were upset and felt betrayed by the forced refund. The reason was clear. During the three years from February 1994 to December 1997, LTCM had quadrupled their portfolios. Investors asked: *What fund in its right mind would force its investors to take their money and go home?* But the LTCM principals had grown rich. The $146 million of equity capital they invested in 1994 had grown to $1.9 billion, and these funds along with the equity

---

[56]Robert Goldwyn Blumenthal. "Life After Long-Term Captial May Be Very Sweet, Indeed." *Barron's* 80(32) (7 August 2000), 10.

[57]John Meriwether's house was a 67-acre estate in Westchester County, NY, a wealthy suburb north-east of New York City.

[58]Eric Rosenfeld, Larry Hilibrand, Victor Haghani, Richard Leahy, and Arjun Krishnamachar.

and financial support of a core group of strategic investors and key banks were all it needed.

All together, during their four-year roller-coaster ride (i.e., from fortune to despair), John Meriwether and his band of arbitragers netted outside (non-principal) investors average annual returns of slightly less than 20%, which is not a bad return. But these investors made out as well as they did because they were forced to take a refund. Therefore, when the collapse occurred, they had nothing (or relatively less) invested in LTCM. In the end, it was John Meriwether and the other principals who were most harmed by the LTCM failure.

THE CONSORTIUM

The consortium had mixed results. Spreads did not converge rapidly and economic conditions remained tenuous. As a result, some, but not all, of LTCM's positions were closed with profits, but overall the results were satisfying because the full $3.65 billion invested by the consortium was paid back.[59]

Review Questions

1. Given the economic and political turmoil that took place in 1998, what bet would have earned John Meriwether and his team of arbitrageurs the highest profits?

2. Suppose the yield on a two-year Treasury note was 4%, and the yield on a five-year Treasury note was 6%. If you expected this yield spread to widen, explain the spread trade you would execute.

   a. After a year, suppose the yield on a two-year Treasury note fell to 3.5%, and the yield on a five-year Treasury note rose to 6.5%. Would you profit or lose on your trade? Explain.

   b. After a year, suppose the yield on a two-year Treasury note rose to 6% and the yield on a five-year Treasury note fell to 5.5%. Would you profit or lose on your trade? Explain.

3. Using the information from Exhibit 8.2, calculate the return on assets and the return on equity if LTCM had earned only a 1% net return (instead of a 5% net return) on the investment assets purchased with borrowed funds.

---

[59]Joseph Kahn, "Long-Term Capital Said to Earn a Small Profit for Its Rescuers," *New York Times* (11 November 1998), 10.

4. Why did LTCM have difficulty raising its level of risk?
5. Why was long-term funding crucial to LTCM's strategy?
6. What were LTCM's major assets? What were its major financing sources?
7. Given its strategy, why was it vital for LTCM to have a high credit rating?
8. Explain how LTCM minimized its use of equity.
9. Explain the endogenous (i.e., hedge-fund-related) factors that caused LTCM's portfolio to lose the normal protections afforded by diversification.
10. How did LTCM secure long-term funding?
11. Explain the three major catalysts that caused LTCM to fail.
12. What is Value at Risk (VaR), and what role did it play in the LTCM failure?
13. Explain the major benefits of a total return swap.
14. Explain the causes of the Asian Tiger crisis and how it affected LTCM.
15. Explain the Russian ruble crisis and how it affected LTCM.
16. What role did the Federal Reserve play in the LTCM rescue? Why was the Fed involved?

Further Reading

Please visit http://www.prenhall.com/marthinsen, where you can find the following embellishments on and extensions of this chapter.

- Appendix 8.1: LTCM's Major Trades
- Appendix 8.2: What Are the Problems With Value at Risk?
- Appendix 8.3: UBS and the LTCM Warrant Fiasco

Bibliography

Adrian, Tobias. "Measuring Risk in the Hedge Fund Sector." Federal Reserve Bank of New York *Current Issues in Economics and Finance* 13(3) (March/April 2007), 1–7.

Anonymous (Editorial) "Decade of Moral Hazard." *Wall Street Journal* (25 September 1998), A14.

Anonymous. "Finance and Economics: Economics Focus: When the Sea Dries Up," *The Economist* 352 (8134) (25 September 1999), 93.

Anonymous. Hedge Fund Association. "About Hedge Funds" (23 February 2003). http://www.magnum.com/hedgefunds/abouthedgefunds.asp. Accessed 28 December 2007.

Blumenthal, Robert Goldwyn. "Life After Long-Term Capital May Be Very Sweet, Indeed," *Barron's* 80 (32) (7 August 2000).

Bollerslev, Tim. "Generalizing Autoregressive Conditional Heteroskedacity." *Journal of Econometrics* 31 (1986), 307–327.

Brown, Stephen J. and Steenbeek, Onno W. "Doubling: Nick Leeson's Trading Strategy." *Pacific-Basin Finance Journal* 9 (2001), 83.

Dunbar, Nicholas. *Inventing Money: The Story of Long-Term Capital Management and the Legends behind It.* New York: John Wiley & Sons, 2000.

Engle, Robert F. "Autoregressive Conditional Heteroskedacity with Estimates of the Variance of U.K. Inflation," *Econometrica* 50 (1982), 987–1008.

Jennings, Kate, *Moral Hazard.* London: Fourth Estate, 2000.

Kahn, Joseph. "Long-Term Capital Said to Earn a Small Profit for Its Rescuers," *New York Times* (11 November 1998), 10.

Knorr Cetina, Karin and Bruegger, Urs. "The Market as an Object of Attachments: Exploring Postcocial Relations in Financial Markets." *Canadian Journal of Sociology* 25 (2000), 141–68.

Lipin, Steven, Murray, Matt, and Schlesinger, Jacob M. "Bailout Blues: How a Big Hedge Fund Marketed Its Expertise and Shrouded Its Risks—Regulators and Lenders Knew Little About the Gambles at Long-Term Capital—'Stardust' in Investors' Eyes," *Wall Street Journal* (25 September 1998), A1.

Loomis, Carol. "A House Built on Sand," *Fortune* 138 (8) (26 October 1998), 110–118.

Lowenstein, Roger. *When Genius Failed: The Rise and Fall of Long-Term Capital Management.* New York: Random House, 2000.

MacKenzie, Donald. "Long-Term Capital Management and the Sociology of Arbitrage." *Economy and Society* 32(3) (August 2003), 349–380.

Muehring, Kevin. "John Meriwether by the Numbers," *Institutional Investor* 30 (11) (November 1996), 68–81.

Pacelle, Mitchell, Scism, Leslie, and Lipin, Steven. "How Buffett, AIG and Goldman Sought Long-Term Capital, but Were Rejected," *Wall Street Journal* (30 September 1998), C1.

Perold, André F. "Long-Term Capital Management, L.P. (A)," Harvard Business School, case 9-200-007 (5 November 1999).

Perold, André F. "Long Term Capital Management, L.P. (B)," Harvard Business School, case 9-200-008 (27 October 1999).

Perold, André F. "Long Term Capital Management, L.P. (C)," Harvard Business School, case 9-200-009 (5 November 1999).

Perold, André F. "Long Term Capital Management, L.P. (D)." Harvard Business School, case 9-200-010 (28 October 1999).

Perrow, Charles. *Normal Accidents: Living With High-Risk Technologies.* Princeton, NJ: Princeton University Press, 1999.

President's Working Group on Financial Markets. *Hedge Funds, Leverage, and the Lessons of Long-Term Capital Management: Report of the President's Working Group on Financial Markets.* Washington DC: Department of Treasury, 28 April 1999.

Raghavan, Anita and Pacelle, Mitchell. "Key Figures Set to Leave Hedge Fund—Long-Term Capital Losing Two Partners," *Wall Street Journal* (3 February 1999), C1.

Scheifer, Andrei and Vishny Robert W. "The Limits of Arbitrage." *Journal of Finance* LII(1) (March 1997), 35–55.

Scholes, Myron S. "The Near Crash of 1998: Crisis and Risk Management." *American Economic Review* 90(2) (May 2000) 17–21.

Schroeder, Michael and Schlesinger, Jacob M. "Fed May Face Recrimination over Handling of Fund Bailout," *Wall Street Journal*, (25 September 1998), A8.

Seely, Beth. "Long-Term Capital Management- An Analysis of Intervention As a Prisoners' Dilemma." Working Paper No. 99–01 Commodity Futures Trading Commission (24 February 1999), 1–20.

Spiro, Leah Nathans, with Laderman, Jeffrey M. "How Long-Term Rocked Stocks, Too. It Wasn't Just the Bond Market That LTCM Endangered," *Business Week* (9 November 1998), 160.

9

Amaranth Advisors LLC

Using Natural Gas Derivatives to Bet on the Weather

Introduction

Nicholas Maounis must have been filled with pride and a bit of amazement at how far and fast the hedge fund he founded in 2000 had come in six years. From a relatively small group of about 30 portfolio managers, analysts, traders, and support personnel, Amaranth Advisors LLC and the funds it managed (hereafter, Amaranth) had grown to become the 39th largest hedge fund in the world, with a net asset value of about $9 billion and a global team of employees numbering more than 400.[1] Amaranth posted double-digit profits each year from its founding in 2000 to 2005, and at the end of April 2006, annualized returns were on course to hit 114% by year's end. What happened during the next five months that caused this company to lose $6.4 billion—most of it during one week in September? How could so much be lost so quickly by so few?

The purpose of this chapter is to explain Amaranth's natural gas strategy and the risks it faced. We begin our analysis in

[1]There were about 9,000 hedge funds in the world at that time.

2005, when the company ramped up its natural gas trading desk, and end in 2006, when Amaranth suffered devastating losses. Our discussion will show how faulty strategies, large bets, and dramatic changes in market conditions all combined to earn Amaranth the unfortunate distinction as the largest hedge-fund disaster in history. But if our story stopped there, Amaranth might be remembered as *just-another-tale* about a large hedge fund gone bust; it was not. Amaranth was accused of excessive speculation, price manipulation, and regulatory arbitrage, which immediately made this financial fiasco a broader concern because natural gas is so tightly and intricately woven into the fabric of American citizens' everyday lives.

Amaranth Advisors LLC

Amaranth Advisors LLC began operations as a multistrategy hedge fund specializing in convertible bonds, mergers, acquisitions, corporate restructuring, and utilities.[2] Its founder and CEO, Nicholas Maounis started his career in 1985 working for New York–based LF Rothschild, Unterberg, Towbin Holdings, an investment bank, and then moved to Angelo, Gordon & Co., a hedge fund. In 1992, he joined Paloma Partners Management Company (Paloma), a 25-year-old hedge fund specializing in relative-value trades and other structured investments. At Paloma, Maounis managed approximately 25 traders and assistants and was in charge of an assortment of arbitrage portfolios that focused on the U.S., Japanese, European, and Canadian markets. It was during his eight years at Paloma that Maounis sharpened his trading skills and eventually managed a $400 million convertible bond fund. Maounis left Paloma in 2000 after raising $200 million to start Amaranth.[3]

---

[2]Amaranth Advisors LLC was a Delaware Limited Liability Company that managed Amaranth Partners LLC, Amaranth Capital Partners LLC, and Amaranth International Ltd. These funds were part of a master feeder structure.

[3]Much of Amaranth's initial funding came from Paloma. Later, Amaranth was funded by insurance companies, fund-of-funds, retirement and benefit programs, high net-worth individuals, financial institutions, endowments, and insider capital. Its investor list reads like a *who's who* of the financial world, including well-known institutions, such as Arden Asset Management, Credit Suisse, Glenwood Investments, Goldman Sachs Asset Management, Ivy Asset Management, Man Investments, Morgan Stanley, New Market Capital Partners, Pine Grove Associates, Rock Creek Management, and UBS Asset Management.

The minimum investment in Amaranth was $5 million, and, initial investors were subject to a 13-month, lock-up period with 90-day notice.[4] After the lock-up period, withdrawals of annual profits required 45-day written notice and could be made only four times a year (January, April, July, and October), subject to a 2.5% fee. There was also a gating provision that restricted quarterly withdrawals to no more than 7.5% of an investor's net asset value. These provisions reduced the risk of sudden runs on the fund and provided Amaranth with greater assurances that it would not have to abandon positions due to customer withdrawals. Like many hedge funds, Amaranth charged a management fee of 1.5% and a 20% incentive fee on the gains above an investor's high-water mark. In addition, employees were required to invest one-third of their bonuses each year in Amaranth, and there was a three-year vesting period before the funds could be withdrawn.

By 2002, Amaranth had expanded its palette of investments to the energy sector. Diversification into energy coincided with the scandal and subsequent failure of Enron Corporation during the previous year. As a leading market maker of energy products, Enron's departure left a large vacuum into which companies, like Amaranth, jumped. To head its new effort, Amaranth hired Harry Arora, a former energy trader at Enron. Cognizant of the energy market's high volatility, Amaranth intended to limit exposures in this area to no more than 2% of its capital.

From 2001 to 2003, Amaranth earned impressive profits amounting to 29%, 15%, and 21%, respectively, but half way through 2004, investment returns from its core areas of expertise were less than 4%. Plummeting stock market volatility and declining spreads between corporate and government bond yields caused convertible bond trades, which at their peak accounted for 60% of Amaranth's portfolio, to fall by 6.5% during the first five months of 2004. During this period, Amaranth also incurred losses on its credit bets when Standard & Poor's cut the credit ratings of General Motors Corp. and Ford Motor Co. to below investment grade.

In an effort to boost profits, Amaranth decided to focus more of its resources on energy-related investments, but for this, it needed an experienced trader and leader to build an energy arbitrage desk. Amaranth hired Brian Hunter, a 6-foot-5-inch, Canadian-born natural gas trader who had recently left Deutsche Bank after a rather turbulent relationship. Hunter, who had a penchant for driving Ferraris and Bentleys, reinvigorated Amaranth's profitability almost immediately, earning $200 million during the first six months.

By mid-2005, the company's energy arbitrage operations had earned more than $1 billion in profits, and Amaranth was devoting about 30% of its equity

---

[4]In February 2005, the lock-up provision was increased to two years.

to this activity. Hunter was a hero, and he was rewarded with greater trading authority, promotion to co-head of Amaranth's commodities group, a $75 million bonus (for 2005 alone), and 15% draw (up from 10%) on his future trading profits.[5] To accommodate Hunter's desire to work in his hometown, Maounis moved Amaranth's trading desk to Calgary, Alberta. Maounis gladly paid the bonus and offered these generous fringe benefits because he also earned bonuses ($70 million in 2005 alone!) from Hunter's profits.

In early 2006, the net asset value of Amaranth's portfolio had grown to about $9 billion, and the company had U.S. offices in Greenwich, Connecticut and Houston, Texas, Canadian offices in Toronto and Calgary, and offices in London, England and Singapore. It looked as if Amaranth found the formula for steady, solid growth and profitability. Equally important, its chief risk manager, Robert Jones, and his 12 risk lieutenants seemed to possess the skills needed to navigate between the tricky shoals of risk and return.[6]

Natural Gas Markets

Natural gas fuels our lives. In 2006, it accounted for about 22% of all U.S. energy consumption, and more than 60% of U.S. families used natural gas to heat homes, fuel water heaters, dry clothes, or juice their household appliances with electricity generated from it. Natural gas was also used to make products as varied as aluminum, bricks, chemicals, clothing, electricity, fertilizer, glass, insulation, medicine, paper, paints, plastic, and steel. Even the propane used to grill kabobs on the back patio comes from natural gas, and to top it off, natural gas is the cleanest of all fossil fuels.[7]

Natural gas competes vigorously against oil, but the two markets are quite different, and these differences are important. In contrast to the oil market, where prices are determined by global supply and demand conditions, natural gas is locally produced and consumed. Most of the natural gas that Americans consume is produced in the continental United States. Relatively little is imported, and what is imported comes mainly from Canada via pipelines or from countries such as Algeria, Egypt, and Trinidad in the form of liquid natural gas (LNG).

---

[5]The decision to compensate Hunter so liberally was heavily influenced by a job offer he received from Steven Cohen's SAC Capital Advisors LLC, which was an $8.5 billion, Stamford-based hedge fund. The offer came with a $10 million up-front bonus for Hunter.

[6]Amaranth differentiated itself from other hedge funds by having a designated risk manager sit at the desk with traders for each of its trading books.

[7]Energy Information Administration, *Natural Gas Basics 101*. Available at http://www.eia.doe.gov/basics/naturalgas_basics.html. Accessed 28 December 2007.

About 20 large natural gas suppliers account for 60% of all U.S. natural gas production. Unlike oil, natural gas is not easily transported by ships. Therefore, it is stored during the spring and early summer months (i.e., the off season) in underground salt caverns, mines, aquifers, depleted (oil and gas) reservoirs, and hard-rock caverns. There are about 400 storage facilities in the Lower 48 States, which are owned, managed, or leased by about 120 pipeline companies, local distribution companies, independent storage facilities, and third-party operators. The ability to store natural gas is important because it enables market participants to profit from arbitrage opportunities between the spot and forward/futures markets (more about this later in the chapter).

In 1978, Congress passed the Natural Gas Policy Act, which removed most federal regulations on natural gas during the subsequent six-year period. Therefore, since 1984, the well-head price of natural gas in the United States has been determined mainly by market forces of supply and demand. In the short run, the relationship between changes in the price of natural gas and production is very inelastic. Rising prices encourage production and the discovery of new wells, but the increased amount supplied is usually relatively small and requires time to reach the market. The demand for natural gas is also inelastic. Overall, the price elasticity of demand for natural gas (over a two-year period) in the United States is about −0.14, which means that a 10% increase in price causes the amount demanded to fall by only 1.4%.[8] Because of the highly inelastic supply and demand, natural gas prices tend to be rather volatile, which encourages speculation and, unfortunately, lends itself to market abuses.

From 1985 to 1999, the price of natural gas in the United States was relatively low, costing, on average, $1.85 per million British thermal units (MMBtu), and it fluctuated within a narrow band of about $2/MMBtu (i.e., between $1.22/MMBtu and $3.30/MMBtu) (Exhibit 9.1). Consumption rose steadily during this 14-year period, but domestic production lagged behind. Nevertheless, natural gas prices remained low and stable because any excess demand was filled by imported natural gas and LNG.

From 2000 to 2006, conditions changed dramatically. The average price of natural gas increased by almost 160% to $4.81/MMBtu, and it varied within a broad range of about $8/MMBtu (i.e., between $2.12/MMBtu and $10.04/MMBtu). Volatility also increased significantly. Critics argued that underlying market fundamentals no longer explained the dramatic increase in spot prices, and equally important, they did not account for the growing difference between spot and futures prices. Something else was causing prices and spreads to change. It was in this environment of volatile prices

---

[8]See Dave Costello, *Reduced Form Energy Model Elasticities from EIA's Regional Short-Term Energy Mode RSTEM)*, 9 May 2006. Available at http://www.eia.doe.gov/emeu/steo/pub/pdf/elasticities.pdf. Accessed 28 December 2007.

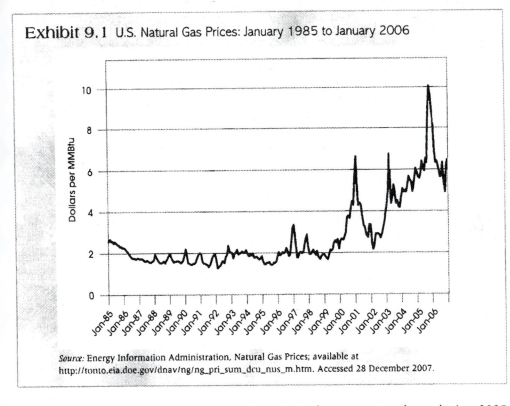

Exhibit 9.1 U.S. Natural Gas Prices: January 1985 to January 2006

Source: Energy Information Administration, Natural Gas Prices; available at
http://tonto.eia.doe.gov/dnav/ng/ng_pri_sum_dcu_nus_m.htm. Accessed 28 December 2007.

and uncertainty that Amaranth made its bets on natural gas during 2005
and then increased the stakes in 2006.

Amaranth's Natural Gas Trading Strategy and Performance: 2005 to 2006[9]

Amaranth was a sophisticated user of derivative contracts, and its trading
strategies were nuanced and adapted to the natural gas industry's constantly changing conditions and forecasts. The company fluidly opened,
mixed, and matched futures, forwards, swaps, and options to make both
directional bets and price-spread bets on natural gas prices. For example, if
the company felt that natural gas prices would rise, it made directional bets
by taking long positions in futures, forwards, swaps, and call options. If it
felt natural gas prices would fall, it took short positions in futures, forwards,
and swaps, and bought put options.

[9]Except where noted, the facts for this section come from United States Senate Permanent Subcommittee on Investigations Committee on Homeland Security and Governmental Affairs, *Excessive Speculation in the Natural Gas Market and Appendix, Washington D.C. Government Printing Office, 25 June 2007.
Staff Report—Excessive Speculation in the Natural Gas Market;* available at http://hsgac.senate.gov/_files/
062507Report.pdf. *Appendix—Excessive Speculation in the Natural Gas Market;* available at http://hsgac.
senate.gov/_files/062507Appendix.pdf. Accessed 28 December 2007 (hereafter referred to as *PSI
Report, 25 June 2007*).

Amaranth's spread trades were bets on the difference between the prices of two energy-related contracts, and most of these bets were on calendar price spreads, which means they were on the price difference between two contract months. For example, if Amaranth felt that the price spread between natural gas contracts for January 2007 and November 2006 would increase,[10] it would purchase the January 2007 futures contract and simultaneously sell the November 2006 futures contract. Once the buy and sell sides of the transaction were set, it made no difference to Amaranth whether natural gas prices increased or fell; all that mattered was whether the spread changed.

2005: USING LONG CALL OPTIONS TO BET ON THE WEATHER

During the four-year period between 2000 and 2004, natural gas prices spiked every winter except in 2002. At the beginning of 2005, chief trader Brian Hunter wagered that natural gas prices would spike again during the coming year. To profit from this expectation, he purchased a large number of out-of-the-money call options on natural gas. For the first half year, his bet seemed likely to fail, and it looked as if Hunter's options might remain underwater for the rest of the year. Gas stockpiles were abundant and weather forecasters were predicting subdued hurricane activity in the late summer and early fall. As a result, natural gas prices remained relatively flat from January to June

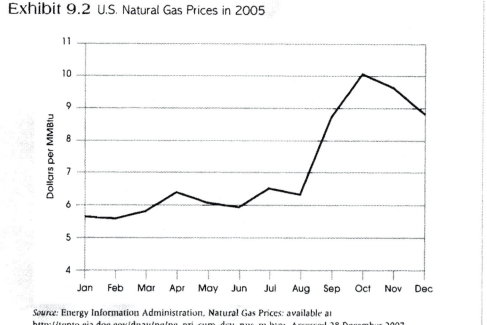

Exhibit 9.2 U.S. Natural Gas Prices in 2005

Source: Energy Information Administration, Natural Gas Prices: available at http://tonto.eia.doe.gov/dnav/ng/ng_pri_sum_dcu_nus_m.htm. Accessed 28 December 2007.

[10]It is conventional to mention the buy side of a spread trade first and then the sell side. Therefore, buying the January 2007/November 2006 spread means buying the January 2007 futures contract and selling the November 2006 futures contract.

(Exhibit 9.2). When Amaranth reported its 2005 midyear performance, the results were disappointing, with losses amounting to about 1%.

Industry conditions changed quickly in late summer. Hurricane Katrina hit the Gulf Coast and New Orleans with a vengeance in late August 2005 and was followed, less than a month later, by Hurricane Rita. These severe storms destroyed scores of natural gas platforms and miles of pipelines, causing supply to plummet. Natural gas prices soared, and when they did, Amaranth's out-of-the-money call options suddenly became highly valued assets. By year's end, Amaranth's profits on energy-related investments accounted for almost 98% of its 21% annual return.

2006: USING FUTURES AND SPREADS TO BET ON THE WEATHER

The economic effects of Hurricanes Katrina and Rita dissipated quicker than expected and were followed by relatively mild winter weather. As a result, Amaranth shifted energy strategies to benefit from these new conditions and its revised expectations. The company reasoned that a glut of natural gas would continue to put downward pressure on prices throughout the summer of 2006, but it would vanish by the winter 2006/2007 heating season because of anticipated weather-induced disruptions in supply, delivery bottlenecks, and/or cold snaps. Once the surplus was eliminated, Amaranth figured that winter prices would spike, just as they had during four of the past five years, causing winter 2006/2007 natural gas prices to rise relative to prices in the summer and fall of 2006. To profit from these expectations, Amaranth made both directional and relative value bets.

Amaranth's Directional Bets: Short Futures Positions

Expecting natural gas prices to fall during the spring, Amaranth began in January 2006 taking short positions in the March 2006 futures contract. By the beginning of February, it had built a position of about 40,000 contracts. Amaranth stood to gain considerable amounts if the natural gas price fell below the average strike price but could incur significant losses if it rose above this level. If its expectations proved correct and natural gas prices fell, Amaranth intended to roll over its short March position into April, and then April into May, May into June, and so on until either its expectations changed or the fall 2006/winter 2007 months arrived.

An example might help to explain how Amaranth profited. On 24 February 2006, when the March 2006 futures contract matured,[11] Amaranth was short about 20,000 March 2006 futures contracts. Let's assume the average

---

[11]Natural gas futures contracts on NYMEX and ICE expire three business days before the first day of the contract month. The March 2006 futures contract expired on February 24 because the weekend fell on February 25 and 26.

price of the contracts in Amaranth's portfolio was $9.80/MMBtu. To roll over this position, the company purchased 20,000 March 2006 futures contracts, thereby offsetting its short position, and it simultaneously sold the number of April 2006 futures contracts it wanted for its new position.[12] On 24 February 2006, the price of a March 2006 futures contract was about $7.10/MMBtu, and the price of an April 2006 futures contract was about $7.30/MMBtu. Therefore, the fund earned, on average, $2.70/MMBtu (i.e., $9.80/MMBtu − $7.10/MMBtu) on each of its 20,000 March 2006 futures contracts (Exhibit 9.3). Because Amaranth wanted to increase its short exposures, it ended up establishing a futures position in April 2006 that was a bit larger than the March 2006 position (i.e., about 25,000 contracts).

Even though many of the storm-damaged natural gas platforms remained nonoperational in spring 2006, production returned to prehurricane levels, mainly because of the discovery of new wells. Stored reserves of natural gas began to rise, and the prospect for increased supply combined with reduced demand caused natural gas futures prices to fall. As long as they did, Amaranth earned profits at each rollover date, and by rolling over its investments, the company simultaneously set the stage to earn even more profits

Exhibit 9.3 Payoff Profiles: Rolling Over a March Futures Contract into April

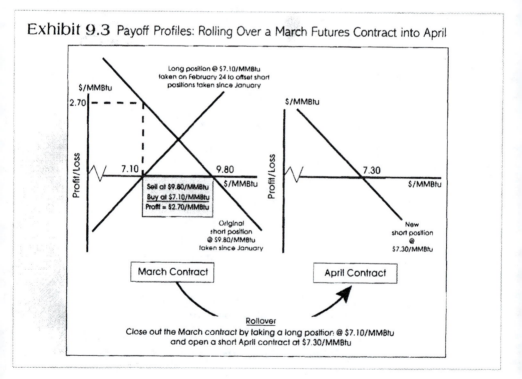

---

[12]Actually, Amaranth had been building its short April 2006 futures position during March; so it only had to top up its April position to the level it wanted.

in the next month. Except for some brief periods, when futures prices followed a rollercoaster pattern (Exhibit 9.4), Amaranth's strategy was effective and profitable during the January to August 2006 period. What was troublesome about Amaranth's directional bets was their size. By August 29th, Amaranth's short September 2006 futures position had increased to about 105,000 contracts![13] (See Risk Notepad 9.1.)

Amaranth's Relative Value Bets: Long Spread Positions

Starting in January 2006, Amaranth began making two major spread bets that would prove to be fatal. Expecting winter 2007 prices to rise relative to fall 2006 prices, Amaranth purchased natural gas futures contracts that expired in winter 2007 and sold contracts that matured in fall 2006.[14] Its second major gamble was based on the March 2007/April 2007 price spread. Expecting the price of natural gas in the last month of the winter

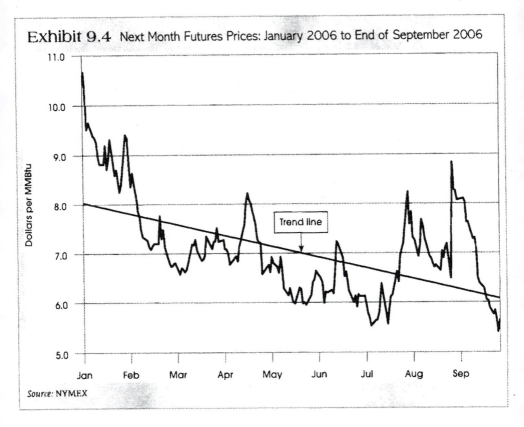

Exhibit 9.4 Next Month Futures Prices: January 2006 to End of September 2006

Source: NYMEX

[13]The date, 29 August 2006, was significant because it was the expiration date for the September 2006 contract.

[14]Actually, Amaranth placed its winter/fall price spread bets for maturities out as far as 2010. The positions that eventually brought the company to its knees were bets on the contracts for winter 2007/fall 2006 and March 2007/April 2007; so, we will focus our attention there.

Risk Notepad 9.1

Measuring Natural Gas and Putting Amaranth's Positions into Perspective

Two ways to measure natural gas (NG) are by its energy content and quantity. Energy content is measured in British thermal units (Btu), and quantity is measured in cubic feet (cf). In the United States, the Commodity Futures Trading Commission (CFTC) considers a *large trader* to be anyone with 200 natural gas contracts or more. At times during 2006, Amaranth held more than 100,000 natural gas futures contracts in just one contact month (e.g., September 2006)! How much natural gas does a position of 100,000 futures contracts represent? How much of a financial stake does it represent? Let's provide some perspective.

- NYMEX is the New York Mercantile Exchange
- ICE is the IntercontinentalExchange
- 1 NYMEX NG futures contract = 10,000 million Btu (i.e., 10,000 MMBtu)
- 1 ICE NG futures contract = 2,500 MMBtu
- 1 NYMEX NG futures contract = 4 ICE NG futures contracts[15]
- 1 cubic foot (cf) of NG = 1,031 Btu
- 1 NYMEX NG futures contract = 9,699,321.05 cf of NG
- 100,000 NYMEX NG futures contracts = 969,932.1 million cf of NG
- U..S. residential consumption of NG (2006) = 4,355,333 million cubic feet (MMcf)[16]
- 100,000 NG contracts ≅ 22% of U.S. residential energy consumption in 2006
- Margin requirement for 100,000 NYMEX NG gas contracts ≅ $675 million
- A one-cent price change for 100,000 NG gas futures contracts = +/− $10 million

season (i.e., March) to increase relative to the first month of the spring season (i.e., April), Amaranth bought the March 2007 futures contract and simultaneously sold the April 2007 contract.

Exhibit 9.5 shows the payoff profiles of a long January 2007 futures position at $11/MMBtu and a short November 2006 futures position at $10/MMBtu. Purchasing the January 2007 contract and simultaneously selling the November 2006 contract is called *buying the spread* because any combination of price changes that increases the spread between January's price relative to November's price earns a profit and, of course, reductions

---

[15]In this chapter, all the references to natural gas futures contracts have been standardized in terms of the NYMEX contract. Therefore, the purchase of one NYMEX contract and four ICE contracts would be cited as two contracts.

[16]U.S. Energy Information Administration, Official Energy Statistics from the U.S. Government. Updated 21 December 2007. Available at http://tonto.eia.doe.gov/dnav/ng/hist/n3010us2A.htm. Accessed 28 December 2007.

Exhibit 9.5 Amaranth's Long January 2007/November 2006 Spread Position

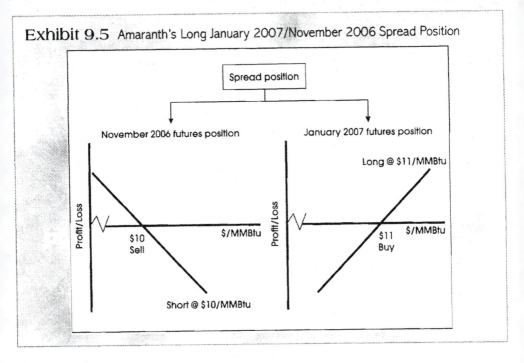

in the spread cause losses. Risk Notepad 9.2 provides a detailed example of how profits are earned on spread trades.

In early February 2006, when the spread was below $1.30/MMBtu (Exhibit 9.6), Amaranth began to build up a large position in the January 2007/November 2006 natural gas futures contract, and by month's end, it held more than 25,000 contracts (i.e., about 25,000 long January 2007 contracts and about 25,000 short November 2006 contracts). During March and April, Amaranth increased this long spread position to about 30,000

Risk Notepad 9.2

Understanding How Profits Are Earned on Spread Trades

One easy way to understand how profits are earned on a long January 2007/November 2006 position is to increase the price spread by fixing one of the two futures prices, changing the other one, and seeing what happens. For instance, suppose that on 10 April 2006 Amaranth locked in the January 2007/November 2006 spread by purchasing the January 2007 natural gas futures contract and selling the November 2006 futures contract. Suppose the November 2006 price was $10/MMBtu and the January 2007 price was $11/MMBtu, which means the spread equaled $1/MMBtu. One month later (on 10 May 2006), suppose the January 2007 futures price rose to $12/MMBtu.

and the November 2006 futures price remained constant at $10/MMBtu, causing the spread to rise from $1/MMBtu to $2/MMBtu. Amaranth could unwind its position by selling the January 2007 futures contract and buying the November 2006 futures contract. In doing so, it would earn nothing on the November 2006 futures contract because the buy and sell prices would be the same. But it would gain $1/MMBtu on the January 2007 contract because it agreed to buy natural gas for January 2007 delivery at $11/MMBtu and simultaneously sell it for $12/MMBtu[17] (Exhibit RN9.2.1).

Exhibit RN 9.2.1 Profits on Amaranth's Spread Position if the January 2007 Price Rises

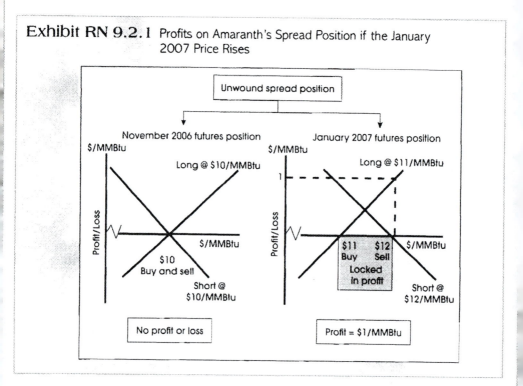

Now, let's begin again, but this time, suppose that between 10 April 2006 and 10 May 2006 the January 2007 futures price remained constant at $11/MMBtu, and the November 2006 futures price fell from $10/MMBtu to $9/MMBtu; therefore, the spread rose from $1/MMBtu to $2/MMBtu. Amaranth could unwind its position by purchasing the November 2006 contract and selling the January 2007 contract. As a result, it would earn nothing on the January 2007 contract, but it would earn $1/MMBtu on the November 2006 contract (Exhibit RN9.2.2).

Any combination of changes in natural gas prices that increases the January 2007/November 2006 spread would earn Amaranth profits. For example, suppose the spread widened by $1/MMBtu because the January 2007 futures price increased by

---

[17]The futures contract on NYMEX is for 10,000/MMBtu; so this $1/MMBtu increase in the price of natural gas would earn a total of $10,000.

Exhibit RN 9.2.2   Profits on Amaranth's Spread Position if the November 2006 Price Falls

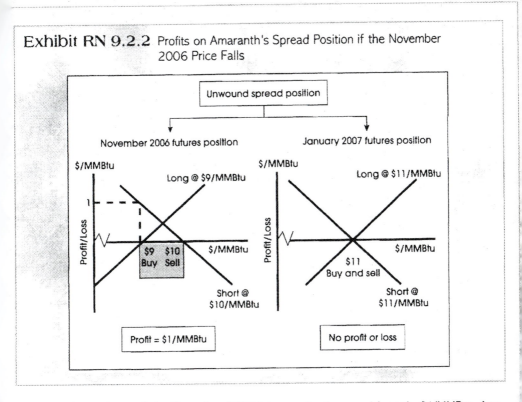

$2/MMBtu and the November 2006 futures price increased by only $1/MMBtu. Amaranth would incur a $1/MMBtu loss on its short November 2006 contract but earn $2/MMBtu on its long January 2007 contract. Similarly, if the January 2007 futures price fell by $1/MMBtu and the November 2006 futures price fell by $2/MMBtu, the company would incur a $1/MMBtu loss on its long January 2007 contract but earn $2/MMBtu on its short November 2006.

contracts.[18] By late April 2006, the January 2007/November 2006 price spread had already increased to more than $2.20/MMBtu, and it looked like Amaranth had uncovered a goldmine; many thought that Brian Hunter had the Midas touch. In April alone, Amaranth's portfolio had gained (*on paper, at least*) more than $1.2 billion. If conditions continued as they had during the first four months, annualized profits for 2006 would have been about 114%!

Amaranth Seeks to Unwind Its Positions Sensing that these profits were vulnerable, Amaranth decided in May to capture some of its gains, unwind positions, and reduce risks. To do so, it tried to employ a two-pronged strategy. First, Amaranth wanted to offset its long winter exposures

---

[18]During March, Amaranth reduced the number of November 2006 futures contracts it held but still kept the company's spread position by increasing its holdings of short October 2006 futures contracts. The company went back to holding mainly November 2006 futures contracts in April 2006.

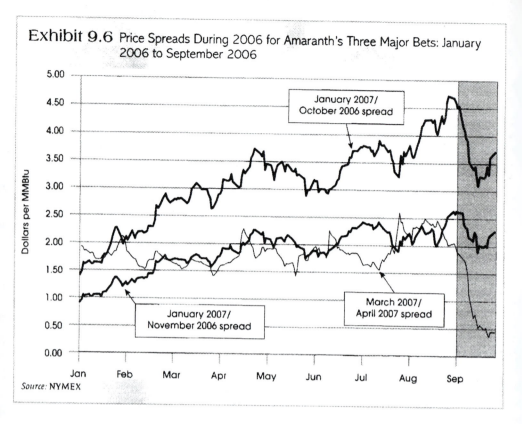

Exhibit 9.6 Price Spreads During 2006 for Amaranth's Three Major Bets: January 2006 to September 2006

Source: NYMEX

with short futures contracts. Second, the company wanted to reduce its short summer positions by allowing its financially settled contracts to expire and by offsetting or rolling over into a later month its physically settled contracts.

The problem was finding counterparties for these deals at prices that would earn Amaranth a profit, and they just were not available.[19] Amaranth held between 60% and 70% of the open interest on the New York Mercantile Exchange (NYMEX) for the November 2006 contract, and it held between 50% and 60% of the January 2007 contract.[20] The company also held a hefty portion of the contracts on the IntercontinentalExchange (ICE) and had numerous open positions in the OTC market. Amaranth's fear was that selling these positions into illiquid markets would cause its

[19]See letter from Michael Carrieri, Amaranth Compliance Director, to Anthony Densieski, Senior Director, Market Surveillance, New York Mercantile Exchange, 15 August 2006. Source: Permanent Subcommittee on Investigations Selected Excerpts from Instant Messages and E-mails Obtained from Amaranth LLC. *Exhibit List: Hearing on "Excessive Speculation in the Natural Gas Market," July 25 & July 9, 2007.* (Hereafter referred to as *PSI Report. Exhibit List: Hearing on Excessive Speculation in the Natural Gas Market," July 25 & July 9, 2007*).

[20]*Open interest* is the number of contracts (i.e., pairs of buy and sell orders) that have been transacted but not exercised, closed out, or expired. If open interest rises, funds are flowing into the market, and if it falls, funds are flowing out.

returns to nose-dive, thereby turning these positions into the natural-gas-market equivalent of toxic waste.

During May, price spreads began to drop (see Exhibit 9.6), erasing almost all the gains the company had earned during April. To make matters worse, Amaranth incurred losses on many of its non-energy investments.[21] Had Amaranth closed out its positions at this point, its losses would have been approximately $1.1 billion. But management was unwilling to concede such large losses when it had been so successful in the past and its energy strategy still looked so promising. As a result, the fund decided to hold its positions and wait for market conditions and liquidity to improve.

Unable to exit profitably, Amaranth not only kept its spread positions but, from June to August 2006, aggressively increased them (i.e., *doubled up*). By doing so, Amaranth accumulated its largest absolute and relative market positions to date. For example on August 29th, which was expiration day for the September 2006 futures contract, the company's winter 2007/fall 2006 position was short (approximately) 90,000 October 2007 contracts,[22] long 50,000 November 2006 contracts, and long 70,000 January 2007 contracts. Its March 2007/April 2007 position was long (approximately) 55,000 March 2007 contracts and short 75,000 April 2007 contracts.

During late August and into September 2006, natural gas spreads plummeted (see Exhibit 9.6). On August 29th alone, Amaranth lost about $600 million, but, fortunately, the company managed to finish August with net profits equal to about $635 million, as a result of earnings on the rest of its portfolio. Nevertheless, the foundation of Amaranth's investment strategy was crumbling. JP Morgan Chase (JPM), Amaranth's clearing agent, held more than $2 billion in margin deposits and was growing increasingly concerned that Amaranth may not be able to meet future demands. JPM owed a responsibility to the exchange clearing houses that sufficient funds would be present to meet any sudden and dramatic shifts in prices. Natural gas supplies were plentiful and the hurricane season, while far from over, had passed some significant milestones; so during the last week of August, natural gas prices and spreads fell rapidly, causing Amaranth's margin payments to rise. The bounce in winter futures prices and spreads that Amaranth hoped for (and bet on) looked increasingly less likely to occur. It was time to get serious about damage control.

---

[21] At the beginning of May 2006, Amaranth allocated 38% of its capital to energy, 23% to credit products, 12% to international convertible arbitrage and volatility, 8% to long/short equity, 9% to statistical arbitrage, 6% to commodities, 3% to U.S. convertible arbitrage, and 1% to merger arbitrage. See *Amaranth May 2006 Update to Investors*, prepared by Amaranth. Source: *PSI Report, Exhibit List: Hearing on Excessive Speculation in the Natural Gas Market,"* July 25 & July 9, 2007.

[22] In late July 2006, Amaranth switched its November 2007 futures position from short to long and replaced it with a short October 2006 futures position to balance its long January 2007 position.

Disadvantageous price movements at the end of August saddled Amaranth with a $944 million margin call, bringing its total payments to more than $2.5 billion. By 8 September, Amaranth had made more than $3 billion in margin deposits. To get a sense for how fast and sharply spreads fell, consider this. Between 1 September and 20 September, the January 2007/October 2006 spread fell by more than 30% (from $4.69/MMBtu to $3.28/MMBtu). After falling by nearly 12% during the week between August 25 and September 1, the March 2007/April 2007 spread fell by nearly 72% (from $2.05/MMBtu to $0.58/MMBtu) during the following three weeks. On 14 September alone, Amaranth lost about $560 million, due to declining natural gas prices and narrowing spreads caused by burgeoning inventories and cooler weather, which reduced the demand for air conditioning.

On Friday, September 15, Amaranth knew that it would not have sufficient funds to meet its margin calls the following Monday morning. Desperate for a counterparty to purchase Amaranth's portfolio, Nick Maounis spent the weekend trying to sell his energy book to potential buyers, such as Goldman Sachs Group (GS), Merrill Lynch (ML), Morgan Stanley, and Centaurus Energy. On Saturday, Maounis was able to sell a $250-million portion of the portfolio to ML, but it was still not enough.

After all-night negotiations with GS on Sunday, Maounis thought he had reached an agreement, but it came with a hefty price tag. GS would take over Amaranth's positions only if Amaranth made a concession payment of $1.85 billion. Maounis was jubilant that a deal had been reached at the last minute but, at the same time, thunderstruck that his hedge fund had been captured at such a bargain basement price. There was only one major problem standing in the way of concluding the GS deal, and it materialized later that Monday morning. To make the concession payment to GS, Maounis needed to use some of the collateral Amaranth had posted with JPM, but JPM was unwilling to release it. The Amaranth-GS deal did not free JPM from its risks as the clearing agent. Most likely, JPM feared that GS would strip the Amaranth portfolio of all its good positions and leave the toxic waste. If GS wanted Amaranth's energy portfolio, then it should also assume the clearing responsibilities from JPM with all its rights and responsibilities. JPM's refusal broke the deal.

Unable to come to terms with GS and with no other credible suitors in line, Maounis agreed on 20 September 2006 to sell Amaranth's energy book to JPM and Citadel Investment Group LLC (Citadel), a $12-billion hedge fund run by Kenneth Griffen. JPM and Citadel initially agreed to share the risks and returns from the 20,000 trades in Amaranth's energy book. As compensation for assuming these risks (i.e., to sweeten the deal),

Amaranth agreed to make a cash concession payment of more than $2.5 billion to JPM and Citadel.[23] In his letter to investors, Nick Maounis said that these "actions have eliminated the prospect of further significant mark-to-market losses in the natural gas portfolio and helped us avoid the termination of our credit facilities and the risk of a consequent forced liquidation by our creditors."

Now that the end was at hand, Amaranth needed to skillfully and efficiently liquidate the rest of its portfolio, paying what remained to creditors and investors. Therefore, Maounis suspended client redemptions and hired Fortress Investment, a $24-billion New York–based investment firm, to help sell its remaining $3 billion in assets. Fortunately, positive market conditions allowed Amaranth to sell a large portion of its remaining assets at healthy prices. On 31 March 2007, Amaranth officially closed its doors, after losing about 70% of its net asset value and leaving Amaranth's 400 plus employees in Greenwich, London, Toronto, Singapore, Calgary, and Houston without jobs.[24]

What Caused Amaranth's Catastrophic Losses?

Amaranth's demise was the result of three major interdependent factors: inadequate risk management practices that led to an excessively concentrated portfolio in energy investments, lack of liquidity, and extraordinarily large, unfavorable changes in market prices. All hedge funds make mistakes, but there are three cardinal rules that must be followed to overcome them. The first one is to make sure that your good bets outnumber the bad ones or that the good bets have heavier weights. The second rule is to cut your losses and run with your gains and, finally, to plan for the worst. Amaranth violated all three rules.

INADEQUATE RISK MANAGEMENT PRACTICES

By focusing only on the change in Amaranth's net asset value and profits from January to August 2006, one could easily be fooled into thinking that this hedge fund had a solid, well-reasoned natural gas strategy. With the exception of May and July, Amaranth's net asset value increased each month between January and August. At the end of August 2006, Amaranth's net asset value stood at approximately $10.2 billion, its highest month-end balance ever, and an increase of about $1.3 billion from January

[23]Read the epilogue at the end of this chapter if you wish to find out how much JPM made on this deal and how fast these profits were captured.
[24]Read the epilogue at the end of the chapter to find out what happened to Brian Hunter, Nick Maounis, and other players in the Amaranth fiasco.

Exhibit 9.7 Amaranth's Monthly Net Asset Values, First-Day Contributions/ Withdrawals, Month-End Contributions/Withdrawals, and Performance: January 2006 to August 2006

(Millions of Dollars)

Month	Beginning NAV*	First Day Contributions/ Withdrawals	Adjusted Beginning NAV	Net Performance	Month-End Contributions/ Withdrawals	Ending NAV
January	8,464	86	8,550	544	−191	8,904
February	8,884	7	8,890	357	−127	9,121
March	9,123	−38	9,086	264	·109	9,240
April	9,238	19	9,256	1,241	−173	10,325
May	10,347	155	10,502	−1,135	−48	9,319
June	9,297	274	9,571	633	−31	10,173
July	10,173	52	10,225	−46	−567	9,611
August	9,611	39	9,650	635	−56	10,228
Change from January			1,100			1,324
Total		593		2,493	−1,302	

* NAV is the sum of net of asset values for Amaranth LLC, Amaranth Partners LLC, and Amaranth Global Equities. These funds accounted for about 80%, 15%, and 5%, respectively, of Amaranth's total net asset value.

Source: Amaranth's CP Leverage Funds Due Diligence, prepared by JPMorgan Chase & Co. (Permanent Subcommittee on Investigations, *PSI Report, Exhibit List: Hearing on Excessive Speculation in the Natural Gas Market,* July 25 & July 9, 2007).

2006 (Exhibit 9.7). Profitability was also strong, with net accumulated earnings between January and August 2006 equal to about $2.5 billion (Exhibit 9.7) and a year-to-date compounded return of more than 30% (Exhibit 9.8).

But strategy should not be judged solely by return and top line growth. The risks inherent in a portfolio must also be considered. Despite employing 12 risk managers, who produced an avalanche of daily risk management measures, Amaranth was woefully overexposed.[25] Exhibit 9.9 shows the disproportionate weight (56%) that energy played in Amaranth's portfolio. Nick Maounis advertised Amaranth as a multi-strategy hedge fund, with the implication that its assets *and* strategies would be diversified. Who would have guessed that, to Amaranth, a multi-strategy hedge fund was one that plunged from sector to sector, depending on where the prospects looked the best? By placing more than 50% of the company's assets in leveraged energy bets,

---

[25]Amaranth's group of risk managers produced daily position statements as well as reports on profits and losses, value at risk, premium at risk, stress tests, Greek sensitivities (delta, gamma, theta, rho, and vega [sic]), leverage, concentrations, and industry exposures.

Exhibit 9.8   Amaranth Monthly Returns and Weighted Average Return: January to August 2006

Month	Amaranth LLC		Amaranth Partners LLC		Amaranth Global Equities		Weighted Return
	Return	% NAV	Return	% NAV	Return	% NAV	
January	6.45%	80%	5.23%	15%	3.91%	5%	6.13%
February	4.30%	80%	3.49%	15%	1.26%	5%	4.03%
March	2.91%	80%	2.49%	15%	4.02%	5%	2.90%
April	14.42%	80%	11.98%	15%	2.04%	5%	13.48%
May	−11.66%	79%	−9.58%	16%	−0.41%	5%	−10.78%
June	7.07%	81%	5.79%	16%	−0.98%	3%	6.63%
July	−0.53%	82%	−0.45%	15%	1.64%	3%	−0.45%
August	6.98%	82%	5.67%	15%	0.68%	3%	6.59%
Cumulative compound return: January to August 2006							**30.16%**

Source: Amaranth's CP Leverage Funds Due Diligence, prepared by JPMorgan Chase & Co. (Permanent Subcommittee on Investigations, *PSI Report, Exhibit List: Hearing on Excessive Speculation in the Natural Gas Market,* July 25 & July 9, 2007).

Exhibit 9.9   Amaranth's Investment Portfolios: September 2006

Investment	Portion of Equity Devoted to Investment (%)
Energy	56.0
Credit Products	17.0
Volatility	7.0
Long/Short Equity	7.0
Commodities	6.0
Statistical Arbitrage	4.0
U.S. Convertible	2.0
Merger Arbitrage	1.0
Total	**100.0**

Source: Amaranth's CP Leverage Funds Due Diligence, prepared by JPMorgan Chase & Co. (Permanent Subcommittee on Investigations, *PSI Report, Exhibit List: Hearing on Excessive Speculation in the Natural Gas Market,* July 25 & July 9, 2007).

the fund was not well diversified, and by building single-mindedly its long winter 2007/fall 2006 spread positions, its strategies were not multi-faceted.

LACK OF LIQUIDITY

Ultimately, Amaranth's decision to sell its energy book and close the fund was forced by a lack of liquidity. Not only was the company desperate for funds to meet its margin calls, but Amaranth also needed funds to make new investments. Normally, every decrease in natural gas prices was perceived by Amaranth as a buying opportunity, but with enormous margin calls to meet and a portfolio that was becoming increasingly more difficult to sell, Amaranth had no ability to take advantage of new deals in the market.

These liquidity problems had three major sources. First, Amaranth had such large open positions in the futures markets that there were no natural counterparties who could assume them at prices that would earn Amaranth profits. Second, Amaranth was the victim of large net withdrawals by investors, and finally, competitors quickly realized Amaranth's desperate position and exploited it mercilessly.

Huge Open Positions in Natural Gas Futures Contracts

At various times during 2006, Amaranth held between 46% and 81% of the open interest in NYMEX' most active natural gas futures contracts (Exhibit 9.10). At the same time, it held similarly large positions in less active futures contracts stretching out as far as 2010. Reducing these positions in a short period of time and at a profitable price turned out to be almost impossible.

Exhibit 9.10 Amaranth's Positions in NYMEX Natural Gas Futures Contracts

Natural Gas Futures Contract	Amaranth's Percent of Open Interest (at Various Times Throughout 2006)
August	46
September	51
October	60
November	70
December	81
January	60
March	60
April	60

Source: PSI Report, 25 June 2007.

Net Investor Withdrawals

Exhibit 9.7 shows that from January to September 2006, investors' net withdrawals from Amaranth were $709 million.[26] Withdrawals were particularly large in July 2006 when they reached $567 million.[27] It appears as if the smart money knew to leave—and for good reason. During April, May, and June, Amaranth's monthly profits fluctuated wildly by about 11%, −24%, 17%, respectively (Exhibit 9.8). What saved the company from even greater withdrawals were Amaranth's lock-up and gating provisions.

Competitors' Reactions to Amaranth's Financial Crisis

Amaranth's liquidity problems were exacerbated by market reaction to the company's impending crisis. When competing traders got wind of Amaranth's financial difficulties, they reacted predictably, skillfully, and immediately by adjusting their portfolios, causing market prices to move significantly against Amaranth's positions. Between Friday, September 15 and Wednesday September 20, Amaranth lost about $800 million because of deteriorating spreads. Having sold the most liquid assets from its not-so-diversified portfolio (e.g., convertible bonds and leveraged loans), the company was unable to liquidate enough other positions in time to pay its mushrooming margin calls.

EXTRAORDINARILY LARGE MOVEMENTS IN MARKET PRICES

Value-at-Risk (VaR) analysis would have enlightened many investors to the fact that Amaranth was a risky investment.[28] Based on monthly historic data, the company's VaR (with a 99% confidence level) was 28%, which meant that for 99 months out of 100, Amaranth stood to lose 28% or less of its portfolio's value, which implies that for one month out of 100 months (about once every 8.3 years), it stood to lose more than 28%.[29] Using the month-end figure for August 2006, 28% of Amaranth's portfolio translates into about a $2.9 billion loss. But Amaranth ended up losing more than $4.6 billion in just one week! Based on historic data, a monthly loss of this magnitude should have occurred about once every 27.4 quadrillion years.[30]

---

[26] $593 million first-day net contributions minus $1,302 million in month-end net withdrawals equals −$709 million (Exhibit. 9.7).

[27] About $400 million of these withdrawals were by fund-of-funds investors who were concerned about the increase in Amaranth's volatility.

[28] See Appendix 9.1: What are the Problems with Value at Risk, which can be found on the Prentice Hall Web site at http://www.prenhall.com/marthinsen.

[29] See Hilary Till, *EDHEC Comments on the Amaranth Case: Early Lessons from the Debacle.* Lille, France: EDHEC Risk and Asset Management Research Centre and Principal and Premia Capital Management, LLC. EDHEC Business School, 2006. Available at http://www.edhec-risk.com/features/RISKArticle.2006–10–02.0711/attachments/EDHEC%20Comments%20on%20Amaranth%20Case.pdf. Accessed 28 December 2007.

[30] A quadrillion is a one followed by 15 zeros (1E+15). On 15 September 2006, market prices changed by nine standard deviations. Assuming returns were normally distributed, a movement of nine standard deviations has a one-sided probability of happening equal to 1E-19. See Hilary Till, Ibid.

Christopher Fawcett of Fauchier Partners, a U.K. hedge fund with $4.3 billion under management, would have been a good spokesman for investors who saw Amaranth for the risky investment it was. In December 2005 (before it collapsed), Fawcett withdrew $30 million of Fauchier's funds from Amaranth because of at least 11 warning signals he recognized during an on-site visit.[31] In his letter to investors, he stated that Fauchier was willing to pay an early redemption penalty because "Amaranth had just about every characteristic we do not look for in a hedge fund," including the lack of an independent third-party administrator to verify the fund's returns, insufficient risk management supervision, high leverage, poor transparency, overconfident management, overreliance on a narrow trading strategy, and loose accounting controls that allowed employees to pass company expenses to the fund. For Fawcett, Amaranth's losses were "anything but unforeseeable."[32]

Explosion or Implosion? Who Got Hurt?

Amaranth lost more money than any hedge fund in the history of the world, and it lost it faster than was almost imaginable. Yet, the damage seemed to be contained to Amaranth's investors, shareholders, and employees. Amaranth met all its margin calls, followed all NYMEX directives, and remained solvent because of the purchase of its energy book by JPM and Citadel. The purchase prevented a default that could have triggered the sale of Amaranth's collateral by creditors and counterparties. Amaranth's traders did not falsify transactions or their values, as Nick Leeson did with the Barings Bank fiasco (1994), and unlike Metallgesellschaft (1993), Brian Hunter's strategies seemed to be fully understood and supported by upper management (i.e., Nick Maounis and the board of directors).

There was no need for Federal Reserve involvement, no domestic or international financial disruption, and there were almost no fears of financial contagion. A prepared statement by Amaranth for the Senate Subcommittee hearings indicated that the company was "unaware of any financial institution that lost money as a result of Amaranth's experience, and some institutions profited handsomely."[33] CFTC Commissioner Annette L. Nazareth indicated that, despite Amaranth's losses totaling

---

[31]Fauchier's investment in Amaranth came from an acquisition and not from an independent decision to invest in Amaranth.

[32]See Patrick Hosking, "Investor Paid Out Extra Penalties to Quit Amaranth," *The Times Online*, 13 October 2006, Available at http://business.timesonline.co.uk/tol/business/markets/united_states/article599997.ece. Accessed 28 December 2007.

[33]*Statement of Amaranth Advisors L.L.C. Before the Senate Committee on Homeland Security and Governmental Affairs Permanent Subcommittee on Investigations Concerning "Excessive Speculation in the Natural Gas Market" July 25, 2007.* Analysis by David J. Ross, Lexecon, Inc.

more than $6 billion, "there were no significant effects on the markets from a systemic risk point of view."[34]

Most of the victims of the collapse were investors, but then as early as 2005, Amaranth warned investors that it intended to make large directional bets, and Amaranth's prospectus stated clearly that the company was "a speculative investment that involves risk, including the risk of losing all or substantially all of the amount invested." Pension funds, like the San Diego County Employees Retirement Association,[35] and utilities, such as the Municipal Gas Authority of Georgia,[36] were stunned by the losses. If Amaranth's trades actually increased natural gas prices, then many consumers (e.g., families, hospitals, schools, businesses, and electrical plants) were hurt. Similarly, if Amaranth increased the volatility of natural gas prices, then many businesses may have felt forced to hedge early, and as a result, ended up paying significantly more for natural gas than those who waited and either paid the spot price or locked in futures prices later in the year.

The greatest damage may have been to the confidence many participants had in the market system. If natural gas prices and spreads were totally out of whack with fundamental economic conditions because of one trader's actions (which is a charge that has not been proved), then the usual market yardsticks appeared random until the fundamentals reasserted themselves. But how long does it take for this to happen? The answer is crucial because futures positions are marked-to-market daily, and meeting unexpected margin calls can force traders to liquidate their positions before they yield their expected profits. John Maynard Keynes once said "in the long-run we are all dead," but anyone who has played the futures market knows that the landscape can be littered in the short-run with the corpses of traders who missed margin calls.

Aftermath

The aftermath of Amaranth's financial crisis divided into two overlapping debates. One debate was mainly among regulators, exchanges, and traders who focused on how the futures markets functioned under the stress of

---

[34]Annette L. Nazareth, Commissioner, U.S. Securities and Exchange Commission, *Speech by SEC Commissioner: Remarks before the PLI Hedge Fund Conference*. Available at http://www.sec.gov/news/speech/ 2007/spch060607aln.htm. Accessed 28 December 2007.

[35]San Diego County Employees Retirement Association sued Amaranth and Brian Hunter for more than $150 million in lost retirement investments. See SDCERA v. Maounis, No. 07-CV-2618 (S.D.N.Y., complaint filed 29 March 2007).

[36]Municipal Gas Authority of Georgia testified that it hedged expected future natural gas purchases early in the year due to fears of rising prices and increasing volatility. As a result, it ended up paying $18 million more than it would have paid if it had not hedged.

Amaranth's financial crisis and whether built-in financial safeguards functioned effectively. The other debate was mainly among elected officials, utilities, and consumer groups, who focused on whether Amaranth hurt consumers. Very few involved in either debate were troubled much by the demise of Amaranth and the losses inflicted on its well-heeled investors. Amaranth guessed wrong, and its investors paid; it was as simple as that.

DID THE FUTURES MARKETS FUNCTION EFFECTIVELY?

The regulatory system and exchanges seem to have functioned effectively. Even though losses on the scale of Amaranth were disconcerting, NYMEX' major concern was with JPM, an exchange clearing member, and not particularly with Amaranth. Amaranth always deposited sufficient margin with JPM, and JPM was never in jeopardy of insolvency. Federal regulators and NYMEX communicated as early as June 2006 about Amaranth and followed up in August. Amaranth never missed a margin call and, in the end, was purchased. As a result, its credit facilities were not terminated, and the fund did not go bankrupt, which would have caused its collateral to be dumped on the market. There was no need for the Federal Reserve to intervene and there was no contagion to the financial markets. As for Amaranth's incredibly large losses, it is not the job of regulators or exchanges to protect traders from themselves. As long as markets are fair, function efficiently, and are free from price manipulation, fraud, and trading abuses, we can expect no more from our regulators and exchanges.

DID AMARANTH DOMINATE FUTURES MARKETS, ENGAGE IN EXCESSIVE SPECULATION, AND/OR CONDUCT REGULATORY ARBITRAGE?

In October 2006, barely a month after Amaranth's crisis, the U.S. Senate Permanent Subcommittee on Investigations (PSI) started a nine-month inquiry into the causes of this financial fiasco and possible cures. The PSI Report, entitled *Excessive Speculation in the Natural Gas Market*, was published in June 2007; hearings followed in late June and early July 2007. Among the major conclusions of the fact-filled PSI Report were that Amaranth dominated the U.S. natural gas market in 2006 and engaged in *excessive speculation* that distorted natural gas prices, widened price spreads, and increased volatility. The report also concluded that the regulatory structure of U.S. futures markets permitted Amaranth to evade federal rules and regulations.

Did Amaranth Dominate the U.S. Futures Markets for Natural Gas?

PSI's accusations of market domination were based on two pillars, namely, the significant portion of open interest that Amaranth held in the futures markets and the strong correlation between the fund's positions and the price of natural gas futures contracts. Exhibit 9.10 shows that, at various times during 2006, Amaranth held between 46% and 81% of the open interest in NYMEX' most active natural gas futures contracts. The fund held similarly large open interest positions for longer maturities. PSI was concerned that Amaranth's large purchases and sales could distort prices away from underlying energy market fundamentals, which might cause calamitous spillover effects on consumers and the financial and commodity markets. Surely, if a manufacturing or primary products company controlled such a large portion of total market sales, its activities would be scrutinized by antitrust authorities for abusive practices.

Exhibit 9.11 shows the extremely high correlation between Amaranth's January 2006 open interest and the price spread of the January 2007/November 2006 futures contract. Perfect positive correlation is 1.0; so, these correlations, which range from 0.75 and 0.93, appear to be so large as to leave little doubt that Amaranth dominated the natural gas futures markets during 2006.

There are problems with both arguments used by the PSI Report to connect Amaranth's activities to market domination. For one, the link between open interest and futures market domination is quite different from the link between market share and product market power. Physical goods have relatively high production and distribution costs, as well as relatively long production and distribution cycles. Therefore, physical products are supplied to the market rather slowly because they have to be produced, transported, and then sold. An individual or company can corner a physical market by purchasing a large portion of the available supply, storing it, withholding delivery, and driving up the product's price.

Exhibit 9.11 Correlations Between Amaranth's January 2007 Futures Position and the January 2007/November 2006 Price Spread

	Correlation Between		
	Amaranth's NYMEX Positions and Spread Price	Amaranth's ICE Positions and Spread Price	Amaranth's Total Positions and Spread Price
3 January to 28 April 2006	0.86	0.90	0.93
1 January to 31 August 2006	0.78	0.75	0.87

Source: PSI Report. 25 June 2007. P. 66.

By contrast, the marginal cost to create a new futures contract is almost zero, and it can be delivered instantaneously whenever there is a demand. Futures contracts cannot be stored with the intent to later withhold them from the market. Therefore, having a large share of a contract's open interest carries almost no power to restrict supply. In fact, most individuals holding long futures positions end up reversing (i.e., selling) them before maturity.

A second problem with the PSI Report is its use of correlation analysis. Correlation is not the same as causation; therefore, the high correlation between Amaranth's open interest and the price spread on futures contracts does not mean that one caused the other. To understand why, consider the high correlation between a child's foot size and her vocabulary. No one would argue that foot size has anything to do with the number of words a child possesses. Foot size does not influence vocabulary, and vocabulary does not influence foot size; rather the high correlation is caused by a third variable, age, which influences both foot size and vocabulary. Exhibit 9.12 uses the same data as Exhibit 9.11 but removes trend as a causal factor.[37] Notice how the correlations fall from a range between +0.75 and +0.93 to a much lower range between −0.15 and +0.31. These trend-adjusted figures provide ambiguous results. They indicate that the correlation between *changes in* Amaranth's open interest and *changes in* the price spread could be negative, a relatively insignificant positive value, or even zero.[38]

Exhibit 9.12 Correlations Between Changes in Amaranth's January 2007 Position and Changes in the January 2007/November 2006 Price Spread

Time Period	Adjusted Correlation between Changes in		
	NYMEX Positions and Spread Price	ICE Positions and Spread Price	Total Position and Spread Price
3 January to 28 April 2006	0.29	0.16	0.31
3 January to 31 August 2006	−0.15	0.07	−0.06

Source: Statement of Amaranth Advisors L.L.C. Before the Senate Committee on Homeland Security and Governmental Affairs Permanent Subcommittee on Investigations Concerning "Excessive Speculation in the Natural Gas Market" July 25, 2007. Analysis by David J. Ross. Lexecon, Inc.

[37]The time factor was removed by differencing the data by one period, thereby eliminating linear trend.

[38]Regression analysis (rather than correlation analysis) might have been a more insightful way for Amaranth to prove this point.

Finally, Amaranth was just one of many well-capitalized players in the natural gas futures market. Among the others were about 200 financial institutions (e.g., Goldman Sachs, Morgan Stanley, Deutsche Bank, and Lehman Brothers), hedge funds (e.g., Citadel Investment Group, D.E. Shaw, Centaurus Energy, BP Capital, and Ivy Asset Management Corp.), and producers (e.g., BP-Amoco, Sempra Energy, and Chevron-Texaco). Normally, these large players account for about 80% of the open interest on NYMEX.[39] If Amaranth dominated the natural gas markets, then one wonders what prevented these other key players from exercising their financial muscle to prevent it.[40]

Did Amaranth Engage in Excessive Speculation?

Since its inception in 1974, the U.S. Commodities Futures Trading Commission (CFTC) has been charged with protecting the integrity of U.S. futures and options markets for commodities by preventing *excessive speculation*.[41] Congress felt that excessive speculation caused highly abnormal price fluctuations, which hindered interstate commerce. Therefore, CFTC's mandate has been to shield U.S. financial markets for commodities from "sudden or unreasonable fluctuations or unwarranted changes" in prices.[42] The problem has been that Congress never defined *sudden or unreasonable fluctuations or unwarranted changes* in prices. As a result, there is a rather wide playing field of interpretations.

Congress did not make excessive speculation a *per se* violation of any law, such as the U.S. Commodity Exchange Act (CEA). Therefore, if Amaranth (or any trader) engaged in excessive speculation, it was not an illegal act. Rather, this provision was written into CFTC's charter to assign responsibility and to empower the Commission with authority to implement restraints that would stop or prevent excessive speculation.

Excessive speculation may be harmful to a nation, but normal speculation is not. Speculators can contribute to healthy, dynamic economies by providing liquidity to markets that would otherwise be relatively shallow. Speculators are particularly important in the natural gas industry because the quantity of futures contracts supplied by individuals who produce and/or store natural gas and want to protect their future revenues is normally much greater than the amount demand by consumers who want to lock in future costs. Speculators bridge this gap.

---

[39]Testimony of Dr. James Newsome, CEO New York Mercantile Exchange, Inc. before the Senate Subcommittee on Homeland Security and Government Affairs Permanent Subcommittee on Investigations Concerning "Excessive Speculation in the Natural Gas Market" July 9, 2007.

[40]See Risk Notepad 9.3: A Tale of Two Hedge Funds.

[41]The *excessive speculation* clause originates in legislation passed during the 1920s, but it was eclipsed by the *price manipulation* clause. PSI resurrected the excessive speculation clause in its report.

[42]CEA Section 4a (a) U.S.C. § 6a (a).

Did Amaranth Commit Regulatory Arbitrage?

On 8 August 2006, Amaranth's share of open interest for the September 2006 futures contract exceeded 44%.[43] Because this contract was due to expire in about three weeks, NYMEX contacted Mike Carrieri, Amaranth's compliance officer, and requested that he reduce, in a commercially reasonable trading manner, Amaranth's September 2006 open interest to between 30% and 40%. Amaranth also had a large October position; so Carrieri was instructed not to roll Amaranth's September positions into October 2006. Within three days of the notification, Amaranth reduced its September exposures on NYMEX to 29%, thereby satisfying NYMEX' demands. Shortly thereafter, its October position was also reduced.[44]

Only insiders and Amaranth's clearing agent (JP Morgan Chase) knew that Amaranth reduced its September and October 2006 positions on the regulated NYMEX by switching them to the unregulated ICE (Exhibit 9.13). By the end of the month, Amaranth was well within the NYMEX' position limits,[45] but its September 2006 position on ICE was actually higher than when Carrieri was warned by NYMEX in early August.

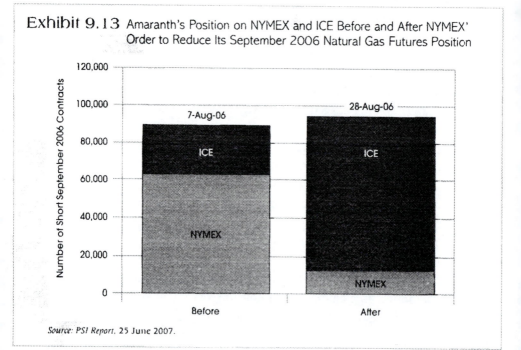

Exhibit 9.13 Amaranth's Position on NYMEX and ICE Before and After NYMEX' Order to Reduce Its September 2006 Natural Gas Futures Position

Source: PSI Report, 25 June 2007.

[43]In June 2006, NYMEX was contacted by the surveillance staff of CFTC's Division of Market Oversight about Amaranth's large positions and its losses, but active surveillance and monitoring began only in August.

[44]Amaranth actually increased its open interest in the October 2006 contract from 52% on 9 August, which was the day after NYMEX requested that Amaranth reduce its September 2006 exposure, to 63.5% on 10 August, but quickly thereafter, it reduced this position to an acceptable level.

[45]See Appendix 9.2: Position Limits versus Accountability Levels, which can be found on the Prentice Hall Web site at http://www.prenhall.com/marthinsen.

Amaranth was able to avoid NYMEX regulations because of a provision in the Commodity Futures Modernization Act of 2000 (CFMA 2000) that created a special trading unit called an *exempt commercial market* (ECM). An ECM is an over-the-counter (OTC) entity that is not required to be registered, designated, recognized, licensed, or approved by the CFTC.[46] To qualify, the exchange must deal in bilateral transactions between *eligible commercial entities*, and an eligible commercial entity is any institution or high-net-worth individual who trades either financial derivatives or exempt commodity derivatives, such as metals and energy.[47]

Congress reasoned that well-heeled investors who use ECMs do not need the protections and safeguards provided to smaller investors. It also understood that electronic exchanges operate in a competitive twilight zone between fully regulated exchanges and the totally unregulated OTC markets. Moreover, electronic exchanges were recognized as experimental proving grounds for new and innovative contracts, which is an area the United States needs to promote if it wants to continue playing a leadership role in global financial markets. By passing CFMA 2000, Congress statutorily removed most federal regulations and oversight from electronic trading platforms and gave legal certainty to OTC transactions.

Amaranth, therefore, was able to pull off this act of contract prestidigitation undetected because, as an unregulated exchange, ICE had no reporting obligations and was not required to impose any limits on Amaranth's positions. Amaranth's contract-switching operation may, therefore, have defied the spirit of NYMEX' position limits, but it did not violate any law. During fall 2007, two bills were introduced in the U.S. Senate and House to bring regulated exchanges, like NYMEX, and unregulated electronic exchanges, like ICE, under a common regulatory umbrella.[48] If Congress decides more regulation is necessary, it must make sure that the cure is not worse than the disease because harsh regulations will push derivative transactions away from regulated exchanges and toward OTC and/or foreign markets. Currently, about 75% of all U.S. energy trades are conducted on the unregulated OTC markets, and these markets are not going away because so many customers rely on them for customized contracts (e.g., hedging new plant construction costs). Congress must also make sure that it pinpoints the markets it wishes to regulate. For instance, ICE offers more than 400 specialty

[46]ECMs did not totally escape CFTC purview. See Appendix 9.3: Reporting Requirements for an Exempt Commercial Market, which can be found on the Prentice Hall Web site at http://www.prenhall.com/marthinsen.
[47]CEA Sections 2(h) (3)-(5), 7 U.S.C. §§ 2(h) (3)-(5).
[48]S.2058, *Close the Enron Loophole Act* was introduced in the U.S. Senate on 17 September 2007 by Sen. Carl Levin (D-MI), Chairman of the Senate Permanent Subcommittee on Investigations. H.R.4066, *Close the Enron Loophole Act* was introduced in the U.S. House of Representatives by Congressmen Peter Welch (D-VT) and Robert Andrew (D-NJ) on 1 November 2007.

contracts, many of which have only a handful of positions and, therefore, are very illiquid. Would all of these contracts be regulated or just the ones with a large number of open positions?[49]

DID AMARANTH MANIPULATE PRICES?

Within a month of the PSI Report on *Excessive Speculation*, CFTC filed a civil enforcement action suit against Amaranth and Brian Hunter. The suit accused the defendants of intentionally and unlawfully *attempting* to manipulate the price of NYMEX natural gas *futures* contracts on two expiration days—24 February 2006 and 26 April 2006.[50] The day after CFTC filed suit, the Federal Energy Regulatory Commission (FERC) issued a "Show Cause Order"[51] after making a preliminary determination that Amaranth entities,[52] Brian Hunter, and Matthew Donohoe, an Amaranth trader, had manipulated prices on NYMEX and affected *physical* gas prices on three futures contract expiration days—24 February 2006, 29 March 2006, and 26 April 2006.[53] The suit against Amaranth was FERC's first prosecution of a price manipulation case under the Energy Policy Act of 2005, and the civil penalty for this offense was $1 million per day per violation. In its Show Cause Order, FERC proposed penalties equaling $291 million.[54]

CFTC was created in 1974 as an independent agency with exclusive jurisdiction over the accounts, agreements, and transactions involving commodity *futures and options contracts* that are *transacted on regulated exchanges*.[55] By contrast, FERC was created in 1977 to ensure fair and competitive natural gas markets in the United States. Therefore, FERC has been charged with the regulation of markets for *physical* natural gas, and CFTC has been charged with the regulation of *financial* exchanges for natural gas (i.e., futures and options).

CFTC and FERC did not base their charges on Amaranth's enormous open interest on NYMEX; rather they charged the fund with manipulating prices

---

[49] In 2006, CE's Henry Hub swap had more than 140,000 trades per day, but the second largest contract had fewer than 20,000, and the number of trades per day for other contracts fell considerably from there.

[50] *Perfected manipulation* is a much more serious charge.

[51] A *Show Cause Order* is a judge-directed charge that requests Party A (e.g., Amaranth) to provide convincing reasons why a charge brought by Party B (e.g., FERC) should not be granted. See 18 C.F.R. § 1C.1 (2006) (Anti-manipulation). CFTC's charge against Amaranth was made on 25 July 2006. FERC filed its Show Cause Order on 26 July 2006.

[52] Amaranth entities included Amaranth Advisors LLC, Amaranth LLC, Amaranth Management Limited Partnership, Amaranth International Limited, Amaranth Partners LLC, Amaranth Capital Partners LLC, Amaranth Group Inc., and Amaranth Advisors (Calgary) ULC.

[53] CFTC's charge was for attempted price manipulation, and FERC's charge was for actual price manipulation.

[54] See Daniel P. Collins, "Manipulating a Hedge Fund Blow-up," *Futures* 36(11) (7 September 2007). 66–68. Amaranth was sued for $200 million, Hunter for $30 million, and Donohoe for $2 million, and a $59 million disgorgement of profits claim was placed on Amaranth.

[55] See Commodity Futures Trading Commission, *About the CFTC*. Available at http://cftc.gov/aboutthecftc/index.htm. Accessed 28 December 2007.

by selling extraordinarily large amounts of NYMEX futures contracts during the last 30 minutes of selected contract-expiration days. CFTC immediately claimed jurisdiction over the case because Amaranth dealt in natural gas futures and option contracts, which fell within the CFTC's exclusive territory. FERC also claimed jurisdiction, arguing that Amaranth affected the cash market prices for physical natural gas. Even though Amaranth never traded in the cash market and never took (or made) physical delivery of natural gas on a futures contract, the settlement price for NYMEX' natural gas futures contract is used as the basis for many cash market transactions. Therefore, FERC argued that Amaranth's trades increased natural gas prices to wholesale market participants, thereby harming natural gas customers.

What is Price Manipulation?

FERC's suit was based on the Energy Policy Act of 2005 (EPA 2005), which prohibited "the use or employment of manipulative or deceptive devices or contrivances in connection with the purchase or sale of natural gas." The EPA 2005 standard for price manipulation came from language in the U.S. Securities Exchange Act of 1934.[56] By contrast, CFTC's price manipulation suit was a *per se* violation of the U.S. Commodity Exchange Act (CEA) because it threatened two of the most fundamental functions that markets perform, which are risk management and price discovery. Specifically, CEA makes it unlawful for "[a]ny person to manipulate or attempt to manipulate the price of any commodity in interstate commerce, or for future delivery on . . . any registered [exchange], or to corner or attempt to corner any such commodity." Amaranth immediately cried foul, claiming that it was being prosecuted under two different sets of price manipulation rules.

The usual standard for price manipulation is the ability and intention to unduly influence prices. It also matters whether prices actually changed as a result of the behavior. When price manipulation occurs, it is usually because someone:

- Controls the supply, transportation, and/or storage of a physical asset;
- Plays one exchange off another, or
- Makes erroneous booking entries, reports fictitious trades, falsifies trading information, and/or circulates false stories/rumors.[57]

[56]Energy Policy Act of 2005, Pub. L. No. 109-58, 119 Stat. 594 (2005).

[57]See Federal Energy Regulatory Commission, *Discussion on Commission Use of Natural Gas Price Indices.* Washington, DC: Federal Energy Regulatory Commission, (October 2002). Available at http://www.ferc.gov/legal/maj-ord-reg/land-docs/Harvey-01-15-03-CommissionPresentation-A-5.pdf. Accessed 28 December 2007. Also see Federal Energy Regulatory Commission, *Derivatives and Risk Management in the Petroleum, Natural Gas, and Electricity Industries: Natural Gas Spot Markets: How Accurate Are Reported Prices?* Federal Energy Regulatory Commission. Washington, DC: Federal Energy Regulatory Commission, (October 2002). Available at http://www.eia.doe.gov/oiaf/servicerpt/derivative/ngsm.html. Accessed 28 December 2007.

Manipulating Price Spreads by Affecting Storage Opportunities for risk-free arbitrage occur when a futures price is greater than or less than the spot price plus the cost of carry. The cost of carry is basically the net cost to purchase an underlier on one date (say, in April) and then sell it later (say, in December). Therefore, the cost of carry is the sum of all interest and storage expenses to purchase and warehouse an underlier minus any investment returns earned from owning the underlier. As the price spread between the winter 2007/fall 2006 contract and the March 2007/April 2007 contact increased, why didn't arbitragers hammer the markets to earn risk free returns? All they had to do was borrow sizeable amounts, use the funds to purchase natural gas on the spot market, store it, and then sell the fuel at futures prices that guaranteed profits. Where were the arbitragers?

In fact, they were there! But there was one big problem. Amaranth bought a huge number of futures contracts for winter delivery, thereby bidding up the winter 2007/fall 2006 price spread. These higher winter prices encouraged natural gas storage, but as arbitragers bought increasingly more natural gas in the spot market and sold more futures contracts, the limited capacity of U.S. storage facilities was gradually exhausted. As a result, the ability of arbitragers to engage in further arbitrage reached its limits. Brian Hunter's strategy was based, in part, on his expectation that higher futures prices would encourage storage and storage would be exhausted by fall 2006. Once the storage facilities were full, he expected natural gas to be dumped on the spot market, causing futures prices in autumn 2006 to drop relative to winter 2007.

Risk Notepad 9.3

A Tale of Two Hedge Funds

During 2006, a common refrain among market traders was they were frightened to take positions counter to Amaranth because market fundamentals no longer seemed to be the basis for natural gas price swings. The risk of paying margin until the market corrected itself was just too great. MotherRock LP (MR) and Centaurus Energy (CE) were two hedge funds that took on Amaranth. One failed and the other succeeded.

MOTHERROCK LP

Founded by Bo Collins, former chairman of NYMEX, MR was a $300 million hedge fund that traded heavily natural gas futures contracts. Realizing that the March 2007/April 2007 spread was too wide, MR sold the spread, which was diametrically opposite to what Amaranth was doing. In the long run, MR's bets were winners and would have paid off handsomely, but the fund never got the chance to collect the profits because it was killed off by escalating margin calls. The final straw for MR came on 31 July 2006, when the March 2007/April 2007 spread increased by 72 cents. Coincidentally, on the same day Amaranth purchased more than 10,000 March 2007 contracts on NYMEX and sold about an equal number of April 2007 contracts, thereby accounting for about 70% of volume trades on the exchange for those two contracts. Amaranth also purchased about 13,000 March 2007 contracts on ICE and sold 11,000 April 2007 contracts, which constituted about 60% and 50%, respectively, of the total volume for those two contracts on that exchange.

Did Amaranth's transactions increase the spread and kill off MR, or did the March 2007/April 2007 spread widen as a result of breaking news stories about expected natural gas storages and revised weather forecasts? Proving cause and effect is difficult. Ironically, in early September 2007 when MR failed, it was Amaranth that bought MR's portfolio from ABN Amro, the clearing house that presided MR's bankruptcy. By acquiring these positions, the acquisition helped offset, and thereby improve, some of Amaranth's extreme loss-making positions.

CENTAURUS ENERGY

Centaurus Energy was a $3 billion, Houston-based hedge fund founded by former Enron trader, John Arnold. On 29 August 2006, which was expiration day for the September 2006 natural gas futures contract, Amaranth and CE engaged in head-to-head combat on NYMEX. The surveillance team at NYMEX ordered Amaranth not to transact any large trades during the last half hour of trading because, during this brief period, the exchange's final settlement price for the September contract was determined. Amaranth spent the day selling September contracts in an attempt to build its long October 2006/September 2006 spread position, and, on the other side, CE spent the day buying. The match between Amaranth's supply and CE's demand held the September futures price relatively steady for most of the day.

To comply with NYMEX' order to limit its trades during the last half hour of trading, Amaranth exited NYMEX at about 1:15 P.M. and then ICE shortly thereafter, a little more than an hour before the end of the trading sessions. With Amaranth gone, CE became the dominant player for the last hour, and it appears to have taken advantage of the situation. During the last 45 minutes of trading alone, CE purchased almost 10,000 September contracts on ICE and 3,000 on NYMEX. The September futures price rose by 60 cents, an approximate 10% increase. Similarly, the October 2006/September 2006 spread, which had opened at 36 cents and rose to 50 cents by noon, plummeted by about 40 cents to fewer than 10 cents by market close. Amaranth's position hemorrhaged cash and lost millions in value.

Amaranth complained immediately to NYMEX, convinced that CE artificially spiked the September price and squashed the October 2006/September 2006 spread, and it requested that NYMEX conduct an investigation. CE responded to these accusations by saying that it was prepared to continue buying the September contract until its price rose to a level consistent with the spot price of natural gas and until the October 2006/September 2006 spread fell to normal levels. Clearly, there were no fundamental changes in the underlying natural gas conditions during the last 45 minutes of trading. The spike was artificial, but at the same time, if you live by the sword, you must expect to die by it. The consensus seemed to be Amaranth was complicit in driving up the October 2006/September 2006 spread, which historically was between 7 cents and 8 cents, to 50 cents during the summer of 2006 and to about 35 cents at the end of September. Therefore, Amaranth was being cut by the double edge of its own blade.

Manipulating Prices by Playing One Exchange Off Another To understand the price manipulation charges against Amaranth, it is important to recognize the similarities and differences between settlement on NYMEX and ICE. These two exchanges compete vigorously against each other, and their contracts are functionally (i.e., financially) identical. On both exchanges, natural gas futures contracts expire three business days before a new month begins. One important difference between the exchanges is that NYMEX futures contracts require physical delivery for the natural gas futures contracts that are held to maturity.[58] ICE contracts are settled financially (i.e., with no obligation to deliver natural gas). Many price manipulation schemes require control of the production, transportation, and/or storage of physical natural gas; so this difference could be important.

NYMEX requires physical delivery of natural gas futures contracts held to maturity, and the final settlement price is a weighted average of the prices during the final 30 minutes of trading (i.e., from 2:00 P.M. and 2:30 P.M. EST).[59] Most individuals who trade NYMEX futures contracts have no intention of taking physical delivery. Delivery is just too inconvenient. If they wanted to actually purchase natural gas, they would do so on terms that suited their needs (e.g., delivery location) instead of NYMEX' standardized terms. Therefore, the overwhelming majority of NYMEX contracts are closed prior to maturity, thereby nullifying the physical delivery requirement. One problem with having to close out a position on NYMEX is the transaction, if it is large enough, can move the contract price in a disadvantageous direction. For example, a trader with a large short position would benefit if the price of the futures contract fell. But to offset a short position, the trader must purchase futures contracts, which would raise the price and reduce profits. Similarly, a long position would benefit if the price rose, but to offset a long position, the trader must sell futures contracts, which would lower the futures price and reduce profits.

Natural gas futures contracts on Atlanta-based ICE are financially settled, and the final settlement price in 2006 was taken directly from NYMEX.[60] Because ICE contracts are settled for cash, rather than physical natural gas, they are called *swaps*, but as far as hedgers, speculators, and arbitragers are concerned, the two contracts are functionally equivalent. With no possibility for physical delivery, traders simply let their ICE contracts expire and then collect or pay the difference between the spot price of natural gas and their previously negotiated futures prices. Because there is no need to unwind these positions, traders do not engage in offsetting transactions that could move futures prices disadvantageously.

---

[58]Actually, NYMEX also has an electronic trading platform that is classified as an ECM (just like ICE) and, therefore, is exempt from CFTC regulations. NYMEX' financially settled natural gas contract did not play a role in this financial fiasco.

[59]Information on NYMEX can be found at http://nymex.com. Accessed 28 December 2007.

[60]Information on ICE can be found at https://www.theice.com/homepage.jhtml. Accessed 28 December 2007.

Expiration day for the March 2006 contract was 24 February 2006. The day before expiration, Amaranth was short 1,700 March 2006 contracts on NYMEX, and, at the same time, it was short 12,000 March 2006 swap contracts on ICE. If the price of natural gas fell, Amaranth stood to gain handsomely. Brian Hunter wrote text messages to colleagues saying he wanted to make a "bit of an expiriment (sic)" . . . so, "make sure we have lots of futures to sell MOC [market on close] tomorrow" . . . because we "just need [March] to get smashed on settle then [the] day is done."

On expiration day, Hunter kept his enormous short position on ICE but reversed his short position on NYMEX, ending up with a long position equal to about 3,000 natural gas futures contracts. Then, during the last half hour of trading, when NYMEX' settlement price was determined, he sold all 3,000 long contracts, which put downward pressure on the price of NYMEX' March 2006 natural gas futures contract.[61] Even though the lower price may have hurt Amaranth's profits for the 3,000 contracts Hunter sold on NYMEX, it increased the fund's profits on his 12,000 contract ICE position. We know this because ICE took its final settlement price directly from NYMEX.

Regulators claimed that Hunter manipulated prices in the same way on 26 April 2006, the day the May 2006 futures contract expired. In the days prior to expiration, Amaranth was charged with accumulating a net long position on NYMEX equal to 3,000 May 2006 natural gas futures contracts and, at the same time, taking a short position on ICE for 19,000 May 2006 futures contracts. Of the 3,000 contracts sold on 26 April, 2,527 were traded during the last 30 minutes, of which 2,517 were traded in the last four minutes, and 1,897 were traded in the last minute. During the day, the natural gas futures price for May 2006 rose from $7.15/MMBtu at 2:00 P.M. to $7.27/MMBtu at 2:22 P.M., and then plummeted to $7.10 at the close of trading.

Issues Relating to the Price Manipulation Charges against Amaranth

Charges of price manipulation raise a number of important economic issues. Do speculators destabilize prices? Do changes in futures prices affect the underlier's price? CFTC and FERC accumulated a considerable body of circumstantial evidence against Amaranth, but still there were many who questioned the claims.

Do Speculators Stabilize or Destabilize Prices? If they are successful, speculators earn profits by purchasing natural gas at prices lower than they sell it. This means they buy natural gas when the market price is

---

[61]Hunter sold 2,000 of these 3,000 contracts during the last eight minutes of trading.

below where it should be and then sell it when the price rises back to or above the (steady state) equilibrium level. When speculators purchase natural gas, their actions raise the price, and when they sell, their actions lower it. Therefore, if they are profitable over time, speculators should reduce natural gas price volatility and not increase it because they are buying when the price is too low and selling when it is too high.[62]

In a 2005 study, CFTC's Office of Economic Analysis concluded that managed market traders (MMT), such as hedge funds, do not change their positions as frequently as hedgers.[63] Reinforcing these conclusions, a March 2005 study by NYMEX found that hedge funds tend to hold positions significantly longer than the average market participant and actually reduced market volatility, rather than increased it.[64] Therefore, these studies support the view that speculators tend to dampen volatility and not increase it.

Does Futures Speculation Affect the Underlier's Price? Futures contracts are supposed to derive their value from the underlier—hence the name *derivative*. As the spot price of an underlier changes, the futures price should change in tandem, and it should differ from the spot price by the cost of carry. If this were not the case, then opportunities for risk-free arbitrage should arise. Options on commodities also derive their value from the spot price of the underlier, but these values are also influenced by four other variables, namely the strike price, maturity, volatility, and risk-free interest rate. Again, causation is supposed to run from the cash market to the derivative market and not the other way around.

The International Swap Dealers Association (ISDA) responded forcefully to CFTC's and FERC's attempt to regulate electronic exchanges by saying "[t]ired allegations that activity in the privately negotiated derivatives industry somehow adversely affects consumers have been thoroughly rejected by the federal agencies charged with their policing."[65] The CFTC's Office of Economic Analysis concluded that changes in the positions of MMTs were reactions to commodity price changes and not the cause of these price changes. Moreover, the analysis found that MMTs shifted their

[62]Of course, during a speculative bubble or if a trader has some monopoly advantage, artificial profits could be generated from speculative trading, which would take the price away from the (fundamental-based) equilibrium level.

[63]Michael S. Haigh, Jana Hranaiova, and James A. Overdahl. Office of the Chief Economist, U.S. Commodity Futures Trading Commission. *Price Dynamics, Price Discovery and Large Futures Trader Interactions in the Energy Complex*, Working Paper: First Draft: April 28th 2005. Available at http://www.cftc.gov/files/opa/press05/opacftc-managed-money-trader-study.pdf. Accessed 28 December 2007.

[64]Testimony of Dr. James Newsome, CEO New York Mercantile Exchange, Inc. Senate Subcommittee on Homeland Security and Government Affairs Permanent Subcommittee on Investigations Concerning "Excessive Speculation in the Natural Gas Market" 9 July 2007.

[65]Jeremy Grant. "Amaranth Gas Trades Hit US Consumer." *FT.Com* (24 June 2007). Available at http://us.ft.com/ftgateway/superpage.ft?news_id=fto062420072242331551&page=2. Accessed 31 December 2007.

positions in reaction to and inversely with changes in the positions of other large hedge funds, thereby supplying the market with needed liquidity.[66]

In his appearance during the Senate Subcommittee hearings, CFTC's chief economist said, "The [PSI] analysis failed to conclude that Amaranth's trading was responsible for the price spread level observed during 2006."[67] Rather, CFTC interpreted the evidence as showing two-way causality, with Amaranth influencing the market price and the market price influencing Amaranth.[68] The chief economist went on to say that "[a]ll the data are consistent with the hypothesis that the March/April spread, and similar winter/summer spreads, declined due to changes in the perception of market fundamentals."[69] CFTC's Acting Chairman, Walt Lukken, agreed and testified that Amaranth did not have any effect on prices in the natural gas market.

Did Amaranth's Large Open Interest Affect Futures Prices? Futures markets are not bidding arenas for a fixed number of contracts. The marginal cost of transacting a new deal is virtually zero and delivery is instantaneous. Two counterparties can create a new contract even if a third party holds 100% of the existing open interest. Therefore, holding a large portion of the open interest in a futures contract is not a barrier to entry because the price is determined by the flow of supply and demand transactions and not by the stock of existing positions.

Other Doubts about the Price Manipulation Cases against Amaranth Other doubts surfaced about the price manipulation charges against Amaranth. First, there was a timing issue. Amaranth began building its March 2007/April 2007 positions in the spring of 2006, but price spreads for this contract were already wide due to Hurricanes Katrina and Rita in 2005. This means that the spread increased and remained high for *months before* Amaranth took its large positions. Second, Amaranth's demise caused its demand for and supply of futures contract to fall to zero. If Amaranth were such a large portion of the market, one would have expected its departure to reduce open interest on NYMEX, but it didn't. Instead, open interest "remained fairly stable at record levels."[70] Finally, when Amaranth exited the market, it should have substantially reduced the demand for NYMEX' January 2007 natural gas futures contract, thereby lowering the

---

[66]Michael S. Haigh, Jana Hranaiova, and James A. Overdahl. Office of the Chief Economist, U.S. Commodity Futures Trading Commission, *Price Dynamics, Price Discovery and Large Futures Trader Interactions in the Energy Complex*, Working Paper: First Draft: April 28th 2005. Available at http://www.cftc.gov/files/opa/press05/opacftc-managed-money-trader-study.pdf. Accessed 28 December 2007.

[67]Daniel P. Collins, "Manipulating a Hedge Fund Blow-up," *Futures* 36 (11) (7 September 2007), 66–68.

[68]This finding was for a subset of the data from 15 April 2006 to 25 August 2006.

[69]Daniel P. Collins, Ibid.

[70]See Winter 2006–07 Energy Market Assessment Item No.: A-3 19 October 2006 at 6. Available at http://www.ferc.gov/EventCalendar/Files/20061019110945-A-3-talking.pdf. Accessed 28 December 2007.

January 2007 futures price. But the price of this contract rose with Amaranth's departure. Independent studies came to the same conclusion, indicating that Amaranth simply made a bad bet on the weather and paid a hefty price for its reckless gambling.[71]

Conclusion

It is hard to argue with success, but it is not at all difficult to see that Brian Hunter's *success* in 2005 was due more to luck than to skill. Incorporated into the option prices he paid in early 2005 were market expectations about the spot prices of natural gas in the future. These expectations were captured by volatility estimates, which made their way into traders' option-pricing models. Hunter bet that natural gas prices would be more volatile than the market expected. Therefore, he bought (what he thought were) underpriced call options. By midyear, it was clear that he had totally misjudged the market.

Nevertheless, he was bailed out in August by two hurricanes that no one at Amaranth could have predicted in early 2005. One problem with such unmerited, random success is that it often attracts large inflows of funds with hallucinogenic visions about what can be earned and with romantically high expectations about the capabilities of the money managers charged with earning it. Investing these massive volumes of new funds with mediocre talent is a recipe for disaster because it usually means increasing risk in the hopes that lightening (in the form of a favorable random event) will strike twice.

The demise of Amaranth was not due to irrational strategies or the misguided use of sophisticated risk management tools that suddenly went awry. Nor was it due to the complicity of rogue traders, incompetent managers, or any lack of understanding about how derivative markets work. Rather, Amaranth's demise was the result of the exceptionally large bets it made on a faulty strategy. These large bets led to a liquidity crisis, as looming margin calls of colossal size could not be financed. Reining in these large bets was primarily the responsibility of Amaranth's risk managers, and they failed. During just one week in September, Amaranth lost about $4.6 billion on its natural gas bets. By month's end, the losses totaled $6.4 billion, which was about 70 percent of Amaranth's net asset value.

To be sure, there were victims, but most of them were Amaranth's investors, shareholders, and employees. In fact, a truly remarkable feature of Amaranth's crisis was how easily it was absorbed by the financial system and

---

[71]For example, see Hilary Till, Ibid.

how little collateral damage occurred. Amaranth was like an enormous ocean liner sinking in the middle of the ocean—a tragedy to be sure, but one swallowed up easily by a sea of liquidity. It is a tribute to the massive liquidity in U.S. capital markets that Amaranth was ruined with so little fallout. Part of this tribute goes to financial institutions, like Citadel and JPM, that were able to whip out their computerized risk management models at the speed of light and, over a weekend, value the complicated positions of a sinking fund like Amaranth. Nevertheless, the amounts these rescuers earned in such a short amount of time might tempt others to start drilling for their natural gas profits on Wall Street rather than the Gulf Coast.

At the time of publication, no ruling or settlement had been made on whether Amaranth manipulated or attempted to manipulate natural gas prices, even though we know that, if Amaranth were actually able to manipulate prices, it did a pretty bad job of it. Debate continued, as well, about whether the futures markets functioned properly and whether Amaranth hurt consumers by dominating the natural gas futures markets, engaging in excessive speculation, and/or conducting regulatory arbitrage. Congress will have to sort out these issues with the ultimate goal of improving financial transparency so investors and regulators can make better decisions.

Amaranth's enormous losses and demise point to four recurring maxims of risk management, namely, size does matter, you can't float without liquidity, don't buy what you can't sell, and don't put all your eggs in one basket—in fact, don't put most of them there. Amaranth advertised itself as a multi-strategy hedge fund, with the implication that its assets *and* strategies would be diversified, but as it turned out, that was not the case. More than 50% of Amaranth's assets were focused in energy; the company took massive, highly leveraged, off-balance sheet positions in natural gas futures contracts, and it used strategies that proved to be wrong.

Epilogue

What Happened to the Amaranth's Traders and Managers?

BRIAN HUNTER: CHIEF TRADER AT AMARANTH

- Six months after the Amaranth fiasco, Brian Hunter and some other Amaranth traders (among them were Karl Roster, Shane Lee, and Matthew Calhoun) tried to start a new hedge fund called Solengo Managed Funds, in which Hunter would be president and own a 60% interest. Hunter and others had spent the half-year after they left Amaranth developing a proprietary trading desk at a cost of $1.7 million and recruiting 11 employees. Hunter was also able to get preliminary financial commitments for $800 million from about 25 high-net-worth individuals. On 3 August 2007, Hunter filed a complaint with U.S. District Court for the District of Columbia claiming that investor interest had dwindled to less than $100 million because of FERC's and CFTC's price manipulation charges.[72] Hunter filed a temporary restraining order against FERC.

- In late 2007, Hunter became an adviser/consultant to a Bermuda-based fund connected to Helmsmen Advisors and to Peak Ridge Commodities Volatility Fund Segregated Portfolio, a newly developed commodities hedge fund run by Peak Ridge Capital, a private equity firm.
- Hunter reportedly hired two bodyguards after there were several attempted attacks on him. The attacks were by colleagues—not by investors!
- As of December 2007, the CFTC and FERC charges against Hunter were still pending.

NICK MAOUNIS: CEO AND FOUNDER OF AMARANTH

- As of October 2007, Nick Maounis was trying to start a new hedge fund. Two possible names for the firm were *Continuum* and *Segue*.

HARRY ARORA: TRADER AND FORMER HEAD (AND LATER CO-HEAD) OF AMARANTH'S COMMODITY GROUP; BRIAN HUNTER'S FORMER BOSS

- Left Amaranth in March 2006 because of a disagreement over Amaranth's investment policies. He stared a new hedge fund called ARCIM Advisors, which is headquartered in Greenwich, CT.

MATTHEW DONOHOE: TRADER AT AMARANTH WHO WAS ALSO CHARGED BY FERC WITH PRICE MANIPULATION

- While at Amaranth's office in Calgary, Donohoe executed trades on behalf of Brian Hunter.
- After leaving Amaranth, Donohoe was employed by Bank of Nova Scotia (Canada's third largest bank) in its global energy derivatives group in Toronto.
- As of December 2007, the price manipulation charge against Donohoe was still pending.

[72]See Daniel P. Collins, "Manipulating a Hedge Fund Blow-up," *Futures* 36 (11) (7 September 2007), 66–68.

Assorted Other Things That Happened

JPMORGAN CHASE & CO.: AMARANTH'S CLEARING AGENT, PURCHASED PART OF AMARANTH'S ENERGY BOOK IN SEPTEMBER 2006

- Fewer than two weeks after purchasing Amaranth's positions, JPM sold them to Citadel, earning profits of $725 million. The proceeds helped JPM offset poor third-quarter earnings from its energy book.
- On 13 December 2007, Amaranth sued JPM for more than $1 billion in damages. The suit accused JPM of using its position as Amaranth's clearing broker to prevent the fund from making a better deal, extracting a massive concession payment, and inflicting other damages.

CITADEL: HEDGE FUND THAT PURCHASED PART OF AMARANTH'S ENERGY BOOK IN SEPTEMBER 2006

- Citadel needed only two weeks to reduce Amaranth's risks by about two-thirds.
- Within two weeks of Amaranth's financial crisis, Citadel purchased JPM's positions in Amaranth and, thereby, assumed all the remaining concession payments Amaranth agreed to make.
- According to Bloomberg, Citadel's profits from purchasing Amaranth's energy book were responsible for its two main hedge funds earning a 3% return on their September energy investments.

PALOMA PARTNERS MANAGEMENT COMPANY: HEDGE FUND THAT NICK MAOUNIS LEFT BEFORE STARTING AMARANTH AND WHICH PROVIDED MUCH OF AMARANTH'S INITIAL FUNDING

- Paloma withdrew its funds from Amaranth in 2004, feeling that Amaranth had become too large.

Review Questions

1. In 2005, Amaranth made substantial option bets on the price of natural gas. Suppose the price of natural gas had fallen by as much as it increased. Would Amaranth have lost as much as it gained in 2005?
2. Suppose it is August 29th, and you are trading on NYMEX. Explain how you would roll over 40,000 long September futures contracts into 50,000 long October futures contracts.

  a. Suppose your original September futures price was $10.50/MMBtu, the close-out September price was $10.75/MMBtu, and the October futures price was $11/MMBtu. Calculate your profits. (Remember that a NYMEX futures contract is for 10,000 MMBtu.)

3. Is it accurate to say that the reason for Amaranth's devastating losses was because the chief trader and CEO just did not understand the derivatives markets in which they were trading?

4. In the end, what caused Amaranth to lose so much so quickly?

5. In what major ways are the regulatory responsibilities of FERC different from CFTC?

  a. Both regulators prosecuted Amaranth. Explain the grounds on which each regulator felt it had jurisdiction.

6. The NYMEX natural gas futures contract is different from the ICE natural gas futures contract in terms of delivery. What is this difference, and why is it important in cases of price manipulation?

7. On what grounds did the PSI Report claim that Amaranth dominated the natural gas futures market during 2006?

  a. What arguments are there against PSI's claims?

8. Did Amaranth evade NYMEX regulations in August 2006? Explain.

  a. If it did, was this evasion illegal?

9. Did Amaranth engage in natural gas speculation? Did it engage in excessive speculation? What is *excessive speculation*?

10. Explain two ways by which Amaranth might have manipulated natural gas prices in 2006.

11. Explain how profitable speculators should stabilize prices if they make profits over a long time period.

12. What is the difference between a financial explosion and a financial implosion? Was the Amaranth fiasco an explosion or an implosion? Explain.

Further Reading

Please visit http://www.prenhall.com/marthinsen, where you can find the following embellishment on and extension of this chapter:

- Appendix 9.1: What Are the Problems with Value at Risk?
- Appendix 9.2: Position Limits and Accountability Levels
- Appendix 9.3: Reporting Requirements for Exempt Commercial Markets

Bibliography

Collins, Daniel P. "Manipulating a Hedge Fund Blow-up." *Futures* 36(11) (7 September 2007), 66–68.

Commodity Futures Trading Commission. *About the CFTC.* Available at http://cftc.gov/aboutthecftc/index.htm. Accessed 28 December 2007.

Commodity Futures Trading Commission. *FY 2008 President's Budget and Performance Plan.* Available at http://www.cftc.gov/aboutthecftc/2008budgetperf-txt.html. Accessed 28 December 2007.

Costello, Dave. *Reduced Form Energy Model Elasticities from EIA's Regional Short-Term Energy Mode RSTEM.* 9 May 2006. Available at http://www.eia.doe.gov/emeu/steo/pub/pdf/elasticities.pdf. Accessed 28 December 2007.

Energy Information Administration. *Natural Gas Basics 101.* Available at http://www.eia.doe.gov/basics/naturalgas_basics.html. Accessed 28 December 2007.

Energy Information Administration. *The Basics of Underground Natural Gas Storage.* Available at http://www.eia.doe.gov/pub/oil_gas/natural_gas/analysis_publications/storage-basics/storagebasics.html. Accessed 28 December 2007.

Federal Energy Regulatory Commission. *About FERC: What FERC Does.* Available at http://www.ferc.gov/about/about.asp. Accessed 28 December 2007.

Federal Energy Regulatory Commission. *Derivatives and Risk Management in the Petroleum, Natural Gas, and Electricity Industries: Natural Gas Spot Markets: How Accurate Are Reported Prices?* Federal Energy Regulatory Commission, (Washington, D.C., October 2002). Available at http://www.eia.doe.gov/oiaf/servicerpt/derivative/ngsm.html. Accessed 28 December 2007.

Federal Energy Regulatory Commission. *Discussion on Commission Use of Natural Gas Price Indices.* Washington, DC: Federal Energy Regulatory Commission, October 2002. Available at http://www.ferc.gov/legal/maj-ord-reg/land-docs/Harvey-01-15-03-Commission Presentation-A-5.pdf. Accessed 19 October 2007.

Federal Energy Regulatory Commission. *Natural Gas Market Summary, An Annotated Bibliography, 2005-06 FERC.Gov/Market Oversight.* Available at http://www.ferc.gov/market-oversight/reports-analyses/overview/gas-report.pdf. Accessed 28 December 2007.

Haigh, Michael S., Hranaiova, Jana, and Overdahl, James A. Office of the Chief Economist, U.S. Commodity Futures Trading Commission. *Price Dynamics, Price Discovery and Large Futures Trader Interactions in the Energy Complex, Working Paper: First Draft,* April 28th 2005. Available at http://www.cftc.gov/files/opa/press05/opacftc-managed-money-trader-study.pdf. Accessed 28 December 2007.

Hosking, Patrick. "Investor Paid Out Extra Penalties to Quit Amaranth." *The Times Online* (13 October 2006). Available at http://business.timesonline.co.uk/tol/business/markets/united_states/article599997.ece. Accessed 28 December 2007.

Nazareth, Annette L. Commissioner, U.S. Securities and Exchange Commission. *Speech by SEC Commissioner: Remarks before the PLI Hedge Fund Conference.* Available at http://www.sec.gov/news/speech/2007/spch060607aln.htm. Accessed 28 December 2007.

United States Senate Permanent Subcommittee on Investigations Committee on Homeland Security and Governmental Affairs. *Excessive Speculation in the Natural Gas Market and Appendix, Washington D.C. Government Printing Office, 25 June 2007. Staff Report - Excessive Speculation in the Natural Gas Market* is available at http://hsgac.senate.gov/_files/

062507Report.pdf. *Appendix - Excessive Speculation in the Natural Gas Market* is available at http://hsgac.senate.gov/_files/062507Appendix.pdf. Accessed 28 December 2007.

Shapiro, Robert J. and Pham, Nam D. *An Analysis of Spot and Futures Prices for Natural Gas: The Roles of Economic Fundamentals, Market Structure, Speculation, and Manipulation.* Sonecon (August 2006) Available at http://www.pulp.tc/Nat_Legal_Policy_Center_Gas _Manip_August_29_2006.pdf. Accessed 28 December 2007.

Till, Hilary. *EDHEC Comments on the Amaranth Case: Early Lessons from the Debacle.* Lille, France: EDHEC Risk and Asset Management Research Centre and Principal and Premia Capital Management, LLC, EDHEC Business School, 2006. Available at http://www .edhec-risk.com/features/RISKArticle.2006-10-02.0711/attachments/EDHEC%20 Comments%20on%20Amaranth%20Case.pdf. Accessed 28 December 2007.

United States Energy Information Administration. *Official Energy Statistics from the U.S. Government.* Updated 21 December 2007. Available at http://tonto.eia.doe.gov/dnav/ng/ hist/n3010us2A.htm. Accessed 28 December 2007.

United States Senate Permanent Subcommittee on Investigations Committee on Home-land Security and Governmental Affairs. *Excessive Speculation in the Natural Gas Market and Appendix.* Washington, DC Government Printing Office, 25 June 2007. Available at Staff Report—Excessive Speculation in the Natural Gas Market, http://hsgac.senate. gov/_files/062507Report.pdf. Appendix—Excessive Speculation in the Natural Gas Market, http://hsgac.senate.gov/_files/062507Appendix.pdf. Accessed 28 December 2007.

Glossary

Accountability level When a trader's net position reaches the exchange-set (accountability) level, a notification is sent to the exchange's surveillance staff. The exchange can decide to do nothing, increase the trader's limits, ask for more information, or request that the position be reduced. Accountability levels are not strict position limits; they are information triggers.

Administration Administration is a legal proceeding that is like Chapter 11 bankruptcy in the United States.

Agency trading Buying and selling assets and derivatives for customers' accounts.

American option An option that can be exercised on any business day before and including the maturity date.

Arbitrage The simultaneous purchase and sale of an underlier or derivative to earn a risk-free return.

Arm's length transaction A transaction in which the buyer and seller act independently and are on equal footing. The counterparties have no association with each other that would make the price or performance of duties special from any other buyer or seller.

Ask rate The rate at which a dealer sells an underlier or derivative to a counterparty.

Asset management Professionally investing funds according to the risk-return preferences of customers.

At-the-money If the market price of the underlier is equal to the strike price, an option is at-the-money.

Back office The back office handles the administrative functions of a company's (e.g., bank's or brokerage house's) business. Its specific duties include, among other things, trade confirmation, settlement, recordkeeping, accounting, regulatory compliance, reconciling, and clearing.

Backwardation When the spot price of the underlier exceeds its forward/futures price.

Bear spread instrument An option strategy that caps an investor's downside losses (or gains) and caps the upside gains, but there is a range of underlier prices for which the investor's return increases as the price of the underlier falls.

Bid rate The rate at which a dealer buys an underlier or derivative from a counterparty.

Binomial lattice model A risk-neutral option pricing model that traces changes in the price of the underlier for discrete time periods. The resulting array of possible prices and option outcomes is latticelike in structure, and the option price is derived from this array of outcomes.

Black-Scholes formula An option pricing model based on six variables: price, expected volatility, expected dividend return, risk-free interest rate, strike price, and maturity.

Bridge loan A short-term loan that is taken out by a company until long-term or intermediate-term financing can be arranged. A bridge loan *bridges* the gap between immediate financing needs and the optimal long-term financing strategy. Bridge loans are also called "swing loans."

Bull spread instrument An option strategy that caps an investor's downside losses (or gains) and caps the upside gains, but there is a range of underlier prices for which the investor's return increases with the price of the underlier.

Call option The right, but not the obligation, to buy the underlier at a specific price (i.e., the strike price) on or before maturity.

Close-out (termination) rights Close-out (termination) rights allow a counterparty to terminate an agreement if a certain contractually defined event occurs. After termination, the contract is closed, and counterparties settle the net balance due. Because they reduce counterparty exposures and reduce market risk, close-out rights enhance market stability and reduce systemic risk.

Contango When the spot price of the underlier is less than its forward/futures price.

Constant maturity swap (CMS) Similar to a regular interest rate swap, except the floating interest on the deal is reset periodically relative to a fixed maturity market rate of an underlier with a duration extending beyond that of the swap's reset period (e.g., a swap based on 12-month LIBOR but reset every six months).

Convergence trade The simultaneous purchase and sale of an underlier (or underliers) at two different prices that *must* converge in the future. If held to maturity, a convergence trade *must* earn a profit.

Convertible bond arbitrage Buying a convertible bond and simultaneously selling short various amounts of the underlying common stock into which the bond can be converted.

Convertible debt Debt financing that allows the holder, under certain conditions, to convert debt into equity.

Cost of carry The sum of all interest expenses minus the value of all investment returns plus the value of all storage costs when an underlier is purchased on one date and then sold at a later date.

Convenience value The value an individual places on owning an asset that has some practical use in trade, production, or consumption. It is the advantage of possessing an asset and not just having the right to buy it in the future.

Counterparty A counterparty to a transaction is one of the (two or more) parties involved in a deal.

Credit arbitrage Buying and selling different classes of securities to benefit from their priced credit spreads. This arbitrage is often used in conjunction with credit default swaps.

Credit risk The chance that a borrower will be unable or unwilling to repay a debt.

Cross-trades Cross-trades occur when a trader matches internally customers' buy and sell orders for the same contract (e.g., with the same underlier, maturity, and price) instead of on the exchange floor.

Deutschemark The German currency until 1999 when it was replaced as an accounting unit (i.e., checking account form) by the euro and, finally in 2002, when it was replaced in physical form (i.e., bills and coins) by the euro.

Doubling Doubling occurs when a trader doubles his/her bets each time he/she loses in the hopes of recovering all previous losses (or making a small profit) when the market moves in a favorable direction.

Elastic When the absolute value of the elasticity measure is greater than one it is elastic. Therefore, a relationship is elastic when the percentage change in response (e.g., quantity consumed) is greater than the percentage change in the stimulus (e.g., price).

Elasticity The percentage change in response (e.g., quantity consumed or produced) divided by the percentage change in the stimulus (e.g., price).

Energy arbitrage Trading energy-related contracts in either the same or different locations. Among the many variations are trading different grades of energy, expected changes in the volatility of energy prices, and expected changes in calendar spreads.

Euro-market The euro-market is a short-term market for borrowing and lending a currency outside the country of issue. For example, a short-term U.S. dollar deposit in (or loan from) a Canadian bank is an example of a euro–dollar deposit (loan).

Euro–dollar market A U.S. dollar deposit in (or loan from) a bank outside the United States.

European option An option that can be exercised only on the maturity date.

Euro–yen deposit A yen deposit in (or loan from) a bank outside Japan.

Exercise To exercise a call option means to employ the right to purchase the underlier at the strike price. To exercise a put option means to employ the right to sell the underlier at the strike price.

FAS 123 (R) FAS 123 (R) is an abbreviation for Financial Accounting Standards Board Rule 123 (revised). This Rule was passed in December 2004 and is important because it requires U.S. companies to report employee stock options as expenses and to use fair-value-based methods to determine their worth.

FASB 133 FAS-133 is a direct and unequivocal U.S. accounting statement that disclosure of off-balance-sheet transactions is crucial to understanding the financial health of any company.

Federal funds rate The interbank borrowing and lending rate for U.S. dollars. Normally, these deposits or loans are overnight, but longer maturities can be negotiated.

Firm-fixed contract Contracts that require customers to take delivery of oil or gas on fixed contract dates.

Firm-flexible contract Contracts that allow customers to alter the timing of oil or gas deliveries but, at the same time, require these customers to purchase any deferred quantities by the end of the contract period.

Five Eights Account The errors account used by Nick Leeson to book unauthorized trades at Barings Bank.

Front office The front office is involved with direct customer interface and other operating aspects of the business.

Gating provision A restriction that limits the ability of hedge fund investors to withdraw their investments. Gating provisions are imposed to prevent investors from running on a hedge fund. They provide hedge funds with the assurance of longer-term financing. The size of the gating provision varies from fund to fund.

Haircut A haircut is the difference between the market value of an asset and its value as collateral. It is a small portion (usually 1% to 2%) that is deducted from the principal when a bond is shorted. The creditor, therefore, can borrow only 98% to 99% of the bond's market price.

Hedge The purchase or sale of an asset and/or derivative to neutralize the cash flow or profit/loss effects of an existing or expected position.

High water mark A provision in an investment contract that stipulates an incentive fee will not be collected unless the amount invested grows above its highest former level. In other words, losses must be completely recovered before an incentive fee applies.

Hybrid instrument A financial instrument that blends the risk-return characteristics of fixed-income securities, equities, and/or derivative instruments. Usually, they are not backed by collateral, and their derivative-related characteristics come from warrants with embedded options. Also called a "structured note."

Inelastic When the absolute value of the elasticity measure is less than one, it is inelastic. Therefore, a relationship is inelastic when the percentage change in response (e.g., quantity consumed) is less than the percentage change in the stimulus (e.g., price).

In-the-money A call option is in-the-money if its strike price is lower than the market price of the underlier. A put option is in-the-money if the strike price is higher than the market price of the underlier.

Inter-exchange arbitrage The purchase of a contract on one exchange and the simultaneous sale of a similar contract on another exchange. Also called "switching."

Intrinsic value For a call option, intrinsic value is the amount by which the strike price is below the market value of the underlier. For a put option, intrinsic value is the amount by which the strike price exceeds the market value of the underlier.

Leverage Using borrowed funds to increase the risk and expected return profile of a portfolio or business activity.

LIBOR The London Interbank Offered Rate. It is the short-term, interbank interest rate that a London bank earns when it lends to another London bank. This rate is used as a basis for other floating rates because the credit risk among these London banks is very low.

Liquidity Liquidity is the ability to turn an asset into cash quickly and without substantial loss of value.

Liquidity risk The chance of not having sufficient cash on hand to meet demand.

Lock-out provision A restriction on invested funds that prevents investors from making withdrawals (e.g., from a hedge fund) for a certain period of time.

Long position A long position occurs when an underlier or derivative is purchased.

Long/short equity A directional bet on shares.

Long straddle The simultaneous purchase of a call option and put option at the same strike price and maturity.

Loss threshold A loss threshold is the limit below which a counterparty has to pay additional margin. For instance, a hedge fund may have a loss threshold of $1 million, which means if mark-to-market losses exceed $1 million, it has to pay additional margin.

Maintenance margin payments Disbursements that must be made on a daily (or intraday basis) for exchange-traded derivative contracts due to adverse movements in the price of the underlier. Also called "variation margin payments."

Margin A fixed payment amount per contract made to an exchange, which is usually a very small percent of the contract's overall notional value. Margin is not really a down payment on the underlier as much as it is a performance bond that ensures the broker and exchange that the contract will be settled in due course.

Margin call If a margin account falls below the maintenance (variation) margin requirement (i.e., the minimum level to which the margin account is allowed to fall before broker calls the trader for more funds), a margin call is issued, and the account must be brought immediately up to the full initial margin level.

Market risk The variation in the price of an underlier due to changes in market variables, such as interest rates, exchange rates, stock prices, and commodity prices.

Mark to market Derivative contracts are revalued each trading day, and funds are transferred from the loser's margin account to the winner's margin account, as if the contract had been closed out and then reopened. An exchange does this to protect itself because, if a trader went bankrupt, the exchange would have to honor the trader's commitments.

Market neutral portfolio A portfolio that earns returns regardless of whether market prices are rising or falling. A market neutral portfolio is usually attained by taking simultaneous long and short positions in a variety of assets and/or derivatives.

Merger arbitrage Buying and/or selling securities of companies that are expected to be involved in a future merger, acquisition, restructuring, or recapitalization.

Merchant bank A merchant bank is similar to a current-day investment bank. It provides financial services, such as underwriting and loans, to customers and invests its own capital.

Monte Carlo model An option pricing model that relies on changes in expected payoffs that are generated by simulating price movements of the underlier.

Naked position An unhedged (speculative) position.

Net asset value Net asset value (NAV) is calculated by subtracting a fund's liability value from its asset value and dividing by the number of outstanding shares. NAV also adjusts for the value of all open positions that must be marked to market.

Netting Netting means arriving at a net position by deducting the amount a counterparty is owed from the amount it owes. By netting, counterparties can avoid entering the market (in the case of a default) to reverse each open position. Netting enhances market stability and reduces systemic risks.

Nikkei 225 Index An index of share prices for the 225 largest stocks trading on the Tokyo Stock Exchange. Since its initiation in 1950, the Nikkei 225 Stock Average has been the most widely used measure of Japan's stock market activity.

Non-clearing member A broker who cannot independently register or settle trades with the clearing house. It must rely on a clearing member for these activities.

Notional value The face value of an underlier that is not exchanged in a transaction. In a swap transaction, it serves only to determine the periodic cash flows.

Off-the-run security A seasoned (i.e., already issued) security that usually has a less active market than an on-the-run (i.e., newly issued) security.

On-the-run security A newly issued security that usually has a more active market than an off-the-run (i.e., seasoned) security.

Open outcry trading Open outcry trading takes place when traders communicate on a physical exchange by shouting and using hand signals to communicate their buy and sell orders.

Open interest The number of contracts that has not been exercised, closed out, or expired. An initial buy and sell transaction increases open interest by one unit. The subsequent sale to an existing owner reduces open interest by one unit, and the sale to a new owner keeps it the same. At initiation and maturity, open interest is equal to zero.

OSE Osaka Stock Exchange

Out-of-the-money A call option is out-of-the-money if its strike price is higher than the market price of the underlier. A put option is out-of-the-money if the strike price is lower than the market price of the underlier.

Over the counter Trades with dealer networks that are executed and settled using global telephone, telex, fax, and high-speed Internet connections.

Payoff profile The relationship between the price of the underlier and the *value* of the underlier or derivative position.

PLC PLC is an abbreviation for Public Limited Company, which is like an incorporated public stock company (i.e., Inc.) in the United States.

Position Limit Strict rules on the quantity of exchange-traded contracts a customer can hold during a set period (e.g., three days before a futures contract matures).

Profit/loss profile A profit/loss profile includes both the payoff from an underlier or derivative and its initial cost.

Proprietary trading Buying and selling assets or derivatives for a house's (e.g., dealer's) account and not for a customer's account.

Put option The right, but not the obligation, to sell the underlier at a specific price (i.e., the strike price) on or prior to maturity.

Reconciliation Matching payments and receipts to a specific customer's account.

Relative value trade The simultaneous purchase and sale of an underlier (or underliers) at two different prices that *should* converge in the future. If held to maturity, there is no guarantee that a relative value trade will earn a profit.

Repurchase agreement In a repurchase agreement (repo), a securities dealer sells securities to a counterparty (i.e., the counterparty is the buyer) with a simultaneous commitment to repurchase the same or similar securities at a fixed price on a specific date in the future.

Restricted share Equity-based compensation that grants shares to employees with certain restrictions on their sale, transferability, and/or risk of forfeiture until they are vested.

Reverse repurchase agreement In a reverse repurchase agreement (reverse repo), a securities dealer buys securities from a counterparty (i.e., the counterparty is the seller) with a simultaneous commitment to sell back the same or similar securities at a fixed price on a specific date in the future.

Risk aversion Risk aversion is an individual's dislike for unexpected results. Faced with two alternatives, both having the same expected return but different risks, the risk-averse individual will choose the alternative with the lower risk.

Short position A short position occurs when an underlier or derivative is sold.

Short straddle The simultaneous sale of a call option and put option at the same strike price and for the same maturity.

SIMEX Singapore International Monetary Exchange. On 1 December 1999, SIMEX merged with the Stock Exchange of Singapore (SES) to form Singapore Exchange Limited (SGX).

Speculation A transaction in which risk determines part of or the entire outcome. Also called an "unhedged transaction" or an "unhedged position."

Spread trade The simultaneous purchase and sale of an underlier (or underliers) to profit from changes in the price or yield differential.

Stack-and-roll hedge The purchase or sale of enough futures contracts in near-dated maturities to offset the total exposure of a series of long-term forward contracts.

Statistical arbitrage Trading that takes advantage of inconsistencies among price correlations for an underlying index (e.g., Russell 2000), basket of securities, or exchange rates.

Strike price The price at which an option can be exercised

Structured note A financial instrument that blends the risk-return characteristics of fixed-income securities, equities, and/or derivative instruments. Usually, they are not backed by collateral, and their derivative-related characteristics come from warrants

with embedded options. Also called a "hybrid instrument."

Summary judgment A summary judgment is made when there is no dispute between interested parties over the facts of the case. When this occurs, the judge can rule on the matter based on the presented statements and evidence.

Swap rate The interest rate paid by the party responsible for the fixed payment in an interest rate swap.

Switching The purchase of a futures contract on one exchange and the simultaneous sale of a similar futures contract on another exchange. Also called "inter-exchange arbitrage."

Tailing a hedge Adjusting the hedge ratio based on the expected interest earned or paid due to the daily marking to market of derivative contracts.

Time value The value of an option that is derived from the time left until maturity. It is equal to the amount by which an option's price exceeds its intrinsic value.

Trading "for the house" Taking a proprietary position with equity of the firm and not with customers' funds.

TSE Tokyo Stock Exchange

Variation margin payments Disbursements that must be made on a daily (or intraday basis) for derivative contracts due to adverse movements in the price of the underlier. Also called "maintenance margin."

Vesting period The time period an individual must wait before he/she unconditionally owns an option and can exercise it or until he/she unconditionally owns the underlier (e.g., share) and can sell it.

Volatility arbitrage Buying or selling options on an underlier and then selling or buying various amounts of the underlier.

Warrant A financial instrument that is often issued with a bond and gives its owner specific rights concerning the purchase of shares in the future. Usually, warrants are issued by a company.

Index